THE DEVELOPMENT
OF THE THEATRE

Fig. 1. The Orchestra of the Theatre of Dionysos at Athens
Photo Alinari.

THE DEVELOPMENT OF THE THEATRE

A STUDY OF THEATRICAL ART FROM THE BEGINNINGS TO THE PRESENT DAY

BY

ALLARDYCE NICOLL M.A.

PROFESSOR OF THE HISTORY OF DRAMA AND DRAMATIC
CRITICISM IN YALE UNIVERSITY
AUTHOR OF "MASKS MIMES AND MIRACLES" "BRITISH DRAMA"
"THE THEORY OF DRAMA" "FILM AND THEATRE" ETC.

WITH THREE HUNDRED AND THIRTEEN
ILLUSTRATIONS

NEW EDITION REVISED

NEW YORK
HARCOURT, BRACE AND COMPANY
1937

Made in Great Britain.   Printed at THE BALLANTYNE PRESS
by SPOTTISWOODE, BALLANTYNE & CO. LTD.
Colchester, London & Eton

PREFACE

MUCH has been written about the theatre. The Greek stage, the Elizabethan stage, the stage of our own day—all these have received more or less adequate treatment; but there is no book in the English language which presents a summary of theatrical art from the beginnings to the twentieth century. There is, of course, the monumental work of Mantzius, but that, noble as it is, is not always accurate, and is often clogged with biographical data unnecessary and distracting. It is my object, therefore, in this book to present a brief outline of the art of the theatre, with special reference to the English stage. For this purpose I have dealt with the Greek theatre, the Italian Renascence theatre, and the theatre of modern France and Germany, but have neglected the development of nineteenth-century Continental theatres, as these merely ran parallel to the English playhouses of the same time.

As such an outline as this would be useless without pictorial illustration, I have selected for reproduction what seemed to me the most typical drawings, plans, and engravings of the various periods. Some of these are necessarily well known (for one cannot escape de Witt's sketch of the Swan), but in general I have endeavoured to choose for this purpose designs more out of the way, so that this book contains a number of illustrations which either have never been reproduced at all or have not appeared in a modern work on this subject. I should desire to call special attention to the Buontalenti designs to be found in Chapter IV and those by Juvarra presented in Chapter VIII.

Necessarily, in a book which covers the history of theatrical decoration and arrangement from the times of Aeschylus to those of the present day, much detailed comment has had to be omitted, but I have aimed at devoting special attention to certain neglected aspects of the playhouse of former times, such as the orientation of the *mansions* in medieval plays and costume on the English stage up to 1750. Also I have devoted more space to the theatrical tendencies of past times than to those of the present, not because I believe the past to be greater than the present, but because there is fuller opportunity for gaining first-hand knowledge of the scenic art of to-day than for acquiring a knowledge of the art of the Bibienas and their fellow-workers. Above all, I have endeavoured to indicate what seemed to me the main tendencies in the various periods and to stress the continuity of tradition from earliest times to latest.

For those who wish to pursue further researches into individual aspects of this larger subject I have added a fairly full bibliography. No pretence is made in this to absolute completeness, but the selection will, I think, be found to be catholic.

A final note may be added on the general scope of the book. In dealing with the modern period I have made no attempt to discuss the technical terms of the stage or to describe scenic apparatus. At the same time I should not wish this book to be thought of as merely theoretic. The study of the theatre of the past is one which is necessary not only for the scenic artist, but for the true playgoer. Unless we can appreciate the stage of Sophocles and the stage of Shakespeare (not separately, but in their interrelations) we cannot hope to understand their works aright; unless we have a knowledge of past theatrical effort we can barely form an opinion concerning the more recent developments in scenic artistry. I have, therefore, a

3

strictly practical purpose in the penning of this book, and if even in a slight way I may be the means of inducing others to study this subject more closely I shall feel myself to be amply rewarded.

In the course of preparing the volume for the press I have received helpful advice from my colleague Professor Earp, and from Mr James Laver, of the Victoria and Albert Museum. I desire also to express my thanks to the publishers and authors of the following books for permission kindly granted to reproduce designs and photographs :

Alexander Bakshy, *The Path of the Modern Russian Stage, and other Essays* (Cecil Palmer) ; A. C. Baumeister, *Denkmäler des klassischen Altertums* (R. Oldenbourg, München) ; Margarete Bieber, *Denkmäler zum Theaterwesen im Altertum* (Walter de Gruyter, Berlin) ; Sir Edmund Chambers, *The Mediaeval Stage* (Oxford University Press) ; W. Creizenach, *The English Drama in the Age of Shakespeare* (Sidgwick and Jackson) ; P. L. Duchartre, *La Comédie italienne* (Librairie de France, Paris) ; E. R. Fiechter, *Die baugeschichtliche Entwicklung des antiken Theaters* (C. H. Beck'sche Verlagsbuchhandlung, München) ; R. C. Flickinger, *The Greek Theater and its Drama* (University of Chicago Press) ; Gsell, *Monuments antiques de l'Algérie* (E. Boccard, Paris) ; A. E. Haigh, *The Attic Theatre* (Oxford University Press) ; C. Lanckoroński, *Städte Pamphyliens und Pisidiens* (F. Tempski, Vienna) ; Émile Male, *L'Art religieux* (Librairie Armand Colin, Paris) ; Karl Mantzius, *A History of Theatrical Art in Ancient and Modern Times* (Duckworth) ; Octave Navarre, *Le Théâtre grec* (Payot, Paris) ; George C. D. Odell, *Shakespeare from Betterton to Irving* (Charles Scribner's Sons and Constable) ; Paul Reyher, *Les Masques anglais* (Librairie Hachette) ; Corrado Ricci, *I Bibiena* (Alfieri e Lacroix, Milan) ; Carl Robert, *Die Masken der neueren attischen Komödie* (Max Niemeyer, Halle) ; Oliver M. Sayler, *Max Reinhardt and his Theatre* (Brentano's, N.Y.) ; Theodor Wiegand, *Priene* (Georg Reimer, Berlin).

My thanks are also due to the following for facilities and help generously given in connexion with the reproduction of illustrations : His Grace the Duke of Devonshire, the Most Honourable the Marquess of Bath, Sir Israel Gollancz, Professor F. J. Curtis, and the authorities of the Victoria and Albert Museum, the British Museum, All Souls College, Oxford, Worcester College, Oxford, the Provinzialmuseum, Bonn, and the Landesbibliothek, Darmstadt.

A. N.

PREFACE TO THE NEW EDITION

THE preparation of this new edition of *The Development of the Theatre* has afforded an opportunity to bring the work up to date. The last chapter has been entirely rewritten, but the topics dealt with there have still been kept general in theme, since it would have been impossible to discuss in detail the work of individual scene-designers, and also since it seems that in a book of this kind one should rather concentrate upon fundamental principles than present masses of scattered facts. I cannot, however, refrain from drawing attention to the truly remarkable achievements of contemporary scenic artists in New York. The American public appears to be specially sensitive to visual appeal, and as a result there has grown up in New York within the past twenty years a remarkable group of designers, distinguished for their versatility and inventiveness. Men like Lee Simonson, Donald Oenslager, Jo Mielziner, and Robert Edmond Jones have brought a freshness to the stage which gives distinction to the New York theatre.

In addition to the rewriting of the final chapter, Appendix B, which originally contained some short extracts from the *Dialogues* of Leone di Somi, now includes a translation of the entire text of these interesting disquisitions. From Leone di Somi we may get an excellent picture of Renascence ideals and practice. A further appendix, specially prepared for this edition, presents a number of illustrations derived from the work which is being done at Yale University in gathering material for a comprehensive photographic collection of theatrical designs and plans. Over thirty thousand prints and drawings in English, American, French, German, Italian, Austrian, Belgian, and Dutch museums have now been reproduced and filed in this collection for reference. I should have wished to include a section on the Chinese, Japanese, and Indian theatres, but such an addition would have been likely to lengthen overmuch the text of the volume. Emphasis, however, should be laid on the fact that from the conventions of the Oriental stage we may learn a great deal which might be of service to our theatres.

For assistance in preparing the version of Leone di Somi's *Dialogues* I wish to thank Professor Angelo Lipari, of Yale University. Some information regarding di Somi's life was kindly brought to my attention by Dr Harvey Cushing.

A. N.

YALE UNIVERSITY
April 1937

5

CONTENTS

ILLUSTRATIONS

THE DEVELOPMENT OF THE THEATRE

ILLUSTRATIONS

ILLUSTRATIONS

13

ILLUSTRATIONS

B

The
DEVELOPMENT OF THE THEATRE

CHAPTER I

THE GREEK THEATRE

(i) INTRODUCTORY

THE Greek theatre is, in more ways than one, the ancestor of all the theatres of modern Europe. Not only was Greece the first European country to raise dramatic performances to the level of an art, not only were the Greek dramatists among the finest masters whom the world theatre has ever known, but the forms and conventions of the classic playhouses set an indelible seal upon the theatres of Renascence Italy, and thence were carried over, through the Elizabethan and Restoration periods in England, to modern times. It is through a disinclination to study these facts that so many able writers on Greek or on Elizabethan stage conditions have failed; it cannot too often be emphasized that those who segregate the Theatre of Dionysos at Athens or the Globe theatre in London, treating each as a separate entity, must inevitably fail to appreciate many of the most salient features of each. It is only when we take a bird's-eye view of the whole and trace the larger developments that we can reach a final synthesis.

In any discussion concerning the Greek stage it must be noted first of all that when we speak of the Greek theatre we are referring not to one thing, but to several things. Usually, in employing the phrase, we think of the original theatre at Athens, but besides that original theatre there were scores of centres where plays were performed and where scenic remains have been discovered. It must be realized that not only different localities in Greece but also different generations witnessed the building of these playhouses, and that, as a consequence, no two theatres are identically alike. There can thus be no absolute 'ideal' of a Greek theatre, although for convenience we may divide the existing buildings into three main types, recognizing that these types are used only to aid in our general survey and are not employed in any strict and narrow sense. The *classical Athenian* is the first of these types, and belongs to the fifth century B.C. Next comes the *Hellenistic*, so called because it is the type of playhouse erected from the fourth century onward, mostly in territories outside of Greece, but under the impress of Greek or Hellenic culture. It corresponds, in theatrical art, to that movement which, in history, is symbolized in the conquests of Alexander the Great. Finally, when the Greek civilization was coming to an end, it met with the rapidly spreading Roman ideas, and out of these two forces sprang a third type of theatre, which is usually called *Graeco-Roman*. Classical Athenian, Hellenistic, and Graeco-Roman playhouses are all distinct from one another, and must, as a consequence, be studied separately. Greatest literary interest undoubtedly attaches to the first because of its association with the masters of old Greek tragedy and comedy, but from the point of view of the student of the theatre the later types have equal, if not greater value, for it is a well-attested fact that, although mimic action (acting) comes before drama, the fuller development of scenic art is arrived at only after an age of great plays. No excuse, therefore, is offered for the relative portions of this book devoted to the three main forms of Greek playhouses.

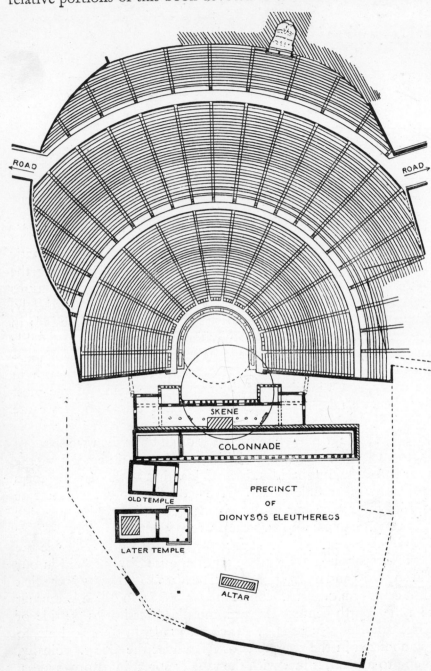

Fig. 2. THE LYCURGOS THEATRE OF DIONYSOS AT ATHENS
The inner circle shows the position of the earliest orchestra.
From Flickinger, *The Greek Theater*, p. 64.

In any discussion concerning the nature of the first type, that in which the dramas of Aeschylus, Sophocles, and Euripides were produced, attention must first be drawn to the meagreness of the available information. The greater Greek dramatists reached their culmination by the middle of the fifth century B.C., yet only a few stones dating from that period exist among the ruins of the famous Dionysian theatre at Athens, while nearly all the theatres outside of Athens itself are of much later construction. Three sources of information only are open to us, each possessing grave disadvantages. (1) The literary evidence taken from the works of Vitruvius and Pollux is perhaps chief in value, partly because these are the only two writers who retained touch with the ancient Greek traditions, and partly because these two authors gave to Renascence architects almost all that was known in the sixteenth and seventeenth centuries of the classical stage. For several reasons, however, we must be on our guard when reading their books. In the first place, Vitruvius penned his famous work on classic architecture about the year 15 B.C., or four centuries at least after the time of Sophocles; while Pollux, whose *Onomastikon* contains so many valuable passages of information, lived in the second century A.D. It stands

to reason that neither of these writers could speak with first-hand authority concerning that which interests us most—the antique theatre of Athens; while, in addition, we discover that even their remarks on the theatres of their own time, Graeco-Roman and Roman, partake of a decidedly idealistic tendency. The description of a Roman theatre in Vitruvius thus corresponds with no exactitude to the ruins found of playhouses belonging to that date. While Vitruvius and Pollux remain invaluable, therefore, they can in no wise be trusted when their views run counter to the weight of evidence gathered from other sources. (2) Second come the extant relics of the ancient theatres, but again the warning note must be sounded. We cannot permit ourselves to argue back from the more completely preserved playhouses of the second century B.C. to those of the fifth century. But a few sparse relics remain of the theatres of the latter date, and consequently we have to work largely on theory or on imaginative reconstruction, our ideas being framed largely by hints given to us from other sources. (3) Finally, and perhaps of chief importance, there is the evidence to be derived from the plays themselves. While of stage direction there is practically nothing, we must remember that these works were penned by practical dramatists and that unless our imaginary or reconstructed theatre is of such a form as to provide full opportunities for their production we must lay aside our most dearly treasured theories in favour of others more practical. Such a statement may seem a truism, yet only too many writers on this subject have erred through disregard of facts of this kind. Our object, therefore, must be to sift such scattered items of evidence as are presented to us by different authorities, and from a union of these items of evidence endeavour to re-envisage the theatres in which the tragedies and the comedies were played.

(ii) The Origins of Tragedy and of Comedy

Perhaps for our purpose a rapid glance at the origin and development of drama previous to the building of the first theatre may not be inopportune. Although theories are innumerable concerning this subject, and although hardly any two modern scholars hold identical views, the general movement toward the elaboration of dramatic form may be stated in broad outline. It is generally agreed that the origin of tragedy lies in the dithyramb sung in honour of Dionysos, the Bacchus of the Greeks; that this dithyramb was originally improvised and rhapsodical in essence; and that, as time passed by, it was 'poetized' or rendered literary, possibly by Arion of Methymna. The dithyramb was not confined to any one region of Greece, and the movement toward literary composition was one which probably saw developments in widely different regions, the whole coalescing in a type of formal chant, sung by the devotees of the god, and no doubt directed by one man as leader or guide. Then came Thespis, who, probably merely developing ideas which had come into existence before his time, elaborated the part of the leader, making him a genuine *actor* whose words were answered by the chanting chorus, and who turned to subjects not intimately connected with the stories of Dionysos. This was in the sixth century B.C.; the drama as such, and fundamentally if not outwardly dissociated from the worship of Dionysos, had been born. Only the further elaboration of dramatic forms and conventions was left to Aeschylus (525–456 B.C.), Sophocles (495–406 B.C.), and Euripides (480–406 B.C.), the masters of Greek tragic drama.[1]

Comedy had a similar development. It arose out of the less decorous mummery associated with the κῶμος (comos; the Latin *comus*), or voluntary procession organized by the townsfolk in honour of Dionysos and ending with a phallic song. Our 'comedy' is derived directly from this word κῶμος added to ᾠδή (odē, song). Apparently the *comus* revels consisted fundamentally of a procession, a sacrifice, and the final song; but, owing to the fact that the words of the *comus* revellers were often satiric, what had been originally the back-chat of the crowd of onlookers became eventually part of the *comus* merriment itself, so that comedy, when at last it emerged as an independent entity, was distinguished from tragedy by the presence in it of two choruses instead of

---

[1] The presence of satyric plays as part of a series is explained as due to religious conservatism, which was shocked by the complete departure from Dionysiac subject-matter. Only two of these are extant—the *Cyclops* of Euripides and the *Trackers* of Sophocles.

only one.   The first form of true comedy, that to which has been given the title of Old, found its chief representative in Aristophanes (c. 448–388 B.C.).   This Old Comedy was followed by the Middle Comedy (c. 375–325 B.C.), full of literary criticism and parody, while that in its turn was supplanted by the New Comedy—chiefly championed by Menander (342–291 B.C.)—in which domestic life was humorously drawn.

(iii) THE ANCIENT ATHENIAN THEATRE: MAIN FEATURES

From this more than inadequate sketch of the rise of tragedy and comedy in the sixth and fifth centuries B.C. two facts become evident.   (1) Religion colours the whole of the drama, and as a consequence the drama appeals to the vast mass of the people.   This is no class affair, but a form of art essentially popular and democratic.   When theatres come to be built there is therefore the obvious necessity for ample standing, and later for ample sitting, room.   The playhouses must be vast and capacious.   (2) The chorus, both in tragedy and in comedy, as the very essence of each, remains the central element in drama.   Consequently the theatres, when they are erected, must provide a considerable acting space, or, to speak more correctly, a considerable space in which the chorus could make those elaborate terpsichorean movements which always were associated with the verses of the lyric chants.   The solution for both these necessary requirements was found in the selection of a hill-slope at the bottom of which was marked out a circle as the ὀρχήστρα (orchestra), with, in the centre, a θυμέλη (thymele, altar) erected in the honour of the god.   The upper slope of the hill provided natural opportunities for the witnessing of the action.   The bare hill-side, then, with the round orchestra and the altar was the first theatre [1] known to the Greeks.

Starting from this simple arrangement, where a circular dancing-place was all that converted natural ground into an artificial theatre, the Greek playhouse easily and logically developed.   The process is not difficult to follow.   First came a few wooden seats toward the inner edge of the orchestra, designed for the principal men of the district or for honoured guests.   These naturally would be arranged in a semicircle to follow the circumference of the dancing-place, and would form the commencement of a regular auditorium.   From this stage to that in which wooden benches, or ἴκρια (ikria), arranged up the hillside, completed the auditorium, or to that in which stone seats supplanted the wooden benches, was of course but a simple step.   It was the collapse of the wooden seats at Athens in 499 B.C. which led to the erection of a stone auditorium there.   Obviously, owing to the fact that the hillside sloped only one way and that even in the most primitive form of drama there was one side to the action, these seats did not completely encircle the orchestra, but it was found that an unrestricted view of the actors was still possible when the seats were carried somewhat beyond an exact semicircle.   Hence we reach the norm of the primitive Greek theatre—dancing-place and altar, seats arranged in an extended semicircle, with the terminating sides running obliquely to the diameter of the auditorium.

The excavations undertaken at Athens by Professor Dörpfeld have shown that in the original Dionysian theatre there the orchestra stood 50 feet to the south of the present orchestra and had a diameter of 78 feet.[2]   As it was placed on the slope of the Acropolis itself the ground-level could not be obtained without banking up at the rear, which left a drop of some 6½ feet, beyond which stood the ancient Temple of Dionysos (Fig. 3).   It is the fact that up to 465 this simple arrangement endured which explains the settings and some of the conventions in the earliest plays of Aeschylus.   Thus the *Suppliants* (c. 490 B.C.), the *Persians* (472 B.C.), and *Prometheus Bound* (c. 470 B.C.) are all laid, in contradistinction to later plays, in open, desert countryside unflanked

---

[1] It may be noted that the word θέατρον (theatron, theatre) signified in Greek not a building or a stage, but what the Romans called the *cavea* and we the auditorium.   θέατρον is derived from the verb θεᾶσθαι (theasthai, to see).

[2] The old orchestra is shown in Fig. 2.

by any building, proving the non-existence then of any background. Aeschylus adapted these early plays to the requirements of the stage, just as later he and other playwrights made use of the scenic wall erected after 465 B.C. Still further, Aeschylus utilized for dramatic purposes the trench or drop formed at the rear edge of the orchestral circle. In *Prometheus Bound* a dummy figure was evidently used for the captive fire-bringer, and this figure at the close of the drama sank into the abyss, to give place to a live actor who ascended at the commencement of the lost *Prometheus Unbound*. The drop, inconvenient as it might seem, had provided an opportunity for Aeschylus, who, like all dramatic masters, realized that success could come only if all the physical conditions of his theatre were utilized for the purposes of art. In many other ways physical conditions which might well seem at first sight inconvenient or unadaptable to the purposes of dramatic

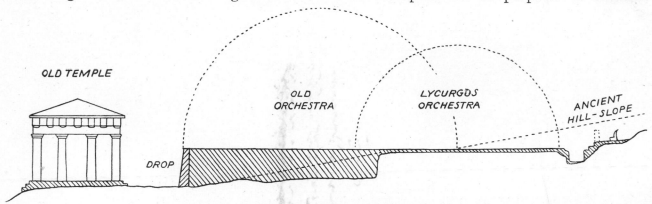

Fig. 3. CROSS-SECTION THROUGH THE OLD AND NEW ORCHESTRAS AT ATHENS
The drop at the rear of the former should be noted.

art were freely made use of by the playwrights. Thus the fact that the performance of the dramas commenced usually at sunrise led to time references in the dialogue which made dramatic action and actual surroundings harmonize. In Euripides' *Iphigenia at Aulis* the setting starts with the last darkness before dawn. "What star is that there sailing?" asks Agamemnon, to which his attendant replies, "Sirius, in his middle height near the seven Pleiads riding." Some time later the dawn begins to break:

> That silver light
> Shows the approach of morn, the harbinger
> Of the sun's fiery steeds.

The rest of the action takes place in the broad light of day. What an effect this synchronization of dramatic setting and actual physical phenomena must have had may well be imagined.

(iv) THE SCENE-BUILDINGS AND STAGE

With the advent of two and later of three actors whom the necessities of the drama constrained to perform in a diversity of parts it became imperative that a hut should be erected for the convenience of the performers. In Athens the close proximity of the old temple of Dionysos would have rendered the building of such a hut or dressing-room almost impossible, and it is probable that about this date the ancient orchestra was moved 50 feet northward, leaving a space at the back which had been formerly part of the dancing space. On this ground was erected, about the year 465 B.C., a small wooden σκηνή (*skene*, scene-building),[1] designed originally as a mere dressing-room,

---

[1] While σκηνή regularly signified the scene-building or dressing-hut, it was also used at a later date to indicate both the stage and the scenic decorations. Obviously our word 'scene' is derived from it.

but soon found to offer many opportunities when considered as a scenic background. It is from this time that plays, instead of being set in some open country, are presumed to take place before a temple or a palace. What this early scene-building looked like we cannot tell; unpretentious undoubtedly it was, presenting in all probability a plain front unadorned save for possible paintings erected to symbolize the scenic action. Within a few years, however, something more ornate had been planned and executed. About 425 B.C. a firm stone basis was laid for an elaborate scene-

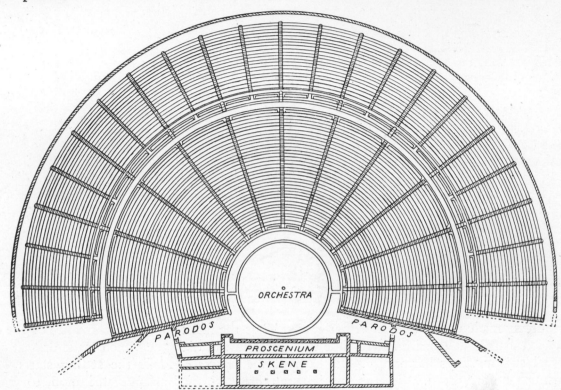

Fig. 4. Plan of the Theatre at Epidauros

After Dörpfeld-Reisch.

building consisting of a long front wall interrupted at the sides by projecting wings or παρασκήνια (*paraskenia*). Between these projecting wings we may suppose that there existed a very low stage, possibly raised but a foot from the orchestra level, yet providing that elevation which actors of all ages and of all climes have sought and used. Immediately behind this stage may have come a columned προσκήνιον (*proskenion*, proscenium), built of wood like the rest of the scene-building.[1] The front wall of the scene-building itself was probably pierced by three doors for the exits and the entrances of the actors.

It is obvious that this scene-building, often extending to beyond the diameter of the orchestral circle, nearly met the oblique lines formed by the seats in the auditorium. In other words, a passageway was made at each side by the edge of the auditorium and the ends of the scene-building. These passageways, used by both chorus and spectators, gained the name of πάροδος (*parodos*), and were in later times adorned with richly sculptured gates.

In all probability the wooden scene-building thus erected on a stone foundation at the end of

---

[1] The word προσκήνιον was used in various senses. Sometimes it was applied to the stage (*i.e.*, that which was προ or in front of the σκηνή); sometimes it signified the decorative wall in front of the σκηνή (*i.e.*, the back wall in front of which the actors performed). The latter sense is used here. (See *infra*, p. 30, n.)

the fifth century B.C. was of two stories, the upper of which was the ἐπισκήνιον (*episkenion*) and was utilized for the ' machines,' of which an account will be given below. It is likely that the slightly raised stage was called the λογεῖον (*logeion*, speaking-place), although that word and the term θεολογεῖον (*theologeion*, speaking-place of divinities) have both been applied to the top of the proscenium or first story of the scene-building itself. By the time that the scene-building was thus

Fig. 5. THE THEATRE AT EPIDAUROS
This theatre is among the best preserved and the most beautiful of the earlier type.
Photo E. P. Co.

elaborated and sometimes constructed of stone, the regular palace convention for tragedy had become fully established, to pass on in imitative forms to the dramatists of the Renascence.

(v) THE HELLENISTIC THEATRE

The simple arrangement described above, consisting of round orchestra, *parodoi*, rectangular *skene* with projecting *paraskenia*, and low platform or stage, is all we can confidently assert for the earliest Athenian playhouse. Attempts have recently been made to deny to it, and to later theatres, any raised stage at all, but the phrases used by Aristophanes [1] as well as those used by Aristotle [2] seem to prove definitely that there was some slight erection at Athens for the use of the actors,

[1] ἀναβαίνειν (to go up) and καταβαίνειν (to go down). [2] ἐπὶ τῆς σκηνῆς (upon the stage) and ἀπὸ τῆς σκηνῆς (from the stage).

23

but sufficiently low to allow of free intercourse between the chorus on the orchestra level and the actors proper. Nor can there be any reasonable doubt that the Hellenistic and Graeco-Roman playhouses boasted stages of an increasingly ornate kind.

Some half a score of fairly well preserved theatres, in addition to the reconstructed portions of the Athenian Theatre of Dionysos, reveal to us the main features of the Hellenistic type. Epidauros, Eretria, Oropos, Delos, Priene, all possess playhouses which, in spite of many divergencies,

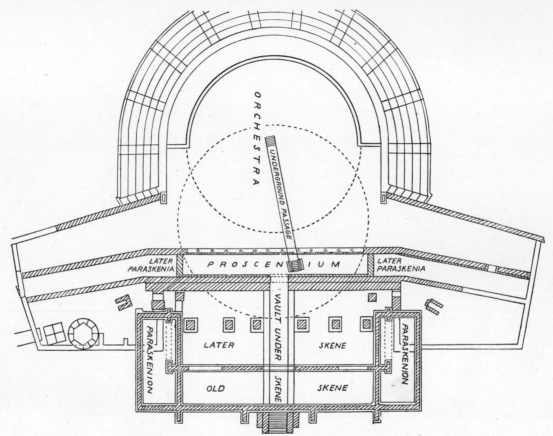

Fig. 6. PLAN OF THE THEATRE AT ERETRIA

Note should be taken of the old passageway leading to " Charon's steps " in the centre of the orchestra.

present to us the realization of a common ideal or plan. Each one has an orchestra, either completely circular as at Epidauros or capable of being continued circularly as at Priene. Each too has an auditorium which stretches slightly over a semicircle, the edges of the seats at the side of the *parodoi* forming a sharp angle with the front of the *skene*. So far all agree. Each has a *skene* with various parts, and it is at this point we must pause to consider the common qualities and the divergencies in those theatres when considered as a group. For this purpose we may glance at particular examples. In the beautifully symmetrical theatre at Epidauros, described by Pausanias as the most perfect in Greece, we have a playhouse begun under the direction of the younger Polyclitus in the fourth century B.C. and added to or altered in the two following centuries (Figs. 4 and 5). Here the *skene* is a rectangular building, divided into one large and two smaller rooms. Some few feet in front runs a set of half-columns of the Ionic order, roughly 11 feet 7 inches in height and 8 feet 8 inches from the front wall of the *skene*. At the ends there are two small projections (*paraskenia*), and a ramp or sloping ascent connects the extreme edges of the top of the row of columns with the beautifully proportioned gateways which stand at the openings of the *parodoi*.

At Eretria in Euboea the theatre also dates from the fourth century B.C., although all traces of the original scene-buildings have disappeared (Figs. 6 and 7). Some time about 300 B.C. and again in the first century B.C. its *skene* was altered. The first arrangement consisted of a rectangular scene-room with a row of columns flanked by two fairly large *paraskenia*. The second had the rectangular scene-room as before, but the columns, some 11 feet 6 inches high, continued straight across until they were met by side-walls which were continued along the *parodoi*.

Of later date is the theatre of Oropos in Attica, which was erected during the second or first century B.C. (Fig. 8). Here the formation of the scene-buildings corresponds more or less exactly to those at Eretria. The columns, of the Doric order, stretch at a distance of some 10 feet from

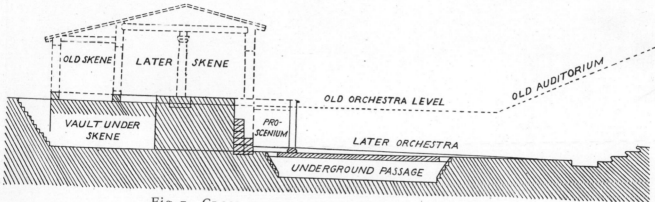

Fig. 7. Cross-section of the Theatre at Eretria

Comparison with Fig. 6 shows clearly the arrangement of the underground passage.

the front wall of the *skene* and are met by side-walls which slope off directly along the *parodoi*. The height of the columns, together with the entablature, is 8 feet 2 inches.

At Delos the columns, which are peculiarly carried right round the four walls of the *skene*, are 8 feet 3 inches high and set some 9 feet 10 inches from the wall of the scene-building (Fig. 9). In spite of later remodelling the original scene-buildings can be discerned in the theatre at Priene (Fig. 10). Here were ten Doric half-columns with two corner-pieces, the height being 8 feet 8 inches and the distance from the wall of the *skene* 8 feet 10 inches. So at Ephesus, where later Roman work has remodelled the whole, the Hellenistic *skene*, nearly 44 yards long, had in front a row of columns 8 feet 6 inches high and 9 feet 10 inches distant from the *skene* wall.

Finally one may look at the reconstructions undertaken during the second century B.C. in the Dionysian theatre at Athens. At this time the *paraskenia* were drawn back some 6 feet, and a series of stone columns, 13 feet high, was built about 9 feet from the front of the scene-building. This theatre, as indeed all the others, had a fairly lofty *episkenion* rising above the *skene* itself.

(vi) The Proscenium and Stage of the Hellenistic Style

In the theatres which have been briefly dealt with in the preceding section we have found as a common factor the presence of a series of pillars, at the most 13 feet high, but chiefly about 9 feet, placed some 8 or 10 feet from the scene-building and normally enclosed either by the *paraskenia* or by the abutting wall from the side of the *skene* itself. According to the view of Dörpfeld and others the actors stood on the ground-level with the columns behind them, and over that the

Fig. 8. THE SKENE OF THE THEATRE AT OROPOS

The proscenium pillars and the front wall of the scene-building are here shown.
Photo Deutsches Archaeologisches Institut.

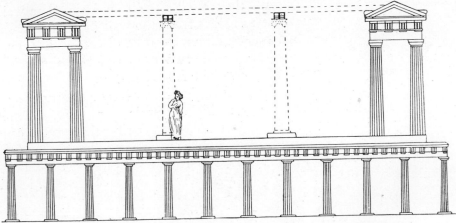

Fig. 9. RECONSTRUCTION OF THE STAGE AT DELOS

After Navarre, *Le Théâtre Grec*, p. 72.

towering height of the *episkenion*.   Several facts, however, make us pause ere we accept this view. (1) The actor with his κόθορνος (*kothornos*, cothurnus) and ὄγκος (*onkos*)[1] must have stood well over 7 feet in height.   Even the 13 feet of the Hellenistic stage at Athens was hardly imposing enough

[1] See *infra*, p. 39.

26

Fig. 10. THE THEATRE AT PRIENE

From Wiegand, *Priere*, Plate XVI.

to correspond with his appearance, and the top of his head must have been nearly level with the architrave over the columns in some theatres. (2) These columns, placed close together, frequently show no trace of doors, whereas doors are freely provided in the *episkenion*. (3) *Pinakes*, or painted boards, were undoubtedly placed between the proscenium pillars. Dörpfeld assumes that these served as scenery, but if this was their purpose surely the effect presented must have been ludicrous, for each *pinax*, or panel, was sometimes no larger than 8 feet by 5 feet. (4) Evidence as to the real nature of these front *pinakes* is provided by some records of money payments in connexion with the theatre at Delos. It is found there that the carpenter who made *one* of such *pinakes* was paid no less than 30 drachmae [1], whereas the painter

FIG. 11. SCENE FROM A PHLYAX COMEDY
Note should be taken of the plain wooden stage.
From Baumeister, *Denkmäler des klassischen Altertums*, iii, No. 1827.

who dealt with *two* of them received only 3 drachmae 1 obol.[2] The obvious implication is that the proscenium *pinax* was painted, not representationally, but merely with a wash of colour or at the most a formal design. (5) The stage at Epidauros shows an incline running to the top of the columns. It is assumed by Dörpfeld that the space at the top (made into a platform with wooden boards) was used only by divinities, but if this was the case the erection of the incline seems hardly to have been necessary. In itself it suggests that the platform so provided was used regularly by impersonators of ordinary characters in the dramas of the time.

Irresistibly, therefore, we are driven back from the acting-ground-level theory, and have to presuppose a wooden stage built on the top of the pillars, the *pinakes* being merely wooden panels, painted perhaps in simple colour, erected between the pillars to form a complete wall. Almost

FIG. 12. SCENE FROM A PHLYAX COMEDY
From the original in the Petrograd (Leningrad) Museum.

at once light is thrown on the subject by a comparison between this hypothetical stage and some vase-paintings depicting scenes of that farcical comedy of Magna Graecia known as the Phlyakes.

[1] Θεοδότῳ πίνακα εἰς τὸ προσκήνιον ποιήσαντι μισθὸς δραχμαὶ ΔΔΔ ("To Theodotos for making one *pinax* in the *proskenion*, 30 drachmae"). Here *proskenion* is used to refer to the row of columns in front of the skene. See *supra*, p. 22.

[2] Ἡρακλείδῃ εἰς τὸ προσκήνιον γράψαντι πίνακας δύο μισθὸς δραχμαὶ ⊢⊢⊢ Ι ("To Herakleides for painting two *pinakes* in the *proskenion*, 3 drachmae 1 obol").

Fig. 11 shows one of these. Attention may be drawn to the wooden platform and the obviously wooden supports. Similar wooden supports are delineated in Fig. 12. Next we may take Fig. 13, which clearly shows a burlesque of heroic drama. Here a wooden platform, supported by wooden props, is filled in with panels on which is painted a purely formal design. Steps lead from the stage-level to the ground. The wooden platform occurs again in Fig. 14, but here the place of the panels is taken by draped curtains. Finally, in Fig. 15 we reach the conclusion. Here the stage is not so clearly of wood, and formal pillars have taken the place of rough-hewn or square props. Behind the actors appear what look like larger painted panels on the proscenium or, as it is sometimes styled, the *episkenion*. The evidence of these scenes from the Phlyakes seems complete. But, it may be said, how could the actors and the chorus have intercourse if there was this high stage of from 7 to 10 feet in height? The answer is twofold. Firstly, such intercourse, by the later centuries, was hardly necessary.

Fig. 13. SCENE FROM A PHLYAX COMEDY
From the British Museum *Guide to Greek and Roman Life*.

By the third and second centuries the tragedy chorus had practically disappeared, while in comedy the choral odes had degenerated into mere detached entertainments. Secondly, there is always the possibility that a flight of steps led from the stage to the orchestra-level. Such steps are indicated in the vase-paintings mentioned above. Pollux [1] distinctly declares that the stage, the locality of the actors, was connected with the orchestra, the locality of the chorus, in this manner, [2] and steps are to be found in at least one theatre of Roman style.

Fig. 14. SCENE FROM A PHLYAX COMEDY
Note should be taken of the platform stage and of the decorated doorway.
From Bieber, *Denkmäler des Theaterwesens im Altertum*.

For the Hellenistic theatre, therefore, we have the following characteristics:

(1) A circular orchestra, or an orchestra capable of being extended in a circular form.

(2) An auditorium slightly larger than a semicircle.

(3) A rectangular *skene* usually divided into various rooms, and with from one to three doorways in the front wall of the second story.

---

[1] The quotations from Pollux, save for one or two minor deviations, are from the edition published at Leipzig in 1824 (*Iulii Pollucis Onomasticon cum Annotationibus Interpretum, curavit Gulielmus Dindorfius*).

[2] εἰσελθόντες δὲ κατὰ τὴν ὀρχήστραν, ἐπὶ τὴν σκηνὴν διὰ κλιμάκων ἀναβαίνουσι (" Mounting from the orchestra to the stage, they ascend by means of steps ") (*Onomastikon*, iv, 127).

29

(4) A series of pillars with panels set between, situate some 8 to 10 feet in front of the *skene*.

(5) A resultant stage normally 9 feet high and about 8 to 10 feet deep, stretching the entire length of the *skene*.

(6) An *episkenion* or *proskenion* [1] usually pierced by three doors, which, as will be seen later, had each a definite significance.

(vii) GRAECO-ROMAN THEATRES

To a certain number of theatres, notably those at Termessos, Sagalassos, Patara, Myra, Tralles, Magnesia, and Ephesus (in the altered form), has been given the title Graeco-Roman, these theatres displaying a combination, as it were, of Greek and Roman characteristics. It may be simplest, perhaps, to take the main features of these playhouses and consider them together. (1) In the first place, the auditorium for the most part still retained its old form, stretching beyond the regular semicircle (Fig. 16). (2) The orchestra, which had been completely circular in purely Greek hands, was encroached on by the scene-buildings, but always remained more than a semicircle (Figs. 16 and 17). In many of these theatres the orchestra if carried round in a complete circle would touch with its circumference the front of the scene-building proper, the stage jutting forward for about half its radius. (3) The lowest row of seats usually abutted directly on the orchestra, although this is by no means an invariable rule. (4) The stage-front was changed and the background elaborated. These are the most important points and require greater consideration.

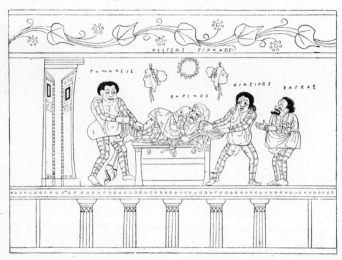

Fig. 15. SCENE FROM A PHLYAX COMEDY

Note should be taken of the formal stage supports and the suggestion of scenery.

From Baumeister, *op. cit.*, iii, No. 1830.

The dramatic fare in the Graeco-Roman theatres consisted mainly of comedy, and comedy of the type which deals with ordinary life. It is clear that this would demand greater verisimilitude, and that the columns supporting the Hellenistic stage might well seem out of place. As a consequence the normal frontage of the stage in a Graeco-Roman theatre was perfectly plain, or merely panelled, broken by two or three doors leading on to the orchestra-level. In height this stage was not quite so great as had been those of the Hellenistic style. A drop of a few feet is noticeable in almost all, and there is nothing so high as the Hellenistic stage at Athens. On the other hand, the depth is generally very much greater, reaching even to 20 feet. This, of course, is exactly what might have been expected, as the Hellenistic stage, although it was of plentiful length, was often extremely narrow.

Most characteristic of the Graeco-Roman theatre, however, was the elaborate scenic façade. Instead of a comparatively bare scene-building wall pierced with doors we find many varieties of

---

[1] In view of the later use of the word 'proscenium' it is perhaps better to use that term here for the wall at the back of the actors, which, according to this reconstruction of the Hellenistic theatre, would be that of the second story of the *skene*. As we have seen, the word *proskenion* is frequently used to indicate (1) the stage and (2) (more frequently) the row of pillars in front of the *skene*. This use, however, was not continued to later times, and may give rise to considerable confusion. The term ὑποσκήνιον (*hyposkenion*) or under-stage was evidently applied both to the space beneath the stage and to the row of pillars on which the stage was supported.

architectural adornment. At Termessos it takes the form of a series of pillars set on a solid foundation and broken by three doors (Fig. 17). At Ephesus varied architectural embellishment reaching to three stories makes a lofty and conventional background for the actors. There seven doors of entrance were provided, a large one in the centre flanked at each side by three of diminishing height. It is quite obvious that in these playhouses the stage and the 'setting' have grown

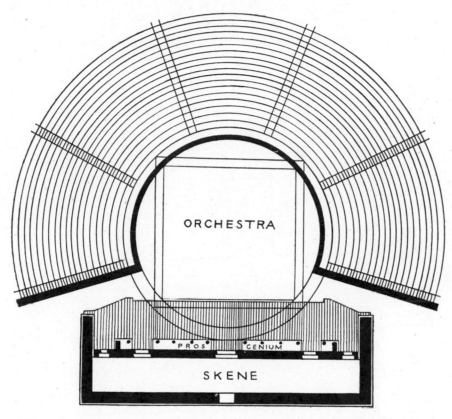

Fig. 16. PLAN OF THE GRAECO-ROMAN THEATRE AT TERMESSOS

Redrawn from Flickinger, *op. cit.*, p. 110.

to possess an almost dominating importance (Fig. 18). By this time Roman influence had come to oversway that of ancient Athens, and these Graeco-Roman playhouses form a fitting link between the Theatre of Dionysos and the theatre at Orange.

(viii) MACHINES

Although all these theatres were open-air structures the performances given there were not entirely without scenic embellishment ; machines and even scenery were utilized much more freely than one might have imagined possible. Pollux provides us with a list of some nineteen theatrical devices, and, although his account is exceedingly meagre, we can divine from it that scenic effects of a kind were regularly secured both in tragedy and in comedy. Some indication must now be given of the nature of these devices.

In the first place Pollux indicates the conventional nature of the three main doors in the background. The middle door, usually larger than the others, was the 'royal' entrance. It was regarded as the doorway of a palace or was presumed to belong to the protagonist in the drama.[1] That on the right was the door by which the second actor entered, or was supposed to lead to guest-chambers,[2] while that on the left belonged to a minor person, or formed a fictitious ruined temple, desert, or prison.[3] These were the doors which led directly into supposedly actual buildings, and for persons who were presumed to come from a place outside the two doors in the side-wings, or *paraskenia*, had to suffice, one leading toward the forum, the other to the outskirts of the city.[4]

These doors were, of course, permanent scenic features, and provided what may be styled symbolic or conventional settings, but besides that something must have been attempted in the way of representational effects. Vitruvius[5] declares that Aeschylus invented scene-painting, while Aristotle[6] ascribes the credit of this to Sophocles. Painted scenes of some kind, therefore, must have been in use, and we may assume that these came into existence at a time when the activities of these two dramatists coalesced, or, in other words, at some period immediately previous to 458 B.C. We have evidence that *pinakes* were used not merely to fill in the spaces between the proscenium pillars, but for the purpose of providing a scenic background. Some of these may have been fixed to the wall behind the actors, but normally they seem to have been attached to the περίακτοι (*periaktoi*), which are described for us by Pollux and Vitruvius.[7] These seem to have been triangular prisms, on each side of which was painted a certain scene. Placed on a central pivot, they could thus be revolved in order to display a change of scene. Probably they were fitted with a small ledge which could, if need be, accommodate the god who, in Vitruvius' words, is to appear with sound of "sudden

Fig. 17. The Theatre at Termessos
After Lanckoroński, *Städte Pamphyliens und Pisidiens*.

thunder." The exact position of the *periaktoi* has not yet been definitely determined, but it would seem probable that they stood in or by the two side-doorways—a suggestion which corresponds

---

[1] τριῶν δὲ, τῶν κατὰ τὴν σκηνὴν θυρῶν, ἡ μέση μὲν βασίλειον ἢ σπήλαιον, ἢ οἶκος ἔνδοξος ἢ πᾶν τοῦ πρωταγωνιστοῦ τοῦ δράματος (*Onomastikon*, iv, 124). Vitruvius speaks also of the *aulae regiae*. The convention cited by Pollux, whereby the doors belonged to definite characters, has a peculiar parallel in medieval times. Is the latter a relic of the mime tradition?

[2] ἡ δὲ δεξιὰ, τοῦ δευτεραγωνιστοῦντος καταγώγιον . . . ἐν δὲ τραγῳδίᾳ ἡ μὲν δεξιὰ θύρα ξενών ἐστιν (*op. cit.*, iv, 124–125). Vitruvius classes both the right and left doors as *hospitalia*.

[3] ἡ δὲ ἀριστερὰ τὸ εὐτελέστατον ἔχει πρόσωπον ἢ ἱερὸν ἐξηρημωμένον, . . . ἢ ἄοικός ἐστιν. ἐν δὲ τραγῳδίᾳ . . . εἱρκτὴ ἡ λαιά (*op. cit.*, iv, 124–125).

[4] παρ' ἑκάτερα δὲ τῶν δύο θυρῶν τῶν περὶ τὴν μέσην ἄλλαι δύο εἶεν ἂν μία ἑκατέρωθεν, πρὸς ἃς αἱ περίακτοι συμπεπήγασιν (*op. cit.*, iv, 126). Vitruvius refers to these: "Secundum ea loca versurae sunt procurrentes, quae efficiunt una a foro, altera a peregre, aditus in scaenam" (v, 6).

[5] *Op. cit.*, vii, Praefatio § 11.   [6] *Poetics*, 1449 A, 18.

[7] καταβλήματα δὲ, ὑφάσματα, ἢ πίνακες ἦσαν, ἔχοντες γραφὰς τῇ χρείᾳ τῶν δραμάτων προσφόρους· κατεβάλλετο δὲ ἐπὶ τὰς περιάκτους (Pollux, *op. cit.*, iv, 131).

"Secundum autem spatia ad ornatus comparata, quae loca Graeci περιάκτους dicunt ab eo, quod machinae sunt in his locis versatiles trigonoe habentes singulares species ornationis, quae, cum aut fabularum mutationes sunt futurae, seu deorum adventus cum tonitribus repentinis, versentur mutentque speciem ornationis in fronte" (Vitruvius, *op. cit.*, v, 6).

with the conventional significance of these doors, for the *periaktos* on the left displayed distant country scenes, while that on the right showed parts of the city.[1]

More important still is a consideration of the machines regularly employed at least in the Hellenistic period, and here Pollux becomes our principal guide. (1) First comes the ἐκκύκλημα (*ekkuklema*).[2] Described by Pollux as a platform upon which a throne is set and obviously derived from the verb ἐκκυκλεῖν (*ekkuklein*, 'to roll out'), it was clearly some device whereby the result of interior action, such as dead bodies after a murder could be shown. Many references to it are made both in the plays themselves and by later commentators, and considerable discussion has been devoted to it by modern scholars. A view which is commonly held gives to it a semicircular shape, so that the low platform could be swung out at any of the three main stage-doors. (2) Evidently associated with this machine is the ἐξώστρα (*exostra*), which Pollux identifies with the *ekkuklema*.[3] It is possible that the machine indicated here was a low platform, not revolved as the *ekkuklema*, but pushed out on wheels or rollers. (3) Still more common was the machine proper, or μηχανή (*mechane*), described by quite a number of classical writers.[4] This appears to have consisted of a hook and pulley set at the very top of the *skene* to the left-hand side of the stage. By its means divinities could be raised or lowered. Examples of its use are numerous after about 430 B.C., when, no doubt, it was introduced in a perfected form. Aristophanes hangs Socrates in a basket by its help in the *Clouds*, while a similar device is to be noted in the *Birds*. In tragedy it seems implied in at least two plays of Aeschylus, and occurs frequently in Euripides. It is from this use of the *mechane* that there arose the phrase θεὸς ἀπὸ μηχανῆς, repeated in Latin as *deus ex machina*, which, originally applied solely to the physical appearance of the divinity, came to signify a dramatic device introduced for the purpose of bringing a problem or an action to a swift, and often to an unsatisfactorily artificial, conclusion.

The *mechane* possibly appeared under a variety of different names. Thus Pollux enumerates

Fig. 18. Terra-cotta Relief showing a Stage Wall

From Ernst R. Fiechter, *Die baugeschichtliche Entwicklung des antiken Theaters : Eine Studie.* 130 Seiten Text und 132 Abbildungen auf 43 Tafeln. C. H. Beck'sche Verlagsbuchhandlung, München, 1914.

---

[1] παρ' ἑκάτερα δὲ τῶν δύο θυρῶν τῶν περὶ τὴν μέσην ἄλλαι δύο εἶεν ἄν, μία ἑκατέρωθεν, πρὸς ἃς αἱ περίακτοι συμπεπήγασιν, ἡ μὲν δεξιὰ τὰ ἔξω πόλεως δηλοῦσα, ἡ δὲ ἑτέρα τὰ ἐκ πόλεως, μάλιστα τὰ ἐκ λιμένος. καὶ θεούς τε θαλαττίους ἐπάγει, καὶ πάνθ' ὅσα ἐπαχθέστερα ὄντα ἡ μηχανὴ φέρειν ἀδυνατεῖ. εἰ δ' ἐπιστραφεῖεν αἱ περίακτοι, ἡ δεξιὰ μὲν ἀμείβει τόπον ἀμφότεραι δὲ χώραν ὑπαλλάττουσιν (Pollux, *op. cit.*, iv, 126). It has already been seen that the *pinakes* were sometimes merely panels connecting the pillars which supported the stage. These must be carefully distinguished from the scenic panels. The former were probably painted in one colour only, or with purely formal designs.

[2] καὶ τὸ μὲν ἐκκύκλημα, ἐπὶ ξύλων ὑψηλὸν βάθρον, ᾧ ἐπίκειται θρόνος. δείκνυσι δὲ τὰ ὑπὸ σκηνὴν ἐν ταῖς οἰκίαις ἀπόρρητα πραχθέντα, καὶ τὸ ῥῆμα τοῦ ἔργου καλεῖται ἐκκυκλεῖν. ἐφ' οὗ δὲ εἰσάγεται τὸ ἐκκύκλημα, εἰσκύκλημα ὀνομάζεται, καὶ χρὴ τοῦτο νοεῖσθαι καθ' ἑκάστην θύραν, οἱονεὶ καθ' ἑκάστην οἰκίαν (*op. cit.*, iv, 128). [3] τὴν δὲ ἐξώστραν ταὐτὸν τῷ ἐκκυκλήματι νομίζουσιν (*op. cit.*, iv, 129).

[4] ἡ μηχανὴ δὲ θεοὺς δείκνυσι, καὶ ἥρως τοὺς ἐν ἀέρι . . . καὶ κεῖται κατὰ τὴν ἀριστερὰν πάροδον, ὑπὲρ τὴν σκηνὴν τὸ ὕψος (*op. cit.*, iv, 128). Suidas declares it was also called the ἐώρημα (*eorema*). The hook at the top was the ἅρπαξ (*harpax*) or ἀγκυρίς (*ankuris*). See Haigh, *The Attic Theatre*, p. 209.

also (4) the *theologeion*, (5) the crane, and (6) the suspension machine, while Suidas, as we have seen, suggests ἐώρημα as a synonym for the *mechane*. Concerning the *theologeion* opinions differ; by some it is thought to have been merely an upper platform, by others it is assumed to have been a regular piece of theatrical machinery. Pollux says little to guide us save that here gods made their appearance. The crane (γέρανος) seems to have been a machine used for swifter effect, particularly employed when a body had to be snatched from the stage.[1] The suspension machine (αἰῶραι, *aiorai*) may simply be a name for the ropes by which divinities were suspended in the air, but was probably distinguished from the *mechane* by the fact that the ropes were invisible and that there was no platform.[2] Finally (7) Pollux mentions as the equivalent of the *mechane* in comedy the *krade* (κράδη), or 'fig-branch';[3] this is referred to also by Plutarch.

A peculiar machine is suggested by Pollux when he deals (8) with the *skope* (σκοπή), which he tells us is made for those who view the action. It seems probable here that he is referring to a particular vantage-point from which the 'director' could supervise the play being performed below. (9) Little information is given us of the 'wall' (τεῖχος, *teichos*) save that it and (10) the tower (πύργος, *purgos*) were raised parts from which persons might look down upon the stage. It may have been that these were lofty practicable platforms. (11) The beacon-tower (φρυκτώριον, *phruktorion*), as Pollux notes, indicates its purpose in its very name. (12) The *distegia* (διστεγία), literally 'the second floor,' provided the means whereby actors could mount to the roof of a house and thence survey the characters below.[4] (13) The κεραυνοσκοπεῖον (*keraunoskopeion*), or 'lightning-machine,' is described by Pollux merely as a kind of *periaktos*.[5] It may have been, as Weismann conjectured, a prism with the three sides coloured black, across each of which was painted a lightning-flash. (14) With it naturally goes the βροντεῖον (*bronteion*), or 'thunder-machine'; this machine consisted of jars filled with stones, the latter being poured noisily into a vessel of brass.[6] (15) The 'semicircle,' says Pollux, is sufficiently indicated by its name. It stood by the orchestra and gave a view of a far-distant landscape—a portion of a city or sailors upon the sea.[7] The description seems to suggest some kind of a cyclorama. (16) The στροφεῖον (*stropheion*), which from its name seems to have been a revolving machine, showed Heroes who had been taken into the company of the gods, or those who had met their deaths by sea or in battle.[8] (17) 'Charon's steps' must simply have been trap-doors, possibly in the orchestra, through which ghosts and spirits made their appearance, a simple device, elaborated perhaps in the (18) ἀναπιέσματα (*anapiesmata*), which apparently raised the spirits mechanically from the deeps.[9]

Perhaps scholars have not made quite as much of these machines as they deserve. It is true that we are unaware when the majority of these came into being, but we have the testimony of Pollux, supported by many other scattered authorities, that they existed at one period or another during the career of the Greek or Graeco-Roman theatre. Their importance lies in the facts that they show the Greek stage-managers to have been almost as eager as managers of to-day to

---

[1] ἡ δὲ γέρανος μηχάνημά ἐστιν ἐκ μετεώρου καταφερόμενον ἐφ' ἁρπαγῇ σώματος, ᾧ κέχρηται Ἡὼς ἁρπάζουσα τὸ σῶμα τοῦ Μέμνονος (*op. cit.*, iv, 130).

[2] αἰώρας δ' ἂν εἴποις τοὺς κάλως οἳ κατήρτηνται ἐξ ὕψους ἀνέχειν τοὺς ἐπὶ τοῦ ἀέρος φέρεσθαι δοκοῦντας ἥρως ἢ θεούς (*op. cit.*, iv, 131).

[3] ὁ δὲ ἐν τραγῳδίᾳ μηχανή, τοῦτο ἐν κωμῳδίᾳ κράδη (*op. cit.*, iv, 128).

[4] ἡ δὲ διστεγία ποτὲ μὲν ἐν οἴκῳ βασιλείῳ διῆρες δωμάτιον, οἷον ἀφ' οὗ ἐν Φοινίσσαις ἡ Ἀντιγόνη βλέπει τὸν στρατόν, ποτὲ δὲ καὶ κέραμος, ἀφ' οὗ βάλλουσι τῷ κεράμῳ. ἐν δὲ κωμῳδίᾳ ἀπὸ τῆς διστεγίας πορνοβοσκοί τι κατοπτεύουσιν ἢ γράδια ἢ γύναια καταβλέπει (*op. cit.*, iv, 129). Contrast the 'upper stage' of the Elizabethan theatre. [5] See p. 32. κεραυνοσκοπεῖον . . . ἐστι περίακτος ὑψηλή (*op. cit.*, iv, 130).

[6] τὸ δὲ βροντεῖον, ὑπὸ τὴν σκηνὴν ὄπισθεν, ἄσκοι ψήφων ἔμπλεοι διωκόμενοι φέρονται κατὰ χαλκωμάτων (*op. cit.*, iv, 130).

[7] τῷ δὲ ἡμικυκλίῳ, τὸ μὲν σχῆμα, ὄνομα. ἡ δὲ θέσις, κατὰ τὴν ὀρχήστραν. ἡ δὲ χρεία, δηλοῦσα πόρρω τινὰ τῆς πόλεως τόπον, ἢ τοὺς ἐν θαλάττῃ νηχομένους (*op. cit.*, iv, 131–132).

[8] ὥσπερ καὶ τὸ στροφεῖον, ὃ τοὺς Ἥρως ἔχει, τοὺς εἰς τὸ θεῖον μεθεστηκότας, ἢ τοὺς ἐν πελάγει, ἢ πολέμῳ τελευτῶντας (*op. cit.*, iv, 132).

[9] αἱ δὲ Χαρώνιοι κλίμακες, κατὰ τὰς ἐκ τῶν ἑδωλίων καθόδους κείμεναι, τὰ εἴδωλα ἀπ' αὐτῶν ἀναπέμπουσι. τὰ δὲ ἀναπιέσματα, τὸ μέν ἐστιν ἐν τῇ σκηνῇ ὡς ποταμὸν ἀνελθεῖν ἢ τοιοῦτον πρόσωπον, τὸ δὲ περὶ τοὺς ἀναβαθμούς, ἀφ' ὧν ἀνέβαινον Ἐρινύες (*op. cit.*, iv, 132). These 'Charon's steps' are preserved in the theatre at Eretria.

secure spectacular effects, and that these passages of Pollux were eagerly conned by the theatre innovators of the Renascence. Perhaps a performance in an ancient theatre was not so statuesque, so innocent of purely 'theatrical' devices as sometimes we think; by these machines it was put in touch with the theatres of the modern world.

It will be readily understood what a service the elaborated scene-building and its accompanying contrivances did to the dramatists of the time. We have only to analyse the difficulties which must have faced any contemporary playwright to realize the fresh realms which were opened before him by successive improvements in the theatrical craft. Thus as a typical example one might take the prohibition imposed on the dramatist in regard to the presentation of murder on the stage. Originally due, apparently, to the religious associations of dramatic performances, this prohibition was almost absolute. In the earliest period the only method of informing the audience of some scene of violence was by introducing a messenger—a device rendered necessary by the physical conditions surrounding the dramatist, but essentially dull and uninspiring. With the appearance of the scene-building, however, a further means of overcoming the prohibition was presented. Behind the closed doors the cry of a Clytemnestra could be heard; or, still more effective, an actor could stand at the door and in broken words tell the audience of what he sees within. The last stage is reached when the ἐκκύκλημα is invented. Now the dramatist can present not merely the cries of the victim, but the dead body of the victim itself. All that he has to do is to arrange a tableau of murderer and murdered on the semicircular platform, wheel that round and display it to the wondering and terrified gaze of the spectators. It is obvious that this effect could not have been secured by the mere opening of the central doors. Only those directly in front could have seen the tableau; it would have remained out of the line of sight of those who sat toward the sides of the auditorium. Partly because of the ease with which the results of violent scenes might be shown, this convention, which forbade murder upon the stage, was passed on as a tradition to later times, being rephrased by Horace in classical Latin and imitated in Italian by critics and creative authors of the Renascence.

(ix) FESTIVAL ARRANGEMENTS AND THE CHORUS

There are many other things which have to be studied if we wish to understand the Greek drama and its theatre aright. Thus, for example, when we are reading a Greek play we want to know at what season of the year it was produced, at the City Dionysia in March or at the Lenaea in January. The reason for this is that, navigation being unsafe in the latter month, few strangers were present at the Lenaea. The performances were regarded as more homely and intimate than those which took place at the City Dionysia, when Athens was crowded with representatives of the allied states. It was at the City Dionysia that Aristophanes produced the *Babylonians*, in which he represented the allies as ground down by the tyranny of Cleon. The result was the impeachment of the author by the enraged demagogue, not because the former had dared to make fun of the government, but because he had done so παρόντων τῶν ξένων—in the presence of strangers. Such slips as this of Aristophanes were, however, not frequent, and we can generally trace a restraint and a marked care in the dramas, particularly the comedies, written to be performed at the more mixed festival.

So, too, the reader requires to know that plays in Greece were written in competition, a prize being awarded to that dramatist who succeeded in winning the favour of the judges selected by the people. The judges were not always uninfluenced by popular clamour, and as a result the play-wrights often made direct efforts to capture the plaudits of the mass. Openly the comic poets bid for success, sometimes going so far as to present titbits to the crowd—a practice ridiculed by Aristophanes when, in the *Peace* (421 B.C.), he caused one grain of corn to be given to each member of the audience. More decorously, but not less eagerly, the tragic authors vied with one another, writing, sometimes with tongue in cheek, passages which were calculated to gain the applause of patriotic Athenians.

Many peculiar difficulties which an Athenian dramatist had to overcome depended upon the materials at his command in the shape of performers and chorus. Aeschylus, at the beginning of his career, had to struggle on with only two actors and a chorus. Even in the days of Euripides three actors appear to have been all that was allowed to the playwright. Not only so, but the tragic poet had to obey the rules of dignity laid down without actual enunciation by his audience. Traditionalism ruled dominant. Even when three actors were permitted no playwright succeeded in evolving that three-character dialogue which plays such a marked part in modern drama, and which was developed, because of the greater freedom and realistic licence of the *comus*, in Greek comedy. A certain conventional grandeur clung to the characters, even as their number was settled by convention. The manners depicted were mostly those of an heroic age, not of contemporary times. Women moved on a social equality with men such as was unknown in Athens of the fifth century B.C., but which had been described in immortal words by Homer centuries before.

The chorus by itself presented difficulties to the playwrights. The original dithyrambic chorus seems to have consisted of fifty performers, those for whom Aeschylus created the fifty daughters of Danaus in his *Suppliants*. By 487 B.C., however, the number was reduced to twelve, the reason being probably the convention of presenting at one time four plays—three tragedies and a satyric drama. A chorus of fifty persons for each would have been costly and difficult to rehearse ; while fifty performers in all could easily be split into four separate divisions. Under Sophocles the number was raised to fifteen, possibly because of some exigencies of the dance evolutions. The presence of this chorus throughout the entire action of the drama offered to the author the problem of explaining to the audience the reason of their position on the stage. The earlier dramatists normally escaped from problems such as this by making the chorus the centre of the action, but Euripides displays in many of his tragedies his dissatisfaction with a traditional dramatic element which he must have come to regard as a mere encumbrance. In his plays the presence of the chorus is often deliberately slurred over ; and in this way he stands as intermediary between Aeschylus and those later dramatists who virtually banished it completely. In the third century B.C. we discover that the comic chorus has been reduced to seven persons ; in the second century B.C. it has shrunk to four and is evidently non-existent in tragedy. More than this, by the time of the New Comedy, and perhaps before, the chorus no longer stood in the orchestra throughout the whole of the action. It came on solely to present entertainments not necessarily associated with the plot of the play, in what may be styled the *entr'actes*. The process which led to this culmination is easily studied. In Aeschylus always and usually in Sophocles the words given to the chorus are intimately related to the action which has preceded on the stage and to the fate of the main tragic characters. In Euripides, on the contrary, the choral chant is often merely an independent lyric, of great beauty perhaps, but of no value for the development of the play. A stage further is marked in the works of Agathon, who, according to Aristotle, was the first to diversify his choral odes with ἐμβόλιμα (*embolima*, things thrown in), and in those of Aristophanes. The latest comedies by the latter present a peculiarity to our view. Sometimes, where we should have expected a formal ode from the chorus, there is marked in the manuscript merely the word *XOPOY* (*chorou*, of the chorus). This is evidently a stage direction and implies : 'Let the chorus perform here, singing and dancing as it will.' These ἐμβόλιμα and this *XOPOY* prepare the way for the undramatic choral entertainments which, we know, accompanied the New Comedy of later years. It is unquestionable that the choral element would have disappeared long before it did, had religious conservatism not dictated its retention. In later ages, of course, it reappeared, but only because of a kind of literary traditionalism.

THE GREEK THEATRE

(x) THE UNITIES AND THE ACTS

Perhaps in dealing with the chorus a word or two may be said concerning the famous unities and concerning the division of dramas into acts. It has been often pointed out by critics that the unities, as elaborated and expressed by Renascence critics, were almost wholly unknown in Greece. On the other hand, Greek drama does present the basis on which the later theories were based. The unity of time was referred to vaguely by Aristotle when he declared that tragedy, in contradistinction to the epic, was generally limited in duration, often being confined to twenty-four hours. It is obvious, first of all, that this general statement is strictly true, and, secondly, that it was more imperative to confine the duration of the action in Greek than in modern drama. The chorus, we must remember, stood continuously in the orchestra. Because of its presence the dramatic action had to be rushed forward to its conclusion. On the other hand, we must observe that the Greek dramatists evidently felt the restriction, for they have employed in the words of the chorus itself a certain species of idealized time. Indeed, we meet in Greek drama that peculiar phenomemon which, by critics of Shakespeare, is called a 'double clock,' where two separate impressions, or sets of facts, are presented before an audience. It is observable also that the tradition of the trilogy, by which three plays on the same general theme were produced together, provided the Greeks with a method of escape. Where the *Orestes* story would hardly be fully intelligible by itself, the conjunction of an *Orestes* with a preceding *Agamemnon* and a succeeding *Furies* supplied the spectators with what a modern dramatist would have to include in a single play. The unity of action, in the broadest significance of the term, has naturally to be preserved in all drama ; but even in the narrower sense as implying an insistence upon one theme and upon one theme alone, it was never strictly adhered to in the realms of the Greek drama. Even in what seems at first sight to be the purest tragedy, comic elements were occasionally introduced. Old nurses and messengers were depicted with frequent touches of humour, so that the impression could not have been so simple and mono-emotional as Renascence critics declared it ought to be. Finally, there is the unity of place not mentioned at all in Aristotle's *Poetics*. At first glance it might seem as if this unity of place would have been indelibly impressed upon Greek drama because of the physical conditions of the play-house ; but even in this respect the stricter assumptions of the pseudo-classic critics are not justified. Both in Aeschylus' *Eumenides* and in Sophocles' *Ajax* the rules are broken, even if there is nothing of that violent and frequent alteration of locality which is such a marked feature of modern theatres. Undoubtedly there were limits beyond which the Greek dramatists could not go; undoubtedly, as compared with playhouses of to-day, their theatres imposed upon them restrictions which proved ultimately the basis for the theories of Renascence philosophers. At the same time we must note that the restrictions were not final and critically imposed; that there was always a margin of licence ; and that the dramatists, not being critic-bound as were those of later days, succeeded in securing an even greater concentration of effect and sometimes an even more delicate subtlety in the seizing of situation, through the conventions within which they, as artists, had to work.

This question of the unities, itself dependent on the structure of the Greek playhouse, is intimately connected with the division of dramas into portions or acts. The Old Comedy of Aristophanes knew naught of formal dividing, and, although we can trace in general various portions fairly clearly marked, there is no norm which we can establish as the ideal to which the dramatists looked for their model. We may on the other hand state in bold terms that the comedies of Aristophanes do as a rule fall into seven separate parts or collections. There is, first of all, the πρόλογος (*prologos*, prologue), in which the general outline of the plot is presented, followed by the πάροδος (*parodos*, entrance), the entrance-song of the chorus. These two parts are preparatory for the ἀγών (*agon*), or dramatized debate between the principal characters of the comedy. The ἀγών over, the chorus comes forward to address the audience in the παράβασις (*parabasis*, from παραβαίνειν, *para-bainein*, to come forward), a part which is itself apportionable into many subdivisions. This choral ode is followed by a number of ἐπεισόδια (*epeisodia*), or episodes, in which action enters more into play, the episodes for the most part illustrating the theme which in the ἀγών had been treated in an abstract and theoretical manner. When the histrionic action has ceased the chorus sings its στάσιμα (*stasima*) or χορικά (*chorika*), in which, addressing the audience once more, it draws conclusions from the ἐπεισόδια and sometimes from the ἀγών. Finally, leaving the theatre, the chorus sings its last song, the ἔξοδος (*exodos*, exit-song), often addressing the audience directly and pointing out salient features of the play. In tragedy a simpler division is apparent. Here, in spite of a certain amount of variation, we can trace a general tendency toward the presenting of five main portions of histrionic action (ἐπεισόδια) separated by four or more choral chants. It seems probable that, when the chorus disappeared as an integral part of the drama, these five portions, indicated even in Greek days as τὰ πέντε μέρη (the five parts), were standardized and that this example was that which Horace followed when he advised the would-be writer to make his tragedy of neither more nor less than five acts, while Horace's advice was, in its turn, taken over by the critics of the Renascence.

(xi) MASKS AND COSTUMES

The performance of a Greek play, whether comedy or tragedy, differed from a modern production not only in the facts that the theatre was an open-air structure and that a chorus played so large a part in the dialogue. The costumes, and above all the masks, gave to it a special character of its own. In any consideration of the costumes of the tragic actors it must be remembered that the manners portrayed in the tragedy as well as the themes of the plays reached back to the cycle of Homeric legend. For the Greeks, however, no thoughts of historical accuracy prescribed a dress which copied exactly that worn in previous centuries, and a solution seems to have been found in a conventionalized stage-costume which was similar to, yet differed widely from, the dresses of ordinary life. That this typical tragic costume was fully established, if it was not actually invented by him, in the time of Aeschylus is amply proved from references in later writings, and it endured down to Roman days, traditional conservatism having forbidden experimental alteration.[1] This actual dress may claim our attention first, as being the subject most easily disposed of. In simple terms we may say that the fundamental article of dress was the χιτών (*chiton*), a loose-flowing garment which extended from the neck to the ankles. The χιτών, of course, was worn in daily life as well, but the stage χιτών was distinguished from the ordinary χιτών by several peculiarities. (1) Because they were thought to be degenerate and effeminate, sleeves were eschewed by the Athenians. The stage-garment, however, was provided with such sleeves extending to the wrists. (2) Whereas the ordinary χιτών was usually belted at the waist, on the stage the girdle was worn just below the breast. This, as will be seen, was due to the exaggerated height of the tragic actor. (3) Instead of being always composed of white or of self-coloured materials, this χιτών was often adorned with many bright hues and was ornamented, now with formal designs, now with painted animals, figures, or symbolical forms (Fig. 19).[2] This richness of colouring must ever be borne in mind when we speak of the 'statuesque' quality of classical Athenian performances.

Above the χιτών was thrown a cloak, which might either be the ἱμάτιον (*himation*) or the χλαμύς (*chlamus*). The former was a long covering thrown over the right shoulder, the latter a short

---

[1] It will be understood here that the costume referred to is that of the actors and not of the chorus.

[2] καὶ ἐσθῆτες μὲν τραγικαί, ποικίλον. οὕτω γὰρ ἐκαλεῖτο ὁ χιτών (Pollux, *Onomastikon*, iv, 115).

mantle cast over the left shoulder. These, like the χιτών, were gorgeously coloured, and, judging from the account of Pollux, we may hazard the conjecture that the colours were employed for symbolic effect. Thus it would seem that dark or dim colours signified grief or mourning (symbolism of emotion), and that queens wore garments in which purple played a predominant part (symbolism of station). In all probability the Greek dramatists were aided in their delineation of character and of soul-state by these means. It is undeniable, also, that while normally the principal figures in a Greek tragedy all wore this conventional costuming, special garments were occasionally employed to signify

either the profession of the wearer or his immediate condition. Thus Pollux informs us that
Telephus and Philoctetes, being in a state of abject
misery, were clad in rags, and we may presume
that the lower-class characters, such as servants or
messengers, wore garments nearer to those in
ordinary use. Small details of apparel too helped
to make distinctions. Kings wore their crowns as
they did in the Elizabethan theatre. A Persian
sported his turban over the ordinary stage-dress.
Hercules carried his club and lion's skin. Old men
rested wearily on a stick or crutch. Granted that
there was an understanding on the part of the
audience, this conventional symbolism of attire must
have gone far toward making the natures and the
status of the various characters perfectly plain.

In connexion with the garments worn mention
may be made of two peculiar features which the
Athenian stage shared with the stage of China to-
day. Probably because of the vastness of the
Grecian playhouse the actor was usually raised to
an abnormal height by the use of the κόθορνος
(*kothornos*, cothurnus), variously known as the
ἐμβάτης (*embates*) and the ὀκρίβας (*okribas*). These
were boots with a heavy wooden sole, generally
painted, no doubt with symbolic colouring. If the

Fig. 19. Andromeda in Stage Dress
After Navarre, *op. cit.*, p. 205.

origin of the cothurnus, however, was due to the desire to make the actor seem taller than he was in reality, the prevalent wish for symbolism certainly entered in to give it a subordinate importance. Thus the height of the cothurnus varied in accordance with the importance of the character. A monarch was entitled to a loftier boot than was one of his attendant lords, and possibly the gradation passed down until, among the chorus, the heavily raised boot was non-existent. Along with this cothurnus must be taken the ὄγκος (*onkos*), a lofty headdress which towered over the mask, reminding us at times of the feathered head-gear of Restoration heroes and of the weirdly dressed performers in Chinese drama. This *onkos* and cothurnus, as is obvious, must have raised an actor of 6 feet to well over 7 feet 6 inches, and, to prevent his appearance from seeming unduly slim, padding was freely used to increase the bulk as well as the height. Perhaps this bulk corresponded also with the dignity of the characters. We know that kings wore a special short garment, heavily padded, to which was given the name of κόλπωμα (*kolpoma*).

The great characteristic of the Greek tragic actor was, however, not a portion of his dress, but the mask which rendered in conventional forms an indication of his age, station, and prevalent mood.

Fig. 20. COTHURNUS, MASKS, AND ONKOS ON THE MODERN CHINESE STAGE

While the mask owes its being without question to the religious ceremonies from which tragedy was born, it was, partly at least, dependent upon the theatre in which the performances were given.

Fig. 21. TERRA-COTTA FIGURE OF AN ACTOR
From Bieber, *op. cit.*

Facial expression would have been lost in the vastness of the Athenian playhouse; the mask gave typical expression in more easily visible form. The small number of actors allowed could not, without its help, have sustained their many parts. The aid given through the resonance of the widely opened mouth must have proved a welcome assistance even in theatres where, as we know, the acoustic properties were well-nigh perfect. For many reasons, then, traditionally religious as well as theatrical, the mask was retained as a prime feature of the actor's attire. Made of linen, cork, or wood, these masks provided much information to the audience. For our knowledge of the typical varieties the account given by Pollux, if meagre, is invaluable. In his work are enumerated nearly thirty masks for tragedy, and we gather that the mask-maker endeavoured, above all other things, to indicate the age of the person represented. Six old men are described in the *Onomastikon* as follows: (1) First comes the shaven type, the oldest of all, with a few white locks attached to the *onkos*. His mask depicts extreme age. This is the type of Priam. (2) Then there comes the man who is not quite so old—the " white " man, so he is styled by Pollux—with grey locks, a thick white beard, hanging eyebrows, and, above, a small *onkos*. Thus, no doubt, was Cadmus played. (3) Coming downward, we meet with the grey-haired man, of a dark or sallow complexion, the Oedipus of these type-characters, on the verge of old age. (4) Middle-aged men come next. The tyrant with thick black locks and beard, sharp face, and lofty *onkos* is nearest the age of Oedipus. Aegisthus must have been of this nature.

40

(5) Blonde hair seems to have indicated extremer youth, for there next comes the "fair" man, of a pleasant complexion and sporting a lower *onkos*, the "hero" proper, companioned (6) by the "fairer" man, rather paler and displaying a countenance which betokens distress or sickness.

This list of the older men in Pollux is followed by a list of eight young men, again distinguished by the colour of their hair, complexions, and *onkos*. (1) The eldest of these is the "good-for-all-

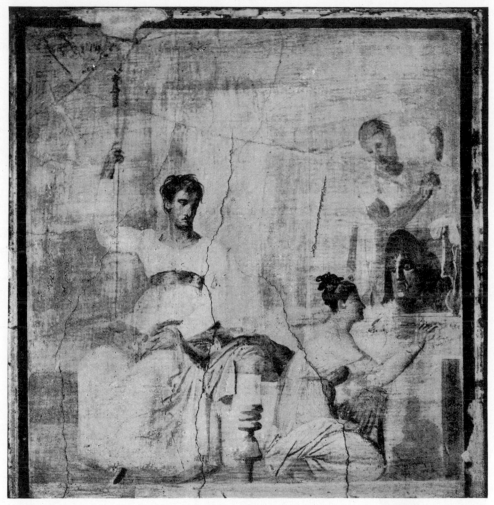

Fig. 22. A Tragedy King

The actor is shown with hair disarranged, as if he had but newly taken off the mask which is placed on the table to his left.

Photo Alinari.

work," a character who has no beard, but is granted thick black hair and locks. He is somewhat tanned in face, but has a good complexion, and is typified in the person of the youthful hero. (2) The character with crisp flaxen hair, fierce countenance and bushy eyebrows comes next, accompanied by (3) another, just a little younger. The description seems to be that of the youthful hero, corresponding in temperament with the last two types of middle-aged men, who obviously belong to the hero class. (4) Contrasted with these comes the "soft" type, pale of face, jocund of appearance, shining, as Pollux says, with a godlike beauty. A youthful divinity, such as Dionysos or Apollo, may well have appeared in such a mask. Perhaps Castor and Pollux belong to the same group.

41

(5) There come next the "squalid" characters with livid cheeks, light hair, and eyes downcast through misery. These are the youths whom misfortune has driven into despair. (6) Finally we reach the "pale" type and his companion (7) the quasi-pale type, the first very fair-haired, with lean, emaciated cheeks, the second more like the " good-for-all-work " but wasted by suffering. The former appears as Polydore's ghost in *Hecuba*, the latter as the fainting Orestes and as the lovelorn Hemon in *Antigone*.

Fig. 23. MASK OF A TRAGIC HERO
From Bieber, *op. cit.*

The servants of tragic drama appear next in Pollux' account, three varieties being noted. (1) The old man clad in leather, with a leather cap in place of an *onkos*, white locks, sallow face, sharp nose, and raised eyebrows, is the more intelligent servitor or the old tutor. (2) The servant with the peaked beard is middle-aged. He bears a high and wide *onkos* hollowed round the circumference. His hair is light in colour and his countenance ruddy. He is the typical messenger. (3) With him appears another snub-nosed messenger, fair also, with a ruddy complexion and hair parted at the middle of the head.

The three servants complete the list of male parts, so that we may now turn to the women characters. These, like the men, are arranged by Pollux in order of age. (1) There is first the grey-haired old woman, above the rest in years and position. She wears a medium-sized *onkos* and is pale of face. (2) The free old woman has grey hair, pale features, a smaller *onkos*, and locks streaming down to the neck. (3) Next comes the old woman slave with ruddy cheeks and a sheepskin bonnet instead of an *onkos*. This is a typical old nurse. (4) The middle-aged servant has a small *onkos*, is pale of face, and has hair streaked with grey. (5) The *diphtheritis*, or leather-clad woman, is younger than this type. She has no *onkos*. (6) "The woman with flowing hair" is dark, with pale, sad complexion, companioned by (7) another with long hair at the sides and short hair on the forehead. (8) The newly violated woman has a special tonsure. (9 and 10) The young girl with shorn locks has a pale complexion; of this type there seem to be two varieties. (11) Finally we find the very young child.

Both in tragedy and in comedy, of course, these type-masks were supplemented by the use of special masks which indicated either the mental or physical state of the wearer, or the legendary attributes of the fictitious person. The horned Actaeon, the blind Phineus or Thamyris, the many-eyed Argus, Achilles

Fig. 24. STATUETTE OF A TRAGIC HERO
Note will be taken of the *onkos*, the *cothurnus*, and the ornamented robes.

in despair over the death of Patroclus, Rivers, Hours, Muses, Furies—these are among the many similar characters which, as Pollux notes, were performed in this manner.

While comedy in many ways reproduced for another purpose forms found in tragedy, naturally the comic actor wore a dress fundamentally different from that of his tragic colleague. Padding (which was named σωμάτιον, *sōmation*), as in tragedy, was regular, but it was designed to create a ridiculous, not a dignified appearance. Puffed out in front and behind, and without the long χιτών, the comic actor bustled his way, Falstaff-like, on the stage. Over his padded stomach he sometimes wore an abnormally short χιτών, with occasionally an equally short χλαμύς. Sometimes, however, he was completely clad in a tight-fitting skin-like garment which clung closely to his limbs and was coloured to represent flesh or was striped with some dyes. Characteristic of his appearance was the phallus, which symbolized the prevailing licence and, to our minds, indecency of the Athenian comedy. Apparently these typical garments were carried over to the New Comedy, in which, however, a greater realism prevailed, some of the persons at least wearing the dress of ordinary life.

Fig. 25. MASK OF THE LONG-HAIRED HEROINE
From Bieber, *op. cit.*

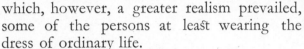

Like the tragic actors the performers in comedy wore masks, although without the *onkos* so typical of tragic grandeur. Pollux again provides us with a long list of these, differentiated once more according to age. (1 and 2) First come two characters called *pappos*. The first of these, an ancient grandfather, is almost bald but long-bearded. His face is pale and lean, his eyes dim; but his whole countenance betokens cheeriness. He is thus contrasted with his companion, who is still thinner, but is given a severe look with a ruddy, cantankerous appearance. Callipho and Simo in *Pseudolus* are later representatives of these types. (3 and 4) Alongside of these are the two 'old men' or stock comedy fathers, of whom Menedemus and Chremes in *Heautontimoroumenos* are typical. The former is called by Pollux the "chief." He has a hooked nose with a broad mask. The eyebrows have a certain peculiarity in that the right side is raised, the left horizontal, so that one profile indicates anger, the other calm, the actor being forced to turn his face one way or the other to reveal the fictitious emotions of the character he is representing. The second old man has a long, trembling beard, thick hair, and a certain phlegmatic appearance. (5 and 6) The Hermonios and Second Hermonios gain their names apparently from that of an actual actor-contemporary of Aristophanes. The chief of these two has a bald head, raised eyebrows, and a severe countenance. The second is barely described for us, but the short, pointed beard seems to have been a characteristic feature. (7) A pointed beard is worn also by another character, called by Pollux simply "the man with the pointed beard." He is marked by an air of intractability, which is indicated in his raised eyebrows. Lyco in the *Curculio* is of this type. (8) The brothel-keeper, the *leno* of the Roman stage, resembles the next-described character, Lycomedeios, save that he is bald and has

Fig. 26. TERRA-COTTA STATUETTE OF A COMIC ACTOR

From Haigh, *The Attic Theatre*, p. 258.

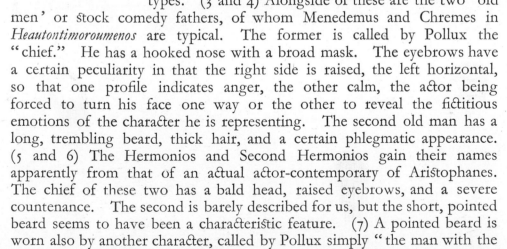

Fig. 27. TERRA-COTTA STATUETTE OF A COMIC ACTOR DE-CLAIMING

From the original in the British Museum.

43

Fig. 28. Menander Relief, showing Masks of Youth, Courtesan, and Old Man

Photo Anderson.

contracted brows and distended lips. (9) Lycomedeios sports crisp hair and a double expression, one eyebrow being raised, the other horizontal. He is the sycophant and busybody of the comic dramas.

The youths come next in order. Of these there are eleven, to correspond with the nine old and elderly men. (1) First comes the young man, " good-for-all-work." He is ruddy in colour, has raised eyebrows and a crown of hair on his head, with the general appearance of a robust, athletic youth—the lover, the 'juvenile lead' of to-day, the Clitipho of the classical *Heautontimoroumenos*.

Fig. 30. SET OF MASKS: OLD MAN, FAIR YOUTH, YOUTH WITH CURLY HAIR, AND SERVANT

Photo Moscioni.

(2) The " dark young man " is a trifle his junior. His eyebrows are not raised, and he looks like a student or a follower of the gymnasium. He is obviously not so riotous as his elder brother. He is opposed to the (3) " young man with curled hair," who is more beautiful of feature and ruddy of complexion, with one wrinkle on his brow. His well-tended hair and general appearance betoken the man of luxurious life. (4) Still more effeminate is the " delicate young man " with a pale complexion, obviously reared in ease and unathletic habits. He too has a crown of hair on his head. He is the youngest of all and is typified in the Dinarchus of *Truculentus*. (5) In addition to these typical young men, lovers and their kin, appear seven other class types, of whom the " rustic " first claims our attention. His hair is black and bound in a crown on his head. His cheeks are tanned, his lips wide, and his nose flat. (6 and 7) Next comes the " boasting soldier," of which type there are two varieties, one having black hair and dark complexion, the other blond hair and fair complexion. Both are distinguished by the enormous headdress of threatening proportions.

Obviously Pyrgopolinices in the *Miles Gloriosus* of Plautus is the type representative of this class. (8 and 9) The flatterer and the parasite naturally go together, the former distinguished by evil eyebrows, the latter by a cheerier and more obsequious countenance.   Both have dark hair, hooked

Figs. 31–34.   TERRA-COTTA MASKS
From the originals in the British Museum.

noses, and broken ears.   (10) With these goes the " Sicilian," a kind of third parasite, who is not described for us.   (11) Finally there is a character called by Pollux merely a "portrait mask," that is, a stranger, well dressed, with a clean-shaven chin.   He is probably the gull of the rascal crew described above.

The servants of comedy in some respects follow closely on the lines of the other characters. (1) Thus the first servant mentioned by Pollux is the *pappos*, a grey-haired old man who has been liberated for his long service, as is shown by the arrangement of his hair, which is as worn by freemen.   (2) Next to him is the " chief slave," distinguished by a

Fig. 35.   TERRA-COTTA STATU-ETTE OF AN OLD MAN
From the original in the British Museum.

coil of red hair, raised eyebrows, and contracted brows.   (3) There is a servant who is lean and ruddy, with raised eyebrows and a head partly bald.   (4) The " crisp slave " has also red hair. His eyes are peculiarly screwed up and his lips distended.   (5) With these goes Maison, the Greek cook, who is bald and has hair of a yellowish red.   (6) Tettix, the foreign cook, boasts a bald head streaked with two or three black locks, a dark complexion, and a deceitful face.   (7) Finally, there is a type of boasting servant with enormous headdress, a kind of double of type 2, represented in the Sceledrus of *Miles Gloriosus*.

The women's masks, some seventeen in all, now must occupy our attention.   First there comes a group of three " old hags."   (1) The lean or " wolfish " old woman, with thin net of wrinkles, white-haired and pallid, has crooked

Fig. 36.   MASK OF A TRAGIC HERO
From the original in the Museo Nazionale, Rome.

eyes, which correspond with the general rapacious nature of the type.   (2) The " fat old woman " has deep wrinkles on her face, while her hair is caught in a band.   (3) Thirdly, there is the old domestic servant, flat-nosed, with two molar teeth only in each jaw.

The " young women " correspond to the " young men," ranging in age from about forty-five

47

D

down to extremest youth. (1) First comes the "talkative woman," a perennial type. She has long hair, straight eyebrows, and a fair complexion. (2) The "crisp woman" is distinguished by

the appearance of her hair, and it has been thought that this is the type of the silent, modest spouse. No doubt the two are represented in the Philumena and Pamphila of Plautus' *Stichus*. (3) The "virgin" is the young heroine, with straight dark eyebrows and a pale countenance. (4 and 5) Next come two "false virgins," girls of good family who have fallen into distress and have been the victims of violation. Whereas the virgin wears the usual maiden's headdress, the plaited locks separated by a parting, the first false virgin has her hair in a knot after the custom of young brides, and the second wears the maiden's locks without the parting. Both are pallid in complexion. With these we leave the world of upper-class life and pass to the *demi-mondaine*. (6) The "talkative mistress" is an elderly courtesan who has become a bawd. (7) The "mistress" has her hair done in the style of married women, which indicates the fact that she has been accepted by some wealthy man as his concubine. (8) The "accomplished courtesan" is somewhat like the false virgin, but is ruddier and has locks of hair about her ears. (9) The "young courtesan" is largely un-

Fig. 37. MASK OF A MESSENGER
From the original in the Museo Nazionale, Rome.

adorned and only has a fillet binding her head. (10 and 11) The courtesan proper has, however, two companions, the "golden courtesan" and the "courtesan with the bandeau." The former, as her name shows, wears a profusion of golden ornaments in her hair; the latter binds her head with a gaily coloured bandeau. Both are older and more experienced than the young courtesan. (12) Among the courtesans we find, last of all, the *lampadion*, so called because of the fact that the hair is caught in a pointed tress on the head. Perhaps, as has been thought, this is the mask of the young noble-born girl who, seized away from her parents in youth, is thought to be a courtesan until discovery is made of her birth—the Marina of the classical stage. (18) The "dainty servant," clad in a white undergirdled tunic, is the lady's maid *par excellence*, while (14) the "servant with smooth hair," dressed in scarlet and snub-nosed, is clearly the confidante of the courtesan, typified in the Milphidippa of *Miles Gloriosus*.

So ends the list of the masks in Pollux, and we can see from the indications given by him how age, class, birth, and nature were symbolized by special features. Colour of hair indicates the first; while snub-noses are apportioned to those of low birth. Colour and ornaments characterize the courtesans, and hair-dress the married and unmarried women. Eyebrows, lips, and complexion are freely used to indicate temperament and mental condition, the

Fig. 38. MASK OF A TRAGIC HEROINE
From the original in the Museo Nazionale, Rome.

object of the whole being to allow the spectators at a glance to grasp the main features of the persons represented. All these indications, of course, serve to make the masks less real and individual.

It is thought by some that in the Old Comedy an attempt was made to provide some masks with lifelike features; that Cleon, Socrates, and others, appearing in the comedies of Aristophanes, were costumed and 'made up' to resemble their originals. This theory, however, has seen some discussion in recent years, and it would seem as if even then the types predominated to the exclusion of individual portraiture. Mr F. M. Cornford, analysing the main qualities of the characters presented in Aristophanic comedy, discovers there some half a dozen main forms : (1) the *miles gloriosus*, typified in Lamachus of the *Acharnians* and in Aeschylus of the *Frogs*; (2) the learned doctor,

as in Socrates of the *Clouds* and Euripides of the *Frogs*; (3) the cook, as in Agoracritus in the *Knights*; (4) the parasite, shown as Cleon in the *Knights*; (5) the old man ; (6) the young man ; (7) the old woman ; (8) the young woman with (9 and 10) a comic slave and another buffoon. To these types correspond not only the list of masks given by Pollux, but equivalent persons in the farce comedy of the Phlyakes type. In Pollux, as we have seen, we get various species of old men, including among them a pandar ; we get young men, swaggering soldiers, flatterers, and parasites. Maison and Tettix (one fair and one dark) are slaves and correspond to the cook. Old women and young women (including the courtesans) are described, and from the extant records of New Comedy itself we can trace a learned doctor. In other words we have a set of stock characters corresponding with fair accuracy to the types discovered in Aristophanic comedy. So in the Phlyax mimedrama of Megara and Magna Graecia we find a corresponding set of stage figures. Two types of comic slave are present—a foolish and a sly one. There is a bald-headed type who

Fig. 39. MASK OF THE GOLDEN COURTESAN
From Robert, *Die Masken der neueren attischen Komödi*.

reminds us of the parasite ; a glutton ; a doctor ; a testy old man ; a cook ($\theta\epsilon\rho\acute{a}\pi\omega\nu$). In addition to these we know of a Myllus, an Acco, and a Macco, of whose characteristics we are ignorant. When we remember that in the Roman *fabulae Atellanae* one of the chief types is a foolish gull called Maccus, we are bound to connect him with the Phlyakes' $M\alpha\kappa\kappa\acute{\omega}$ (Macco). In any case, without anticipating by entering the field of Roman comedy, we find established a number of corresponding stock figures :

OLD COMEDY	NEW COMEDY	PHLYAKES
Old Man	Old Man	Old Man
Young Man	Young Man	
Old Woman	Old Woman	Old Woman
Young Woman	Young Woman	
Soldier	Soldier	
Parasite	Parasite	Baldhead (parasite)
Cook	Cook (Maison and Tettix)	Cook
Doctor	Doctor	Doctor
Stupid Slave } Clever Slave }	Many slaves	Macco and other Comic Slaves

The correspondence is remarkable, and perhaps enough has been said to show the inherent traditionalism of comedy and the importance of these stock types when considered in relation to later Roman and Renascence drama.

CHAPTER II

THE ROMAN THEATRE

(i) THE PLAYHOUSES

BY the time that Rome first thought of theatres the old religious feeling which had dominated early Greek drama was dead. Even although the initial dramatic performance in Rome itself was held to placate the angry gods, the fact remains that the theatre for the Romans was nothing but a theatre; its association with the temple had vanished. For some considerable time the Senate opposed the erection of anything but wooden structures for dramatic shows or entertainments. A stone playhouse built in the year 154 B.C. was forthwith destroyed by them. The first permanent stone theatre,

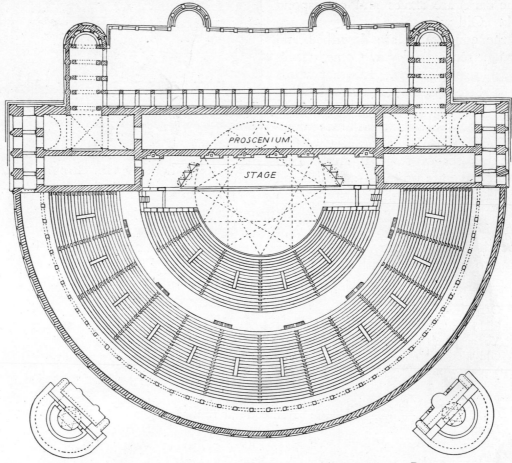

Fig. 40. PLAN OF THE MARCELLUS THEATRE AT ROME
From Streit, *Das Theater*, Plate VIII.

accordingly, was not constructed till 55–52 B.C., under the direction of Pompey. This was the Roman theatre *par excellence*, and came to be a model on which architects of those and of later times worked.

50

THE ROMAN THEATRE

The Roman theatre, many examples of which have been preserved in various cities of the old Empire, differed from the Greek, whether classical, Hellenistic, or Graeco-Roman, in many respects.

(1) The first peculiarity we note is that seldom were those theatres set on the slopes of hills. Almost always they were built on level ground, whereas under Greek influence, with one or two exceptions, the auditoria rested on a natural proclivity. It is difficult at first to divine the reason of this, but it is probable that the desire of architects to have the wall-space for elaborate embellishment may have been one determining factor. As we shall find, one of the peculiarities of the Roman theatre is the attention paid to the beauty of the outer structure. Save in one or two instances the Greeks left the rear of their scene-buildings severely unelaborate.

(2) More important are the changes made in the arrangement of the auditorium, or *cavea*, and of the stage itself. The most characteristic of these is the new form given both to the orchestra and to the rows of seats. A Roman theatre is fundamentally differentiated from a Greek by the fact that the *cavea* is exactly a semicircle (Fig. 40), the benches occupying the side portions being cut away, probably because they gave only a partial view of the stage. At the same time the orchestra was cut sharply in half, also exhibiting a semicircle bounded on the diameter by the front of the stage itself (Fig. 40), generally styled the hyposcenium (ὑποσκήνιον, or under-stage). Sometimes, perhaps, the orchestra was used for extra seating accommodation; sometimes, as in the Nero reconstruction of the theatre at Athens, arrangements

Fig. 41. STAGE FRONT AT DJEMILA
Note will be taken of the steps leading from stage to orchestra.
From Gsell, *Monuments de l'Algérie*, vol. i, Plate XLV.

were made whereby the whole of the orchestral space could be flooded for the presentation of mimic sea-fights or the like. In Athens a marble balustrade was erected probably for this purpose and also to form a protection for those occupying the lowest seats during gladiatorial displays.

(3) Possibly because the orchestra may have been occasionally used by spectators, the stage in the Roman theatre was comparatively low, rarely reaching above 5 feet in height, but, owing to the encroachment on the orchestra, it was considerably deeper than even the stage in Graeco-Roman structures. Doors were usually provided in the front or hyposcenium wall, while steps from the stage-level to the ground appear to have been usual. Permanent stone steps for this purpose are still to be seen in the theatre of Djemila in North Africa (Fig. 41).

(4) The *frons scaenae*, or what was originally the *episkenion*, was, as in Graeco-Roman theatres, gorgeously decorated. The best-preserved example is perhaps that of the theatre at Orange in France (Figs. 45–47), where an imposing architectural façade, broken by three doors, forms the background for the actors. It will be noted that in this theatre, as in the Graeco-Roman theatre at Aspendos (Figs. 42–44), a roof covers the stage itself.[1] Although definite information is lacking

[1] The roof is now no longer in existence, but is shown in the reconstruction in Fig. 44.

51

it is probable that this was a usual feature of the Roman playhouse. Sometimes, as in the Phaedrus alterations in the theatre at Athens (third or fourth century A.D.) the desire for decoration was carried to the hyposcenium; an elaborate frieze introducing kneeling figures was erected there to

Fig. 42. THE THEATRE AT ASPENDOS
From Lanckoroński, *Städte Pamphyliens und Pisidiens*, Plate XX.

take the place of what was before a comparatively blank wall (Fig. 48). In other theatres the hyposcenium front was indented with niches and rounded recesses (Fig. 49).

(5) Important too are the changes made in connexion with the *parodoi*, or entranceways. At Epidauros and elsewhere in Greece these *parodoi* were often enclosed in monumental open gateways; but, even when the gateway extended from the edge of the scene-building to the banks of seats the theatres remained divided into two parts—auditorium and stage. In the Roman theatres the open entrances disappeared, their place being taken by *vomitoria*, or covered passages, which bound the stage and the *cavea* architecturally into one. This, as is obvious, had immense consequences, for architects now were occupied with a new problem—the creation of a playhouse

Fig. 43. Reconstruction of the Frons Scaenae at Aspendos
From Lanckoroński, *op. cit.*, Plate XXIV.

Fig. 44. Reconstruction of the Frons Scaenae at Aspendos
From Lanckoroński, *op. cit.*, Plate XXVII.

Fig. 45. THE OUTSIDE WALL OF THE THEATRE AT ORANGE

N. D. Photo.

which should have unity of design, where various parts were not to be considered separately, but where stage and auditorium were organic portions of a greater whole.

(6) In general we may say that the Roman theatre presented an appearance more ornate than, and at the same time not so beautiful in its simplicity as, the Greek. The richly decorated *frons scaenae*, the long low stage, or *pulpitum*, the friezes, and the decorations removed it far from the bare grandeur of the first Athenian playhouse. This impression must have been increased by various other subsidiary appurtenances. Awnings spread

Fig. 46. THE THEATRE AT ORANGE

N. D. Photo.

Fig. 47. THE THEATRE AT ORANGE
N. D. Photo.

over part or over the entirety of the *cavea* seem to have been not uncommon, while to cool the fetid air slaves passed up and down the passageways spraying the audience with rose-

Fig. 48. RELIEFS ON THE HYPOSCENIUM OF THE THEATRE AT ATHENS
Photo Sebah.

scented waters. New efforts were made to secure theatrical effect. Besides the machines utilized by the Greeks, we find the introduction of an *auleum*, or curtain, which, unlike modern curtains, dropped down into a hollow recess placed toward the front of the stage. How far this *auleum* was

Fig. 49. A ROMAN STAGE
Pompeiian wall-painting.
Photo Alinari.

used we have little means of judging, but it brings the antique theatre yet one step farther forward toward the modern type.

(ii) Actors, Costume, and Masks

One fundamental cause of the decline of Roman drama lies in the social position occupied by the actors. While originally it would seem the comic or tragic poet engaged his own company and perhaps took a leading part in it himself, the custom soon arose of having permanent dramatic troupes. These troupes were gathered together by a manager, and consisted of slaves whom he could flog or put to death if he chose. Naturally the profession of acting was as a consequence despised, and, even after Roscius had won for himself fame and esteem, there never was in Rome that dignity surrounding a performer which is evident in records of the Greek theatre. Still more did the acting profession decline on the introduction of the *mimi*[1] when women first appeared on the stage, prostituting themselves to the degenerate tastes of a vulgar audience.

The costumes used by the Roman actors were, almost invariably, modelled on the Greek. For tragedy there were the long sweeping robes (*syrmata*) which corresponded to the χιτών, and for comedy various short garments which at once recall the costumes both of the Phlyakes and of the regular literary comedy. Wigs (*galeri* or *galearia*)

Fig. 50. Masks for the "Andria" of Terence
From a Vatican MS. as reproduced in Robert, *Die Masken der neueren attischen Komödie*, p. 89.

were usually worn, and the tragic actor sported buskins, or *cothurni*, as in Greek times. Still symbolism in colour seems to have been employed. Old men were usually dressed in white, young men in purple, parasites in grey, courtesans in yellow. Originally, it would seem, masks were not used, but became later, as in Greece, familiar accompaniments of the comic actor. These masks were sometimes more or less natural, sometimes highly exaggerated. In this connexion there is an interesting miniature preserved in a manuscript of the *Andria* of Terence,

[1] See *infra*, pp. 60–62.

showing the masks for that piece arranged in rows (Fig. 50).   The various masks here are lettered by the copyist of the manuscript, but it would seem that some mistakes have been made in the apportionment of the characters.   As Robert has shown,[1] while the first two masks in the top row are rightly marked as Simo, the ἡγεμὼν πρεσβύτης, and Sosia, the δοῦλος πάππος, the third cannot be Panphilus, as marked, but must represent Davos, the slave.   The last mask in the first row seems to be that of Archylis, the friend of the heroine. The second row contains Mysis, a maid, Panphilus, the lover, Charinus, a youth, and Byrria, a slave.   In the third row we have Lesbia, the wife, Glicerium, the heroine, Chremes, an old man, and Crito, the second πάππος, while in the fourth row comes Dromo, a slave.   It would appear that, as in Greece, the colour of the hair aided in differentiating the types.   White hair was a symbol of age, black of youth, while red distinguished the slaves.

Fig. 51. SYRUS IN THE "HEAUTON-TIMOROUMENOS" OF TERENCE

From a Vatican MS. reproduced in Robert, *op. cit.*, p. 96.

(iii) TYPES OF ROMAN DRAMA

For the most part the Roman drama was imitative—imitative of the Greek.   Tragedy, under Ennius and Seneca, has no interest for us here; but something may be said of forms of comic drama.   The most famous of all types of Roman comedy is, of course, the *fabula palliata*,[2] patronized by Terence (P. Terentius Afer, *c.* 195–159 B.C.) and T. Maccius Plautus (*c.* 254–184 B.C.), who based their work on the New Comedy of Greece, particularly on the plays of Menander and those associated with him—Philemon, Diphilus, and Demophilus.   Their works were thus usually mere adaptations, and the manners described were those of Greece rather than those of Italy.   In these plays we get once more the stock characters which have already been noticed in Aristophanes, the popular comedy of Greece, and the New Comedy.[3]   There are the old men, sympathetic and kindly, as is Philto in the *Trinummus*, or luxurious and libertine like Lysimachus in the *Casina*.   There are boasting soldiers such as appear in the *Miles Gloriosus* and other comedies; rascally servants like Tranio in the *Mostellaria*, Pseudolus and Epidicus; young lovers, young heroines, old pedants, and old women—a series of types, indeed, which shows that we are working on the old lines laid down in Greece.

The *fabula palliata* ended with Terence, giving way to the *fabula togata*, in which Italian rather than Greek manners were presented, and where stress was laid rather on the feminine element. Perhaps because of social considerations, the slaves seem to have been rarely so cunning as the astute rascals of the Plautan and Terentian types.   Italian manners too, but rather those of city than of country-folk, appear in the *fabula tabernaria*, of which little definite is known, but both of these faded before the introduction to the literary theatre of the *fabula Atellana*, brought to popularity under Pomponius of Bononia and Novius in the time of Sulla.   This *fabula Atellana*, although at first sight it seems to be the only form of native drama which the Roman Empire possessed, must have come originally from Greece.   Flourishing in Campania, it gained its title from the small town of Atella, the modern Aversa.   While little is known of this comedy save the titles of some of the plays, we have record of some four chief character-types who seem to have been displayed

---

[1] *Die Masken der neueren attischen Komödie* (1911), pp. 88–91.
[2] From *pallium*, the equivalent of the Greek χλαμύς.   [3] See *supra*, p. 49.

over and over again. Maccus is the first of these, evidently derived from the Greek Μακκώ, a foolish person with hooked nose and rounded shoulders. Next comes Bucco, with bulged-out cheeks, Pappus the bald-headed old man, and Dossennus the hunchback. Perhaps to these may be added a fifth, Cicirrus, or the 'cock.' If, once more, we consider the types of these Atellan plays together with the types of the *fabula palliata* we get a striking correspondence.

FABULA PALLIATA	FABULA ATELLANA
Testy old men	Pappus (Old man)
Miles Gloriosus	Cicirrus (Soldier)
Two Comic Slaves	Maccus ⎫ (Buffoons) Bucco ⎭
Pedants	Dossennus (Learned man)

The importance of this correspondence will become increasingly apparent as we study the drama of Renascence Italy. At present it may be noted that both the popular and the literary stage of Greece and of Rome knew these figures; and, moreover, that the titles preserved of plays of the *fabula Atellana* type bear strange resemblance not only one to another, but also to titles of many centuries later. *Maccus Virgo* (*Maccus a Girl*), *Maccus Miles* (*Maccus a Soldier*), *Bucco Adoptatus* (*Bucco Adopted*), are typical titles of the Atellan farce, and they recall in their forms the *Arlequin Homme à Bonne Fortune*, *Arlequin Misanthrope*, *Arlequin Empereur dans le Monde de la Lune*, of the seventeenth century.[1]

On its introduction to Rome from its Oscan home the *fabula Atellana* declined, and itself gave way to the *mimus*, a type of entertainment intimately connected with the Grecian Phlyakes. In this *mimus*, or *fabula riciniata*,[2] we meet definitely for the first time that theme, so common later, of the doltish cuckold, the frail wife, and the intriguing gallant. No doubt there were many points of correspondence between the Atellan and mime farce; in both no doubt adultery was a stock jest, and indecent phrases were used to evoke laughter among the spectators. Still more vulgar, in all probability, was the *pantomimus*, where licentious terpsichorean entertainments ruled the stage. The Roman drama, as such, comes to an end with these forms of farce and ballet; yet we must remember that even the crudest farce had still something in it of artistic flavour and of social purpose. Grave Roman senators attended the mime performances, and saw in their satirical proportions a salutary object. The mime triumphed for qualities both good and evil, and those good and evil qualities served to keep it alive when, on the fall of the Roman Empire, darkness descended upon the theatres.

[1] See *infra*, p. 114.   [2] From *ricinium*, a sort of mantilla.

CHAPTER III

THE THEATRE IN THE MIDDLE AGES

(i) THE RELICS OF ROMAN MIME

WITH the gradual decay of the Roman Empire the mime, preserved and even encouraged for reasons of polity, came to occupy a position ever more and more debased. Emperors might tax their treasury severely in order to provide entertainments for the populace, but many things combined together to destroy even the mime as a form of theatrical art. The populace may have clamoured over their favourite troupes; three thousand dancing-girls, as Ammianus Marcellinus informs us, may have been allowed to stay in Rome when that city was starving and learned men were driven from its gates; but criticism had already begun to direct its attention to the enormities of the stage. Christian influence soon made itself felt and decrees were issued forbidding baptism to anyone who had been a *scaenicus* or a *scaenica* (actor or actress). Still, however, the shows made their appeal. Both at Byzantium (Constantinople), the seat of the Eastern Empire, and at Rome they endured in spite of all the violent attacks of the early Fathers of the Church. As late as 692 there are records of performances of various kinds in the East, while *scaenici* still played their part when the Ostrogoths wielded power in Italy during the sixth century. At Rome, however, after the coming of the Lombards in 568 we hear no more of *spectacula* or of theatres; while, in the East, Saracen invasions must have set people thinking of things more stern than merry supper-parties with groups of dancing-girls.

It is undeniable, then, that during the sixth century in Italy and during the seventh century at Constantinople theatrical shows as a whole completely disappear; but we cannot, because of this fact, assume that all knowledge of that mime and dialogue which constitutes drama also disappeared. A complete account of the evidence which exists for the presence of *mimi* in the Middle Ages would here take up too much space. All that may be given is the barest summary of some main points.

(1) Theatres by some contemporary writers are treated as separate from mimic shows, and there is an implication that while the playhouses had fallen into disuse the *mimi* continued their entertainments. Thus in the seventh century Isidore of Seville has the following words concerning the former:

> Scaena autem erat locus infra theatrum in modum domus instructa cum pulpito, quod pulpitum orchestra vocabatur, ubi cantabant comici, tragici, atque saltabant histriones.[1]

All this is narrated in the past tense; but the present tense is used when the writer turns to the *mimus*:

> Histriones sunt qui muliebri indumento gestus impudicarum feminarum exprimebant. Mimi sunt dicti Graeca appellatione, quod rerum humanarum sint imitatores.[2]

Throughout the entirety of the Middle Ages these *histriones* are referred to. *Melius est Deo placere quam histrionibus*—" It is better to please God than the actors "—Alcuin warns a young

[1] " The scene *was* the place at the bottom of the auditorium built like a house with a stage. This stage *was called* the orchestra. There comic and tragic actors *sang* and histriones *played* their acrobatic tricks."

[2] " ' Histriones ' *are* those who, dressing as women, presented the doings of common women. . . . ' Mimi ' they *are* called in Greek, because they are imitators of human life."

60

friend. *Melius est, pauperes edere de mensa tua, quam istriones*—"It is better to feed paupers at your table than actors"—declares the same author to the Bishop of Lindisfarne.

(2) The Middle Ages had as their entertainers men known as *jongleurs*,[1] and later as *ministri*. The latter word is derived from the classical Latin *minister*, 'inferior' and hence 'attendant.' 'Minstrel' is the modern English derivative. But the word *jongleur*, which comes from the classical Latin *iocularis*, 'merry,' is regarded by many as the exact equivalent of *histrio* (actor) or *mimus*. Thus an early glossary declares that *istriones sunt ioculatores* ("actors are *jongleurs*"), while *mimi seu ioculatores* ("*mimi* or *jongleurs*") is a common phrase. That is to say, whether the *jongleurs* were merely acrobats and balladmongers or not, medieval writers regarded them as being the direct descendants of the more ancient *mimi*. Their tradition seems proved.

(3) According to Thomas de Chabham, Sub-Dean of Salisbury (*d.* 1313), these entertainers, as we may call them, were of three kinds:

> Tria sunt histrionum genera. Quidam transformant et transfigurant corpora sua per turpes saltus et per turpes gestus, vel denudando se turpiter, vel induendo horribiles larvas. . . . Sunt etiam alii qui nihil operantur, sed criminose agunt, non habentes certum domicilium, sed sequuntur curias magnatum et dicunt opprobria et ignominias de absentibus ut placeant aliis . . . Est etiam tertium genus histrionum qui habent instrumenta musica ad delectandum homines, et talium sunt duo genera. Quidam enim frequentant publicas potationes et lascivas congregationes, et cantant ibi diversas cantilenas ut moveant homines ad lasciviam . . . Sunt autem alii, qui dicuntur ioculatores, qui cantant gesta principum et vitam sanctorum.[2]

There are thus (*a*) *mimi* proper, (*b*) satirists, who may be the wandering scholars or *Goliardi*, (*c*) instrumentalists and singers of a lower type, (*d*) instrumentalists of a higher type. Is it possible that any of these preserved something of the ancient mime tradition? If any did it could not have been the *jongleurs* of classes (*c*) or (*d*), but what of those satirists and of those who indulged in indecent dance and gesture, wearing horrible masks? May these not have preserved something of the mime tradition?

(4) It is obvious that, if they did, little in the shape of literary farce would have come down to us, for the mime itself and much of the *fabula Atellana* was unliterary. Nor would pious chroniclers say much of what they heartily despised and condemned; according to Thomas de Chabham, all but the last class of *histriones* were destined to complete perdition. We may expect then but few records, and must take such records as symbolic rather than as comprehensive. It is impossible here to discuss all these records, few as they are, but two seem of special value. Thomas Aquinas, writing in the *Summa Theologiae* (before 1274), has something to say of the *ludus*, which may mean either 'play' or 'entertainment'—we can hardly tell which. The writer, however, in discussing the kind of *ludus* which is permissible and even "necessary for the conversation of human life," admits a certain species, *non utendo aliquibus illicitis verbis vel factis*—"which does not permit any illicit *words* or *actions*." Unless he is thinking of song and dance merely, Aquinas seems to be describing what are in reality dramatic shows. A century later, in a *Tretise of miraclis pleyinge*, an anonymous, and evidently Wyclifite, English author attacks the miracle cycles, but describes as existing alongside of these miracles "other japis" and parallels "to pley in myriclis" with "to pley in rebaudye"

---

[1] The Latin *ioculator* or *iocularis* has been connected with the Greek γελωτοποιός or μῖμος γελοίων. The word appears in Old French as *iogleor*, in Spanish as *juglar*, in Italian as *giocolatore*, in Old High German as *gougalári*, in Middle High German as *goukelaere*, in modern German as *Gaukler*, and in English as *juggler*.

[2] "There are three kinds of *histriones*. Some transform and transfigure their bodies with indecent dance and gesture, now indecently unclothing themselves, now putting on horrible masks. . . . There are besides others who have no definite profession, but act as vagabonds, not having any certain domicile; these frequent the Courts of the great and say scandalous and shameful things concerning those who are not present so as to delight the rest. . . . There is yet a third class of *histriones* who play musical instruments for the delectation of men, and of these there are two types. Some frequent public drinking-places and lascivious gatherings, and sing there stanzas to move men to lasciviousness. Besides these there are others, who are called *jongleurs*, who sing of the gestes of princes and the lives of the saints."

(ribaldry). These two references seem conclusive. Perhaps we might add to them a sentence written by William Fitzstephen (*c.* 1170–82) in his life of St Thomas à Becket:

Lundonia pro spectaculis theatralibus, pro ludis scaenicis, ludos habet sanctiores, representationes miraculorum quae sancti confessores operati sunt, seu representationes passionum quibus claruit constantia martyrum.[1]

Perhaps Fitzstephen was thinking only of classical times; perhaps, however, in his contrast, he was thinking of secular farces—*ludi scaenici*—than which the London miracles were so much more sanctified.

(5) Literary relics of this secular play are not completely lacking. From the seventh, eighth, or ninth century comes a little dialogue in Latin, spoken by Terentius (Terence) and a *Persona Delusoris*, and evidently intended as a prologue, whether for a revival of a Terentian comedy or of a newer farce we cannot tell. From England comes, in the vernacular, an interesting fourteenth-century text called an *Interludium de Clerico et Puella* ("*An Interlude of a Clerk and a Girl*"). This latter consists of two scenes. In the first a girl repulses a clerk who has offered love to her; in the second the clerk goes to Mome Helwis and begs her to aid him. The piece is incomplete, but it is definitely dramatic. Still further in France there is *Le Garçon et l'Aveugle*, belonging to the thirteenth century and evidently in the farce tradition. Other early pieces remain of various types, but these two, the English *interludium* and the French farce, most clearly preserve the relics of antiquity.

(6) Besides these regular plays performed by living actors, we have also to take into account the production of puppet or marionette plays by strolling entertainers. The marionette tradition is a long one, and there seems to be evidence to show that all through the Dark Ages performances of this kind were given in village and city. At a wedding about the year 1285 "*L'us fai lo juee dels bavastelz*,"[2] while mention of "*cimils*" and "*bavastelz*"[3] is fairly frequent, both in France and in Italy. These men, the *bastaxi* or *joueurs des basteaulx*,[4] must have had playlets for their jointed wooden dolls, and the playlets may well have had some connexion with the ancient repertory of the mimes.

(7) Finally, there is the question of the handing down from Roman times of stock characters—a question, however, which cannot be discussed in this section. At present, it is a point which must merely be borne in mind for later reference.[5] Even without this last piece of evidence there seems plentiful proof for the presence during the so-called Dark and Middle Ages of men who, calling themselves *histriones, mimi, jongleurs*, and *ministri* or *ministralli*, inherited some at least of the traditions of the Roman mime, and who passed these traditions on, now in a debased form freely mingled with acrobatics and dancing, now in the ever-popular puppet-show, and now in a form of more literary proportions, destined ultimately to flourish once again as the interlude.

(ii) The Growth of Medieval Drama

The drama of modern Europe, however, did not ultimately spring from, although it may later have been deeply influenced by, the traditions passed on by wandering entertainers from Imperial Rome.[6] As is well known, the source of that modern drama is to be sought for in the heart of the Catholic Church. Finding its basis in the symbolic nature of the service of the Mass, drama

---

[1] "London, instead of theatrical spectacles and scenic shows, has more sacred plays, representations of miracles which the saintly confessors have wrought or representations of the sufferings by which the constancy of martyrs has been made manifest."

[2] "A puppet show was presented."   [3] "Monkeys and puppets."

[4] The forms in the quotations given above are mostly Provençal.   [5] See *infra*, p. 78.

[6] While the mime tradition has nothing directly to do with the formation of the medieval sacred drama in its origins, it is probable that at least some of the clerics interested in the development of Church drama were inspired by a desire to counteract the licentious entertainments of the wandering *jongleurs*. Later the farce tradition entered in to colour the stock portraits of Noah's wife, Joseph, the shepherds, and the torturers of Christ.

developed out of the desire on the part of the clergy to place the salient facts of Christ's life more realistically before their congregations. At the two great festivals of the Church, Easter and Christmas, arose little dramas, or dramatic scenes, which displayed the birth and the death of Jesus. The story of these two dramatic scenes (generally called liturgical dramas because still associated with the service or liturgy) has often been told and need not be repeated in any detail here. Only such few facts as may serve to make plain the setting are required.

The earliest form of the Easter play is a piece of four-lined dialogue in which a couple of priests, arraying themselves in white as angels, are confronted by two other priests whose robes show that they are women.

> Quem quaeritis in sepulchro, o Christicolae?

" Whom do you seek in the sepulchre, O Christian women? " asks one of the angels.

> Iesum Nazarenum crucifixum, o coelicolae,

" Jesus of Nazareth Who was crucified, O heavenly ones," the women reply, and are immediately answered:

> Non est hic: surrexit sicut praedixerat.
> Ite, nuntiate quia surrexit de sepulchro.

" He is not here: He has arisen even as He foretold. Go, announce that He is arisen from the sepulchre."

It is here evident that we have the foundations of what is true drama, and, the scene pleasing the audience, additions soon crept in. Mary Magdalen lingers behind and meets Christ clad as a gardener; Peter and John run frantically toward the sepulchre, one outstripping the other; the Marys buy perfumes from a little stall set outside the fictitious tomb. At Christmas there is the same development. The shepherds see the star which heralds the birth of Christ, and come to lay their rustic gifts on His cradle. Later three Kings come with their more precious presents; and, still later, Herod rants and raves when he hears that a King of Kings has been born into the world.

All of this, of course, is in Latin, but soon vernacular comes to take its place, and portions of the liturgical drama, as in the English Shrewsbury fragments, are spoken in medieval French or German or English, for, it must be remembered, this was no national development, but a movement which is to be traced in almost every European country. The next stage is the separation of the primitive play from the regular Church services. Partly because these dramas were growing so rapidly in extent, partly because the largest churches were not sufficiently great to accommodate all the vast concourse of people who flocked to see the plays, the drama was moved outside on to the steps of the great west door, the spectators standing in the churchyard without. Then came doubt in the minds of the ecclesiastical authorities. This thing which they had called into being was becoming too great a force in the lives of the people; and accordingly came edict after edict, criticism after criticism, until the clergy were prohibited from taking part in performances —at least in such performances as were conducted outside the walls of the church itself. The drama, however, had been born and had grown into a lusty and lovable child; it could not die now, and the *rôle* of guardian was assumed by the town gilds, which at that time were the greatest of all social forces. While the subject matter of the plays remained still Biblical, they were worked up into regular mystery or miracle cycles, dealing with the entire story of the Old and New Testaments, together with some Apocryphal matter gratuitously thrown in. Thus they were performed by the various gilds on certain days of festival, notably that of Corpus Christi. In France the trades-folk hardly took such a share in the performance, their place being taken by special companies (of amateurs and of professionals), the most important of which was the famous Confrérie de la

E

Passion, which endured to the sixteenth century; but the fundamental development was the same. The famous French *Mystère du Viel Testament* is the counterpart of our Towneley, Chester, York, and Coventry cycles.

Some centuries after the mystery cycles had been established there arose the form of play known as the *Morality*, in which abstract qualities were made the *dramatis personae* and where the story is told of Everyman's temptation, fall, and salvation. Some of these at least may have been professional rather than amateur in character. They were followed, in England, by the *interludes*, rude one-act debates or farces, a type of comic drama which had appeared some considerable time before in France, and which may preserve relics of the Roman mime tradition. It is the theatres, or, more correctly, the acting-places, used in these various performances that we have now to consider.

(iii) Medieval Theatres and Mise-en-Scène

As might naturally be supposed, we cannot describe the appearance of any one theatre used in medieval times. The question is rather one of the theatres (in the broadest sense) employed during those years between the appearance of the first liturgical drama and the comic interludes of the

Fig. 52. The Sepulchre

Note will be taken of the angels who raise the lid of the (practicable) sarcophagus. The original is in the Church of St Paul at Dax.

From Émile Male, *L'Art religieux du xiie siècle en France.*

sixteenth century. In general, we may divide these theatres into several main groups, each to be considered separately: (1) the church as a theatre; (2) the church-like arrangement of the acting-place when first the drama was brought to the open air; (3) the stationary setting; (4) the pageant; (5) the round; and (6) the curtained platform.

(1) We start first, then, with the arrangements made within the church for the performance of the liturgical plays. The sepulchre used at the Easter play could be of various kinds. At first no doubt it was merely an *assimilatio quaedam sepulchri*, a kind of symbol of a sepulchre arranged at the high altar to the east of the church, but this soon gave way to a regularly built tomb, whether of wood or iron, set usually in the north aisle. Some indication of what this sepulchre looked like is provided for us in details of twelfth-century church architecture. The connexion between the dramatic performances and the sculptured art of the medieval period was first suggested by Cahier and Martin in their study of the cathedral at Bourges, and since the appearance of their book in 1841 many efforts have been made by the art critics to trace the influence of the mysteries upon the pictured scenes showing the chief episodes in the scriptural narrative. The principal work in this direction has been that of M. Émile Male, who has devoted chapters of his volumes and special articles to this subject. It is impossible here to indicate the many points of connexion; one must suffice as a typical example. Up to the twelfth century Christ's tomb is nearly always shown, in conventional Byzantine manner, as an architectural building with two arches. With the development of the liturgical play, however, new designs enter in. The tomb is now clearly a sarcophagus, sometimes with the lid half-open or wholly open (Fig. 52) and frequently accompanied by an angel who points within as if saying *Non est hic* (Fig. 53). Still further, Christ Himself, Who is never depicted by Byzantine artists as coming from the sepulchre, is now shown rising out of the

64

sarcophagus as He did in the primitive dramas (Fig. 54). In these liturgical plays, then, we get a double arrangement with the tomb to the east, or, more commonly, to the north, of the church.

Fig. 53. CHRIST RISING FROM THE TOMB

Note will be taken of the realistic treatment both of the sarcophagus lid and of the figures depicted.

From É. Male, *op. cit.*

While costume and accompanying gesture developed rapidly, little more was done at this stage to elaborate the *mise-en-scène* in the theatre-church.

(2) Passing from this, we reach the stage where more than the erection of a simple tomb serves as a background for the actors, but where the church is clearly in the minds of the actors. Here four texts or plans

Fig. 54. CHRIST RISING FROM THE TOMB

Note will be taken of the figure of Christ half seated in the sarcophagus. The original is in the Museum of Toulouse.

From É. Male, *op. cit.*

come to our aid, a twelfth- or thirteenth-century play of the *Resurrection*, a twelfth-century play of *Adam* (both French), an arrangement for a Passion play at Donaueschingen (the extant manuscript of the sixteenth century, but probably preserving traditions of a much earlier date), and another plan of a mystery play given at Lucerne in the same century. In the first of these

there is a kind of preface which informs the reader of the way in which the *mansions* or houses [1] must be arranged. From this preface we learn that the crucifix appears first, no doubt in the position it would have occupied in a church above the high altar (Fig. 55). On one side, no doubt the left, there is a sepulchre, followed evidently by Heaven (Paradise). It seems probable that the Marys, the Disciples, and Nicodemus are also arranged on this left side. To the right is a prison, Hell, Pilate, Caiaphas, and Joseph. Galilee is in the centre along with Emmaus.

As this is the first occasion we have had to mention the typically medieval *mansions* or houses, a word may be said before we pass to the *Adam*. For the liturgical dramas in the churches we have seen that a tomb was set up; where the perfume-selling episode was given a stall was placed elsewhere in an aisle; Herod's Court was at one place, the manger

Crucifix

✝

Monument (*sepulchrum*)	▯		▯	Jaiole
Ciel	▯	—	▯	Enfer
Maries	▯		▯	Pilate
Deciples	▯	▭	▯	Caiphas
		Jemaüs		
Nichodemes	▯		▯	Joseph
		▭		
		Galilée		

Fig. 55. THE MANSIONS IN THE "RESURRECTION"
From Chambers, *Medieval Stage*, ii, 83.

at another. Hence arose the convention of placing all the scenes of action at one time before the people. Boxes or platforms called variously *mansions, lius (lieux), loca, domus, estals, sedes,*

[1] Cf. *infra.*

sièges, and in English *houses*, were placed alongside of each other, their positions being determined in the first instance by the geographical arrangement of the church. The *Resurrection* has thus Heaven to the left (north) of the spectator, Hell to the right (south).[1] Happily the play of *Adam* gives us some additional information. The disposition for the houses is still determined by the structure of the church. To the east stands the crucifix, to the left Heaven, and to the right Hell. This, at least, we may presume from the directions in the text. What is particularly valuable in *Adam* is the description of Paradise and Hell themselves. The Paradise, we learn

> constituatur . . . loco eminenciori ; circumponantur cortine et panni serici, ea altitudine, ut persone, que in paradiso erunt, possint videri sursum ad humeros ; serantur odoriferi flores et frondes ; sint in eo diverse arbores et fructus in eis dependentes, ut amenissimus locus videatur. . . . Quicunque nominaverit paradisum, respiciat eum et manu demonstret.[2]

Of Hell we learn that

> singuli alii diaboli illos venientes monstrabunt, et eos suscipient et in infernum mittent ; et in eo facient fumum magnum exsurgere, et vociferabuntur inter se in inferno gaudentes, et collident caldaria et lebetes suos, ut exterius audiantur.[3]

Evidently verisimilitude of a kind was sought after even in the twelfth century.

Next we may take the plan of the Donaueschingen mystery play (Fig. 56), which presents a more complicated arrangement. Here clearly the three cross divisions indicate sanctuary, choir, and nave. Heaven in this case is in the east (*i.e.*, at the altar), and Hell is placed on the left instead

---

[1] The prologue runs as follows :

" En ceste manere recitom	" In this respect let us recite
La seinte resurreccion.	The Resurrection play to-night.
Primerement apareillons	First of all we detail here
Tus les lius et les mansions :	All the houses that appear :
Le crucifix primerement	First a crucifix we fit ;
E puis apres le monument.	The sepulchre comes after it.
Une jaiole i deit aver	There too must be a prison cell
Pur les prisons emprisoner.	To keep the prisoners in well.
Enfer seit mis de cele part,	On that side Hell must be,
E mansions de l'altre part,	Mansions on the other see.
E puis le ciel ; et as estals	And Heaven is there, and then
Primes Pilate od ces vassals.	A place for Pilate and his men.
Sis u set chivaliers aura.	Six or seven courtiers there,
Caiphas en l'altre serra ;	And Caiaphas on another chair.
Od lui seit la jeuerie,	The Jewish folk are nearby
Puis Joseph, cil d'Arimachie.	With Joseph of Arimachie.
Et quart liu seit danz Nichodemes.	Don Nichodeme comes fourth of all.
Chescons i ad od sei les soens.	Each has his servants within call.
El quint les deciples Crist.	Next the disciples' company we see,
Les treis Maries saient el sist.	And sixth there are the Maries three.
Si seit pourvéu que l'om face	Galilee is placed fair
Galilée en mi la place ;	In the middle of the square ;
Jemaüs uncore i seit fait,	Emmaus also must be reared
U Jhesu fut al hostel trait."	Where Jesus to his friends appeared."

With this prologue may be compared another cited from manuscript in Gustave Cohen's *Histoire de la Mise en Scène*, pp. 76–77. There too Paradise and Hell are on opposite sides.

[2] " Is to be placed on a raised spot ; curtains and silk cloths are to be hung about it at such a height that persons in Paradise are visible from the shoulders. Fragrant flowers and leaves are scattered there ; in it are divers trees with hanging fruit so as to give the impression of a most lovely place. . . . Whoever names Paradise must look toward it and indicate it with his hand." The terrestrial Paradise in the famous *Mystère du Viel Testament* is similarly adorned ; it is " bien garny de toutes fleurs, arbres, fruictz et autres plaisances, et au meilleu l'arbre de vie plus excellent que tous les autres." A technical word for the *loggie* of French theatres—' Paradise'—is a relic of the raised Paradise described here. Its elevated position may be due to the use of choir galleries in the medieval church.

[3] " Certain other devils point at them as they come, and seize them and bear them to Hell ; and in Hell they shall make a great smoke arise, and they shall shout out to each other in Hell in jubilation, and clash their pots and kettles, so as to be heard without."

of on the right, *i.e.*, in the north-west, but its position is determined by the fact that it is the place farthest from Heaven.[1]

The plans of the Easter play presented on two successive days at Lucerne provide a fitting parallel. Here the market square was used as the 'theatre' with Heaven, the seat of the Pater Eternus and His seven angels, at that end on to which abutted the Cornmarket Street and the New Place. The plan showing the arrangement for the second day (Fig. 57) gives a view of the square, while the turreted Heaven mansion is clearly delineated in the first plan (Fig. 58). At the opposite end of the square, and to the left-hand side, a rough sketch of a many-toothed monster marked "Die Höll" indicates the seat of "Lucifer & 6 Tüffel." The other mansions, as is evident, are set along the four sides of the square. From the sketches some of these seem to have been ordinary timbered houses, others decorated in a manner peculiar to their purposes. "Der Tempel" on the right-hand side has thus a kind of Eastern cupola, apparently surmounted by a crescent.

(3) This principle of staging was kept also in the great stationary settings devoted in France to the mysteries. Two illustrations of these give us a clear idea of their scope. The first is the miniature by Jehan Fouquet, showing the martyr-dom of St Apollonia (Fig. 59). Here in the foreground we see the torturing of the saint, and behind is arranged a series of *mansions* with steps leading down to the ground-level. To the left of the spectator there is a box full of angels sur-rounding a throne which is evidently a portion of Heaven. Next comes a house of trumpeters providing celestial music, followed by a large box with an empty throne, probably left vacant by the Emperor, who is standing immediately behind St Apollonia. Immediately to the right of this *mansion* of the Emperor are two boxes, both apparently filled with women and now unidentifiable, followed by Hell on the extreme edge. It will be noted that Hell is in two parts. Above is a platform on which two devils are standing; below is a great gaping monster's head, and from it issues a brute-headed figure.

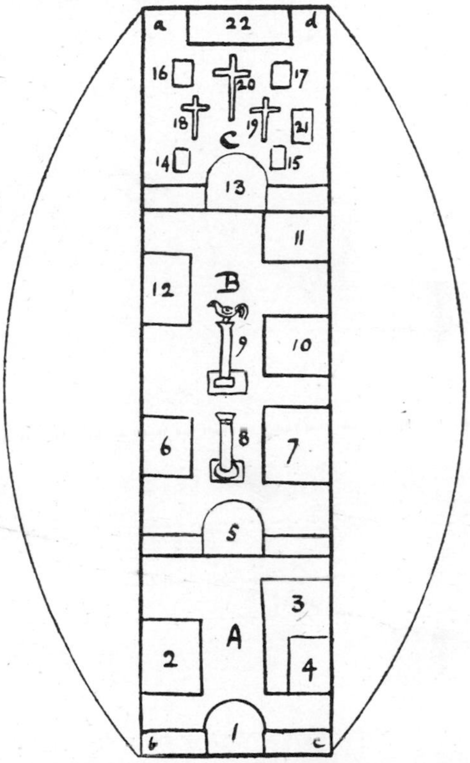

The Valenciennes miniature of the sixteenth century shows us a similar arrangement. The *mansions* here are set in a row with an open acting-place in front. To the extreme left is Paradise (Fig. 60), followed by a small temple before which is a gate. Jerusalem succeeds, and then a castle. The House of Bishops and the Golden Gate lead toward the extreme right, where appear a prison and Hell. It will be noted that in front of the Golden Gate is a small lake with a ship and that Hell is once more of two parts. Behind is a house of torture, peopled by demons. In front is the terrible monster's head from which some devils are issuing.

For our purposes, probably the most interesting of all these *mansions* is the last noticed, because it was to Hell, and after that—*longo intervallo*—to Heaven, that the medieval machinists and

FIG. 56. THE MANSIONS IN THE DONAUESCHINGEN MYSTERY PLAY

1, First door. 2, Hell. 3, Garden of Gethsemane. 4, Mount Olivet. 5, Second door. 6, Herod. 7, Pilate. 8, Pillar of scourging. 9, Pillar for cock. 10, Caiaphas. 11, Annas. 12, Last Supper. 13, Third door. 14, 15, 16, 17, Graves. 18, 19, Thieves' crosses. 20, Cross. 21, Holy Sepulchre. 22, Heaven.

From Chambers, *Medieval Stage*, ii, 84.

---

[1] Whereas the position of Hell to the south seems due to the presence in the church of crypt stairs to the right side of the altar, the position of Hell to the north (*cf.* Figs. 56, 57, 58, and 62) is probably due ultimately to the fact that "evil appeareth out of the north" (Jer. vi, 1).

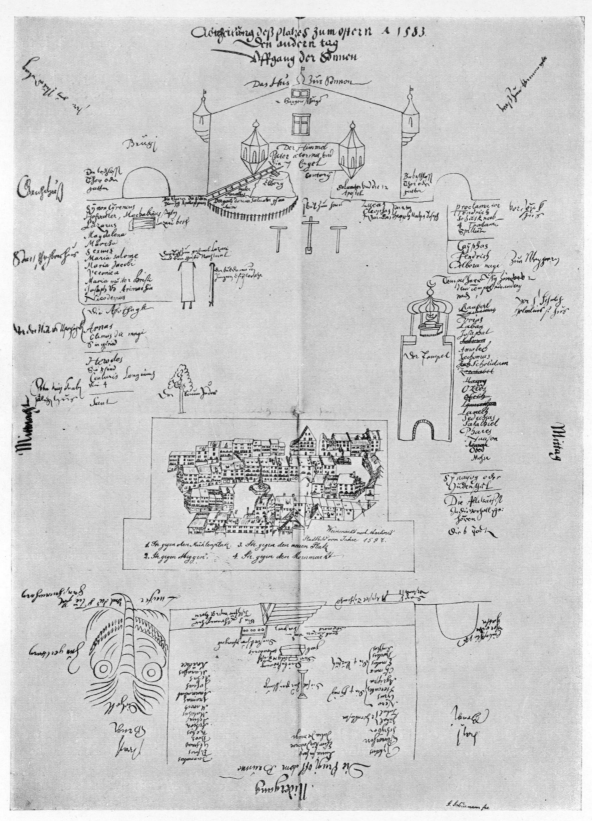

Fig. 57. The Lucerne Easter Play: Second Day

From Leibing, *Die Inscenirung des zweitägigen Luzernes Osterspiels.*

'managers' devoted their attention. The two pictures of it already shown, together with another from Zurich (Fig. 63), give a fair idea of its traditional shape. The monster's head, "faicte en manière d'une grande gueule se cloant et ouvrant quand besoing en est," [1] is probably a reminiscence of Leviathan, and is coloured in the miniatures in striking hues. Here the medieval artist came most near to the modern elaboration of scenic background.

It has been observed in these stationary scenes that the *mansions* or houses were placed semi-circularly or in a straight line, facing an open space in which, as we see from the St Apollonia miniature, the chief action takes place. This open space gained the name of *platea* or, in English, 'playne' (plain) and was an unlocalized stage. [2] The demons in *Adam* run about *per plateas*, that is, on the 'stage,' before they approach Paradise for the purpose of tempting Eve. The *platea* was, in other words, 'anywhere.' It might remain as neutral territory, or, through the words and actions of the characters, it might be thought of by the audience as repre-senting a definite locality. In any case, it stood distinct from the clearly localized *mansions* which remained constant throughout the course of the play. We shall see later how important this convention was in the development of Elizabethan stagecraft.

(4) In England the stationary setting, ex-cept in the form of rounds, does not seem to have been common. There the gilds preferred to stage their plays on what came to be known as pageants, virtually separate *mansions* of the stationary or standing plays placed on wheels. These pageants, apparently, were drawn round a particular town when a mystery cycle was being enacted, various individual plays taking place together. [3] Says Archdeacon Rogers of the Chester plays in the sixteenth century:

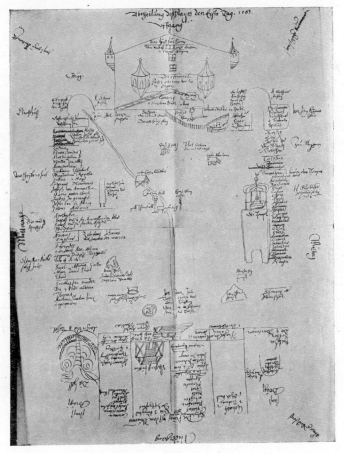

Fig. 58. THE LUCERNE EASTER PLAY: FIRST DAY
From Leibing, *op. cit.*

> They first beganne at yᵉ Abbaye gates; & when the firste pagiente was played at yᵉ Abbaye gates, then it was wheeled from thence to the pentice at yᵉ highe crosse before yᵉ Mayor; and before that was donne, the seconde came, and yᵉ firste wente in-to the watergate streete, and from thence vnto yᵉ Bridge-streete, and soe all, one after an other, tell all yᵉ pagiantes weare played.

Happily we have a good deal of information concerning the character of these pageants. Arch-deacon Rogers appends a little description of those used at Chester as

> a highe place made like a howse with ij rowmes, being open on yᵉ tope: the lower rowme they apparrelled and dressed them selves; and in the higher rowme they played; and they stood vpon 6 [4] wheeles.

---

[1] " Made like a great gargoyle which closes and opens when need be." The phrase is taken from a description of the Hell at Rouen in 1474.

[2] In the unique Italian mystery cycle preserved in an Ashburnham manuscript, there are three main regions, Heaven, Hell, and the World, the last including several independent *mansions* or *luoghi deputati*. The space between them is styled the *campo* or *zafaldo*.

[3] These English pageants are paralleled in the Netherlands by the *wagenspel*, on which see Stecher's *Histoire de la littérature néerlandaise en Belgique*, p. 142.   [4] Probably an error for 4.

"Theatres for the severall Scenes, very large and high, placed upon wheels" is Dugdale's account, while at Norwich in 1565 the Grocers' pageant was "a Howse of Waynskott paynted and buylded on a Carte w^t fowre whelys." These pageants, of course, were made of wood: "Paied to Sampson Carpenter and hys man hewyng and squeryng of tymber for the Pagent" is an entry in the account book of Canterbury. Two of these typical pageants, taken from a miniature in the Bodleian Library, are shown in Fig. 61. The curtained dressing-room is quite apparent here, and there seems to be an upper story from which, in all probability, angels descended.[1] Many of the pageants, however, were made in the representation of some object. Thus at Coventry the Cappers' pageant possessed a "hell-mouth," as did that of the Drapers. The latter was provided also with a windlass, means of showing fire belching from the mouth, a barrel for simulating an earthquake, and some apparatus for setting three worlds afire. In the Digby play of *St Mary Magdalen* we are informed there was a "stage, and Helle ondyr-neth that stage." Other plays had also their special "theatres." At Hull for a Noah drama payments were made "To a shipwright for clinking Noah's ship" in 1483, while in 1494 further money was expended on "making Noah's ship" and "rigging Noah's ship." It is evident that we are not dealing here with a practical vessel such as we find delineated in the Valenciennes miniature, for a farthing was paid in 1483 "to straw and grease for wheels."

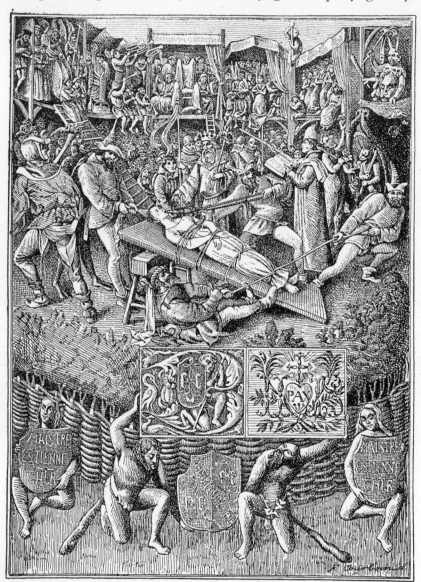

Fig. 59. The Martyrdom of St Apollonia

From Mantzius, *A History of Theatrical Art in Ancient and Modern Times.*

The method of using these pageants is quite clear. The stage-level, no doubt curtained as in the Paradise of *Adam* so as to show merely the upper part of the players, was employed for localized scenes; but the street below served as an open neutral ground. At Coventry, we are informed by a stage direction, "Erode [Herod] ragis in the pagond & in the strete also," while later "the

---

[1] See *infra*, p. 74. It is possible, of course, that the miniature represents puppet-shows, but the puppet-show and the pageant cannot have been far different one from another except as regards size.

70

iij Kyngis speykyth in the ſtrete." The methods in use correspond exactly to those of the ſtationary setting.

(5) In France employment was occasionally made of the ſtill ſtanding Roman theatres, such as those of Nîmes, Arles, and Orange, and it is possibly the ancient Roman tradition which explains

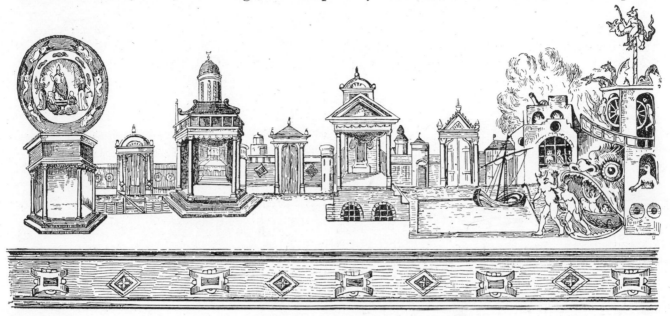

Fig. 60. THE VALENCIENNES MYSTERY PLAY
From Mantzius, *op. cit.*

the 'rounds' in which the Cornish myſteries and some other medieval dramas were performed. Of these the moſt important are the two amphitheatres which can yet be seen at St Juſt and at

Fig. 61. TWO MEDIEVAL PAGEANTS

Perranzabuloe in Cornwall. The former, of ſtone, has a diameter of 126 feet; the latter, of earth, is 4 feet larger. The manuscripts of the Cornish plays themselves are furnished with a plan which shows the arrangement of the various *mansions* during the performances. For the *Origo Mundi* we have *Celum* (Heaven), followed by *Tortores* (Torturers), no doubt equivalent to the Prison in the French dramas, *Infernum* (Hell), *Rex Pharao* (King Pharaoh), *Rex Dauid*, *Rex Salomon*, *Abraham*, and *Ortus*. The arrangement of Heaven and Hell is the same in the *Resurrection* play, and a similar circle is shown for *St Meriasek*. These circular *mansions* of the Cornish plays may be compared with the interesting diagram shown in the manuscript of *The Castle of Perseverance* (reign of Henry VI). Here (Fig. 62) again is a large circle, enclosed with "watyr a bowte the place if any dyche may be mad ther [1] it schal be pleyed; or ellys that it be stronglye barryd al a bowte: & lete nowth [2] ower [3] many stytelerys [4] be withinne the place." a bed for Mankind. What interests us, however,

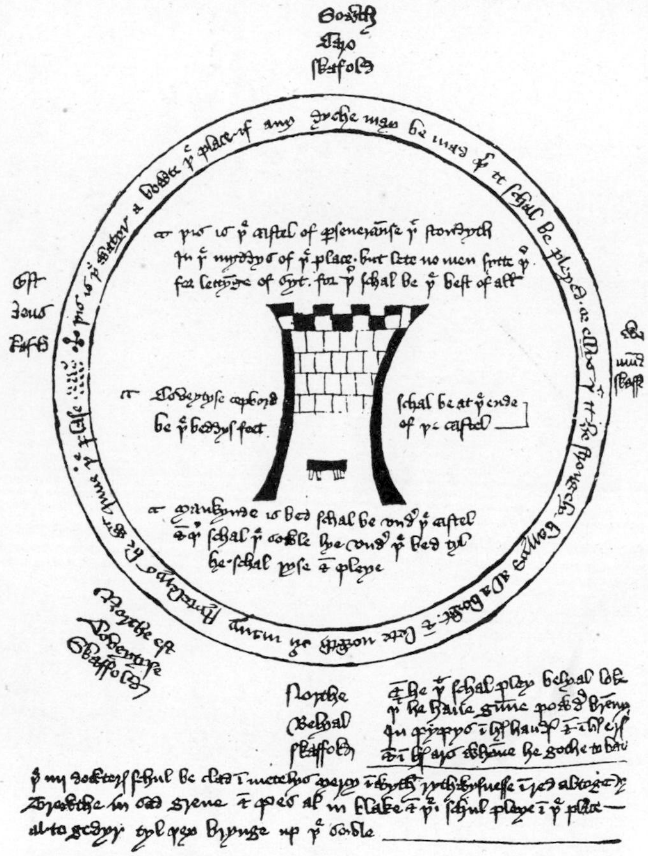

Fig. 62. PLAN FOR "THE CASTLE OF PERSEVERANCE"

The circle represents a ditch; the castle is in the centre with "Mankynde [h]is bed" below it.

In the midst of the circle is a castle, and below is the arrangement of the *mansions* on the edge of the circle. God's scaffold is to the east,[5] Belial comes in the north, with the World in the west and Caro in the south; Covetousness occupies the north-east. Evidently here is an arrangement which still preserves the ancient church setting whereby Heaven is set in the east over the altar. Here obviously is a general arrangement based upon that principle which has already been seen exemplified in the Donaueschingen and Lucerne settings with the north as the seat of evil.

(6) With the passing away of the miracle cycles, or, to speak more strictly, for the performance of those farcical interludes which were common in France and which were revived perhaps rather than instituted in England by John Heywood, such elaborate settings were quite unnecessary. The interludes were commonly played in the houses of the great and the rich; their *mise-en-scène* was of the slightest, consisting rather of properties than of scenic background. In the morality called *The Nature of the Four Elements* (early sixteenth century) a "hall" is definitely mentioned as the place of action, while "dorys" (doors) are referred to in the interlude of *Nature*. The setting of these plays, we must presume, was merely a raised daïs, probably backed by a curtain, containing movable properties such as a "stole" (*Nature*), a "thron" (*The Play of the Weather*), or a fireplace (*Iohan Iohan*). The

platea, in other words, exists without the *mansions*. We do certainly find relics in these dramas of the older tradition; thus Mater in *Thersytes* (mid-sixteenth century) is provided with a "place which is prepared for her," while such a late play as *Mary Magdalene* in the Digby series has a fully crowded set of mansions. In the latter drama six main localities, each subdivided, are placed before the audience. (1) First comes the set used for the Biblical scenes, including the Castle of Maudelyn and the seats of the Emperor, Herod, and Pilate. (2) Hell, in two parts, follows. (3) Next we have Jerusalem with a tavern, the house of Simon Leprous, and an arbour. (4) Marcylle possesses a castle, a temple, and a sea-coast.[6] (5) Heaven above with a wilderness below is

---

[1] where.   [2] not.   [3] over.   [4] Probably 'marshals.'
[5] See *supra*, p. 66.   [6] This seacoast was visited by a practicable ship, which entered "with a mery song."

near by, as is also (6) the Holy Land, which contains a separate mountain. This *Mary Magdalene*, however, really belongs to earlier traditions, and we may say that the majority of the moralities

as well as the interludes had a much simpler setting. Pictorial examples of this platform stage have been preserved in France. Thus Jean de Gourmont (mid-sixteenth century) has one which shows a trestled stage, curtained at the back and full of performers (Fig. 64). A similar scene has been engraved by H. Liefrinck (*c.* 1540–80). It is headed *Comedie ou farce de six parsonnages*, and again shows a bare stage with curtains from which one character is peering (Fig. 65). On the stage in the centre is an old man, somewhat Pantaloonish in appearance. At him a masked servant or another old man is staring; at his side are two women and a character who may be either a young lover or a *capitano*.[1] These illustrations may serve to show the kind of stage which was utilized by the interlude performers.

Fig. 63. MEDIEVAL DEVIL COSTUMES AT ZURICH

(iv) MACHINERY, EFFECTS, AND COSTUMES

That the medieval stage did not lack machinery entirely, in France, in Italy, and in England, is amply proved by stage directions and by eyewitnesses' accounts. In France a head of St Peter, severed, jumped thrice upon the stage, and "à chacun yst une fontaine."[2] There too the Holy Ghost descended like a "grand brandon de feu artificiellement fait par eaue-de-vie,"[3] while a Virgin moved her head and arms, and raised her eyes to heaven. Italy, naturally, because of her artists and painters, was not slow to make full use of these machines—*ingegni*, devices, they were called to correspond with the French *secrets* or *feyntes*. Vasari notes that one of the early masters of Italian perspective, Filippo Brunelleschi, invented or superintended the mechanical arrangements for a Paradise, which may have come near to those described by the same author elsewhere. Here there was—

Fig. 64. A PLATFORM STAGE OF THE SIXTEENTH CENTURY

Print by Jean de Gourmont, from Mantzius, *op. cit.*

Fig. 65. A PLATFORM STAGE OF THE SIXTEENTH CENTURY

Print by H. Liefrinck, from Mantzius, *op. cit.*

---

[1] See *infra*, p. 110.   [2] "At each jump flowed a fountain."   [3] "A firebrand artificially made by spirits."

un altro cielo sopra la tribuna maggiore, nel quale alcune ruote grandi fatte a guisa d'arcolai, che dal centro alla superficie movevano con belissimo ordine dieci giri per i dieci cieli, erano tutti pieni di lumicini, rappresentanti le stelle. . . .[1]

Mechanical effects find frequent mention. In a *Passione* "apronsi li monumenti, e vengono li tremuoti, e tenebre appariscono," [2] while in a *San Lorenzo* play "viene una saetta dal cielo, e fallo rovinar tutto in pezzi." [3]

Effects of a similar kind, although not quite so ornate, were known in England. "Fyftie fadam of lyne for the cloudes" figured in the accounts of Chelmsford in 1562–63; while the Digby *St Mary Magdalene* had a "hevyne" (Heaven) which could open. The Cornish plays presented "the father . . . in a clowde," and when he spoke "yᵉ levys" (leaves) opened. There Paradise, like the Paradise of the French *Adam*, had "ii fayre trees," a "fowntaine," and "fyne flowers." At Dublin we find a camel which is "peynted" and evidently carried by several "Portors." [4] In many of the English mysteries ascents and descents of angels are frequent, while in *The Salutation and Conception* of the Coventry series

þe [5] holy gost discendit with iij bemys [6] to our lady, the sone of þe godhed nest[7] with iij bemys . to the holy gost the fadyr godly with iij bemys to þe sone. And so entre all thre to here bosom.

There are flaming swords and burning altars in the Ludus Coventriae plays of *The Fall of Man* and *Cain and Abel*, while the York cycle abounds in sudden gleams of light.[8] The play of *Mary Magdalene* is likewise rich in visual effects. A "bad angyl" there enters "into hell with thondyr"; some devils set a "house one a fyere"; a "moment" [9] is made to "tremyll and quake"; while later "a clowd" comes "frome hevene, and" sets "þe tempyl one a fyer."

Most realistic, however, must have been the effects connected with Hell. "A skin of parchment and gunpowder" was bought at Kingston-on-Thames in 1520, and from other records we know well what it was used for. In the Cornish plays Lucifer "goeth downe to hell appareled fowle wᵗʰ fyre about hem"; "he that schal pley belyal" (Belial) in *The Castle of Perseverance* is bidden to "loke that he have gunne powder brennying in pypys in his hands and in his ers"; while the Vice in *A Play of Love* "cometh in ronnynge sodenly aboute the place among the audiens with a hye copyr tank on his hed full of squybs fyred." That this was not merely a national custom is proved by a description of similar demons in France:

Adonc fit la monstre de la Diablerie parmy la ville et le marché. Les diables estoient tous capparrassonnés de peaux de loups, de veaulx, et de beliers, passementées de testes de moutons, de cornes de bœufz, et de grands havetz de cuisine: ceinctz de grosses courroies, esquelles pendoient grosses cymbales de vaches, et sonnettes de muletz à bruit horrifique. Tenoient en main aucuns bastons noirs pleins de fusées: autres portoient longs tizons allumés, sur lesquelz à chascun carrefour jettoient pleines poignées de parasine en pouldre, dont sortoit feu et fumée terrible.[10]

---

[1] "Another sky above the great rostrum, in which were some huge wheels constructed as if in the air, moving from the centre to the edges in most beautiful order, ten orbits for the ten heavens, all full of little lamps, representing the stars. . . ."

[2] "The monuments are opened, earthquakes come, and darkness descends."

[3] "A bolt comes from on high and casts it all in ruins."

[4] This, it is true, is in a processional show rather than in a play.

[5] the.   [6] beams. (The word may indicate trumpet-calls.)   [7] next.

[8] *Bethlehem:* A! lord God! what light is þis
    That comes shynyng þus sodenly?
    Harrowing of Hell: A light I woll þei haue
    To schewe þame I shall come sone.

[9] idol.

[10] "Then the show of the Devils was made in the town and square. These devils were all clad in skins of wolves, calves, and rams, surmounted with sheep-heads, bull-horns, and cockscombs: girdles of thick skins, from which hung cows' or mules' bells with horrible noise. Some carried in their hands black rods full of squibs: others long flaming spars, on which at each turn they threw handfuls of powdered resinous pitch from which issued terrible flame and smoke."

This description of the costumes of the medieval devils is exceedingly interesting, and may be compared with the pictures of such characters in Figs. 60 and 63. The animal heads and grotesque dresses seem to have been a traditional stage convention. Of the other costumes of actors in England we have nothing but vague references, but such as they are they have their interest. Masks or " visors " seem to have been fairly common. In 1391 a list of properties at Beverley in Yorkshire included

> j karre,[1] viij hespis, xviij stapels, ij visers, ij wenges angeli . . . j worme . . . ij paria camisarum [2] and j gladius.[3]

Visors formed an entry in the accounts of Bungay, Suffolk, in 1566, and an item in the Canterbury records is the " payntyng of the hede and the Aungell of the pagent." Lucifer in the Cornish mysteries has a serpent form " wth a virgyn face & yolowe heare vpon her head." Wigs, with or without masks, were also freely utilized, as is indicated by a record of 1504 at Leicester :

> Paid for a pound of hemp to mend the angels heads, iiij[d].

In 1585 at Twickesbury there were " eight heads of hair for the Apostles, and ten beards, and a face or vizier for the Devil."

As for the costumes themselves there are many entries, but few descriptions. A Vice's coat at Chelmsford in the sixteenth century is mentioned but not detailed; there also we learn of a coat " of lether for Christ " and are treated besides to a pretty little list of properties :

> ij vyces coats, and ij scalpes, ij daggers (j dagger wanted)
> v prophets cappes (one wantinge).
> iij flappes for devils.
> iiij shepehoks, iiij whyppes (but one gone).

Fig. 66. Hell-mouth from the Cædmon Manuscript (Eleventh Century)

" A new coat & a peir of hoes [hosc] for Gabriell " appears at Coventry in 1544, while three skins were used for Noah's coat at Hull in 1494. Three yards of " dorneck " were used for a player's coat at Kingston in 1513–14, where likewise was demanded a pennyworth of thread " for the resurrection." " Jesus hoose " are mentioned at Leicester in 1504 ; while Norwich provides an interesting record of

> A cote & hosen w[t][4] a bagg & capp for dolo[r],[5] steyned.
> 2 cotes & a payre hosen for Eve, stayned.
> A cote & hosen for Adam, Steyned.
> A cote w[t] hosen & tayle for y[e] serpente, steyned, w[t] a w[t] heare. . . .[6]
> An Angell's Cote & over hoses of Apis Skynns. . . .
> A face & heare for y[e] Father.
> 2 hearys [7] for Adam & Eve.[8]

The costumes of Adam and Eve are more fully described for the Cornish dramas. There " Adam and Eva " are " aparlet [apparelled] in whytt lether," no doubt representing skin, and a stage direction bids " ffig leaves redy to cover ther members," the pair being provided later with " garmentis

---

[1] car or pageant.
[4] with.   [5] dolor, grief.
[2] pairs of shirts.
[6] white hair, or wig.
[3] sword.
[7] hairs, or wigs.
[8] A very similar list of costumes for an Italian play in 1339 is given in A. D'Ancona, *Origini del Teatro Italiano* (1891), i, 164.

of skynnes." [1]   The coſtumes, except for a few thus diſtinctly outlined, were no doubt the ordinary dresses of the day.   At Worceſter in 1576 an inventory hardly diſtinguishes any save a king's and a Devil's:

> A gowne of freres gyrdles.   A woman's gowne.   A Kˢ cloke of Tysshew.   A Jerkyn and a payer of breeches.   A lytill cloke of tysshew.   A gowne of silk.   A Jerkyn of greene, 2 cappes, and the devils apparell.

It is possible, however, that colour played a fair part in the general symbolism of the drama. The ſtage directions in *The Caſtle of Perseverance* thus bid that

> the iiij dowters schul be clad in mentelys, Mercy in wyth,[2] rythwysnesse in red al togedyr, Trewthe in sad grene, & Pes al in blake,

while in the French *Adam* "Chaym sit indutus rubeis vestibus, Abel vero albis." [3]   No doubt this general scheme was followed out in other plays.   Nothing, however, do we have so detailed as certain descriptions such as that written by Jacques Thibouſt of a coſtume worn by Nesron (Nero) in an *Actes des Apôtres* of 1536:

> Nesron . . . eſtoit veſtu d'une saye de veloux bleu toute pourfilée d'or à grands rinceaux d'antique, et découpée a taille ouverte, par ou apparoissoit et flocquetoit a gros bouillons la doublure, qui eſtoit d'ung satin cramoisy, pourfilée semblablement d'ung autre ouvrage de fleurons et entrelacs de fil d'or; elle eſtoit doublée de veloux cramoisy a collet de mesme, faict a pointes renversées, entremesleés l'une dans l'autre, et semées par grands prodigalité de grosses perles, aux quelles pointes pendoient grosses houppes d'autres perles . . . Sa couronne d'or a trois branches estoit remplie de tant de sortes de pierreries . . . Il portait l'un de ses pieds sur une escrin couvert de drap d'argent et semé de quelque nombre de pierreries . . . Portoit en sa main une hache d'armes bien dorée; son port estoit hautain et son maintien magnifique; son dit tribunal et lui dessus estoit porté par huict roys captifs qui estoient dedans, desquels on ne voyoit seulement que les teſtes couronnés de couronnes d'or.[4]

With this account may be compared the notes regarding the coſtumes to be used for the sixteenth-century Lucerne play mentioned above.   There, for example,

> Pater aeternus soll haben das gewöhnliche Diadem, schön altväterisch, graues langes Haar und Bart.   Einen Reichsapfel in der Hand . . . .   Eine weisse Rippe im Aermel.[5]

(v) Actors and Performance

Concerning the actors in the English myſtery plays little more may be said than has been given above.   The gilds, having taken over the management of the cycles, provided the actors from among their own members.   Generally these actors were paid a small fee.   At Coventry one man received three shillings and fourpence " for pleayng God," another fourpence " for hangyng Judas," another fourpence " for Coc croyng [cock-crowing]."   Five shillings was apportioned " to iij whyte [saved] sollys [souls]," five shillings " to iij blake sollys," and one shilling and fourpence " to ij wormes of conscyence."   Similar records occur in the accounts of other towns.   At Hull one Thomas Sawyr received tenpence for " playing God," a Jenkin Smith received one shilling

---

[1] It would seem that in France, if not in England, complete nudity on the stage was known.   In the fourteenth-century *Miracles de Notre Dame* (Anciens textes français, iii, 124–125) a woman disguised as a monk is, on death, revealed on the stage "toute nue."

[2] white.

[3] " Cain is to be clad in red garments, Abel in white."

[4] " Nero was clad in a lined cloak, all blue ſtriped with golden bars after the antique ſtyle, and slit with open seams so that the lining of crimson satin appeared, adorned also with another design of ornaments and knots of gold thread; it was lined at the collar with crimson velvet, made with inverted points, intermingled one with another, and prodigally scattered with large pearls.   At these points hung large ſtrings of other pearls. . . . His golden crown of three tiers was decorated with all sorts of precious ſtones. . . . He supported one of his feet on a ſtool covered with silver cloth and ornamented with a large number of precious ſtones. . . . In his hand he carried a beautifully gilded battleaxe; his carriage was haughty and his demeanour grand; his tribunal and he were carried by eight captive kings who were within and of whom nothing was seen save their golden-crowned heads."

[5] " The Pater aeternus muſt have the cuſtomary diadem.   He is an old man with long grey hair and beard.   An imperial orb is in his hand. . . . A white rib in his sleeve."

for taking Noah, whose wife was awarded eightpence. This was in 1494; eleven years previously Noah and his wife got only one shilling and sixpence between them, and God only sixpence. The salaries of actors were evidently rising.

It is probable that, while the parts of many later morality plays were still performed by amateurs, professional and semi-professional performers were coming to take their share in the development of English drama. These professional players will, of course, be considered when we reach the time of Queen Elizabeth.

In France conditions were similar and dissimilar. The *corps municipaux*, the town gilds, there as in England, took a large part in the organization of the mysteries, but they shared their activities with several others apparently unknown in England.

Fig. 67. THE FOOL AND THE DEVIL
From Barclay's *Ship of Fools*.

The *confréries pieuses* played a prominent *rôle* in the management of the cycles, most famous of all being the Confrérie de la Passion established at Paris by letters patent of Charles VI, on December 4, 1402. It is with the establishment of this company at the Hôpital de la Trinité that we first meet in Europe with a permanent dramatic troupe settled at a definite theatre. The Confrérie de la Passion will also occupy our attention later. Alongside of these *confréries pieuses* there existed a number of peculiar groups of actors, professional and amateur. The Goliardi still busied themselves in the organization of performances. Les Basochiens, famous for their *triomphes* and *tableaux* "sans parler ne sans signer," laid their impress on the interlude stage. Les Sots, clad in hood of yellow and green, ass-ears, and costume of similar colours, the green signifying hope of renewal and the yellow gaiety, passed over great tracts of France, at their head the well-known Enfants Sans-Souci. Finally there were the many *confréries des fous*. Deriving, apparently, from the notorious medieval Feast of Fools, these men, called Cornards or Connards at Rouen and Évreux because of their horned caps, Suppôts du Seigneur de la Coquille at Lyon, Sots at Amiens, Foux at Auxerre, L'Abbaye joyeuse de Lescache Profit at Cambrai, Gaillardons at Chalon-sur-Saône, Diables at Chaumont, Trompettes-Jongleurs at Chauny, and Mauvaises Braies at Laon, played interlude and scandalous farce to the shame of many serious men and the delight of many merry ones.[1]

The fool tradition is an important one in many ways. Not only does it pass on to add gaiety to one great comedy of Shakespeare's and profundity to a great tragedy, but it perhaps gives us one other link between the theatre of the Middle Ages and the mimic entertainments of Greece and Rome. The Sots and the Fols of France, together with the Court fool as immortalized in Feste and the Fool in *King Lear*, at first sight seem to be purely the product of medieval times, but when we discover that in Greece a $\mu\omega\rho\grave{o}\varsigma$ $\phi\alpha\lambda\alpha\kappa\rho\acute{o}\varsigma$ (a bald-headed fool) was a well-known figure,

---

[1] In Italy the actors of the *sacre rappresentazioni* were mostly bodies of young men, called *voci*; sometimes the girls of convent schools also occupied themselves in arranging dramatic performances.

when we find that in Rome the same type was known as the *mimus calvus* or *stupidus*, we begin to trace a resemblance between the antique figures and their later counterparts. The medieval fool seems to have been often bald-headed. Cries a contemporary:

> Mez regardez quel apostol!
> il est tondu comme ung fol,[1]

while another speaks of a kind of entertainer who "rasit capillos suos et barbam."[2] The garments of mixed colours seem to have been known in ancient days as well, while the cocks-

Fig. 68. Terra-cotta Statuettes of Roman Mimes

From the originals in the British Museum.

Fig. 69. Terra-cotta Statuette of a Roman Mime

From the original in the British Museum.

comb, as has lately been shown, was a feature of a type in the classic mime. The fools with their long-eared caps, illustrated in Fig. 67, may be compared with the series of fool-types from Roman times given in Figs. 68, 69, and 70. A whole volume would be required to trace fully the evidence which connects the two, but even these few remarks may serve to call attention to the main points of correspondence.

Another aspect of the medieval theatre must also be hurriedly passed over. It has been seen above that the fools formed important acting companies in France, and it may be suggested that the medieval mystery proper is not so innocent of mime influence as has generally been supposed.

[1] "But look at that apostle!
He is shaved like a fool."

[2] "Shaved his hair and beard."

THE THEATRE IN THE MIDDLE AGES

If we imagine the conditions of life in the Middle Ages; if we think of the wandering vagabonds, the entertainers, with their traditional repertories and their skill in interpretation; and if we contrast with them the wholly inexperienced workmen who set about to perform some great religious cycle—if we think of these things truly, we are almost bound to suppose that the amateurs would call upon the skill of the professional *mimi, jongleurs,* and *histriones.* At York payments were made to "ministrallis in festo Corporis Cristi" in 1446, while the following year twopence was given to "ij ludentibus Joly Wat and Malkyn." How far these records from York can be treated as typical we have, of course, no means of knowing, but we may not be wrong in tracing many of the comic features in the mystery plays to the influence, direct or indirect, of the professionals. Once more, then, the medieval drama and the medieval theatre are seen to be the result of two forces—the traditionally preserved relics of Roman mimic displays and the new spirit which sprang independently from the Church and inspired men toward a form of art entirely different in spirit and in aim from anything which had been seen in classic times.

Fig. 70. TERRA-COTTA SHOWING THE MIMUS CALVUS

From Ficoroni, *De Larvis scenicis*, Plate LXXII.

In presenting their performances these medieval entertainers, having no newspaper press in which to advertise themselves, made free use of the *cri* or *cry.* This *cri* was usually accompanied, as in a present-day circus, by a lengthy procession. A full account of *le cry et Proclamation public* made for the exhibition at Paris of *Le Mystère des Actes des Apostres* in 1540 has been preserved, and a similar proclamation for

Fig. 71. EASTERN MIMI, AS SHOWN IN A FRESCO AT ST SOPHIA (KIEV)

the Chester plays, dated 1544, provides an interesting parallel. The object of both is the same—to announce the plays, present authority, and demand that no disturbance be made.

Normally in medieval drama all parts were taken by men. This is almost certainly true of England; in France there are at least three records previous to 1550 which inform us of women players. One young amateur actress at Metz in 1468 spoke no fewer than 2300 lines as St Catherine—

winning as her reward the hand of a gentleman in marriage. The general level of performance, no doubt, was crude, but a devout air of seriousness pervaded the whole. This acting business was so obviously not merely a game, but something of real importance for the world. Anachronistic as the drama regularly was in main outline, little details had to be scrupulously exact. There must be the bladder of blood and the sheephooks and the instruments of torture. The effect of Christ's crucifixion could not be complete unless the actor himself suffered. M. le curé, one Nicolle, of Metz took the part of Jesus in 1437, and he " cuyda mourir en l'arbre de la croix, car le cœur lui faillit, tellement qu'il fût été mort, s'il ne fût été secouru." [1] From the same locality we learn that a priest named Jehan de Missey " portoit le personnage de Juda," but " pendit trop longtemps " and " fut pareillement transi et quasi mort; car le cueur lui faillit, par quoi il fut bien hâtivement dépendu et fut emporté en aucun lieu prochain pour le frotter de vinaigre et autre chose pour le réconforter." [2] If the Fouquet miniature is at all a representation of the reality we may truly pity the young performer of St Apollonia. The tooth-drawer is most businesslike and the ropepullers most energetic.

As is evident, in this medieval drama and its theatre we have a set of conditions surprisingly like those provided in Greece. A drama, lyrical in origin, which springs from religion; actors devoted to the presentation of the plays; the whole performance a thing not of a class, but of the community—these are features which the Middle Ages possess in common with Athens of the age of Aeschylus. Beyond these similarities, however, there are many differences. The medieval people lacked that classical feeling for simplicity and unity of effect which characterizes Greek sculpture and Greek thought. The gargoyles will always be peering out from behind the soaring windows and the intricate traceries of stonework. The devils with their squibs will ever be pressing among the actors of more serious *rôles*. The medieval theatre is obviously a thing of the " Gothic imagination." Where the Greeks forbade violent action on the stage the audience of the Middle Ages demanded blood and rant. Herod has to rage on the pageant and on the street also. Where the Greeks endeavoured to secure an harmonious unity of effect, the medieval playwrights huddled serious and comic together. The shepherds crack their rustic jokes ere viewing Christ's manger; Noah and his wife have their comic tussle as the Deluge sweeps over the world. No one can say which is higher—the Greek or the Gothic; each is essentially different, even although with both the theatre took its rise out of chants to a divinity.

[1] " Would have died on the rood-tree, for he fainted and was like to have died had he not been rescued."

[2] " He took the part of Judas, but hung too long and fainted and was like dead; for his heart failed him, wherefore he was hastily taken down and carried to a place near by and sprinkled with vinegar and other things to bring him round."

CHAPTER IV

THEATRES OF RENASCENCE ITALY

(i) THE CLASSICAL REVIVAL

THE course of our survey of theatrical settings has carried us to the fifteenth and even to the sixteenth century, but it must be remembered that there is no distinct break between medieval period and Renascence period, that mystery plays were being given on the Continent contemporaneously with the more ornate tragedies and operas at the Italian Courts, that the very years which saw the performance of *As You Like It* witnessed also in some provincial town the ranting of Herod on a pageant stage. As early as 1452 Alberti had designed a theatre proper for Pope Nicholas V, and by the end of the fifteenth century at Ferrara and at Rome performances were being given of classical plays by Terence and Plautus.

Fundamentally, the Renascence meant a rebirth of interest in the life and literature of ancient Greece and Rome. Feverishly men studied the long-forgotten pages of Greek manuscripts, unearthed treasures of statuary, embraced pagan legend, wrote poems and plays in imitation of classic authors. In the midst of this almost universal enthusiasm, which was both artistic and scholarly, it was not surprising that some new knowledge of the Greek and Roman stages should come to light. An ancient work by Vitruvius was rediscovered and eagerly read by the young architects. Out of this were born new theories concerning theatres and the stage, theories which were crystallized in Serlio's famous *Architettura* of 1551, which contained views to be expanded later in Sabbatini's volume on the theatre. The new views and theories gave rise to theatres in Italy and France such as the Middle Ages never knew and such as were finally to revolutionize the whole of European stage and dramatic art.

As we have noted, the first that is heard of the revival of classical plays is toward the end of the fifteenth century. Rome, Florence, and Ferrara all witnessed productions of this type. Under Julius Pomponius Laetus (1425–98) the Roman Academy certainly produced some plays of Seneca and a comedy possibly by Plautus. A description of a tragic performance is given by Sulpicius Verulanus in an Epistle to Cardinal Raffaelle Riario.[1] He says:

> Tu enim primus Tragoediae . . . in medio foro pulpitum ad quinque pedum altitudinem erectum pulcherrime exornasti : eamdemque, postquam in Hadriani mole Divo Innocentio spectante est acta, rursus intra tuos penates, tamquam in media Circi cavea, toto concessu umbraculis tecto, admisso populo et pluribus tui ordinis spectatoribus honorifice excepisti. Tu etiam primus picturatae scaenae faciem, quum Pomponiani comoediam agerent, nostro saeculo ostendisti.[2]

This, as is obvious, tells us little, but what little there is is valuable. The audience sat under awnings, there was a stage five feet high and, most important of all, a *picturatae scaenae facies*. About a quarter of a century or more later P. Palliolo undertook to describe *Le Feste pel Conferimento del Patriziato a Giuliano e Lorenzo de' Medici* when some play or other was given. Here,

---

[1] In his edition of Vitruvius, *c.* 1492.

[2] "You first equipped a stage for Tragedy beautifully. This was erected five feet high in the middle of the square. After the play had been acted *in Hadriani mole* [presumably the Castle of St Angelo] before Pope Innocent, you revived it again in your own palace. The audience sat under awnings, as in the *cavea* of a Circus. The public was admitted and there were many spectators of your own rank. You, too, when the students of Pomponius acted a comedy, first revealed to our age the appearance of a painted scene."

guardando avanti, se appresenta la fronte della scena, in v compassi distinta per mezzo di colonne quadre, con basi e capitelli coperti de oro. In ciascuno compasso è uno uscio di grandezza conveniente a private case. . . . La parte inferiore di questa fronte di quattro frigi è ornata. . . . A gli usci delle scene furono poste portiere di panno de oro. El proscenio fu coperto tutto di tapeti con uno ornatissimo altare in mezzo.[1]

In this instance something more is given to us. There is here a proscenium, and, behind it, a back wall presenting four columns which divided the set into five compartments, each compartment being hung with cloth of gold. So much for Rome.

At Ferrara, under Ercole d'Este, duke of that city, dramatic performances of a similar kind were given with as great enthusiasm. Once more we may turn to the records of these shows. By 1471 a play of some nature had been given there, and then in 1486 comes a revival of the *Menaechmi* of Plautus. A contemporary account of the revival has been preserved, in which we are informed that

in lo suo cortile . . . fu fato suso uno tribunale di legname, con case v merlade, con una finestra e uscio per ciascuna : poi venne una fusta . . . e traversò il cortile con dieci persone dentro con remi e vela, del naturale.[2]

Magnificence and experimentation were developing rapidly. This performance was followed by the *Amphitruo* in 1487 when appeared " uno paradiso cum stelle et altre rode," [3] and the *Menaechmi* was revived again in 1491, with scenery painted by Niccolò del Cogo, showing a " prospecto de quattro castelli." [4] Still later, in 1499, three Roman comedies were presented with " cinque casamenti merlati " executed by the artists Fino and Bernardino Marsigli. For these and for plays given in 1502 the stages were between four and five feet high.

At other cities similar scenes were devised. At Bologna, according to a letter dated July 16, 1496, from Floriano Dulfo to the Duke of Mantua, a farce was presented in which was a

coperto azuro stellato che nè pictore nè sculptore, nè ingegno humano saperebe nè pensare nè fare il più bello.[5]

These descriptions of the performances at Rome, at Ferrara, and at Bologna require careful consideration, for here we have the basis of the Renascence and of the modern stage. First of all, let us see whether there is any pictorial representation which may assist us. This pictorial representation is to be found, as has been divined, in the edition of Terence issued at Lyons under the direction of Jodocus Badius Ascensius in 1493, and in the Venice Terence of 1497. In the former each play is adorned with a series of woodcuts showing various episodes in the plot. At first sight these might be imagined to be merely the fictitious interpretations of an artist, but a more careful study reveals the fact that they must have been taken directly from actual productions of the plays. The chief indication of this fact lies in the grouping of the woodcuts themselves. A reference to Fig. 72 will show that throughout the particular comedy there illustrated the setting is constant. This setting consists of a back wall composed of five simple columns supporting four round arches, the spaces between the columns being closed by curtains, which can be drawn as is shown in the second woodcut in Fig. 72, and behind which are tiny rooms with rear windows (first woodcut in Fig. 72). Each compartment denotes a separate locality, or, to be more exact, denotes the house (*domus* or *mansion*) of one of the characters in the play—Carini, Chreme(tis), Chrisidis, and Do(mus) Symonis being written

[1] " Looking in front we see the scene-front, divided into five compartments by means of four columns, with bases and capitals of gold. In each compartment is a doorway of a size similar to that of doors in private houses. . . . The lower part of the scene-front is decorated with four friezes. . . . At the doors of the scenes were placed curtains of gold cloth. The proscenium was all covered with tapestries and had a heavily decorated altar in the centre."

[2] " In his courtyard . . . was erected a wooden stage with five battlemented houses. There was a window and a door in each. Then a ship came in . . . and crossed the courtyard. It had ten persons in it and was fitted with oars and a sail in a most realistic manner."

[3] " A paradise with stars and other devices [literally, wheels]."

[4] " A prospect of four castles."

[5] " An azure starry covering such as no painter, sculptor, or human genius could imagine or excel."

below the four arches. The back wall, or proscenium, is flanked by two statuettes, symbolizing Phoebus and Liber, while the whole stands on a plain platform stage supported by trestles.

When we turn from these woodcuts of *Andria* to those illustrating the other plays, we note that, while the general principle of the setting is maintained, the actual arrangements differ. It is this fact that leads us to assume the genuinely theatrical origin of the whole series, for while the illustrations vary from comedy to comedy they are constant within the limits of each play of the series. Thus for *Heautontimoroumenos* the four curtained compartments are arranged, not in a straight wall, but as a three-sided figure jutting out on to the stage and supported by formal columns without the flanking statuettes (Fig. 73). For the *Adelphoe* there are five compartments arranged somewhat as in the *Heautontimoroumenos* (Fig. 75, which again shows the interior of one of the sections), while for *Hecyra* the four compartments are arranged as a kind of box toward the right-hand corner of the stage (Fig. 76). Besides these particular settings for the individual plays the Lyons Terence furnishes us with a picture of a *Theatrum* which helps us toward gaining a more comprehensive idea of the type of early Italian experimentation

Fig. 73. Theatre Setting for the "Heautontimoroumenos" of Terence

From the Lyons Terence (1493).

in this direction (Fig. 74), and this might be compared with the "Coliseus sive Theatrum" depicted in the Venice Terence of 1497.

What are we to make of all these? Are they relics of medieval styles or else something new? The problem has been bandied to and fro for some considerable time; but, from the simplicity of the Terence designs, which accord with the descriptions given of the plays at Rome, it would seem that we are dealing here with a classicism not unlike that of our early writers of tragi-comedies. It was a classicism with much of medieval sentiment in it. We must remember that through the *sacre rappresentazioni* of Italy

Fig. 72. Three Theatre Settings for the "Andria" of Terence

From the Lyons Terence (1493).

these humanists must have been acquainted with theatrical performances. Of the Greek stage they knew nothing till about 1484, and they must inevitably have taken over many of the features of the medieval play in their new efforts. No doubt the conventional *case* or houses were the chief of these, and we see in the woodcuts the classical interpretation of medieval practice.

(ii) VITRUVIUS

It has been said that up to 1484 men in general knew nothing of the Greek stage. Perhaps it may be well to consider what they actually did learn when the first Vitruvius was issued. A good deal they read about the proportions and structure of Greek and Roman auditoria, but this is almost all they could find concerning the stage and the *mise-en-scène*:

Ipsae autem scaenae suas habent rationes explicitas ita, uti mediae valvae ornatus habeant aulae regiae, dextra ac sinistra hospitalia, secundum autem spatia ad ornatus comparata, quae loca Graeci περιάκτους dicunt ab eo, quod machinae sunt in his locis versatiles trigonoe habentes singulares species ornationis, quae, cum aut fabularum mutationes sunt futurae seu deorum adventus, cum tonitribus repentinis, [ea] versentur mutentque speciem ornationis in fronte. Secundum ea loca versurae sunt procurrentes, quae efficiunt una a foro, altera a peregre, aditus in scaenam. Genera autem sunt scaenarum tria: unum quod dicitur tragicum, alterum comicum, tertium satyricum. Horum autem ornatus sunt inter se dissimili disparique ratione, quod tragicae deformantur columnis et fastigiis et signis reliquisque regalibus rebus; comicae autem aedificiorum privatorum et maenianorum habent speciem prospectusque fenestris dispositos imitatione, communium aedificiorum rationibus; satyricae vero ornantur arboribus, speluncis, montibus reliquisque agrestibus rebus in topeodis [? topiarii] speciem deformatis.[1]

Fig. 74. A RENASCENCE THEATRE
From the Lyons Terence (1493).

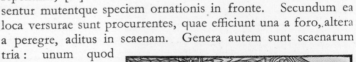

Fig. 75. THEATRE SETTING FOR THE "ADELPHOE" OF TERENCE
From the Lyons Terence (1493).

Fig. 76. THEATRE SETTING FOR THE "HECYRA" OF TERENCE
From the Lyons Terence (1493).

Now, we may ask, what was a humanist toward the end of the fifteenth century likely to seize upon first in Vitruvius? Unquestionably he would take first the arrangement of the auditorium

[1] "The scenes themselves are arranged in such a manner that they have middle doors decorated like those of a royal palace, to right and left the *hospitalia* [? guest chambers], and beyond spaces provided for decoration which the Greeks call περίακτοι because in these places are triangular machines which turn, each having a particular kind of ornamentation, and which, either when an alteration is to be made in the play or when gods with sudden thunderclaps come upon the stage, are revolved and change the appearance of the decoration in front. Beyond these places are projecting wings which afford entrances, one from the forum, the other from abroad. There are three kinds of scenes, one called tragic, another comic, and a third satyric. Their decorations are different and unlike each other, for the tragic scenes are shown with columns, pediments, statues, and other royal appurtenances; the comic scenes show private houses with views of windows after the manner of ordinary dwellings; the satyric scenes are decorated with trees, caves, mountains, and other rustic objects delineated in landscape style."

or *cavea*, but perhaps he would not at once realize that the theatres were open-air structures. He would only note the semicircular arrangement of the seats. Thus in the 1513 Florence edition of Vitruvius illustrations for the first time accompanied the Latin text and both for the Greek and the Roman theatre the artist showed a rectangular building with a semicircular auditorium faced by a fanciful scene-building (Fig. 77). The contemporary humanist is not quite sure what *valvae mediae* and *hospitalia* are; he has seen the popular *sacre rappresentazioni*; and he combines both into one. His *case* are relics of the medieval *mansions*, made now with curtains only, now more firmly with windows and doors.

While the humanist is doing this, however, he puzzles over the various points in Vitruvius. A most interesting illustration of this questioning appears in a sketch by Antonio San Gallo il Giovane (1485–1546), reproduced in *The Mask*. This shows a plan, a front view of a stage, and an explanatory detail. The manuscript text is difficult to read, but seems to run as follows:

> Aula rezio e li ospitalia si facivevano in sul proscenio quello che noi diciamo el parctc c fingieva si una sala e da ogni canto uno ospitio overo Camera donde uscivano li recitanti aveva cosa posti tre perche secondo la materia si facieva varii adornamente come dicie di tre sorte.[1]

Below this is the plan, showing a curved *teatro* (the Greek θέατρον, signifying the auditorium), the *orchestra del teatro*, behind the *aula regia*, and at the rear the *foro* or forum. At the sides are two *machine* or machines *per ogni ascione* (for every action or scene). The front view shows the artist's idea of how these machines were worked. The *aula regia* is evidently composed of buildings to the foreground, and the space to the back is the *foro*.

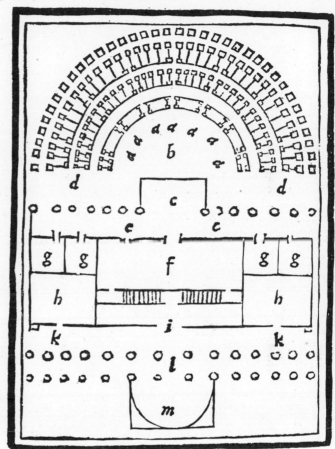

Fig. 77. PLAN OF A GREEK THEATRE IN THE JOCUNDUS EDITION OF VITRUVIUS, 1513

This shows well the early humanist idea of the Greek stage; note that the whole is enclosed within a rectangular wall.

The sides of the stage are formed each by an *ospitio overo hospitalia* (ospitio or hospitalia) with a square space in which the triangular machine is placed. Undoubtedly this design marks a groping toward the truth regarding the theatres of classic days. The interest for us is not that it aids in an understanding of these classic theatres, but that it helps toward an understanding of the theatres of Renascence Italy.

(iii) PERSPECTIVE IN SCENES

Meanwhile, the study of the art and science of perspective had been occupying the minds of many men during the fifteenth century. From the time of Brunelleschi to that of Leonardo da

---

[1] "*Aula regia* and the *hospitalia* were made on the proscenium which we call the 'wall' and a hall was simulated [in them], and at each side an *ospitio* or room whence the actors came forth. This had three stations, so that according to the subject-matter various decorations were given, as I said, of three kinds." *The Mask*, XI, iv, October 1925. Two readings in the text were suggested to me by Mr Hugh Quigley.

Vinci men were striving to learn how most realistically they might present the forms of nature as seen through their eyes. It is not surprising, therefore, that this new art of perspective should have been brought into the early Renascence theatres. The first definite record of the use of this perspective comes with the performance of Ariosto's *Cassaria* at Ferrara in 1508. The scene of Mytilene in this production, contrived by Pellegrino da Udine, presented to the audience " una contracta et prospettiva di una terra cum case, chiesie, campanili et zardini." [1]

The full account of the Mantuan performances of February 1501, provided by Sigismondo Cantelino, seems to indicate, however, that even before this date artists had been devoting themselves to the problems of practical perspective :

> Era la sua forma quadrangula, protensa alquanto in longitudine : li doi lati l'uno al altro de rimpecto, havevano per ciaschuno octo architravi con colonne ben conrespondenti et proportionate alla larghezza et alteza de dicti archi : le basi et capitelli pomposissimamente . . . representavano alla mente un edificio eterno et antiquo, pieno di delectatione ; li archi con relevo di fiori rendevano prospectiva mirabile ; la largheza di ciascheuno era braza quactro vel cerca ; la alteza proporzionata ad quella. Dentro nel prospecto eran panni d'oro et alcune verdure, si come li recitationi recerchavano ; una delle bande era ornata delli sei quadri del Cesareo Triumpho per man del singulare Mantengha : li doi altri lati discontro erano con simili archi, ma de numero inferiore, che ciascheuno ne haveva sei. Doi bande era scena data ad actorj et recitatorj : le doe altre erano ad scalini, deputati per le donne et daltro, per . . . trombecti et musici. [Between the columns] era una grocta, benchè facta ad arte tamen naturalissima : sopra quella era un ciel grande fulgentissimo de varij lumi, in modo de lucidissime stelle, con una artificiata rota de segni al moto de' quali girava mo il sole, mo la luna nelle case proprie : dentro era la rota de fortuna con sei tempi : *regno, regnaj, regnabo* : in mezo residea la dea aurea con un sceptro con un delphin. Dintorno alla scena al frontespitio da basso era li triumphi del Petrarcha, ancor loro penti per man del p° Mantengha ; sopra eran candelieri vistosissimi deaurati tucti : nel mezo era uno scudo colle arme per tucto della Ca Ma ; sopra la aquila aurea bicapitata col regno et diadema imperiale : ciascheuno teneva tre doppieri : ad ogni lato era le insegne. [2]

At Urbino in 1513 an artist painted similar scenes for Bibbiena's *Calandra*, when

> La scena . . . era finta una città bellissima con le strade, palazzi, chiese, torri, strade vere, e ogni cosa di rilevo, ma ajutata ancora da bonissima pintura e prospettiva bene intesa. [3]

These descriptions of early sixteenth-century productions could, of course, be continued almost indefinitely. Perhaps it may be well now to turn to critical precept again, especially as that critical precept is so practical as that contained in the *Architettura* (1551) of Sebastiano Serlio. Serlio was typical of his age. Deeply imbued with the prevalent classicism of his time, he strove to find out the true secrets of the Roman theatre, while at the same time he tried to carry forward ideas he had gained from Rome so as to make them applicable to his own time. His section on scenery therefore has a practical as well as an antiquarian interest. Starting with the

---

[1] " A painting or perspective of a landscape with houses, churches, towers, and gardens."

[2] D'Ancona, ii, 381 : " The shape was rectangular, longer than it was wide : the two sides opposite one another had each eight architraves with columns harmonizing with and proportioned to the breadth and height of the said arches : the bases and capitals were most imposing, the whole giving the impression of a permanent antique building, full of beauty ; the arches with flowers in relief formed a wonderful perspective ; the width of each was about six feet ; the height proportionate. Within the scene were cloths of gold and some shrubs, as the scenes required ; one of the sides was decorated with six pictures of the royal triumph from the hand of the famous Mantegna : the two other sides had similar arches, but fewer in number, each having six in all. Two sides formed the ' scene ' devoted to the actors and performers ; the other two had staircases, apportioned for the ladies and also for the . . . trumpeters and musicians. [Between the columns] was a grotto, although artificial most realistic : above that was a great sky shining with varied lights like clear stars, with an artificial wheel of signs at the movement of which turned now the sun, now the moon, in their proper places : within was a wheel of Fortune with six [? three] states : *regno, regnaj, regnabo* : in the midst stood the golden goddess with a sceptre and a dolphin. Within the scene at the foot of the frontispiece appeared Petrarch's Triumphs, painted also by the hand of Mantegna ; above were most lovely candelabra covered with gold : in the midst was a shield with the arms of His Imperial Majesty ; above the two-headed golden eagle with the imperial crown and diadem : each held three torches ; and these arms were at each side."

[3] " The scene was made to resemble a very lovely city with streets, palaces, churches, towers, real streets, and everything in relief, but assisted by beautiful painting and clever perspective."

description of a theatre, he plans a semicircular auditorium and a stage of a novel plan. In front is a flat platform and behind a stage raked heavily for the better setting of the scenes (Fig. 78). Next, following Vitruvius, he divides his *mise-en-scène* into three types, corresponding to Comedy, Tragedy, and Satyric plays. Designs for each of these are given in his book (Figs. 79, 80, and 81). The Comedy scene has ordinary houses, with in the foreground the house of a courtesan; Tragedy is provided with lofty palaces; the Satyric drama has rustic objects, trees, groves, and cottages. These various stock settings were to be secured by a judicious intermixture of built-up *case* and painted cloths. At the rear of the raked stage

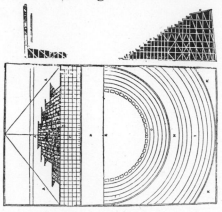

Fig. 78. PLAN OF A THEATRE BY SERLIO

Note should be taken of the rectangular outside walls, and of the two parts of the stage, one level and the other raked.

Fig. 79. THE COMIC SCENE ACCORDING TO SERLIO

Note the steps leading from the stage to the 'orchestra' level.

was the back-cloth, painted in perspective and perhaps the houses nearest to it might also be painted on the flat. Those next the spectator, however, had to have two sides at least so that they should give the impression of solidity, the whole presenting a perspective background for the players who performed not *in* the scene but *against* it, the action proceeding on the flat stage in front. These settings, particularly the tragic and the comic, had an almost incalculable influence upon later scenic endeavour. They were copied, as we shall find, by Inigo Jones in England (Fig. 150); in Italy they had a widely popular career (Figs. 82–84); in France they passed over to the seventeenth century, exercising an

Fig. 80. THE TRAGIC SCENE ACCORDING TO SERLIO

From the English edition of *Architettura* (1611).

Fig. 81. THE SATYRIC SCENE ACCORDING TO SERLIO

influence even in the time of Racine. Again and again we find the palaces and the court-yards and the churches of Serlio facing us in later tragedy and comedy.

It is evident that in the Serlian designs use is made of the old medieval multiple setting, although that multiple setting is classicized; and that there is preserved still the ancient *platea* or open stage in front, all the action proceeding out of doors. Some may describe this as classical; others as medieval; the real truth seems to be that here the medieval multiple setting (the *décor simultané*) and the classical imitation have met. It is needless here to comment on the many peculiar conventions to which this exterior setting of plays gave rise. These are obvious, but attention may be drawn to the very marked influence which this setting had upon all drama of the seventeenth and eighteenth centuries. Even Goldoni in the middle of the latter century was the thrall of this tradition. The scene of *La Bottega del Caffè* (1750) is thus

una piazzetta in Venezia, ovvero una strada alquanto spaziosa con tre Botteghe: quella di mezzo ad uso di Caffè; quella alla diritta di Parrucchiere, e Barbiere; quella alla sinistra ad uso di Giuoco, o sia Biscazza; e sopra le tre Botteghe suddette si vedono alcuni Stanzini praticabili appartenenti alla Bisca colle finestre in veduta della strada medesima. Dalla parte del Barbiere (con una strada in mezzo) evvi la Casa della Ballerina, e dalla parte della Bisca vedesi la Locanda con porte e finestre praticabili.[1]

FIG. 82. AN ITALIAN SETTING OF THE SEVEN-
TEENTH CENTURY

From J. Furtenbach, *Architectura Civilis* (Ulm, 1628).

(iv) THE TEATRO OLIMPICO

Serlio's settings, as we have seen, were temporary erections of lath and canvas, in so far departing from the conventions of the Roman theatre, but there were others who wished to introduce into the modern world, not such flimsy settings, but a permanent *frons scaenae* such as once the theatre at Orange had possessed. New knowledge of the classical stage was being obtained, and this was expressed in visible form by Andrea Palladio in the Teatro Olimpico at Vicenza. This theatre, taking its rise from the Olympic Academy of that town, was begun, it is said, on May 23, 1580, but, Palladio dying on August 19 of that year, the work was entrusted to Vincenzo Scamozzi, who completed it in 1584. The theatre is constructed according to the best classical ideas of the time, although several interesting innovations have been introduced. First, in the ground plan (Fig. 85) we note that the auditorium is arranged as a semi-ellipse, not as a semicircle, the reason being that the former construction provides better sight for the spectators. In general, however, the classical plan is followed, with an orchestra between the front of the stage and the lowest row of seats. The stage proper, or *pulpitum*, is rectangular, long and narrow as in Roman theatres, with a wooden floor painted in the semblance of marble. Behind this is the proscenium, an ornamented architectural façade designed on lines similar to those adopted for the theatre at Orange. Below is a series of four pediments (Fig. 86) with statues, and above a series of six statues surmounted by six decorative panels and a painted roof. Facing the audience is a large open arch, the *porta regia* of Vitruvius, flanked on each side by two lesser doors (*portae minores*). The sides of the stage (*versurae*) are enclosed by walls set at right angles to the proscenium proper and also pierced by doors which have above them boxes, apparently intended both for the action of the play and for spectators. In the original

---

[1] "A small square in Venice, or a fairly broad street with three booths: that in the middle is the Café; that to the right the Barber's; that to the left the Gaming House; and above the three booths are seen some practicable balconies belonging to the Gaming House with windows in view of the street. On the Barber's side (with a street in the middle) is the Ballerina's house, and on the Gaming House side there stands the Inn with practicable doors and windows."

Teatro Olimpico as finished in 1584 the archways seem to have been closed either by doors or by back-cloths, but, probably through the influence of Daniello Barbaro's interpretation of Vitruvius (Fig. 87) where the *periaktoi* are placed immediately behind the main doorways, Scamozzi had the idea of making perspective alleys at each of his arches. These are placed at such angles that every person in the audience may see down one at least. The perspectives are permanent, and are supposed to represent streets running into the courtyard which is the stage. As is evident,

Fig. 83. DESIGN FOR "L'ORTENSIO" BY BARTOLOMEO NERONI (RICCIO)
This should be compared with Serlio's tragic scene. Particular note should also be made of the formal proscenium arch. The production took place at Siena in 1560.
From the original in the Victoria and Albert Museum.

this arrangement was specially suitable for those Renascence plays where two characters, entering upon the stage simultaneously, but from different points, fail to see or hear one another.

The Teatro Olimpico is one of the great landmarks in the history of the European theatre. To it architects of France and of England, including Inigo Jones himself, came for inspiration.

(v) THE TEATRO FARNESE AT PARMA

So far we have found, besides the early efforts of Rome and of Ferrara, two main types of theatrical setting: (1) the rectangular stage as planned by Serlio with canvas 'houses' and back-cloths; and (2) the permanent architectural façade of the Teatro Olimpico. While, as we shall see, various improvements and modifications were being made all through the sixteenth century, the main classical influence held its ground. Serlio and Scamozzi remain the masters of many a theatre worker, and countless designs and suggestions ultimately take their rise from the theatre-plans of the one or of the other. The development of the proscenium arch itself is simply a modification or rather a harmonizing of their efforts. It is clear that the Serlian setting provides for one general background, without, however, any masking frame; it is equally clear that in the Teatro Olimpico we have one large opening for a background and four lesser openings. Imitators of the latter theatre might easily lessen the extent of the architectural façade and so increase the scenic space by (1) widening the central doorway or (2) widening all the three doorways facing the audience until merely a thin column separated one from another.

Fig. 84. An Italian Setting of the Sixteenth Century

From Girolamo Parabosco, *Il Pellegrino* (Venice, 1552). Serlio's influence is clear in this woodcut.

In newer designs of this type there was but a step before a proscenium arch was reached. In other words, the open setting as figured by Serlio might come to occupy the entire width of the stage, and the whole be placed within a framework (our proscenium arch) which was nothing but the attenuated façade of the original Olympic Theatre.

This stage of development is marked in the Teatro Farnese at Parma, completed in 1618 or in 1619, a playhouse which is historically interesting for more than its stage alone (see Fig. 160). Up to this time the auditorium seats had been arranged either semicircularly or in the form of a semi-ellipse. Undoubtedly men had been thinking of the problems presented to an architect in a playhouse auditorium, but one of the very first movements forward is marked in the seating arrangements of the Teatro Farnese. There the semicircular formation is confined to that portion of the theatre which is set farthest from the stage, and the seats are continued at right angles to the diameter of the semicircle until they meet the front portion of the stage itself. While this is neither the best possible arrangement for a theatrical auditorium nor by any means the last word said on this subject, it serves to mark a definite period in playhouse architecture.

Most important of all, however, is the stage arrangement of the Teatro Farnese. Here, as in the earlier Olympic Theatre, a rather long platform faces the audience, but, instead of the heavily sculptured façade in the rear, there is the earliest of the permanent proscenium arches. Behind lies the depth of the stage, designed originally to contain tragic, or comic, or satyric settings planned according to the ideas of Serlio, but soon used for other purposes. Within a few years of the erection of the Teatro Farnese it was realized that the masking frame gave an opportunity for the changing of scenes which was denied to Serlio's open stage. Truly the implications of the Parma Theatre were enormous. Here a third type of Renascence playhouse had been established, a type destined later to influence the whole of European theatre-craft, being imitated, not only in Italy and in France, but in every Western land.

(vi) Changing Scenery

It has been seen that in the Teatro Farnese opportunity was given to the theatre artist to change his settings during the course of a play. This was impossible in the permanent Teatro Olimpico, and rendered difficult in the Serlian type of stage. Already the Renascence humanists had been speculating and experimenting with *periaktoi*, but Vitruvius had suggested to them a further method of changing the *frons scaenae*. Philander in France had engaged on a commentary upon the work of Vitruvius and published his results in 1544. After describing the *scaena versilis* (or *periaktoi*) by the turning of which another scene was presented Philander notes the *scaena*

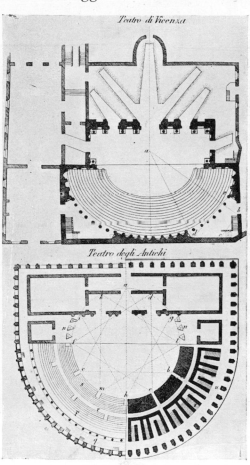

> ductilis, quum tractis tabulatis hac atque illac species picturae nudaretur interior.[1]

This note on the *scaena ductilis* was destined to bear much fruit. It set men thinking and experimenting. By 1638 the experimenting was partly over, as we find in a study of Nicola Sabbatini's *Pratica di fabricar Scene e Machine ne' Teatri* (Ravenna, 1638). Deeming change of scene necessary, if not for plays, at least for *intermedii*,[2] he proceeds to describe how these changes can be secured. Adopting fundamentally the Serlian setting, Sabbatini points out that in any changes of scene the front houses must remain untouched. Apparently he does not take fully into account the innovation introduced at the Teatro Farnese, although he does recommend what is virtually a proscenium arch. Three methods he is aware of for the shifting of the scenery. One of these is the well-known use of the *periaktoi*. Frames are made in the form of an isosceles triangle (Fig. 90) and painted with different scenes on each side. The triangle, set on a central pivot, can then be made to turn by having a rope wound round the central support and carried to a winch under the stage. Besides this there is a second device whereby "houses" are constructed of two sides as in Serlio; duplicates of these are made and painted differently. The duplicates are then concealed behind the houses shown to the audience and, when a change of scene is required, are rapidly slipped in

Fig. 85. Plan of the Teatro Olimpico, Vicenza, compared with that of a Roman Theatre

Note the avenues for street scenes and the five entrances to the stage.

front of the others. A third device consists of the preparation of variously painted canvases which are detachable from the lath frames made to carry them. Besides this, directions are given as to the way in which the back-scene might be altered. This, it would seem, was to be made in two parts, so that the halves could be drawn away or pushed forward as desired. Following upon these general directions, Sabbatini provides information as to the means by which special effects could be produced. The *periaktoi*, if soaked in aqua-vitae, lighted and rapidly

---

[1] "*Scaena ductilis*, by which, through panels drawn to the side, this or that scene is revealed within."
[2] Entertainments of an allegorical kind introduced at the conclusions of the acts of Italian plays.

turned, might give the appearance of a conflagration—although, as the writer realizes, the device at best is fraught with considerable danger. So too houses could be made to fall in ruins by constructing the frames on connecting iron bars which, when pulled away, would remove the necessary support. Seas could be made by painted cloths underneath which rollers could turn, and perhaps crest-like strips of wood might be made to rise and fall between the

Fig. 86. THE TEATRO OLIMPICO
Photo Alinari.

billows. Transformation scenes, by the aid of trap-doors, could easily be arranged, a piece of scenery being suddenly raised to conceal an object on the stage, causing it to disappear and change into something else.

Quite obviously scenic artistry had passed far beyond the Serlian stage. It is said that movable scenes had been introduced first in the opera-house called the Teatro di San Cassiano at Venice, while, a few years later, at the Teatro di SS. Giovanni e Paolo (built 1639), Giacomo Torelli da Fano "inventò il moversi delle scene coll' arzano." [1]

Scenic effects of a kind never dreamt of before were now freely used. Here, for example, is an account of the Teatro Mediceo constructed by Bernardo Buontalenti and of shows given there. The writer is Filippo Baldinucci (1624–96), and the passage, though long, is deeply instructive, for it is typical of Renascence stage endeavour. Buontalenti, we are told,

[1] "Invented a means of moving scenes by a winch."

fece[1] . . . il gran teatro per le commedie . . . di larghezza di braccia 35, di lunghezza 95 e braccia 24 d' altezza, e volle che il pavimento del medesimo due braccia e un ottavo pendesse dal capo al piede, a fine che gli spettatori dalla parte dinanzi a quegli di dietro la veduta degli spettacoli non impedissero; fece poi le prospettive e macchine. . . . Queste medesime macchine furono d'esemplare, dal quale poi dagli ingegneri di tutta Europa furon presi i modi e gli artifizj più novi e più singolari. . . . [At a performance real birds were let loose in the auditorium of a theatre and] tirata che fu la gran tela, apparve la nobilissima prospettiva, dove da più parti ed in diversi punti vedeansi rappresentare le più belle vedute e più singolari fabbriche e piazze della nostra città. . . . Nel primo intermedio apparve una nuvola di così squisito artifizio, che non si vidde mai, nè prima nè poi, cosa simile; conciossiacosachè aprendosi, per dar luogo allo scendere di gran copia di persone, che rappresentavano tutti i Beni del mondo mandati da Giove ad arricchir quel giorno, appoco appoco fu veduta svanire, come disfatta del vento, senza che mai si potesse da chi si fosse osservare che le sue parti andassero in luogo alcuno. Nel secondo intermedio furon fatti vedere tutti i Mali del mondo . . . s'aperse un' orrida caverna piena d'orribilissimi fuochi, con fiamme oscure e fosche; dalla gran caverna scappò fuori la città di Dite assummicata ed ardente . . . eranvi alcune alte torri tutte ardenti, in cima alle quali vedeansi orribil Furie crinite di serpenti, ed in abito sanguinolente. . . . Nel terzo intermedio la scena rappresentò campagna spogliata di frondi, come di crudo inverno; vedeansi letti di fiumi e torrenti del tutto asciutti e secchi, quando in un subito dalla parte di ponente fu veduto uscire d'una sotterranea spelonca Zeffiro, che tenendo per mano la bella Flora, diede con essa principio

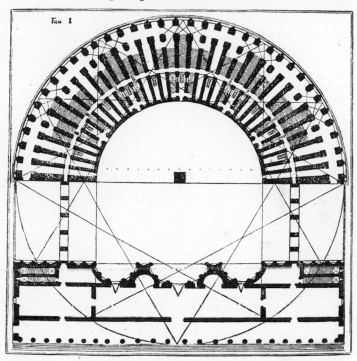

Fig. 87. Plan of a Roman Theatre according to Daniello Barbaro

Note should be made of the *periaktoi* placed at the three doors of entrance.

al dolcissimo cantare; al suon del quale comparve la Primavera, con altre festevoli deità, amoretti, aure, ninfe e satiri; e mentre tutti insieme sollazzavansi col ballo, vedeansi fiorire gli alberi e riempirsi di foglie. . . . Nel quarto intermedio viddonsi comparire nell' estremità del palco scogli e dirupi asprissimi, da' quali acque pendevano di vive fontane, inghirlandate di bianchi coralli, madreperle, nicchi, chiocciole ed erbe marine e palustri. Fra gli scogli comparve la dea Teti con gran comitiva di tritoni e mostri marini. . . . Rendea vaghezza, e terrore insieme, la vista di gran quantità di navigli, che per lo mare venivano agitati dall'

[1] "Made . . . the large theatre for comedies . . . 53 feet wide, 143 deep, and 36 high, and contrived that the floor of the theatre should slope 2 yards and an eighth from top to bottom so that the spectators in front should not prevent those at the back from seeing; he made also perspectives and machines. . . . These machines became the model from which the artificers of the whole of Europe took their ideas and newer and more peculiar devices. . . . When the large curtain was drawn there appeared a most beautiful perspective, where in all directions and at divers points were to be seen represented the most lovely views and most peculiar buildings and squares of our city. . . . In the first *intermedio* appeared a cloud of such an exquisite form as had not been seen before or since; this opened to give place for the descent of a great company of figures who represented all the Virtues of the world sent by Jove to enrich that day; little by little it disappeared, as if it had been carried away by the wind, without anyone being able to see how its various portions vanished. In the second *intermedio* all the Evils of the world were shown . . . a horrible cavern full of the most terrible flames and dark vapours appeared; from this huge cavern appeared the City of Dis all in flame and smoke. . . . There were some high towers all in flames, on the top of which could be seen horrible furies with serpent hair, clad in blood-red garments. . . . In the third *intermedio* the scene represented a bare landscape as in a severe winter; beds of rivers and torrents, all dry and hard, were to be seen, when suddenly from the west Zephyr was seen to issue forth from a subterranean cave; she held the beautiful Flora by the hand, and sang a most lovely song with her; at the sound of this Spring appeared, with other festive deities, loves, winds, nymphs, and satyrs; and while all these together danced on the stage, the trees were seen to flourish again and renew their leaves. . . . In the fourth *intermedio* at the extreme edge of the stage there were seen appearing cliffs and precipitous rocks from which real waterfalls flowed; they were all covered with white coral, mother of pearl, shells, and sea-weeds. The goddess Thetis appeared among the rocks with a great company of tritons and sea-monsters. . . . The sight of a great

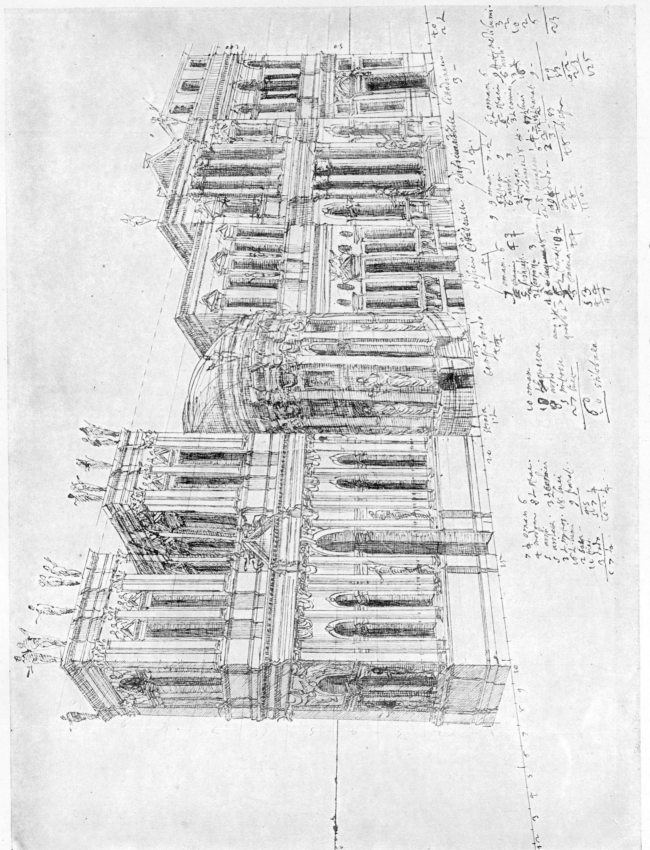

Fig. 88. Design for a Street in the Teatro Olimpico, by Scamozzi

From the original in the possession of the Duke of Devonshire.

Photo Victoria and Albert Museum.

onda e da' venti. . . . Non ebbero questi molto passeggiato per l'onde, che dal fondo del mare venne fuori il dio Nettuno con orrido aspetto. . . . Ma niente meno artifiziose e nuove apparvero le macchine per lo quinto intermedio : viddesi andare oscurando il cielo appoco appoco, e farsi tutto nugoloso, che quasi s'oscurò la luna ; quindi andaron crescendo le tenebre, finchè incominciarono a venir tuoni e lampi, e fra il rumoreggiar di quegli e 'l risplender di questi, fecesi vedere una vaga nugola di color sereno ; sopra questa era un carro tirato da due paoni, grandissimi però e finti, i quali vedeansi camminare e far ruota di lor coda ; sedeasi sopra il carro Giunone

Fig. 89. THE CENTRAL ARCHWAY IN THE TEATRO OLIMPICO
Photo Alinari.

colle ninfe, due delle quali per lo sereno del dì, e due per quello della notte eran figurate . . . da' nuvoli cadeva pioggia . . . fermò la pioggia e viddesi dopo la nuvola comparire l'arcobaleno sì vero, che ognuno ne stupì. . . . Sparve allora la nuvola in modo, che parve cosa soprannaturale e miracolosa. . . . Nel sesto ed ultimo intermedio . . . comparve uno spazioso prato pieno di vaghissimi fiori ed un bosco d'ogni sorta d'alberi selvaggi, le cui cime pareva che quasi arrivassero al cielo, e questi presso ad una grotta ; similmente un nobile palazzo

number of ships, dipping up and down with the waves and the winds, excited both delight and terror in the audience. . . . These had not gone far on the waves, when from the sea's depths appeared the terrible-featured god Neptune. . . . But not less artful and novel seemed the machines for the fifth *intermedio*: the sky grew dark little by little, and all became cloudy as when the moon is obscured ; the darkness crept on until thunder and lightning started. Amid the rumbling of the one and the flashing of the other appeared a lovely cloud of a serene colour ; above that was a chariot drawn by two peacocks, very large and artificial, which were seen to move and make full display of their round tails ; upon the chariot sat Juno with her nymphs, two of whom symbolized the serenity of day and two that of night . . . rain fell from the clouds . . . the rain ceased and a rainbow appeared behind the cloud in such a natural way that all were astounded. . . . The cloud disappeared in a manner that seemed supernatural and miraculous. . . . In the sixth and last *intermedio* . . . appeared a spacious plain full of most lovely flowers and a wood of every kind of forest tree, the tops of which seemed to rise to the

G

con dirupate caverne attorno ; era la selva popolata di molti e varj animali, come capri, daini, cervi, lepri ed altri di quella sorta . . . mentre fecero nobilissima comparsa due schiere di pastori e pastorelle toscanne, diciannove per ischiera, che a suono di liuti, arpi, zampogne, bassi, viole, flauti, traverse, tromboni, cornetti torti e diritti . . . fecero sentire una dolcissima musica.

In such wise was theatrical art developed in Italian *intermedii* and in opera.

(vii) MACHINES AND LIGHTING

Much of what has been said already concerning scenic effects in Italian theatres obviously is also connected with the use of machines of various kinds. Unquestionably, of course, machines would have been invented independently by these enthusiastic Renascence artists, but at first the influence was almost wholly classical. The 'machine' proper or μηχανή was freely utilized for the raising and lowering of divinities. Trapdoors abounded, and some form of the ἐξώστρα was brought upon the stage. Spectacular effects were always looked for in these Renascence shows, in spite of the seeming chill of classic imitation, and such things as the best means of making thunder and lightning were eagerly studied. Pollux had already described machines by means of which both thunder and lightning might be simulated, and those machines of Pollux, varied by suggestions taken from commentators of Vitruvius, found a new lease of life on the Renascence stage. For the Greeks, for the people of the Middle Ages, and for those of the Renascence fulguration with its accompanying thunderclaps, as the prime attribute of stage deity, occupied much attention.

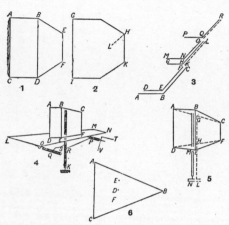

FIG. 90. METHODS OF CHANGING SCENERY ACCORDING TO SABBATINI

Figs. 1 and 2 show the use of separate covers for the Serlian frames, Fig. 3 the use of extra frames concealed within those immediately in front, and Figs. 4, 5, and 6 the use of *periaktoi*.

After L. B. Campbell, *Scenes and Machines in the Renaissance*, p. 155.

To light too the Renascence artists paid due attention, realizing that many of their effects must depend on the judicious placing of candles or of lamps.[1] Leone Ebreo di Somi, a most interesting Renascence theatre-worker, counsels that lights should be placed " per le strade, su per i tetti delle case et sopra le torri "[2] in comedy for the purpose of " imitar la letitia co'l primo aspetto della scoverta scena."[3] This machinist thus believed in symbolism of lighting, anticipating in many ways Jessner's modern Berlin experiments, for in practice he illuminated fully those scenes in a tragedy in which the subject-matter was happy, and " quando cominciò poi per il primo caso dolente "[4] he contrived "che in quell' istante la maggior parte de i lumi de la scena che non servivano alla prospettiva furono velati o spenti."[5]

heavens, and near by a grotto; likewise a noble palace with rocky caverns round about; the wood was populated with many kinds of animals such as goats, deer, stags, hares, and others similar . . . meanwhile two bands of Tuscan shepherds and shepherdesses, nineteen in each group, made a splendid gathering. These sang beautifully to the music of lutes, harps, pipes, bases, viole, flutes, traverse, trombones, straight and bent cornets." The designs from the Chatsworth collection (Figs. 91–95) are given here because, although there is no proof that they are by Buontalenti, they serve to illustrate the above account of the *intermedii* presented at the Teatro Mediceo.

[1] That the medieval theatre also was not unaware of the value of light effects is proved even from the English mysteries. Sudden light dazzles the eyes of Joseph in the York *Bethlehem*, and Peter in *The Descent of the Holy Spirit* could not look at the apparition " so was it light." See *supra*, p. 74.

[2] " In the streets, upon house roofs and towers."

[3] " Imitating the gaiety with the first view of the scene discovered."   [4] " When the first unhappy situation occurred."

[5] " That at that moment the majority of the scene lamps which were not used for the perspective should be shaded or extinguished." For further quotations from Leone Hebreo see Appendix B.

Concerning the placing of these lights there seems to have been considerable diversity of opinion. Some would have them overhead facing the audience, that is to say in the position

Fig. 91. DESIGN FOR CLOUDWORK AND DIVINITIES
This may be by Buontalenti. *Cp.* Figs. 92 to 95.
From the original in the possession of the Duke of Devonshire.
Photo Victoria and Albert Museum.

which they occupied habitually in eighteenth-century English theatres. Others counselled that they should be placed behind the houses or sky borders. To these two theories Sabbatini makes objections, pointing out that side-lighting gives best that brightness and shade which aids in the theatrical illusion. There is also an interesting suggestion in his work regarding foot-

Fig. 92. DESIGN FOR CLOUDWORK

From the original in the possession of the Duke of Devonshire.
Photo Victoria and Albert Museum.

lights. He advises that a parapet should be erected toward the front of the stage some few feet high, and suggests that lights may be placed behind it as well as behind the " heavens " or behind the side *case*. Earlier Serlio had given directions concerning the use of coloured lights. These coloured lights were to be secured by the use of bottles filled, country-chemist-wise, with red or blue liquid, the candles or lamps being placed in immediate proximity to them and probably being aided by putting behind them a bright basin as a reflector. Devices of this kind were,

Fig. 93. Design for a 'Desert' Scene
From the original in the possession of the Duke of Devonshire.
Photo Victoria and Albert Museum.

we know, freely used in Italy, and made their reappearance in the masques contrived in England by Inigo Jones.

Reference has been made above to the 'heavens.' Sabbatini again provides us with a good deal of information regarding this necessary part of a theatre's equipment. As this is a matter of some importance his words may be quoted directly:

Fig. 94. NEPTUNE AND SEA-GODS
From the original in the possession of the Duke of Devonshire.
Photo Victoria and Albert Museum.

Stabilito il piano del Palco, si doverà dar principio a fare il cielo, quale doverà essere ò intiero, ò spezzato ; se intiero, vi sarà poca fatica poichè farassi con tre, ò quattro Centine, ò Arcali fatti in minor portione di cerchio, dando loro (nel metterli in opera) il suo declivio di due oncie per piedi, raccomandogli con buoni e forti tiranti alle Travi del Tetto, ò altro, acciò che ſtiano sicuro. Da poi si ſtenderanno per lo lungo ad esse Centine, legnami lunghi, e sottili in giuſta lontananza bene inchiodati, quali legni da noi volgarmente vengono nominati

Fig. 95. MARINE MONSTERS
From the original in the possession of the Duke of Devonshire.
Photo Victoria and Albert Museum.

Ciavaroni, et in Toscana Correnti. Compita queſta seconda orditura vi si ſtenderanno le Tele, le quali vogliono essere imbrocate più spesso, che sia possibile acciòche non vengano a fare qualche cattivo effetto, e così sarà compito il Cielo intero. . . . Quando bisognerà ne gli Intermedij, che le Machine saliscono al Cielo, ò da esse calino sopra il Palco, in questo caso si dovrà fare il Cielo spezzato, sì per la commodità, che apporta a tale operatione come anco per il gusto, ò maraviglia, che ne prendono gli spettatori, non vedendo come si nascondano le machine venendo da Terra, ò come uscendo dal Cielo esse calino a basso.[1]

What was probably at first but a simple cloth was soon elaborated into a vast series of cloud

Fig. 96. THE SETTING FOR BONARELLI'S "IL SOLIMANO" (1620). DESIGN BY
ALFONSO PARIGI, ENGRAVED BY CALLOT

effects, as in the Buontalenti designs noted in this chapter, where deities could ride on platforms behind gossamer veils and disappear without anyone's noticing how the vanishing trick was done.[2]

[1] "When the stage floor has been arranged first thought must be given to the heavens, which are either 'entire' or 'cut'; if entire, there will be little difficulty, for these are made with three or four rounded frames or arches; when these are placed in action they are

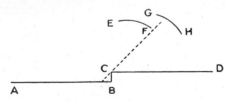

given a slope of 2 inches in a foot, and are fixed firmly and well to the beams of the roof or some other support so that they are secure. Then to these frames there are affixed lengthwise long thin rods, nailed on at suitable distances. These we commonly call *Ciavaroni*, and in Tuscan *Correnti*. When this piece has been finished the cloths are stretched over the rods. These should be nailed down as frequently as possible to avoid any ill effect. So the 'entire' heavens are completed. . . . When in *intermedii* it is necessary for machines to ascend to the sky or descend thence to the stage, one must have a 'cut' heaven, both for convenience and for the delight and wonder which audiences take in it, since they cannot see how the machines which rise from the earth disappear or how they descend from the heavens to the stage."

The accompanying sketch shows the arrangement of this 'cut' sky, where C D is the stage level, A B the auditorium level, and E F, G H part of the cloudwork.
[2] See also the Torelli designs given in Appendix C.

So at least contemporaries said. What exactly we to-day would think of the effects is another matter. That they were striking possibly no one can deny; that they were perfect in lighting and in finish perhaps no one would care to assert. It is noticeable, at least, that, in spite of the fact that so many eulogists have praised the transformation scenes, so practical a man as Sabbatini seems to fear lest the alterations might not take place with sufficient ease. He

Fig. 97. THE SETTING FOR BONARELLI'S "IL SOLIMANO" (1620)

This shows the city (cp. Fig. 96) in flames.
The scene in *Il Solimano* is constant throughout the five acts.

counsels that a man may make a disturbance at the rear of the theatre to distract attention; or that a crash should be made there; or that a sudden noise of drums and trumpets be raised to take away the minds of the audience from the shifting scenery. Curtains, of course, were rarely employed. Sabbatini does describe the method of working one, but his account is only half-hearted. It is peculiar that when Ariosto's *I Suppositi* was revived at Rome there was a painted front curtain which "si lasciò cascare" (was let drop) at the beginning of the performance, even as the Roman *auleum* had done. This curtain, which Ariosto himself refers to in the *Orlando Furioso*: [1]

[1] xxxii, 80.

Quale al cader de le cortine suole
Parer, fra mille lampade, la scena,
D'Archi, et di più d'una superba mole
D'oro, e di statue e di pitture piena [1]—

was designed, however, not to form a means of concealing change of scene but to surprise the audience by the sudden revelation of the scenic glory in the first act. Much as these Renascence theorists experimented, it is surprising to note how they, and their successors, failed to realize the opportunities which a front curtain offered to an ambitious machinist and manager.[2]

[1] " As at the curtain-fall we see appear,
'Mid candles multitudinous, the view,
The arches and the statues, paintings clear
And massive buildings bright with golden hue."

[2] On this question of the Renascence curtain W. J. Lawrence's *The Elizabethan Playhouse and other Studies* may be consulted.

CHAPTER V

THE COMMEDIA DELL' ARTE

(i) The Origins

IN the last chapter we have been breathing the rarefied air of serene humanistic speculation. For the theatres thus built at the Courts of Italian princes were written pseudo-classic tragedies and *commedie sostenute*, comedies based in all essentials upon the best traditions of Terence and of Plautus. Alongside of these more dignified presentations, however, must have been constantly enacted the *sacre rappresentazioni*, or mystery dramas, and there must have been 'interlude' players performing their crude little farces such as we have found in medieval France. Above all we must remember the growth in the sixteenth and seventeenth centuries of the *commedia dell' arte* or the *commedia all' improvviso*, which sprang into sudden fame just about the time when Ferrarese princes were delicately experimenting with classical stages. The *commedia dell' arte* is essentially a popular form of artistic amusement, and its influence upon Continental theatres and upon Continental drama for upward of two hundred years is literally incalculable.

In this book I am deliberately eschewing any study of the drama as such, but the *commedia dell' arte* is not drama in the sense that written plays are. It is fundamentally a thing of the actor, the machinist, the costumier. At times, with Molière and with Goldoni, it may pass into the realm of literature, but it is nevertheless, in essence, unashamedly a creation of the theatre, owing no definite allegiance to a poet. It is for this reason that the *commedia dell' arte* must find a place here. On the other hand, volumes could be written on this subject, and we must deal only with the most outstanding features of this enthralling subject. And first must be explained exactly what the *commedia dell' arte* is. The chief point of interest lies in the fact that the whole of the dialogue was improvised as occasion demanded. The manager, or *concertatore*, drew out his *scenario* which outlined the main elements in the plot and noted pieces of comic business technically known as *lazzi*, in which the humorous characters could horseplay at will. Each actor took a separate part which he performed perhaps to the end of his days—once a Pantalone, always a Pantalone. Each too had his own *repertorio* of *concetti*, *uscite*, and *chiusetti*, series of formal expressions or tags of dialogue which he could use when conversing with others in set situations, or when entering the stage, or when leaving the stage. By means of these he could thus make a fitting exit, or continue conversation in a witty style with his fellow-actors. It must be obvious that, while this style of comedy definitely divorced literature from the theatre, it developed an extremely high technical skill on the parts of the actors. The Italian players soon became the masters of Europe.

How, it may be asked, did this comedy arise? Fortuitously, or springing from some appreciable source? The answer to this question cannot be given with any certitude; but the balance of evidence is on the side of those who see in the *commedia dell' arte* a relic of the old Roman mime. Both the Atellanae and the Phlyakes [1] had been in origin improvisational, and it is, as we have seen, highly probable that, in the darkest days of the Middle Ages, *mimi* had continued the tradition which they had set. It is thus noticeable that, while the *commedia sostenuta* has many features which it shares with the *commedia dell' arte*, in one thing it is distinct both from

[1] See *supra*, pp. 49, 58–9.

the popular Italian comedy and from medieval farce. The stock theme of a Terentian play is the presentation of the love of a youth for a girl who, apparently his inferior in birth, is discovered to be the long-lost daughter of some near friend of his father's. Neither Terence nor Plautus indulges in jests at cuckolds; their satire of old men is kindly and urbane. The Atellanae, however, and the later mimes regularly treated the old man as a dolt and a fool; the woman who is loved is not a maiden but a wife. This theme of old man, wife, lover, is one which reappears again and again in French and English farce of the Middle Ages; it also forms a stock theme for many jests in the *commedia dell' arte*.

Furthermore, when we come to analyse the stock characters presented in classical mime and in sixteenth-century popular comedy we realize at once that there is some clear connexion between the groups. Even in name there is a similarity, for the two comic characters among the Romans were called *sanniones*; their descendants in Italy were styled *zanni*. Harlequin seems to have a clear ancestry, as has Brighella; the *dottore*, the *capitano*, and *pantalone* we have met in earlier times; the young lover, the heroine, and the old men are stock types. The masks which the various characters wore on the stage recall in many ways the masks of antique times.

It must not be supposed, of course, that the tradition was a perfectly simple one, or that it was uninfluenced by cross-currents of national or epoch fashion. Rather must it be asserted that, while connexions are to be discovered among various forms of early drama, the forms remained often distinct as regards their special structure. Already it has been seen that there were inter-relations between the types of the (literary) Aristophanic comedy, the (literary) Roman comedy, the (popular) Phlyakes, and the (popular) Atellan farce. It may be suggested that the first type had as a by-form, or maybe actually sprang from, an indigenous Doric mime-drama, which itself was carried by Greek colonists to Southern Italy, where it flourished in the Phlyakes. Meanwhile an Oscan mime-farce, born in Atella, met with the Phlyakes and developed into a popular form. As we have seen, this type of mime was carried on in a direct line through the Middle Ages, producing that *Interludium de Clerico et Puella* of which mention has already been made. At the same time, this is not the whole of the story. Greece stands between East and West; and an Eastern Empire lorded it at Byzantium during the period when a Western Empire had its capital in Rome. The mime, in various forms, of which the puppet-show was one, moved toward the Orient as well, and there flourished under Theodosius and the later emperors. In the Far East this mime tradition still flourishes in the character of Karagoz, the Turkish Punch, and may be traced perhaps in certain features of Indian, Japanese, and especially Chinese dramatic shows and entertainments. This Eastern mime was introduced to the West during the Renascence period. Not only might *mimi*, after the fall of Byzantium, have come over to Italy, but we have such direct links between East and West as are supplied by Caterina Cornaro, ex-Queen of Cyprus, in whose Court were entertainers from the Orient. If this hypothesis be accepted, it is found that a clear explanation is provided for the sudden popularity of the *commedia dell' arte*. Fundamentally, the *commedia dell' arte* is based on a Western tradition, which is to be found alike in England, France, and Italy; but its particular form in the sixteenth century is due to the new force which came with the introduction of the Byzantine mime, itself sharing a common origin with its Western brother.

(ii) The Stock Characters: the 'Serious' Masks

In discussing the chief stock characters of this immensely popular improvised comedy, we find that nearly all the *scenarii* which are now extant are divided into two parts—that which concerns the non-comic and that which concerns the comic persons. The non-comic characters are, naturally, of least interest, and may be rapidly dismissed. The *comico innamorato* or young lover is an inoffensive gallant of the age. Dressed usually in contemporary garments, he is a representative, albeit a colourless one, of the young men of Roman comedy. He may be called Lelio or Flavio or Orazio or Ottavio, but his uninspired nature remains the same. With him is always and necessarily associated the *comica innamorata*, like her lover, uninteresting and subdued in tone (Fig. 98). She is often a young girl, curbed by hard parents, who desires marriage; sometimes she is merely a kind of doll, a puppet for the plot. Aurelia, Ginevra, Isabella, Flaminia, or Lucinda, she too is a fashionable young person of the time and has no special characteristics. Perhaps her quiet nature depends upon the mute maidens of Plautan comedy. Occasionally there enter in one or two other types of a similar character. The *cantarina*, who is generally also the *ballerina*, does not really play a part in the *scenario*; she is introduced purely to present *intermedii* of a musical kind. If, however, she does not have much interest for us in this way she has a considerable value as a descendant of a type of performer well known in Roman days. Attention has been drawn to the fact that the sketch of Camilla Veronese in the eighteenth century recalls precisely the Franchischina of Callot in the seventeenth century, while the latter might almost have been suggested by the dancing-girl of a Herculaneum frieze (Figs. 99, 100, 101). The young ladies of the Italian comedy are,

Fig. 98. LA COMICA INNAMORATA. DESIGN BY CALLOT

Fig. 99. DANCING-GIRLS FROM A HERCULANEUM FRIEZE
From Ducharte, *La Comédie italienne.*

Fig. 101. CAMILLA VERONESE AS BALLERINA
From Duchartre, *op. cit.*

Fig. 100. FRANCISCHINA AND GIAN FARINA. DESIGN BY CALLOT

of course, attended by their maid-servants, Ricciolina, Nina, Betta, Olivetta, and (by 1683), most famous of all, Colombina. Colombina has many different costumes, extending from an ordinary maid's dress to a fanciful white costume such as has been preserved in pantomime. She is pert, witty, the lover or the loved of Arlecchino.

(iii) THE COMIC MASKS: ARLECCHINO AND BRIGHELLA

These more or less 'serious' characters must, however, be placed on one side in favour of the bevy of exaggerated, blundering, astute, and rascally types who have ever made the *commedia dell' arte* what it is. And chief of all comes Harlequin—Arlecchino—Arlequin—call him what you will. With a spring he leaps on the stage, with a fantastic gesture he is gone; and it is as difficult to catch the real Harlequin as it is for other characters to hold him on the stage.

Fig. 102. ARLECCHINA, LATE SEVENTEENTH CENTURY

From Duchartre, *op. cit.*

Some say he is the god Mercury come to life again, god of thieves and beggars; others declare that he is only a certain wicked serving-man of Arles who took refuge in Bergamo. Some trace his black mask to phalliphoric negro slaves in Roman mime; others see in it only the brown skin of swarthy Bergamese. Some make his name derive from a distinguished Hachille du Harlay, who, as patron of the theatre, gave his own surname to the type; others find in it only a diminutive of *harle* or *herle*, a gaily coloured water-bird. So we go on, he himself jesting at our serious faces, telling us that he was named Harlequin because his father " en langue asinique " cried " Ar lé chin " to his ass. Perhaps we shall never know; perhaps we shall understand him better if we accept him, as he accepts himself, as he is.[1]

When first we meet him he is a rascally beggar, a thing literally " of shreds and patches," boasting a black half-mask surmounted with a hare's tail, a wallet for ill-earned gains and a wooden sword (Fig. 103). So he continues till the sixteenth century when, probably feeling himself raised in social estate, he changes his patches for that chequered costume which he has retained down to the present day. His mask, a peculiar mixture of stupidity and cunning, aptly symbolizes his nature, for Harlequin can be deceived as well as deceive. Sometimes he is the master of the plot; sometimes for him are reserved the lashes and the buffetings which his dull wits prompt him not how to escape.

Fig. 103. ARLECCHINO, LATE SIXTEENTH CENTURY

Note the patchwork garments. From Duchartre, *op. cit.*

Fig. 104. ARLECCHINO, EARLY SEVENTEENTH CENTURY

This shows the transition between the patchwork and the formal checks in Harlequin's costume.

From Duchartre, *op. cit.*

Harlequin is one of the two chief *zanni*, his companion being Brighella or his kin. Where Harlequin has a touch of the human in his fantastic make-up, Brighella is entirely inhuman. His nose is curved and drawn sharply back above his lips, his lips themselves are sensual, his eyes are sated, evil, avaricious. Harlequin will pick a pocket with the best grace in the world; Brighella will think no more of knifing a man in a narrow alley-way. Harlequin's wooden sword

---

[1] For still another suggestion see Driessen's *Der Ursprung des Harlekin* (1904), particularly pp. 66–86.

may do no harm, but Brighella's dagger has a sharp edge. The costume of this unsavoury rascal is well known to us. Moderately wide trousers and a short jacket, laced with green braid, were his from the sixteenth to the eighteenth century, and usually from his shoulders hung a short cloak similar to that worn in Roman comedy. Perhaps of his kin, for he is generally a servant, are Scapino, clad in loose garments in the early seventeenth century, but later dressed as a valet with green and white lace, and Mezzetino, also loosely costumed in the earlier period and, in the eighteenth century, given a costume similar to that of Scapino but laced in red and white. Perhaps, however, Mezzetino belongs rather to the Pedrolino (Pierrot) class than to the kin of Brighella. Whereas in Callot's designs Scapino is clearly a brigandish type, the early Mezzetino seems to be a fool.

(iv) PULCINELLA AND THE CAPITANO

Before dealing with the typical older masks we may turn to one who has remained with us even after Harlequin and Brighella are dead. In treating of Pulcinella or Punch, however, we must bear in mind the fact that, in the earliest *scenarii*, all these characters did not appear, but merely a selection of such as best accorded with the main outlines of the story. For Punch has been dis-

Fig. 105. ARLEQUIN AS CHINAMAN
From a coloured print of the
eighteenth century.

Fig. 106. ARLEQUIN, EIGHTEENTH
CENTURY
From Florian, *Le Bon Ménage.*

covered a wonderful ancestry. He is the descendant, say many, of Maccus of the Atellan farce, perhaps with touches of Bucco thrown in, and owes his name perhaps to the *pullus gallinaceus*, or 'cock' which, it is averred, was a name for Maccus. It is a peculiar fact in this connexion that an Oscan, no doubt a buffoon, is introduced by Horace at a feast. His name is given as Cicirrus. Whether this is, or is not, the name of a character, we find (1) that it is explained as meaning 'cock' by an early commentator, (2) that a Roman vase painting shows an actor with a huge cock's feather in his hat, (3) that a coxcomb is regularly associated with Punch, and (4) (most striking of all) Callot in the seventeenth century depicts a Punch-like figure, boasting two enormous cock's feathers, and calls him *Cucurucu*. Punch, with his pugnacious nature, his hump, his hooked nose, and his coxcomb, appears to have a very respectable antiquity behind him; and it is peculiar to find that it is he, above all the characters of the *commedia dell' arte*, who has most surely retained the affections of the populace. Our street urchins still cluster round the curtained booth, itself a relic of the Middle Ages, to watch the vicious and cunning little tyrant

Fig. 107. BRIGHELLA, OR BUFFET. SEVENTEENTH CENTURY

From Duchartre, *op. cit.*

beat or kill his wife, hoodwink a policeman, and escape in the end gloriously from the gallows.

Punch is most nearly allied to Brighella, but he is older and even more sophisticated. His deeply wrinkled mask with its hooked nose and vicious eyes well symbolizes his nature. He is cruel, inhuman, egoistic, self-seeking—a pleasant rascal perhaps, but one with whom we care not to have overmuch acquaintance. For once we rejoice in the theatre's fourth wall.

Tracing his ancestry likewise to ancient classic times, the Capitano—Capitan Spavento della Valle Inferna, Capitan Cocodrillo, Capitan Rinoceronte, Capitan Spezzafer, or Capitan Sangue y Fuego—strides forward as an arresting personality, full of boasts and vaunting, but an arrant coward as soon as any fighting is toward. He is simply the *miles gloriosus* of the antique stage made popular and more grotesque. Clad in garments which suggest now an Italian *condottiere*, now a Spanish bravo, with a long-nosed mask and fierce moustache,

Fig. 108. SCAPINO. DESIGN BY CALLOT

Fig. 109. SCAPINO AND CAPITAN ZERBINO. DESIGN BY CALLOT

Fig. 110. RICIULINA AND METZETIN. DESIGN BY CALLOT

he vaunts his way through many a *scenario*, creating terror by his appearance and laughter by his poltroonish cowardice.

(v) PANTALONE

Among the old-men types Pantalone is unquestionably the most important. A Venetian merchant by trade, he is, of course, merely the old man of the mime reborn in Renascence Europe. Avaricious to a degree, fearful of any violence, inclined to meddle in high politics, a cuckold, a cheated father, he is always a source of cruel merriment. Euclion in the *Aulularia* is his literary prototype, although nearer models must have existed in the *fabula Atellana*.

Originally he seems to have worn a long, red cloak, which, however, was early changed to black. His gown with the Turkish slippers and the red cap have become definitely traditional. His mask is dark, with a prominent curved nose, white hair, and a long beard.

His companion is the old Dottore—Dottor Partesana, Dottor Graziano Baloardo—later to be translated to literary comedy as Molière's Le Médecin. He is the Pedant of ancient comedy, and appears as philosopher, grammarian, or medical man in a variety of diverting situations. Usually a friend of Pantalone, he serves, like him, as a butt for laughter, mocked at by his wife or his mistress, cheated by a rascally servant of a Harlequin or a Brighella. His costume is obviously that of the professor, black in colour with a dark cloak covering a black garment which falls to his knees. His hat,

Fig. 111. A Roman Mask
This should be compared with the Punch-type of the *commedia dell' arte*.
From Bieber, *op. cit.* Original in the Provinzialmuseum, Bonn

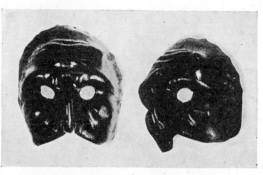

Fig. 112. Mask of Pulcinella
From Duchartre, *op. cit.*

Razullo.   Cucurucu

Fig. 113. Razullo and Cucurucu. Design by
Callot

Fig. 114
Terra-cotta
of a Roman
Mime

From Ficoroni, *De
Larvis scenicis*, Pl. IX

Fig. 115. Capitano,
Seventeenth Century

From Duchartre, *op. cit.*

in contradistinction to that sported by Pantalone, is likewise black. A dark mask with red cheeks and a short beard completes his equipment. He too has his ancestry, for his forefather was called Dossennus in the *fabula Atellana*. There apparently his pedantic wisdom and his real folly caused as much merriment as they did in Renascence times.

(vi) The Significance of the Masks

To outline the many subsidiary characters and the many descendants of these major figures would take up many times the space which can here be allotted to the *commedia dell' arte*, but a few words may be said in conclusion concerning the significance of this type of drama in the history of the theatre. Already it has been indicated that the Italian popular comedy is traceable back to an ancestry in

Fig. 116. CAPITANO, SEVENTEENTH CENTURY
From Duchartre, *op. cit.*

Cap Bonbardon. *Cap Grillo*

Fig. 117. CAPITAN BONBARDON AND CAPITAN GRILLO. DESIGN BY CALLOT

Fig. 118. PANTALONE. DESIGN BY CALLOT

the Roman *mimus*, and this assumption is strengthened instead of weakened by the insistence which some historians have laid on the fact that French farce, independently of Italian,

Fig. 119. PANTALONE
From Duchartre, *op. cit.*

produced stock figures of a similar type. There has thus been adduced the Huret print of Michau (a kind of Pantalone) and Dr Boniface, as well as the print by Abraham Bosse showing a farce at the Hôtel de Bourgogne (Fig. 123). In the latter is shown Gros-Guillaume—

Fig. 120. PANTALONE AND HIS DAUGHTER
This should be contrasted with the Roman comedy scene shown in Fig. 29.
From Duchartre, *op. cit.*

L'ingénieux Guillaume
Contrefaisant l'homme de Cour

Se plaist à gourmander l'Amour
Troussé comme un joueur de paume [1]—

Turlupin, and Gaultier Garguille. It is undoubtedly true that, while we can discover Italian parallels for the two last mentioned, the old fat Falstaffian Gros-Guillaume is difficult to place.

[1] " The clever Guillaume, counterfeiting a courtier, is pleased to chide at love, trussed up like a tennis-player."

THE COMMEDIA DELL' ARTE

His grossly distended stomach, his short trousers and bearded face certainly have but small connexion with the stock masks of Italy, and we may believe that he is a remnant of a French tradition ultimately taking its rise from the same mime source.

At an early date the Italian players came to France. They set up there a permanent theatre, and, when there came into the *commedia dell' arte* a

Fig. 121. IL DOTTORE, SEVEN-TEENTH CENTURY

From Duchartre, *op. cit.*

Fig. 122. DOCTEUR BALOU-ARDO, EIGHTEENTH CENTURY

From Duchartre, *op. cit.*

Fig. 123. SCENE AT THE HÔTEL DE BOURGOGNE

This shows Gros-Guillaume, Gaultier Garguille, and Turlupin. Note the formal setting.

certain infusion of literature, French authors did not hesitate to work out plays for them. *Le Théâtre Italien* prepared by Gherardi has preserved many of these dramas. As an example we may take *L'Opéra de Campagne* (1692) in which part of the story is told in written dialogue; on reaching the fourth scene,

Fig. 124. COVIELLO, SIX-TEENTH CENTURY

From Duchartre, *op. cit.*

Fig. 125. SCARAMUCIA AND FRI-CASSO. DESIGN BY CALLOT

however, this dialogue breaks down. It is a scene between Octave and Arle-quin and is, according to the author,

Fig. 126. SCARAMOUCH

From Duchartre, *op. cit.*

une des plus plaisantes de toute la Comédie, mais c'est une de celles qui ne se peuvent exprimer, & qui n'auroient point d'agrément sur le papier. En un mot, c'est ce qu'on appelle Scêne Italienne, Scêne joüée sur le champ, sans rien apprendre par cœur, & qui dépend entièrement du genie & de l'esprit de l'Acteur. Arlequin contrefait tout ce qu'il a vû, & dit à Octave le dessein qu'il a de faire executer un Opera chez Madame Prenelle, & que par le moyen d'une certaine Colombine qui en est une Actrice, il pretend faire reüssir son mariage avec Thérèse.

113

Octave applaudit à tout, & dit qu'il a parlé à Jeannot, qui luy a promis monts & merveilles. Là-dessus Jeannot arrive.[1]

This may serve, perhaps, as a specimen of a *scenario*.

On the Continent the traditions of the *commedia dell' arte* were kept alive until the middle of the eighteenth century, until, indeed, the opposition of Goldoni brought ruin to the improvised stage. Thereafter only vague relics of its activity persisted.

Fig. 127. An Italian Platform Stage

From Duchartre, *op. cit.*

Fig. 129. Frontispiece to "Les Originaux ou l'Italien" in "Le Théâtre Italien" (1721)

This and Fig. 131 suggest the permanent setting shown more clearly in Fig. 123.

To England the Italian comedians came in the sixteenth and seventeenth centuries. They were popular in London during the Restoration. In the eighteenth century they played for months together in one of the smaller theatres. Then a curious thing happened. They became dumb. It is said that Rich, who, imitating the Italian players, was an excellent Harlequin, finding that he could not speak so well as he could act, turned to dumb show; but, whatever the reason, the traditions of the *commedia dell' arte* passed in England into the pantomime. *Harlequin Dr Faustus, Harlequin Mungo, Harlequin Necromancer* —the titles meet us on page after page of eighteenth-century newspapers, and the pantomimic movement, thus started, was carried over to the nineteenth century. It is dying

Fig. 128. A Platform Stage and Itinerant Players in the Seventeenth Century

---

[1] " [This scene is] one of the most delightful in the whole comedy, but is one of those which cannot be expressed in print and has no value when written down. In a word, it is of the type called 'Italian Scene,' a scene improvised, without any memorizing of words, depending wholly on the genius and spirit of the actor. Arlequin recounts in dumb show all he has seen, and tells Octave of his design of having an Opera performed at Madame Prenelle's house. He thinks that with the aid of a certain Colombine, who is an actress in it, he will be able to arrange Octave's marriage with Thérèse. Octave agrees to everything, and says that he has spoken to Jeannot, who has promised him countless things. At this point Jeannot arrives." The French text is from *Le Théâtre Italien* (1721).

away only in our own days, Christmas laughter rousing annually the palsied limbs to action.

(vii) THE THEATRES OF THE COMMEDIA DELL' ARTE

Fig. 130. THEATRE IN AN ANCIENT AMPHITHEATRE

Fig. 131. FRONTISPIECE TO "LE DÉPART DES COMÉDIENS" IN "LE THÉÂTRE ITALIEN" (1721)

This shows the frames of the side-wings; the audience is supposed to be back stage.

Finally, before we dismiss the actors of the improvised comedy, a word must be said of their theatres. It is not that these actors introduced anything new, but simply that we must place on record the types of stages which they used. One was the outdoor platform. It is the stage of the French *théâtre de foire*, a bare platform backed by a piece of undecorated back-cloth (see Figs. 64, 65). Sometimes more elaborate outdoor theatres were devised, as that shown in Figs. 127 and 128. Generally, however, the acting place was a typical theatre of the Renascence period with a conventional street setting and, in addition, wonderful changes and transformation scenes. Many of the more decorative effects are shown in the frontispiece to Gherardi's *Le Théâtre Italien*, and, making all allowance for the imagination of the artist, we must realize that spectacle here, as in the opera, played a large part. Sometimes the scene shows a simple archway changed for various scenes by the introduction of back-cloths or of movable properties as in Fig. 129; sometimes it is more ornate as in Fig. 132; sometimes it actually shows the secrets of the setting itself, with frames and canvas and side-wings (Fig. 131). In various ways the *concertatori* of the company aimed at novelty, now securing wonderful effects, now no doubt presenting to their audience scenes which would seem to a modern audience meagre and primitive enough.

Fig. 132 FRONTISPIECE TO "LA FILLE SÇAVANTE" IN "LE THÉÂTRE ITALIEN" (1721)

CHAPTER VI

SCENIC DESIGN IN FRANCE (BEFORE 1650)

AT an early date the Italian Renascence penetrated to France, and there, as in its native home, it aroused men to revive the masterpieces of classic drama and so to think of a new stage. At first no doubt the efforts were sufficiently crude, and, in all probability, merely followed along the lines laid down, at Rome and at Ferrara, by Serlio, Palladio, and the rest. A French Terence published in 1552 shows a theatre much of the style familiar to us, save that no curtains divide the pillars at the rear and that those actors who are not speaking apparently sit at the back. In 1561 J. C. Scaliger had noted that the plays acted in France had the peculiar convention that " qui silent pro absentibus habentur." [1] Shortly after, Serlian ideals must have entered in, and no doubt efforts were made after his model. Unfortunately very little information concerning the earlier period has come down to us, and we must note that only one theatre existed which was open to the public. The history of this playhouse is an interesting one. It dates back to December 4, 1402, when the Confrérie de la Passion was given permission " de faire et jouer quelque Misterre que ce soit." [2] On November 17, 1548, this company was formally forbidden to play any " mystères sacrez " but were allowed to perform " autres mystères profanes." The Confrérie, on thus being permitted to produce secular works, converted into a theatre a long rectangular hall in the Hôtel de Bourgogne, situated at the corner of Rue Mauconseil and of Rue Française. Up to 1598 they played there regularly, the theatre once more in 1608 passing into their hands when they were exalted in position by becoming Comédiens du Roi.

It is with the work of these Comédiens du Roi that we are most concerned, for, if little information has been preserved concerning the earlier history of staging in France, ample opportunity for studying the later methods is provided by a *Mémoire pour la Décoration des Pièces qui se représentent par les Comédiens du Roy, entretenus de sa Magesté*, in other words a series of notes and sketches indicating the settings and properties necessary for a number of plays produced by them between 1633 and 1678. The date is late, but the earlier designs are so obviously primitive that we may feel assured they represent in all essentials the settings of the first quarter of the century as well. The chief artist concerned was Laurent Mahelot, and the interest of the volume lies in the fact that both comments and sketches show that the materials preserved were of a highly practical nature. The general style of the *mise-en-scène* presents something to us which is decidedly different from the efforts of the Italians. It borrows from Serlio undoubtedly, but the methods employed are, in the majority of instances, far removed from his. Occasionally we find a scene *tout en pastoralle* in his satyric strain ; occasionally a street- or palace-setting reminds us irresistibly of his tragic and comic designs ; but generally the devices employed carry us far from the unity striven after by Renascence theorists and practicians. In general outline, this *décor simultané* or multiple scenery may be described as the placing on the stage of as many ' localities ' as the action of the drama required. We are dealing, we must remember, with a type of play which is so far ' romantic ' that it disregards the unity of place, that it introduces different localities in different scenes. It is obvious that such

---

[1] " Those who are silent are taken to be off the stage."   [2] " To make and play whatever Mystery they care."

a play can be presented in the theatre in three ways and in three ways only : (1) by the use of curtains, the imagination of the audience creating the surroundings ; (2) by the use of changing scenery ; and (3) by the use of the *décor simultané*.[1] It was the last which Mahelot adopted. A typical example may serve to make the principle clearer. The design shown in Fig. 133 is that executed for the play of *Pandoste*, written on the same theme as that which is used in *The Winter's Tale*. Whereas in Shakespeare's drama the scenes pass from Leontes' palace to Bohemian plains and wild sea-coasts, the French director places everything upon the stage at once. To the left of the audience is a painted sea ; immediately behind it appears the Temple of Delphi. The back of the stage is occupied by the Palace of Epirus, while the right-hand side contains a prison. In all probability the representations of these various *maisons* or *case* were angled, Serlio-wise, con-structed of frames of wood covered with painted canvas, and some at least were practicable. "Une fenestre où se donne une lettre" and "une tour, une corde nouée pour descendre de la tour, un pont-levis qui se lâche quand il est nécessaire"[2]

Fig. 133. A Setting for "Pandoste" at the Hôtel de Bourgogne

At the prompt side are the sea and the Temple of Delphi ; back stage is the Palace of Epirus ; at the actor's left is a prison.

prove that the "houses" were not merely symbolic. All sorts of buildings and of scenes were set on the stage in this manner, and there were even rooms, as if with a "fourth wall" knocked away. One "belle chambre" has in it "une table, deux tabourets, une écritoire." Quite clearly we are here at the meeting point of classic and romantic, or, to be more precise, of medieval and Renascence. We are near the stationary settings of the mysteries, yet we are in touch with Italian ideas. "Une perspective" is spoken of "où il y ait deux passages entre les deux maisons,"[3] and the very word tells its own story.

The importance of Mahelot's designs cannot be overstated. They are invaluable documents for the study, not only of French, but of English theatrical endeavour. In dealing with the staging at Court in London during the sixteenth century, or with the settings indulged in by the boy companies, we must ever bear these in mind.

---

[1] In dealing with French and English theatres of this time we must be careful to note the 'romantic' tendency of some of the dramas of those countries in contradistinction to the 'classic' tendency in Italy. The romantic dramatists were innocent of rules ; and although a Sidney might ridicule their efforts, although a Cervantes might enquire " Que major disparate puede ser en el sugeto que tratamos, que salir un niño en mantillas en la primera escena del primer acto, y en la segunda salir ya echo hombre barbado ? "—the audiences made no such comments or queries, and demanded that all should be represented on the stage.

[2] " A window from which a letter is handed out ; a tower, a knotted cord for descending from the tower, a draw-bridge which can be lowered when necessary."

[3] " Where there are two passages between the two houses."

CHAPTER VII
THEATRES OF ELIZABETHAN ENGLAND (TO 1642)

(i) GENERAL CONSIDERATIONS

IN tracing the development of the theatre in Italy and France we have discovered certain clearly marked types of setting. (1) First, the curtained hall with a simple raised daïs, as in French farce, with, as a variety of this, the *théâtres de foire*, where a raised platform is terminated by a simple back-cloth painted in perspective. (2) The monumental and permanent façade as presented in Palladio's Teatro Olimpico, with streets running down toward the stage proper, five entrances being provided for the actors. (3) The formal designs for comedy, tragedy, and satyric play as planned by Serlio. (4) The *décor simultané* as used at the Hôtel de Bourgogne. (5) The fusion of Palladian and Serlian features as in the Teatro Farnese at Parma, with the elaboration of devices for the shifting of scenery. Clearly, several of these types of staging carry us well into the seventeenth century, but we shall now have to return to the century preceding to deal with what is one of the most interesting and important of all European theatrical developments.

No more than with Italian theatres, however, can we treat the Elizabethan stage as a whole. The first public theatre was opened in 1576, but long before that date elaborate shows had been given at Court, while from 1576 to 1642 is a space of nearly three-quarters of a century. It would, of course, be most advantageous to trace the genesis and slow forward movement of the English theatre chronologically, but that might occupy more space than can conveniently be devoted to the subject here; and as a consequence we shall fall back once more on categorical divisions and deal with each as a separate entity. Some five tendencies or types of setting we can trace in London during the sixteenth and early seventeenth centuries. (1) First there is the hall stage used by the interlude players. (2) Following this there comes the court show of the sixteenth century, with which may be taken the theatres used by the boy-players under Lyly and his companions. (3) Next we come to the public stage proper, typified in the large open-air Globe playhouse. (4) Besides these, however, the public companies used, in the seventeenth century, 'private' theatres such as that at Blackfriars, while (5) there are the masques presented at Court under James I and Charles I, ever increasing in splendour and in artistry, till we reach the closing of the theatres in 1642. While there was a considerable give and take among these theatres, each stands by itself as representative of a special ideal in stage setting.

(ii) THE HALL STAGES

The halls used for the interludes need not detain us for long. Already something has been said of this type of playhouse,[1] and it must be noted that the traditions established in the medieval period itself were extended well to the end of the sixteenth century. Usually all that the actors had here was a slightly raised platform, with, perhaps, a back-curtain or arras through which the performers could enter or leave the primitive stage. That is to say, conditions were almost identical with those of the plain-curtained French hall dealt with in an earlier chapter.[2] The

---

[1] *Supra*, p. 73.   [2] *Supra*, p. 115.

interludes as a whole display practically no change of scene and certainly make but few demands on the scenic-artist, machinist, or 'actor-manager.' For the most part they are but simple one-act playlets with many reminiscences of the medieval poetic *débat*, the characters being few in number and rarely more than two speaking parts being presented at one time. It is just possible, however, that for some there may have been arranged partitions at the back, similar to those early woodcuts in Terence, which were imaginatively given to different localities. We have already seen that *Thersytes* suggests an arrangement of this type and others hint at a similar *mise-en-scène*. The stage directions, however, are slight, and we can make no certain deductions from them.

(iii) STAGING AT COURT AND AT THE UNIVERSITIES

While still in the hazy realm of conjecture, we move on to somewhat surer ground when we pass to the Court shows of this period, for here we possess the invaluable Revels' Office accounts so ably edited and commented upon by Professor Feuillerat. We have, unfortunately, no actual pictorial representation of any setting of this time, but we may, by the exercise of our imagination, conjure up some kind of picture of the manner in which plays were performed. The accounts tabulate the necessary materials for a variety of stage purposes, but on two sets of items alone our attention must be centred. These are the various requirements for "houses" and the canvas for "great cloths." We learn in these accounts of "sparres to make frames for the players howses," of "canvas to cover diuers townes and howses and other devisses and clowds," of "hoopes for tharbour [the arbor] and topp of an howse," and of "nayles to strayne the canvas." Evidently then these were buildings of the Serlian style, made of laths, covered with painted canvas, and surmounted with fitting tops. The number of "houses" used for each particular play seems to have varied from two to five or six. A house and a battlement served for many dramas, but we hear of more for others. Apparently these "houses" were made to represent various objects. The ordinary dwelling-house is there, but besides that there is a "Pallace," "a gret Castell," battlements innumerable, cities, mountains, and similar *mansions*—all recalling the multiple settings employed at the Hôtel de Bourgogne and no doubt being inspired by the stage-manager's efforts there. Sometimes, perhaps, the houses were arranged in a Serlian manner, but more probably they were grouped, French fashion, about the stage with little thought of the laws of perspective. As far as can be judged the authors were not over-careful of the exacter rules insisted upon by their Italian predecessors and contemporaries. Thus, in *Patient Grissell* there is the city of Salucio showing Gautier's house, Janickell's cottage, and that of Mother Apleyarde, besides the city of Bullin Lagras showing the house of the Countess of Pango. Foreshortening is here as it is in the medieval theatre. In the same way a Forest with Bryan Sans Foy's castle and a prison must have stood on one side of the setting for *Clyomon and Clamydes*, the other side being occupied by the Isle of Strange Marshes. It is possible, too, that in some instances doors may have been used with labels indicating the locality they were supposed to represent. The wood and Phrygia in *Common Conditions* seem to have been indicated in this way, while in *Jocasta* we read of "the gates called Electrae" and "the gates called Homoloydes." It seems that the same device was known in France, and possibly was derived from medieval practice. So far, then, we have found ourselves on thoroughly familiar ground.

Some little trouble, however, is caused by the references in the Revels' Office accounts to "curteynes," sometimes called "greate curteynes," along with the poles and "ringes" which were used for opening them. From the indications which are preserved we cannot tell whether these were front curtains or merely coverings for the houses; nor can we say whether the "great cloths" are curtains at all or perspectively painted back-cloths after the Serlian manner. It is noticeable, however, in this connexion that all the references in the accounts point, not to a curtain which rises or falls, but to a curtain which is " drawn " by means of " lynes " and " ringes." That it was used sometimes at least in a front position seems proved by Wilmot's line in *Tancred and Gismund* :

> Now draw the curtens for our Scaene is done,

and by the lines attributed to Sir Walter Raleigh :

> Our graues, that hyde vs from the all-seeing sun,
> Are but drawne curtaynes when the play is done.

In addition to the use of " houses," of course, the Revels' officers made free use of practicable furniture. Chairs, thrones, woods, rocks, wells, caves there are in plenty. Aqua-vitae, as in Italy, provided conflagration effects, and the Elizabethans knew as well as Serlio how to make thunder and lightning.

This method of staging plays by means of multiple scenery with the occasional introduction of perspective—for " the chiefe busynes of the " Revels' Office was to have " skill of deuise " and " iudgment . . . in sight of perspective and architecture "—was, as is natural, adopted both by courtly amateurs and by those companies of choir-boys who, of all actors, were most closely associated with the Court. The practice of the *décor simultané* is referred to clearly in the " magnifica palatia aedesque apparatissimae "[1] mentioned at Oxford in 1566; it is dominant over the performances at the Inns of Court; it flourished at Blackfriars under Lyly and his companions. In *Campaspe* (1584) we find three houses, a palace for Alexander, a tub for Diogenes, and a shop for Apelles, and this principle, sometimes with the adoption of a Serlioesque satyric scene or comedy scene, and frequently with considerable foreshortening made necessary by the romantic freedom which was ever associated with English drama, is carried through to the end. In William Percy's *The Faery Pastorall* (early seventeenth century) we read that " the Properties " required are

> Highest, aloft, and on the Top of the Musick Tree the Title The Faery Pastorall, Beneath him pind on Post of the Tree The Scene Elvida Forrest. Lowest of all over the Canopie ΤΑΠΑΙΤΒΟΔΑΙΟΝ or Faery Chappell. A Kiln of Brick. A Fowen Cott. A Hollowe Oake with vice of wood to shutt to. A Lowe well with Roape and Pullye. A Fourme of Turves. A greene Bank being Pillowe to the Hed but. Lastly A Hole to creepe in and out. Now if so be that the Properties of any These, that be outward, will not serve the turne by reason of concourse of the People on the Stage, Then you may omitt the sayd Properties which be outward and supplye their Places with their Nuncupations onely in Text Letters—

another indication of the use of title-boards on the Elizabethan stage.

(iv) THE PUBLIC THEATRES

The regular companies of actors, however, have now to be considered. These companies, who had taken the place of the amateur performers of medieval times, and who were rapidly ousting both the courtly amateurs and the choir-boys, sometimes acted before Elizabeth, but their regular field of exercise was among the general populace. As is well known, the authorities looked with suspicious eyes at them and at their dramas. Without daring to suggest that the Queen might limit her attendances at comedy or at pageant, they pointed out that public play-houses (originally converted inn-yards) (1) increased the danger of infection in plague years, (2) kept apprentices away from work, and (3) frequently provided opportunity for the devil's work in the way of immorality. It was because of these criticisms, accompanied by galling restraints, that the first public theatres were built outside the bounds of the City proper, so that the London magistrates might have no direct influence upon their activities. The initial playhouse, The Theatre, built by Burbage, was erected near Shoreditch in a locality which had for long been given over to popular games and amusements. Later, the centre of theatrical gravity moved to the south bank of the river, where, in Southwark, was built the famous playhouse called the Globe, the home of Shakespeare's company. Various early panoramic maps show us the locality and the external appearance of this and of other theatres built in its immediate vicinity. That reproduced in *British Drama* shows the Swan (to the extreme left), the Hope (in the centre), and the Globe (to the right). Evidently, from this and other views, the last-mentioned was octagonal outside and possessed a turret rising from one side of the thatched roof. What, however, of the interior? Unfortunately, here we have no such carefully prepared prints to guide us, although we do possess some fairly reliable evidence on the main points. This evidence may be rapidly summarized. (1) There is the de Witt drawing of the Swan theatre, preserved for us at second-hand and not necessarily entirely exact. (2) There are other prints of slightly later date, those which form the frontispieces to Alabaster's *Roxana* (1632) and Richards' *Messallina* (1640) respectively, together with the much later "Red Bull" drawing prefixed to Kirkman's *The Wits* (1672). (3) There is the description of the Fortune playhouse, with other information, contained in the Alleyn papers and in Henslowe's diary (4) Finally there is the evidence to be derived from a study of the stage directions themselves.

Perhaps it may be well to outline the

Fig. 134. THE SWAN THEATRE

main features of points (1) and (3), later comparing them with evidence collected from other quarters. In the Swan drawing (Fig. 134) an open platform stage juts out into the auditorium; behind is a wall with two doors; and over part of the stage projects a roof supported by a couple of pillars. Three galleries run round the sides of what seems to be a circular auditorium. One of these galleries is continued to the back of the stage, and spectators seem to be sitting there. De Witt has evidently attempted to indicate those portions of the theatre which accorded with a Roman playhouse; over the 'pit' he has written—*planities siue arena* (plain or arena), over the stage—*proscaenium*, over the back wall *mimorum aedes* (the tiring house), along the

galleries *orcheſtra*. The roof, the seats, and the *porticus* do not concern us. In addition he has added some observations on the London which he viewed:

> Amphiteatra Londinij sunt iv visendae pulcritudinis quae a diversis intersigniis diuersa nomina sortiuntur: in iis varia quotidie scaena populo exhibetur. . . . Theatrorum autem omnium preſtantissimum eſt et amplissimum id cujus intersignium eſt cygnus . . . quippe quod tres mille homines in sedilibus admittat, conſtruĉtum ex coaceruato lapide . . . ligneis suffultum columnis quae ob illitum marmoreum colorem, nasutissimos quoque fallere possent. Cuius quidem formam quod Romani operis vmbram videatur exprimere supra adpinxi.[1]

De Witt was a Continental visitor and by way of being a scholar, and his account, apart from the drawing, has thus special value. Other records accord with his. Already in 1577 we are informed of "the sumptuous theatre houses"; in 1578 is a reference to "the gorgeous playing place." In 1600 a foreigner was describing the "theatrum ad morem antiquorum Romanorum conſtruĉtum ex lignis."[2] Evidently what ſtruck the onlookers was the "sumptuous" appearance of the theatres and their likeness to Roman models.

Let us now turn to the original indenture regarding the Fortune. Here we learn the following particulars:

(1) the "frame" of the playhouse is "to be sett square"; 80 feet each way outside and 55 feet each way within.

(2) there are to be three ſtories, the firſt 12 feet high, the second 11 feet high, and the third 9 feet high, the width of each being 12 feet 6 inches.

(3) "ffower convenient divisions for gentlemens roomes" as well as 2*d*. rooms are to be provided.

(4) a ſtage and tiring house are to be set up with "a shadowe or cover over the saide Stadge"; the ſtage to be 43 feet long and extending to "the middle of the yarde."

(5) the ſtage is "to be paled in belowe with good, ſtronge and sufficyent new oken bourdes" and the lower ſtory is to be similarly "paled in" and also provided "with ſtrong yron pykes."

(6) there are to be "windowes and lightes glazed to" the tiring house, and the roof is to be tiled.

(7) everything is to be done as in the Globe theatre save that the "poſts" of the frame and ſtage are to be "square and wroughte palaſterwise, with carved proporcions called Satiers to be placed & sett on the topp of every of the same poſtes."

The indications given here may well be compared with those presented by the de Witt drawing, and in addition we may take at leaſt two of the other sketches. The gallery over the ſtage divided into rooms is clearly shown in the *Roxana* print (Fig. 135), but here curtains hide the back wall of the ſtage as they do in the *Messallina* design (Fig. 136) and in *The Wits* (Fig. 137).[3] It is to be noted that in both the *Roxana* and the *Messallina* prints the ſtage tapers toward the front, and is protected by low rails.

Turning now to the plays themselves, we find that the ſtage directions sometimes confirm and sometimes contradict the type of ſtage indicated in the de Witt drawing. (1) In the firſt place, we know of *three* doors in the back wall, with perhaps an additional entrance at each side

---

[1] "There are four beautiful theatres in London which are diſtinguished by their signs; in these plays are daily performed in public. . . . Of all these theatres the moſt outſtanding and largeſt is that diſtinguished by the sign of the Swan . . . this holds 3000 persons on seats. It is built of ſtone . . . based on wooden columns which, painted like marble, could cheat the moſt expert. I have delineated above the shape of this theatre; it is seen to follow the lines of a Roman ſtructure."

[2] "The theatre, built of wood, after the manner of the ancient Romans."

[3] The original print from which the model shown in Fig. 137 was taken is reproduced in *British Drama*, p. 216.

of the stage. Thus in *Patient Grissell* the author bids Urcenze and Onophrio to enter " at seuerall doores, and Farneze in the midst," while there are many directions which indicate entries or exits by the " ends " of the stage. (2) We know that the central aperture at the back was sufficiently wide to make the part behind do service as an inner stage. The directions calling for the use of this inner stage are so numerous and have been discussed so frequently that there is no need to instance any here. (3) From the stage directions we can see that the gallery above the stage was used not only by spectators but by the actors and the musicians as well. The gallery as a whole might represent the walls of a city, or else a single " box " might be a window of a house from which an inmate could address a character standing at the door below. (4) Somewhere below the roof or " shadowe," but above the gallery, there were the " heavens " from which chairs and similar objects could be let down. Already in 1584 Higgins had defined the " heavens " in his *Nomenclator* as " The skies or coûterfeit heauen ouer the stage, from whence some god appeared or spoke."

From these stage directions, therefore, we have fundamentally to alter our conception of the open-air public playhouse. We must imagine a round or rectangular theatre,

Fig. 135. A Seventeenth-Century Stage

set with galleries for the spectators, a large raised stage in the centre of the pit or *orchestra*, backed by a wall, no doubt decorated architecturally with one large and two small openings, perhaps two more doors in side walls, a roof over the stage, supported on elaborately carved and painted pillars, windows above from which spectators may gaze or actors speak (Fig. 138).

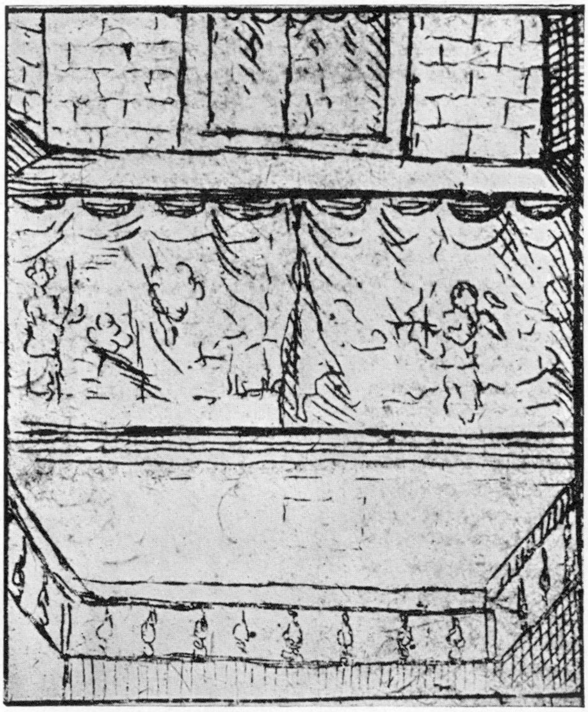

Almost at once a prototype suggests itself in the kind of theatre best exemplified in Palladio's Teatro Olimpico. The central doorway and the two doorways to left and right, the entrances, the windows, the architectural adornment, the roof—all recall that playhouse which had become a model for Italy, just as that itself was based on the type of theatre which has been preserved at Orange. There is, too, the circular auditorium to be considered. While that, as many have thought, may have been merely a relic of the bull-baiting ring or of the inn-yard which

Fig. 136. A Seventeenth-Century Stage

formed the first theatre, it is possible at least that Burbage, who was no illiterate or inartistic boor, may have been inspired by the example set at Vicenza. If this is so, then the Theatre and the Globe represent attempts to reproduce in London the forms of a Roman playhouse.

THE DEVELOPMENT OF THE THEATRE

It has been suggested by Creizenach that the original model of the English playhouse is to be found in some sixteenth-century Low Country theatres, reproductions of which are extant (Figs. 139 and 140). The print of the stage at Ghent shows five doorways and a roof, while in that at Amsterdam are seen three doorways, a roof, and a kind of gallery. It may be, of course, that James Burbage, before he built the Theatre, had seen these erections, but, it seems to me, a more reasonable explanation exists to account for the similarities between the Dutch and the English playhouses. The Palladian model was the final result of much investigation into the form of a Roman playhouse; and one may well believe that it, the Dutch theatres, and the English all were variants of one general line of inquiry into theatrical architecture.[1]

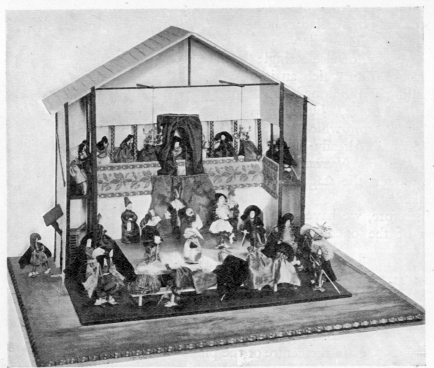

Fig. 137. MODEL OF THE STAGE SHOWN IN KIRKMAN'S "THE WITS" (1672)

Model executed by Mrs Allardyce Nicoll for exhibition at Wembley, 1924. The original print is reproduced in *British Drama*.

At the same time, even while we may admit this direct or indirect influence of Renascence Italian stage practice, we find that the type of playhouse exemplified in the Theatre or in the Globe does not in any way accord with the critical ideal which stands behind the Teatro Olimpico. In that theatre the assumption was that the place of action remained unchanged, that the characters in the drama met and talked at a square flanked by divers houses and served by five intersecting streets. There are, it is true, windows above, which might, on occasion, provide another theatrical plane, but these are small and negligible. When we turn to the English playhouse we find a complete separation from this ideal, for the Globe Theatre catered, not for an academic, but for a general public. The problem which faced Burbage was apparently that which had faced Laurent Mahelot, and he solved it in his own way by providing a Palladian 'scene' and at the same time giving himself the opportunity of using an upper stage and an inner stage. Instead of indulging in the multiple setting, he allowed his actors normally to indicate the place of action, but he bowed to 'scenery' in so far that the inner stage, revealed by the central arch, might serve as a room or as a background to a room. Thus, for example, if we are merely told that a certain character lies in his bed, then we overlook the outer part of the stage and concentrate only on what is behind, but if, as in *Romeo and Juliet*, we are informed that "They all but the Nurse goe foorth, casting Rosemary on her and shutting the Curtens," then the inner stage becomes merely part of the large stage and action proceeds on both, so that the inner stage at one time may serve as a separate locality, and at another may form merely the means of localizing the general action of

---

[1] It is noticeable that the 'window' or upper stage in the English and Continental theatres is no more than the διστεγία of Pollux.

124

the scene. The curtains, or hangings, over the central aperture, covering what was known technically as the 'scene,' shut off at will this back partition. The device, as will be realized, was an exceedingly clever one, but after all it was but the same 'invention' which was carried out by the architect of the Teatro Farnese at Parma in 1618.[1] A Palladian façade has been provided with a back stage on which 'scenery' of a kind may be shown. The only difference is a difference of theory, not of fact; the English theatre manager allows his actors on occasion to delineate for

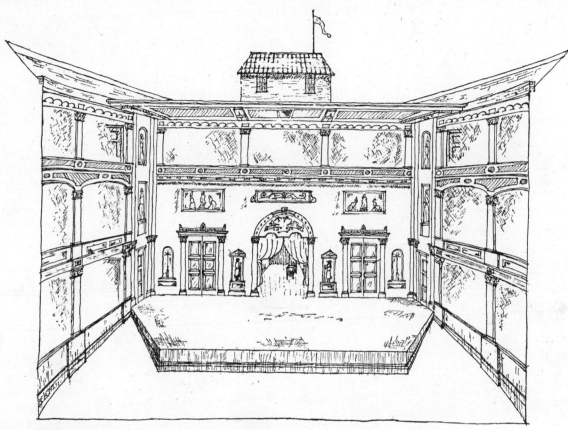

Fig. 138. Reconstruction of an Elizabethan Theatre
Drawn by Mr S. B. Marston with decorations resembling those in the Teatro Olimpico.

the audience those settings which would have remained constant with Palladio or which would have been visually represented by the scenic artists of the theatre at Parma.

In many minor ways the Elizabethan public theatres show their dependence upon the Italian, mingling, as in France, Renascence ideas with medieval. The 'machines' employed may have been relics from the mystery plays, but in many respects they seem to have the impress of the new age upon them. As early as 1546 we have a reference to the use of a κράδη or crane so contrived that there "was great wondering, and many vain reports spread abroad of the means how it was effected." This was at Trinity College, but, quite naturally, experiments in classic machines of this type soon spread to the public stages, and we find many instances of the descent of a *deus ex machina*. The ἐκκύκλημα is, of course, suggested by the curtained inner stage, and

---

[1] If the central aperture is accepted as virtually a proscenium arch, then it is evident that Burbage in England anticipated Italy by nearly half a century. It may be noted here that the word 'proscenium' has moved from an ancient significance—"that which lies before the *skene*"—to indicate the forepart of the stage and even the wall or cloth against which the actors move. See pp. 22, 29-30.

some means similar to the ἐξώστρα was employed to thrust beds and similar objects on to the stage. Various ' effects ' of diverse kinds make their appearance here as in Italy. Trap-doors

seem to have been provided in most of the theatres, and through these figures or solid objects could rise or descend. Many a magician's conjuring is contrived by their means. Thunder and lightning, which had been early used at Court, appear in play after play of the period. A " burning Roabe " and a " burning crowne " occur in Heywood's *The Golden Age*, and the companion play, *The Silver Age*, has " Fire-workes all over the house." Reading these and similar stage directions, we are inclined to credit the Elizabethan theatres with many more means at their disposal than is generally allowed them. We can hardly suppose that travelled gentlemen would have refrained from casting a sneer at primitive effects such as many modern critics assume were all the contemporaries of Shakespeare ever knew. The truth is rather that Burbage and his companions, just as Shakespeare himself, were well abreast of the Italians and the French but moving along lines which, springing from an original Continental source, were bearing them to new ideas and fresh experiments.

Fig. 139. THE THEATRE AT GHENT, 1539

From Creizenach, *The English Drama in the Age of Shakespeare.*

(v) THE PRIVATE THEATRES

Besides these public theatres, and apart from the theatres used at an early period by the choir-boys, we have to reckon with the theatres which, for no very clear reason, were designated ' private.' Blackfriars, the winter home of Shakespeare's company, Whitefriars, Salisbury Court, the Cockpit in Drury Lane were thus all private theatres, differentiated from the others mainly by the fact that they were roofed-in rectangular buildings and consequently used artificial light. Evidently, to judge from the *Wits* print and from later examples the main source of illumination came from the candelabra hung over the stage, together with footlights of a primitive sort.

Unfortunately we know practically nothing for certain concerning the shape of the stage in these private theatres, although, as some were exceedingly narrow, we may presume that the stage itself may have filled up all or nearly all the space from side wall to side wall. When we come to the stage directions of the earlier plays produced in these theatres, however, we find much that must interest us, for it is plain that the private houses preserved more of the Serlian tradition or the tradition of the Hôtel de Bourgogne than did the open-air theatre. Many of the dramas, as Sir Edmund Chambers has demonstrated, could have been performed easily by the use of multiple scenery, and it seems clear that these private theatres preserved a tradition, extending

Fig. 140. THE THEATRE AT ANTWERP, 1561

From Creizenach, *op. cit.*

from the time of Court performances in the sixteenth century, for more academic and chaster effects. We know that the price of admission to those theatres was higher than that to the public playhouses ; we know that the audience was more refined and courtly ; and as a result the effects were more nearly allied to those which Revels officers, aided by the services of foreign artists, busied themselves to provide for captious royalty. It was at the private houses of a slightly later date that movable scenery was first shown to the general public, but with this we cannot deal until we have glanced at the influence of the Court-masque and the efforts of Inigo Jones. Here be it sufficient to note that the private theatres preserved a " fashion," as Marston expresses it, distinct from that of the public theatres, and intimately connected both with the Serlian set-stage and the *décor simultané*. Painted scenery, such as was employed at Court, may well have been utilized for general purposes, and perspective may have played its part as it did in Italy. In this connexion there is an exceedingly interesting sketch, to which attention has recently been drawn,

showing the interior of a theatre. It is included in an English book of the date 1658, a translation from the Dutch.[1] While it may, of course, be Continental in origin, there are one or two minor points which seem to indicate its main features as English. The importance of the design lies in the fact that it shows a simplified multiple setting. On one side is the wall of a house, conventionally arranged; on the other what is evidently intended to be an orchard. At the extreme back of the stage curtains conceal what must be a door or an inner room. Of particular interest, too, is the semblance of theatrical front curtains.

Fig. 141. Frontispiece or Proscenium Arch for "Albion's Triumph" (1609). Design by Inigo Jones

Copyright of the Duke of Devonshire.

(vi) THE MASQUES OF THE SEVENTEENTH CENTURY

Before we can adequately discuss the problems raised by the settings of later plays in the private theatres, some attention must be given to the masque-settings at the Courts of James I and of Charles I. The earlier shows of this kind, interesting as they undoubtedly are, have not any special value for us here, but those which were produced under Inigo Jones in the seventeenth century have more than an ephemeral importance. It was through them that the English theatre most clearly showed its association with the Continent. Jones was "a great Traveller"; he knew his Italy well, and he knew the work on scenic craft which Italy had produced. He was, however, an experimenter, and his own settings show a desire to attempt various styles before coming to a definite decision. Thus for Daniel's *Vision of Twelve Goddesses*, presented on January 8, 1604, something of an Hôtel de Bourgogne *mise-en-scène* seems to have been employed, while at Oxford in 1605 he used a Serlian raked stage [2] backed by a scenic wall in which were set

peripetasmata scaenicaque habitacula, machinis ita artificiose ad omnium locorum rerumque varietatem apparata, ut non modo pro singulorum indies spectaculorum, sed etiam pro Scaenarum una eademque fabula diversitate subito (ad stuporem omnium) compareret nova totius theatralis fabricae facies.[3]

[1] This is reproduced in the present writer's *British Drama*, p. 108.   [2] See *supra*, p. 87.

[3] "Tapestries and scene-houses, artfully prepared with machines for a variety of views and devices, so that, not only for separate performances given on different days, but for a single play, new settings of the entire stage were made to appear with a diversity and suddenness that astonished every one." The *peripetasmata* seem to have been canvas-covered *periaktoi*.

I

In other words, a set of περίακτοι had been established as a back-scene for the changing of the prospect.

From this Jones turned once more to the masque shows at Court. The *periaktoi* he found no doubt a trifle cumbrous, and after all they could show at most but three different views. In principle all his later masque settings demanded an ornate proscenium arch, so that he was adopting or modifying that style of staging which had been popularized by the architects of the Teatro Farnese. This proscenium arch, ornamented with sculptured or painted forms symbolic of the

FIG. 142. PALACE AND ROCKS IN "OBERON" (1611).
DESIGN BY INIGO JONES
Copyright of the Duke of Devonshire.

nature of the masque, and containing usually the name of the show in a central compartment, was a most important part of the general scheme, and to the proscenia Jones devoted considerable attention. An example designed for *Albion's Triumph* is given here (Fig. 141). Within this proscenium arch the stage was set, and the full stage might be concealed by a front-curtain, usually painted with a "perspective." In *The Masque of Blackness* (January 1605) such a curtain represented a "landtschap" or landscape and fell at the beginning of the performance, even as the *auleum* had done in Roman theatres and in the early theatres of Ferrara. Later it was made to rise on rollers in the manner prescribed by Sabbatini. Being painted, it could not, of course, be drawn like the curtains in the public theatres. In this masque mentioned above Jones seems to have made no attempt to change his scenery, but a sea was simulated Sabbatini-wise, and there were many machinist's effects. A reversion to the *periaktoi* for a turning globe and new cloud effects mark the mask of *Hymenaei* (1606). Little but experimentation in various machines is to be found in the masques which immediately followed, although *The Hue and Cry after Cupid* (1608) presents us with the first definite allusion to a fully developed proscenium arch, and *The Masque of Queens* (1609) shows an elaborate use of the *machina versilis* which changed from an "ugly Hell" to "the House of Fame" and thence to "Fama Bona." After this time Jones seems to have turned to other devices. An elaborate alteration of scene, accompanied by moving lights which dazzled the eyes of the spectators, was presented in Daniel's *Tethys Festival or the Queens Wake* (June 1610), and the effects therein were paralleled in *Oberon, the Fairy Prince* (January 1611). In the latter there is shown first "a darke Rocke, with trees beyond it" (Fig. 142) which changed suddenly to a "*Frontispiece* of a bright and glorious *Palace*," evidently by means of wings drawn off or "opened." This in turn was "opened" once again, and within was shown the Nation of Fays. It is possible that Jones was working here with two-sided flats such as Sabbatini described in his book on stage-craft. It is interesting, too, to note that in *The Lords Masque* (February 1613) there was a device similar to that used in Buontalenti's *intermedii* at Rome, for

128

from the side of the Scene appeared a bright and transparent Cloud, which reached from the top of the heavens to the earth :—the cloude brake in twain, and one part of it (as with a winde) was blown overthwart the Scaene.

Spectacular shows in heaven and on earth appear plentifully in succeeding masques, but on these we cannot linger. Rather must we concentrate attention on the extremely valuable plans made for *Florimène* in 1635 and for *Salmacida Spolia* in 1640. These reveal at once the methods

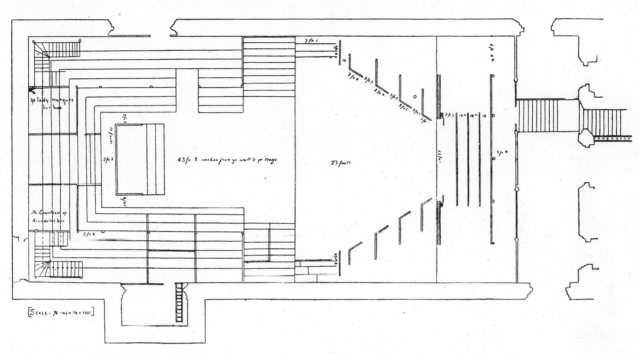

Fig. 143. PLAN FOR "FLORIMÈNE" (1635), BY INIGO JONES

From Reyher, *Les Masques anglais.*

employed. For the former Jones himself drew out a plan of the hall (Whitehall) and caused his assistant, John Webb, to make a fuller ground-plan of the stage for

> that kind of sceane with triangular frames on yᵉ sydes where there is but one standing sceane and yᵉ sceane changes only at the Back shutters.

These plans show that the effects were secured by having a series of two-sided flats running at sharp angles toward the back, with, at the rear, four flat shutters changed when required for the *intermedii* (Fig. 143). Fig. 144 shows the general arrangement of the "standing scene" with a view of the Isle of Delos. Clearly from the plan additional use was made of some flats which ran immediately behind the last triangular frame. Thus when the scene had to change to " a snowy Landschipe with leave-lesse trees," then two side flats of bare trees ran in without meeting, revealing behind a back-cloth, which was thus a "releiue" (relieve) or prospect seen through the rest of the scenery. So the various *intermedii* of the seasons were presented. It is certain that the wings remained unaltered, standing constant amid all the changes in the back-cloths.

Finally we reach *Salmacida Spolia* of which also the ground-plan and section have been preserved (Figs. 145 and 146). The former is inscribed :

> Ground platt of a sceane where yᵉ side peeces of yᵉ sceane doe altogither change with yᵉ back shutters.

129

It is evident that we are dealing here with something entirely different. Four sets of side-wings are placed on each side of the stage, each set consisting of four plain, not two-sided, flats running in grooves. Behind these come a series of four shutters completely cutting off the rear of the stage. These removed, there are revealed the masquers' seats and the perspective beyond. To each set of side-wings and to each of the shutters corresponds a painted sky-cloth, the flats diminishing in height according to the rules of Continental stage designers (Fig. 146). Fig. 147, showing the third scene in this masque, gives a good idea of the arrangement of the setting. The "whole heaven" is illustrated in Fig. 148.

Fig. 144. STANDING SCENE FOR "FLORIMÈNE" (1635). DESIGN BY INIGO JONES
Copyright of the Duke of Devonshire.

From these plans, designs, and inscriptions it is clear that four types of setting were employed in the masques: (1) the Hôtel de Bourgogne simultaneous scene, (2) the triangular machine or *scaena versilis*, (3) the two-sided and stationary flats with movable shutters at the back, and (4) the completely movable series of flats and shutters—the final evolution of the *scaena ductilis*. It is clear, too, that the order of progression was that indicated above, *Salmacida Spolia* being virtually the last word spoken by Inigo Jones on this subject.

(vii) SCENERY IN THE THEATRES

From this rapid and all too brief account of the masques we come to the question which involves a reconsideration of the scenic effects employed in the private theatres. It is almost inconceivable that plays such as *The Tempest* were produced on a bare unadorned stage, and, in point of fact, we do find reason for supposing that there was some give and take between the masque entertainments and the playhouses. The most important document in this connexion is an entry

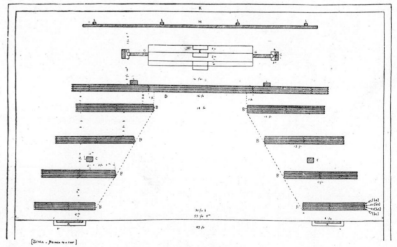

Fig. 145. PLAN OF THE STAGE FOR "SALMACIDA SPOLIA" (1640), BY INIGO JONES
From Reyher, *op. cit.*

in Anthony à Wood's *History of the University of Oxford*. A play by Cartwright, *The Royal Slave*, had been performed with scenery at Christ Church, Oxford, in 1636. It was so beautiful that the

Queen requested the Chancellor to send her the scenery and the costumes to Hampton Court "that she might see her own Players act it over again." The Chancellor thereupon

> caused the Cloathes and Perspectives of the Stage to be sent to Hampton Court . . . [but] desired of the King and Queen that neither the Play, or Cloaths, nor Stage, might come into the hands and use of the common Players abroad.

Unless the scenery could have been made use of by "the common Players" there does not seem to have been much point in the Chancellor's request.

This whole question, it seems to me, has been hopelessly confused by a failure to differentiate between changing scenery and scenery of a set Serlian plan. When Aubrey declares that Sir John Suckling wrote a play which "had some scenes to it, which in those days (1637) were only used at Masques" he was in all probability thinking of changes and not of scenery as such. It will be well then to consider the evidence for the alteration of scene first and apart from the other. It is thus known that Suckling's *Aglaura* produced at the Blackfriars at Christmas 1637 was so provided with scenes. The "Scene magnificent" was girded at in the prologue to Brome's *Antipodes* (1638), and perhaps the "gaudy scene" of the same writer's *The Court Beggar* (? 1638) is another reference.

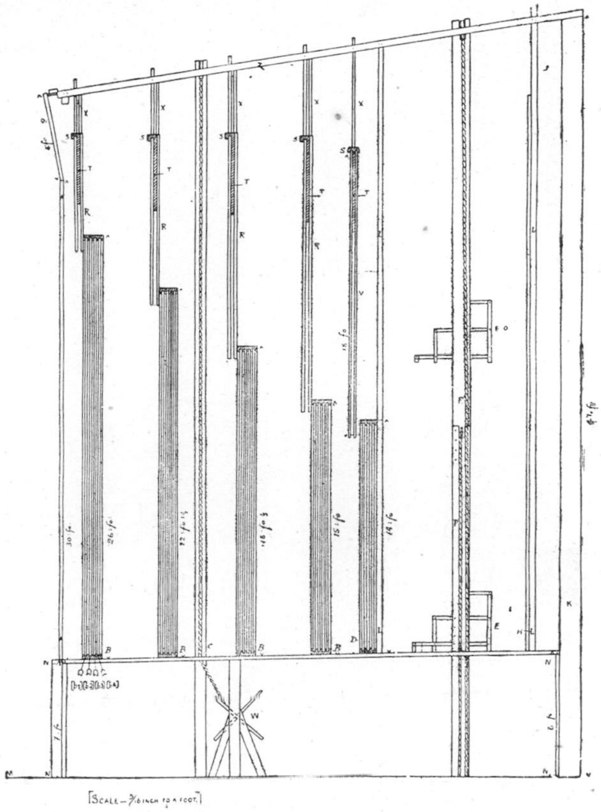

Fig. 146. CROSS-SECTION OF THE STAGE FOR "SALMACIDA SPOLIA" (1640), BY INIGO JONES

From Reyher, *op. cit.*

Fig. 147. THE THIRD SCENE IN "SALMACIDA SPOLIA" (1640). DESIGN BY INIGO JONES

Copyright of the Duke of Devonshire.

Furthermore we know that Habington's *The Queene of Arragon* (1640), after being shown at Court, was also given with scenes at the Blackfriars,[1] while D'Avenant in 1639 received a patent to build a theatre where "scenes" could be employed. At the same time as this movement was being established in the theatres the Court came to take an interest in scenery painted for plays as well as for masques. Thus Fletcher's *The Faithful Shepherdess* was presented at Denmark House in January 1634 with scenery, while *Florimène* was a French pastoral, not a masque. In 1638 Jones sketched plans for Lodowick Carlell's *The Passionate Lovers* as he did in 1640 for Habington's *The Queene of Arragon*. If, then, scenes such as

[1] Inigo Jones' design for a setting in this play is reproduced in *British Drama*, p. 106. Cp. also Fig. 150.

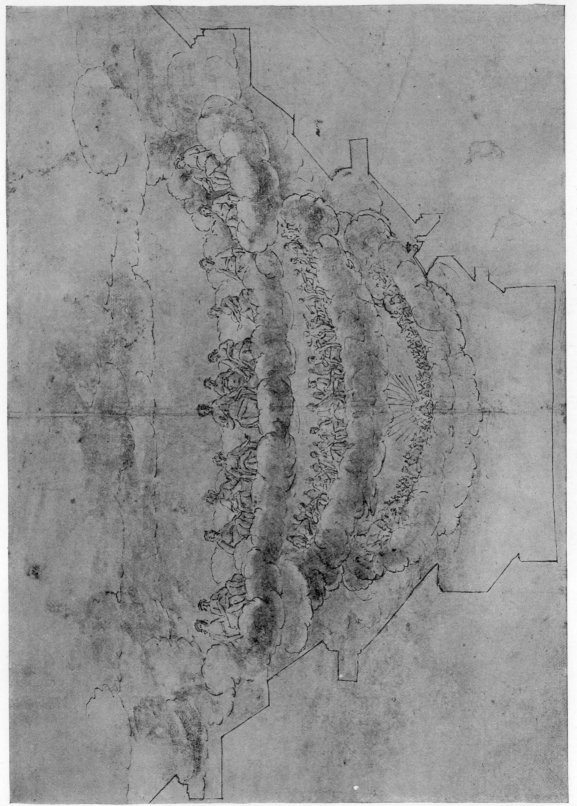

Fig. 148. The Whole Heaven in "Salmacida Spolia" (1640)
From the original in the possession of the Duke of Devonshire.
Photo Victoria and Albert Museum.

were used at Court could be employed in a private theatre, then surely these private theatres had stages capable of making full use of the effects. In spite of the fact that the utilization of changing scenery there is recorded as an innovation, it seems that we must presume (1) that the stage was physically capable of accommodating scenery, and (2) that the love of scenery was growing rapidly on the audiences. Even before 1637 we can trace the attention paid to these devices. The prologue to Nabbes' *Hannibal and Scipio*, given at the Phoenix in Drury Lane in 1635, informs us that "the places sometimes chang'd too for the Scene," while at

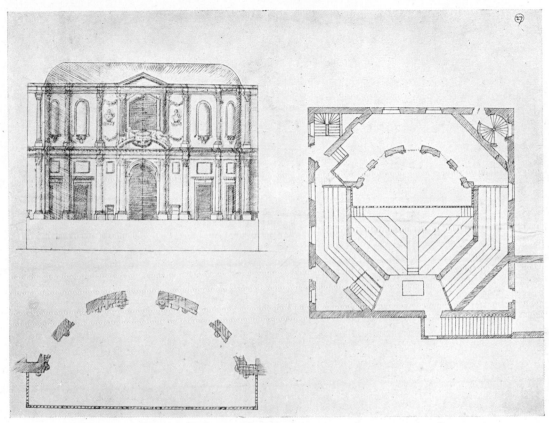

Fig. 149. PLAN BY INIGO JONES FOR THE COCKPIT-IN-COURT
From the original at Worcester College, Oxford.

least five plays of the period 1634–36 have stage directions which seem to imply alteration of setting.

But, if we assume that changing scenery was employed in the theatres about 1633 and used sporadically on to 1642, we are still left with the question of earlier staging. That, I assume, was more or less of the Serlian type, similar to that used in the public theatres, but no doubt at once more ornate and more academic. It probably took the place of the *décor simultané*, which, as we have seen, was originally used at Court and by the choir-boys. That Serlian and Palladian schemes were eagerly thought of in those days is proved by a most interesting set of sketches by Inigo Jones recently discovered. One of these is a plan and elevation conjecturally dated about 1632, which was almost certainly made for the new Cockpit-in-Court (Fig. 149). The arrangement of the seats corresponds to the octagonal setting of the theatre. The stage, 35 feet wide by 16 deep, has a long rectangular front and is backed by a semicircular architectural façade

133

pierced by five doors. Undoubtedly this is but a modification of the Palladian theatre at Vicenza.[1] In connexion with this may be taken another drawing (Fig. 150), even more recently discovered, preserved in Inigo Jones' copy of Palladio. Here the theatre is rectangular, the seats being arranged in concentric curves. The stage is 43 feet wide, and is arranged with two *versurae* or permanent sides and a lofty arch somewhat in the style of the Teatro Farnese. This recedes in the centre and gives way to two side-wings of the usual two-sided sort backed by a perspective. The perspective shown in the elevation is a typical Serlian design. This Serlian design may be compared with the " Tragic Scene " (Fig. 151) of the Chatsworth collection. Evidently Jones was busying himself with plans for some actual theatre, perhaps (may the suggestion be hazarded?) for some private playhouse which thus used a setting which combined a Palladian arch with the scenic device beloved of later audiences. It is remarkable at least that in the sketch for Habington's *The Queene of Arragon* Jones encircled his rough outline of " cloudes," " back-cloth," and " citti of releue " with an archway which recalls the archway in the elevation noted above.

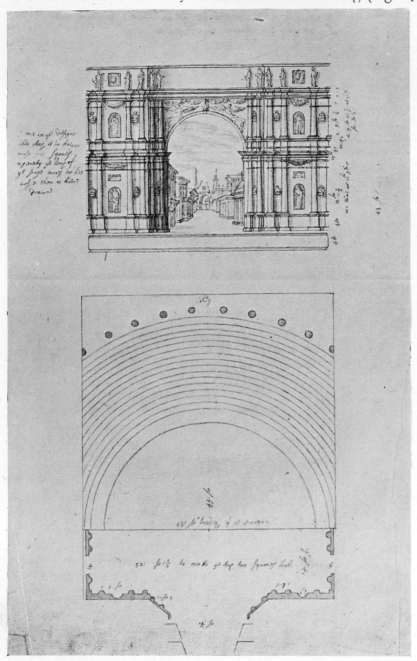

Fig. 150. Theatre Plan by Inigo Jones
From the original at Worcester College, Oxford.

(viii) The Actors, Costumes, and Accessories

So much has been written of the conditions under which Shakespeare wrote that little space need be devoted to that subject here. From being ordinary retainers at the best and " rogues and vagabonds " at the worst, the players slowly won for themselves a position of esteem. Shakespeare could get his coat of arms and a country house at Stratford; Alleyn could leave money to

[1] W. G. Keith in an article on *John Webb and the Court Theatre of Charles II* (*Archit. Rev.*, lvii, 339, February 1925) thinks this design was by Webb and made for a reconstruction of the Cockpit after the Restoration. See also Boswell Eleonore, *The Restoration Court Stage* (1932).

endow an important scholastic centre. Traditions of an earlier time may have clung to such essentially popular houses as the Red Bull, where clownage, squibs, and rant pleased a lower-class public, but at Blackfriars, the Phoenix, and Salisbury Court the actors were gentlemen and the audience critical. Perhaps in the theatres of Shakespeare's time there may occasionally have been noise and tumult—for the Elizabethans were a hot-blooded race—but those who emphasize the rudeness of the gallants upon the stage and the restless clamour of the groundlings seem to me to have misrepresented the conditions of the time. The Elizabethans were still somewhat *naïve*, and obviously looked upon the theatre in a manner entirely different from that of the Restoration courtier. These tales of Italy, these farcical comedies, clearly fascinated them, but I deeply question whether Shakespeare had to contend with those difficulties which later confronted Dryden. As an antidote to the oft-repeated assertions concerning the rude clamour of the multitude let us

Fig. 151. THE TRAGIC SCENE. DESIGN BY INIGO JONES
Copyright of the Duke of Devonshire.

take a portion of an exceedingly interesting letter written by Orazio Busino to the Council of Venice on December 8, 1617. "To distract me," he says,

> they took me at the suggestion of Signore Giovanni Battista Lionello, to one of the numerous theatres here in London where comedies [plays] are recited and we saw a tragedy performed there, which moved me little,

Fig. 152. "TITUS ANDRONICUS" IN 1595
From the original in the possession of the Marquess of Bath.

especially as I cannot understand a single word of English, though one may derive some little amusement from gazing on the sumptuous dresses of the actors and observing their gestures, and the various interludes of instrumental music, dancing, singing and the like. The best treat was to see and stare at so much nobility in such excellent array that they seemed so many princes, *listening as silently and soberly as possible.*

It is but a thumb-nail sketch of an Elizabethan theatre, but an interesting one. This Italian visitor, like so many other earlier Continental visitors, saw nothing in the theatre so crude as to call for an unfavourable comparison with the theatres of his own land. He thought worthy of record the quiet attention of the audience, and he noted the sumptuous apparel of the actors.

That the players were richly dressed we know from many sources. John Northbrooke in 1577 had girded at the "gorgious and sumptious apparell" to be seen in the theatres. Two years later Stephen Gosson declared that

Ouerlashing in apparel is so common a fault, that the very hyerlings of some of our players, which stand at reuersion of vi.s. by the weeke, iet vnder gentlemens noses in sutes of silke.

Unfortunately, although we have many allusions such as these, and although we have some inventories among the Henslowe papers, we possess little sure information concerning the nature of those rich costumes. For many plays certainly the ordinary dress of the time could be used, but often there must have been attempts to secure both a semblance of historical accuracy and something of a symbolic or conventional effect. In a brilliant essay entitled *The Truth of Masks* Oscar Wilde demonstrated with some show of reason that Shakespeare was not so careless in regard to costume as has often been made out, and his case is even stronger now than it was when written. In

Fig. 153. COSTUME OF THE CHARACTER OF NOBODY
From *Nobody and Somebody* (c. 1606).

our survey of the eighteenth century it will be seen that while ordinary costumes were used for many characters, special stage dresses were apportioned (1) to Eastern characters, (2) to Roman and Grecian characters, (3) to special characters outside the usual run of tragedy and comedy.[1] The more we study eighteenth-century theatrical conditions the more we realize that those conditions are largely traditional and consequently that they throw considerable light on the earlier theatre. Thus, while Hamlet invariably wears ordinary dress, Falstaff, Posthumus, Dromio, and others have attires peculiar to themselves, while Othello wears the Eastern garments and Antony the costume *à la romaine*. An interesting commentary on these garments is provided by a drawing of 1595, showing a scene from *Titus Andronicus* (Fig. 152). Tamora wears the ordinary crown of the tragedy queen (*cf*. Figs. 235 and 239).

Fig. 154. THE COSTUME OF FLOODS IN "CHLORIDIA" (1631). DESIGN BY INIGO JONES
Copyright of the Duke of Devonshire.

The two retainers have, apparently, Elizabethan doublets with some kind of breastplate—the costume corresponding with eighteenth-century

[1] *Infra*, p. 178. For more detailed notes on the dressing of actors on the Elizabethan stage see Appendix A.

Roman dress. One of them, be it noted, sports a helmet with plumes just as later tragic characters do (cp. Fig. 217). Alarbus has a peculiar attire, consisting of a breastplate (?) and a kind of cloak flung over his left shoulder, while Aaron the Moor has tight-fitting boots, doublet (or a tunic ?), and an open-necked shirt. While his dress does not agree with that of later Eastern personages, the boots as well as the curved scimitar of one of the guards well merit our notice.

We must remember too "the robe to go invisible in" which is mentioned in one of Henslowe's inventories. What that robe was we have no means of knowing, but it was without doubt a conventional mantle which the audience would automatically accept. It was used later for Ariel in *The Tempest*, and was probably but one of a series of similar allegorical or symbolic costumes made use of by the actors. We certainly know that a character Nobody in the play of *Nobody and Somebody* was represented with breeches up to his neck so that 'no body' should be visible, and we are aware that other conventional costuming was indulged in. Thus in *Henry IV* the King is shown to us in his bed-chamber, lying there in his night-gown with, rather uncomfortably, his crown on his head.

Without question the rich masque suits, specially designed by Inigo Jones and others, must have had their influence upon the public stage. Perhaps the "common players" may, on occasion, have been able to obtain from the Court some garments which, once used, were regarded as no longer valuable. The design for Floods (Fig. 154) in *Chloridia* (1631) reminds us at once of the kingly figure in the *Titus Andronicus* illustration (Fig. 152), while that of a knight masquer in *Oberon* (Fig. 155) gives an idea of the dress *à la romaine*. Other designs, such as those reproduced in the volume of masque-drawings published by the Malone and Walpole Societies, may well be studied in a similar manner. We may imagine that the actors in the public theatres were togged out in finery, which, if not quite so rich, was of the same general character. Court and theatre, we must remember, were closely bound together in Elizabeth's day; Puritan sentiment drew them even nearer in the times of the Stuarts who followed her.

FIG. 155. COSTUME OF A KNIGHT MASQUER IN "OBERON" (1611). DESIGN BY INIGO JONES
This is a typical example of the fanciful, semi-Romanized costume of the seventeenth century.
From the drawing in the possession of the Duke of Devonshire.
Photo Victoria and Albert Museum.

137

CHAPTER VIII

THEATRES OF FRANCE AND ITALY (EIGHTEENTH CENTURY)

(i) GENERAL MOVEMENTS

EXPERIMENTATION in scenic design and in theatrical structure did not, of course, cease with Serlio, Sabbatini, and Jones. Constantly France and Italy were endeavouring to achieve something fresh and new, now planning new auditoria, now devising fresh scenic effects. In general we may say that the movement after 1650 was all in the direction of machines and of changing settings. Palladio became out of date, and Serlio definitely antiquated. Everything was rendered more gorgeous and more spectacular in spite of that pseudo-classic movement which produced a Racine in Paris and an Addison in London. In the French capital Giacomo Torelli till 1660 worked wonders with his teeming brain, and his place was promptly filled by Gaspare Vigarani, a native of Reggio, who called to his aid the services of his son, Carlo. Under his direction rose the great Salle des Machines, the stage of which was 32 feet wide at the proscenium opening and no less than 132 feet deep. There wonderful effects were secured, the immense size of the stage permitting the use of machines as large as 40 feet wide by 60 feet long. There appeared some of those spectacles which were eagerly copied by English managers of the Re-

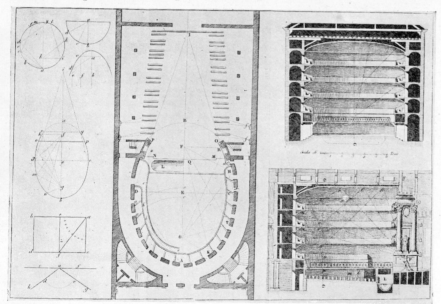

Fig. 156. PLAN OF A THEATRE ACCORDING TO THE PRINCIPLES OF OPTICS AND ACOUSTICS

From Patté (1830).

storation.[1] In Italy the Bibienas carried on earlier traditions, evolving richer and richer settings, until by the eighteenth century the theatres had risen to a height of splendour never known before.

It is impossible here to discuss all the varied aspects of theatrical art in the late seventeenth and eighteenth centuries, but some general notes may be made on theatres that were typical or peculiar, and on the main tendencies which may be traced throughout the scenic art of the eighteenth century. For this purpose it may be well to start with a set of plans for a theatre designed by Andrea Pozzo (Fig. 173). This was published in 1692, but its composition must be

[1] *Infra*, p. 165.

138

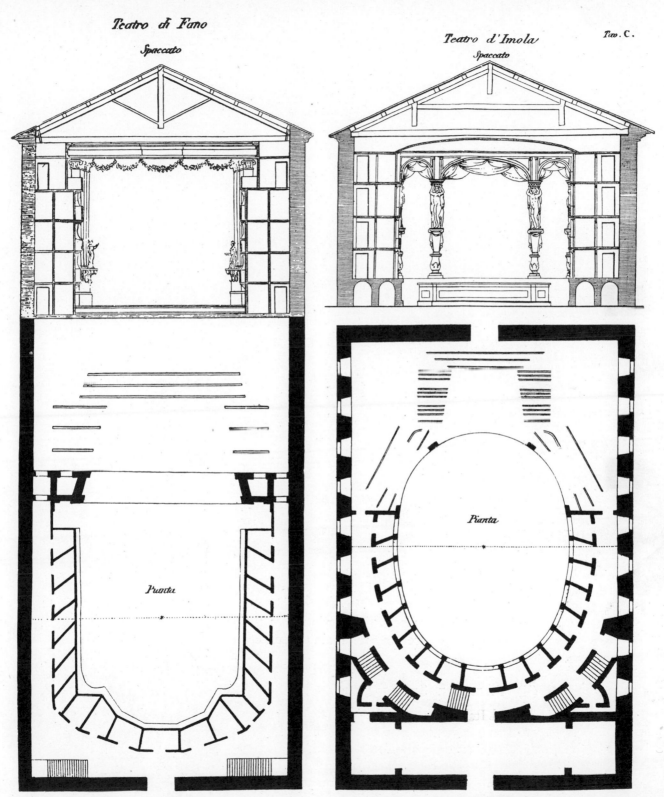

Fig. 157. PLAN AND PROSCENIUM OF THE
TEATRO DI FANO

Fig. 158. PLAN AND PROSCENIUM OF THE
TEATRO D'IMOLA

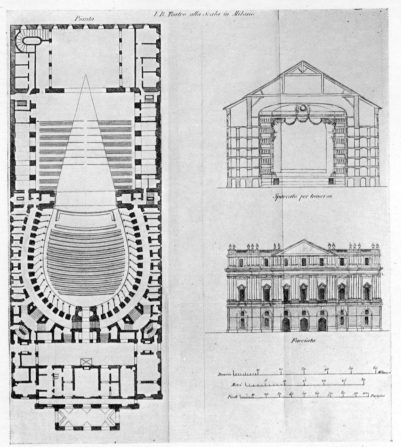

Fig. 159. PLAN OF THE TEATRO ALLA SCALA AT MILAN

of a considerably earlier date. The importance of these plans lies in the fact that they represent what may be regarded as the norm of a late seventeenth-century Italian playhouse, that from which deviations were made, both as regards seating accommodation and as regards setting, in the search for the ideal. The auditorium, it will be noted, is almost a semicircle, while at the same time the seats are arranged, not Roman fashion in a sloping *cavea*, but in a series of five galleries divided into sections by pillars or partitions. On the stage itself there is a set of six side-wings placed obliquely to the

stage-front and decreasing in height as they reach the rear. Farther back are two sets of 'shutters' or cloths, with a space behind for still further and more elaborate perspective effects. On this model the scenic artists worked, now altering the shape of the auditorium, now moving the wings parallel with the stage-front, now attempting built-up designs. With Pozzo's theatre in our mind we may turn to our selected and representative designs for the purpose of gaining some idea concerning the main tendencies of the time.

(ii) THEATRE STRUCTURE

During this period Italy still gave the lead to the artists of other countries. Experimentation there undoubtedly was more active than in France, Germany, or England, and even when, as in Russia, royal money was spent lavishly on theatrical productions, it was to Italy that the managers sent for scenic talent. This experimentation, naturally, takes many forms ; but for our purposes it will be convenient to consider it in so far as it concerns the two parts of the play-

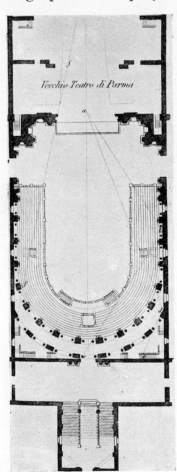

Fig. 160. PLAN OF THE TEATRO FARNESE AT PARMA

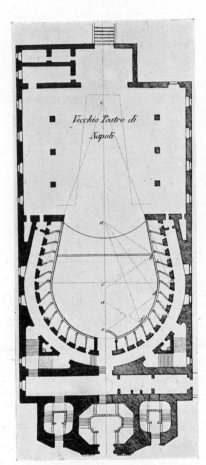

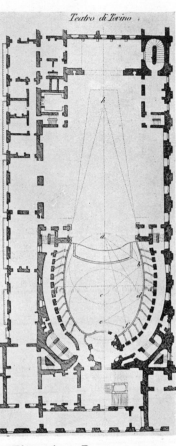

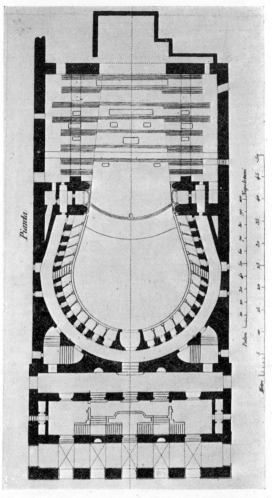

Fig. 161. Plan of the Old Theatre at Naples

Fig. 162. Plan of the Teatro di Torino

Fig. 163. Plan of the Teatro S. Carlo at Naples

house—the auditorium and the stage. Some artists bent all their energies toward the elaboration of the setting; others devoted themselves to the development of machinery; still others strove to construct such seating arrangements as would best aid the spectators in their viewing of the marvels displayed beyond the proscenium arch.

Obviously there are many difficulties which face an architect who would plan a theatre. He has not only to provide adequate seating accommodation for what is frequently a large audience; he has to enable that audience both to hear and to see what passes on the stage. Sometimes the double aim baffles the artist. One man will design a theatre of such proportions that at least one section of the audience cannot see part of the stage; another will construct a playhouse in which only one word out of three can be heard by the spectators in the farther parts of the house. Still, whatever mistakes were made, we can see how surely the generations of experience were teaching the architects and how, out of that experience, new and better forms were being derived.

The semicircular, or Greek, auditorium was often found unsatisfactory, sometimes because of the fact that it did not seat sufficient spectators, sometimes because the plot of land on which the playhouse was being built demanded an oblong and not a round, square, or octagonal outside wall. In general the main tendency was toward the lengthened auditorium, the precise

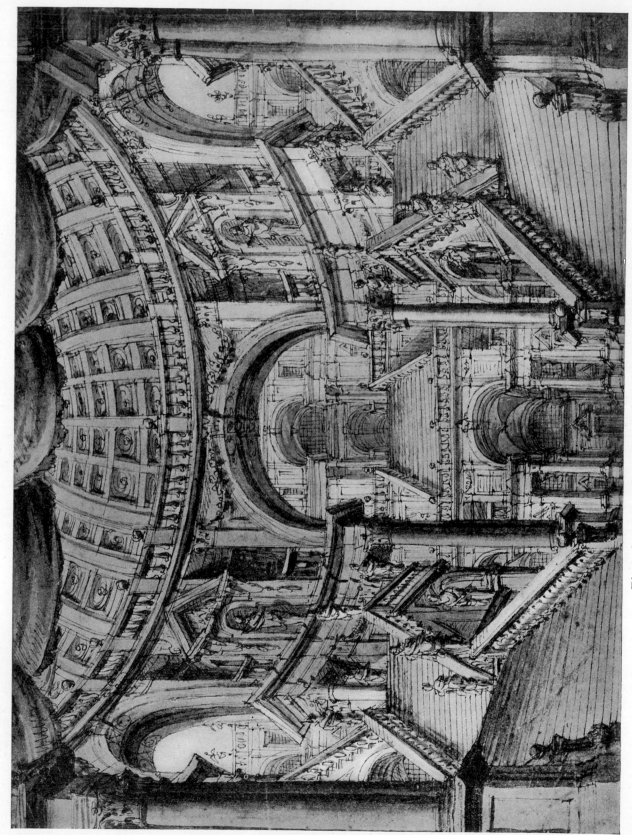

Fig. 164. Theatrical Design by F. da Bibiena
From the original in the Victoria and Albert Museum.

shape taking different forms in the hands of various architects; sometimes with straight galleries running at right angles to the stage-front, sometimes with ovoid galleries, sometimes with an auditorium formed like a horseshoe. The ovoid auditorium is shown clearly enough in the ideal design of Patté (Fig. 156) and in the Teatro di Torino (Fig. 162) with a variant form in the Teatro d'Imola (Fig. 158). The same model dictated the structure of the famous Teatro Tor di Nona, built at Rome in 1671. Other architects preferred the straight-sided type. In the Teatro di Fano (Fig. 157) the galleries run back parallel with the outside walls, and are joined

Fig. 165. Theatrical Design by Giuseppe Bibiena

one to another by a fanciful series of curves and angles. The Teatro Farnese at Parma (Fig. 160), as we have seen, has the same general form save that the two side galleries are gradually arched round at the back of the theatre, the general shape of the auditorium being thus a semicircle with the seats carried forward toward the stage at right angles to the diameter. The horseshoe form was also popular. It is to be seen in the Teatro alla Scala at Milan (Fig. 159), in the Old Theatre at Naples (Fig. 161) and in the Teatro S. Carlo at Naples (Fig. 163). In many of these plans it is evident that the lines of sight were not of the best, and many architects endeavoured to remedy their defects. Most interesting of all these devices is that which we find utilized by Ferdinando Bibiena in the Teatro Ducale Nuovo at Mantua, by Francesco da Bibiena in the Verona Teatro Filharmonico, and by G. A. Falcone in the Teatro Falcone at Genoa, whereby the boxes were made to project slightly in strict order so that necks should not be strained in watching the pirouettes of the dancer or the wonders of the changing scene. In this and other ways, in one design after

K

another, with wider or shallower galleries, with semicircular curves, and ellipses, and straight lines, the architects showed in what respects they were seeking for their Platonic ideal, the perfect theatre.

While noting the various experiments in auditorium structure, we may pay some attention too to the arrangement of the proscenium arch. In general, we may say that three styles attracted the artists. The first of these demands that the proscenium pillars should stand at the extreme corners of the stage, but that there should recede obliquely a kind of false façade which leads the

Fig. 166. Theatrical Design by Giuseppe Bibiena

eye directly back to the scenes themselves. Such an arrangement is clearly shown in Patté's ideal theatre (Fig. 156), in the Teatro di Fano (Fig. 157), and in the Teatro Farnese at Parma (Fig. 160). The second utilized only the proscenium arch itself, without any recessed façade, providing, as is obvious, the model for the typical theatres of to-day. This is illustrated in the Teatro alla Scala (Fig. 159), in the Old Theatre at Naples (Fig. 161), and in the Teatro di Torino (Fig. 162). Finally, there is the peculiar device embodied in the stage arrangements of the Teatro d'Imola (Fig. 158). Here the proscenium pillars appear in front, but the arch is carried round semicircularly and supported on two other pillars further back stage, thus providing not one complete arch but three arches. Behind that in the centre the chief setting appears, but flats and a back-cloth are placed also behind each of the other two, so that even those spectators at the sides of the house may have something wherewith to feast their eyes.

It is clear that each of these three styles derives directly from the original Teatro Olimpico, erected centuries before by Palladio. The three main openings have been preserved most completely in the Imola design, but the formal proscenium arch shown in the Teatro Farnese and in later theatres reveals only a simplification of the triple doorways of the Vicenza playhouse. It is noticeable, however, that the later architects of the Continent almost all moved those archways forward, so that the stage action took place behind, and not before, the façade. In other words there is hardly any relic of an 'apron' in the Continental theatres; that 'apron,' inherited in the Restoration from the Elizabethan platform stage, formed the principal point of difference between the playhouses of England and those of Italy and France. Fully a century

Fig. 167. Theatrical Design by Giuseppe Bibiena

earlier than in London the Continental actors became part of the scenic display, not standing forward, as in Drury Lane, with what was essentially but a decoration, a background, behind them.[1]

(iii) Scenic Design

By far the most important feature of late seventeenth-century and eighteenth-century theatrical endeavour is concerned with the efforts of the scene designers. Opera had become a fully established form of dramatic art, and through the opera came those tremendous architectural fantasies which we associate with this period. The secret of side-wings and flats run in grooves had by this time been fully learned, and numerous changes of setting could be easily secured in the course of one play. In 1671 the *Dario* of Beverini had no fewer than fifteen different

[1] It is obvious that on the Continent the whole of the original Olympic " proscenium " was moved forward to the front of the stage; in England it remained for a century and a half at the rear of the actors.

scenes, and this example can be paralleled by scores of others. These side-wings, first placed obliquely on the stage, were soon set in their accustomed modern position, parallel to the front

Fig. 168. THEATRICAL DESIGN BY GIUSEPPE BIBIENA
From Corrado Ricci, *I Bibiena*.

of the stage, and were also fitted with mechanical apparatus by which they could be drawn up to the flies as well as run off at the sides.

The age teems with a host of men who became famous for their work in the theatres—Gaspare Vigarani (1586–1663), Giovanni Servandoni (1695–1766), Giacomo Torelli da Fano (1608–78), and many others, above whom tower the well-known members of the Bibiena family. Taking his name from his birthplace, Giovanni Maria Galli (1619–65), called Bibiena, first laid the foundations of an artistry which became the hereditary property of his descendants. His sons, Ferdinando (1657–1743) and Francesco (1659–1739), both devoted themselves to scenic work, as did his grandsons, Antonio (1700–74) and Giuseppe (1696–1756), and his great-grandsons, Alessandro (died 1760) and Carlo (born 1725). The two last-mentioned aided in carrying the work of the

family beyond the confines of Italy, the former producing his most characteristic settings in Germany, and the latter serving theatres in that country as well as in Holland and Russia. The Bibiena style has become well known. Employing freely the heavily decorated model of baroque architecture, the various members of the family produced a series of scenic designs which can only amaze through their stupendous grandeur and charm, through their artistic proportions and innate beauty. The majestic columns and spacious proportions shown in Fig. 164 are thoroughly typical of their work, as is the bold massing of light and shade in the design of a city square in Fig. 165. Especially interesting are the engravings contained in a volume of *Architetture e Prospettive* (1740) by Giuseppe Bibiena. Examples of these are presented in Figs. 166 and 168. Particular notice should be taken of the manner in which a bold perspective is called into the service of scenic artistry.

Fig. 169. PROSCENIUM DESIGN BY F. DA BIBIENA
From Corrado Ricci, *op. cit.*

146

Fig. 170. Baroque Italian Design: Bibiena Family

From the original in the Victoria and Albert Museum.

Fig. 171. Theatrical Design attributed to the Bibiena Family

From the original in the Victoria and Albert Museum.

Fig. 172. Theatrical Design by F. da Bibiena

From the original in the Victoria and Albert Museum.

With these most valuable and interesting designs and plans may be considered the sketches for a theatre and flats given in Andrea Pozzo's *Prospettiva dei Pittori e Architetti* (vol. i, 1692; vol. ii, 1700). Fig. 173 has already been noted (see p. 138); Figs. 174 and 175 delineate typical settings.

THE DEVELOPMENT OF THE THEATRE

An important commentary too is provided in a volume of designs executed by the architect F. Juvarra when he was superintendent of the private theatre in Rome belonging to Cardinal Ottoboni.[1] This volume of sketches and thumbnail plans, which is preserved in the Victoria and Albert Museum, not only shows clearly the inventiveness and beauty apparent in baroque scene-designing in the eighteenth century, but provides us with some exceedingly valuable information. We note, first of all, as in the Bibiena designs, how many supposedly modern developments in theatrical art are but revivals of eighteenth-century endeavour. Thus the steps, of which so much has been said of recent years, appear in at least half of the settings of the Bibiena family and are freely used in Juvarra's efforts. Furthermore, there is a suggestion in at least one group

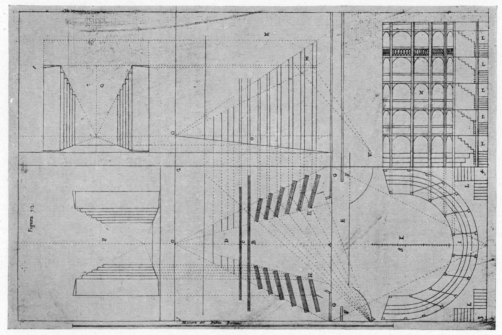

Fig. 173. Plans and Cross-section of a Theatre by Andrea Pozzo
This shows clearly the evolution of the modern playhouse with balconies and flats.

of these sketches that the permanent set such as has been used in our own days was frequently employed by this almost forgotten artist of eighteenth-century Italy. A glance at Fig. 176 will show that the archway presented in the large design is nothing but a permanent set of this kind, alterations being made *behind* the arch to accord with the requirements of the acts of the drama.

Having glanced at these designs, we may pause for a moment to consider how such sketches were realized in actual concrete form on the boards of the stage. As we look at them we think of vast structures solidly built, or at least so manufactured as to give the appearance of solidity. The dreams of scenic artists, however, do not always find full and adequate realization when they are translated into terms of practical stage production, and we must regretfully believe that most of these grandiose effects were carried out with flat wings skilfully painted to simulate reality. At its best the theatrical set of this time could give the illusion of solidity only when it was viewed, in the rather dim light of candles and of lamps, from one particular position on the orchestra floor where was set the chair of state reserved for royalty. From other points in the auditorium there was bound to be a distortion and an awkward view of borders and flats. Juvarra's stage-plan in Fig. 177 indicates

[1] Filippo Juvarra (1684–1735) has hitherto remained almost unknown as a scenic artist. Since the writing of this book, however, several others of his designs have been reproduced, notably by Mr Gordon Craig in *The Architectural Review*. None of these have the exceedingly valuable scene-plans given in the sketches here.

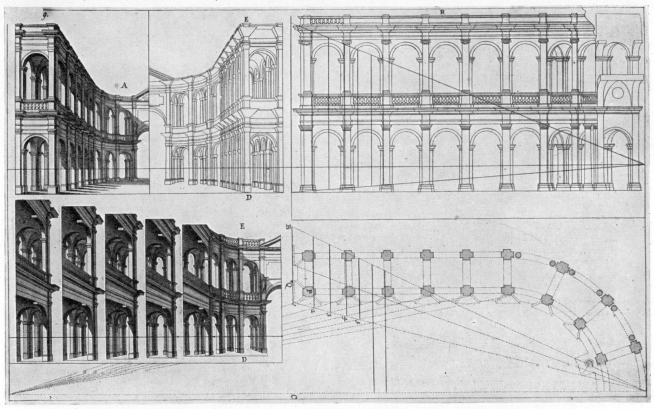

Fig. 174. Theatrical Design by Andrea Pozzo

Fig. 175. Theatrical Design by Andrea Pozzo

Fig. 176. Theatrical Design by F. Juvarra

Note should be taken of the permanent setting used apparently with a variety of back-cloths.
From the original in the Victoria and Albert Museum.

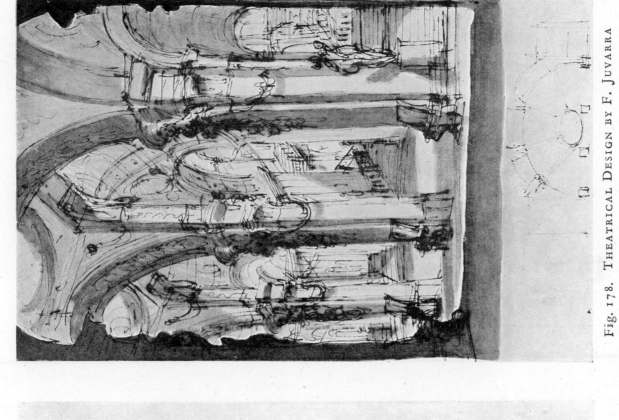

Fig. 178. Theatrical Design by F. Juvarra

Fig. 177. Theatrical Design by F. Juvarra

Note the plan for the scenery immediately below the sketch.
From the original in the Victoria and Albert Museum.

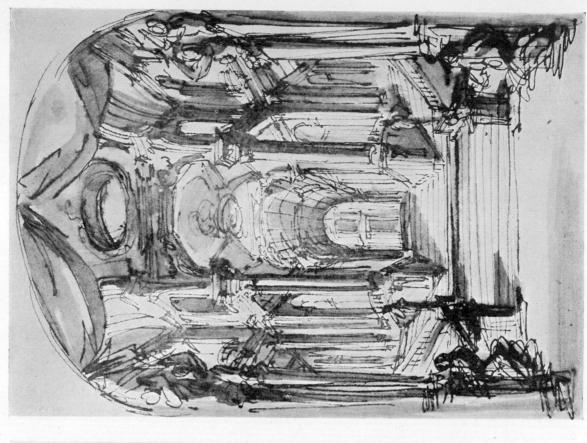

Fig. 180. Theatrical Design by F. Juvarra

"Ingresso nobile della Scala del Palasso Imperiale."

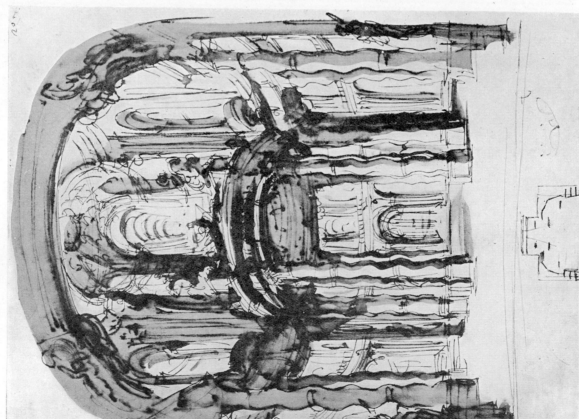

Fig. 179. Theatrical Design by F. Juvarra

Fig. 181. Theatrical Design by Piranesi.

Fig. 182. Theatrical Design by Piranesi

clearly the common method employed. This lofty and richly ornamented palace interior was to be represented by six sets of wings placed in parallel grooves, together with a back-shutter seen through a cut-out. A similar planning is apparent in Fig. 179. That occasionally something in the way of built-up effects in the foreground was employed may be suggested in another design, Fig. 178.

Fig. 183. A PRISON SCENE BY PIRANESI

There the front pillars are indicated 'in the round,' and one might suspect that the stairway on the right was practicable. To assert dogmatically that such devices were used would be somewhat hazardous, particularly in view of the fact that no provision seems to have been made in contemporary theatres for the adequate removal of heavy structures such as these must have been, but the possibility at least remains that on occasion the regular use of flat wings in grooves was supplemented by other means.

The architectural style, with its rich baroque or rococo ornaments, was destined to dominate the Italian —and, through the Italian, the European—stages for over a century. Classicism delighted in it, and the florid styles pleased those who sought for spectacle. Naturally the Bibienas were the inspirers of many a succeeding scenographer. Another family tradition was established by Bernardino Galliari of Andorno (1707–94), whose brother, Fabrizio, and nephews, Giovanni and Giuseppe, carried on a style very similar to theirs. Then comes Gian Battista Piranesi (1720–78), of Venice, even richer of genius, lover of bold light and shade, whose fame was to pass far and wide over Europe. The great courtyard shown in Fig. 182 depends upon the pioneer efforts of the Bibienas, yet it is stronger, more powerful, than the majority of their efforts. Magnificent imagination he has, and can see, as no preceding scenic artist could, the impression that may be conveyed to a spectator by dark near forms with light beyond (Fig. 181). His mind, too, turns occasionally to that which might almost be called romantic, as in his prison scene (Fig. 183), with its gloomy forms and dim-cast gleams of sunlight. Nor was the architectural style killed with the coming of the new realist and romantic movement. Pietro Gonzaga (died 1831), the student of Canaletto, who created such a *furore* in the Imperial Theatre of Russia, merely carries the architecture outside, loving to show an open landscape backed by some towered and mountain-set Italian city. In the hands of others the Gothic arch came to supersede the Roman, but the same lofty columns, the same vistas of palace court remained. Even the Egyptians were brought into the service of the theatre. Both romanticists and classicists united in this common love, and for years the stage of Italy, as well as the stages of nearly all European capitals, was dominated by buildings now in Roman, now in rococo, and now in Gothic style.

CHAPTER IX

RESTORATION THEATRES

(i) STAGE HISTORY

THESE impressive and monumental baroque designs had, of course, their influence in London, but it is a strange fact that while English scenic endeavour up to the time of Inigo Jones kept well abreast of Continental example, after 1660 it lagged lamentably behind, and has not even yet recovered from a position of inferiority which it has thus occupied for two and a half centuries. Experiment went on, and goes on, here as abroad, but there has been lacking in our theatres that tremendous artistic interest and enthusiasm which is so well seen in the designs of Bibiena and of Piranese. An Italian opera at the Haymarket must have been but a poor thing when compared with productions in Rome or Vienna; a Garrick performance, brilliant as it might be in acting, can have presented little that merited comparison with French, German, and even Russian efforts in scenic design. It is this period of often imitative work which now it is our business to consider.

For all practical purposes we may say that acting ceased in 1642 and was not resumed until the restoration of Charles II in 1660. This statement, of course, requires modification. There were sporadic attempts made during those eighteen years to revive plays in London. In the provinces apparently performances still were given. "Drolls," cut down from Elizabethan dramas, were presented with fair frequency. An occasional masque made its appearance. Above all, on May 23, 1656, D'Avenant arranged at Rutland House in Aldersgate an "Entertainment" followed by *The Siege of Rhodes*, given first at Rutland House and later at the Cockpit or Phoenix. This play, in *stilo recitativo*, gave English audiences their first taste of Italian opera, that type of play which, both in France and Italy, had done so much for the encouraging of scenic effect.

A year or two later it was clear to all that the Stuarts would return. The actors gathered together once more, and playing recommenced in earnest. At first, naturally, the old theatres were utilized. The Red Bull, a house famous for rant in the pre-Commonwealth days, was used as early as 1659; the Cockpit was open the year following, as was Salisbury Court. In July of the latter year the King issued patents (or monopolies) to D'Avenant and Thomas Killigrew, thus establishing those two major theatres in London which endured, with occasional rivalry from lesser authorized or unauthorized houses, till the first half of the nineteenth century. The Killigrew, or Royal, troupe started first on November 8, 1660, at a converted indoor tennis court in Vere Street, Clare Market. A Theatre Royal was opened at Bridges Street, Covent Garden, on May 7, 1663. This playhouse was burnt to the ground on January 25, 1672, and a new Theatre Royal in Drury Lane was opened in 1674. The other band of actors, under D'Avenant, known as the Duke of York's company, after playing at Salisbury Court, settled down in a new theatre at Lincoln's Inn Fields, a scene they abandoned only when a theatre at Dorset Garden was opened on November 9, 1671. There is no need here to enter into details concerning the various minor companies which so complicate the theatrical history of this time; rather may we take these new houses as typical, and, along with them, the Court theatre at Whitehall where performances of English and Continental plays were frequently given.

(ii) Webb's Designs for "The Siege of Rhodes"

Happily, a number of drawings and prints aid us in our survey of Restoration stage endeavour. Among the various relics preserved of Webb's efforts are a plan and section of Rutland House, together with five scenes for *The Siege of Rhodes*. The plans (Figs. 184 and 185) show a small

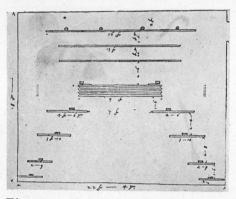

Fig. 184. Plan of the Rutland House Stage for "The Siege of Rhodes" (1656), by John Webb

From the Lansdowne MSS. (1171).

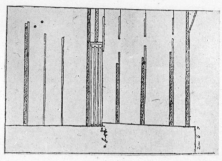

Fig. 185. Section of the Rutland House Stage for "The Siege of Rhodes" (1656), by John Webb

From the Lansdowne MSS. (1171).

stage, similar to some which Jones had contrived for his masques, with a fixed architectural proscenium and a series of three rocky side-wings (Fig. 186), which, as in *Florimène*, were allowed to stand throughout the play (Fig. 144). Then follow a series of back-shutters, showing the city of Rhodes and the fleet of Solyman, the outside of the walls and a "releive" of Solyman's pavilion (Figs. 187 and 188). In the last apparently two side-wings representing pillars were drawn out to reveal the chair of state behind. It is evident that these scenes follow very closely on the masque practice of earlier years, and display a type of scene-shifting at once crude and unsatisfactory. The figures painted on the back-shutters, it may be noted, continued to appear even into the eighteenth century, presenting the peculiar phenomenon of stationary persons on the flat contrasted with the living actors on the stage itself.

(iii) Webb's Designs for "Mustapha"

Of equal interest are the plans and sketches prepared by Webb for a performance at Whitehall of Orrery's *Mustapha*. The first (Fig. 189) is a "Plane of the sceanes for the Queens Ballett in the Hall at Whitehall 1665 To bee vsed also for masques & Playes. 1. The Tragedy of Mustapha." It shows a stage with what is evidently a false proscenium, the supports of which are 3 feet 8 inches wide, leaving a proscenium opening of 25 feet. The width of the hall is evidently 39 feet 6 inches between wall and wall. Behind the false proscenium are set the side-scenes, four in number; these run in grooves, with separate series for each of the scene-changes (Fig. 190). The lowest is 3 feet 5 inches long, the rest 5 feet 3 inches, 6 feet 8 inches, and 6 feet 6 inches. A varying space of 3 feet to 3 feet 6 inches separates each pair, and they are arranged

Fig. 186. Proscenium and Permanent Side-wings for "The Siege of Rhodes" (1656). Design by John Webb

From the original in the possession of the Duke of Devonshire.

in the usual triangular formation. The upper set have 13 feet between them, and are placed so that the shutters are 17 feet from the front of the stage. All these scenes are arranged on a heavily raked stage, but at this point, 17 feet from the front, as in the Rutland House design, comes a drop with a flat stage receding from the audience. A peculiarity of these designs is that the " Musick " was set on a sloping platform resting on the two back supports, rising from 12 feet 8 inches above the stage level to a point in the back wall 14 feet high. This orchestra was concealed by a long sky-cloth, and the audience must have looked underneath the improvised gallery at the back-shutters shown in " relieve." The sketch for a scene of *Mustapha*, given in *British Drama*, shows the arrangement well. The orchestra platform would come just at the cross-line immediately below the cornice of the back pillars.

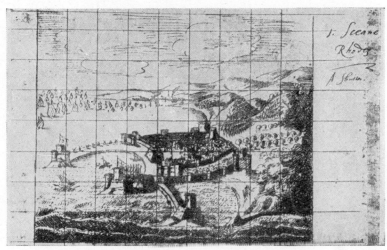

It is perfectly evident that the stage for *The Siege of Rhodes* and the stage for *Mustapha* were, save for the difference in size, planned on the same lines, while both go back for inspiration to the designs of Inigo Jones and to Italian practice. The columns, it may be noted, with the dome at the rear, remind us somewhat of late seventeenth-century baroque settings, so perfectly delineated by the Bibienas.[1]

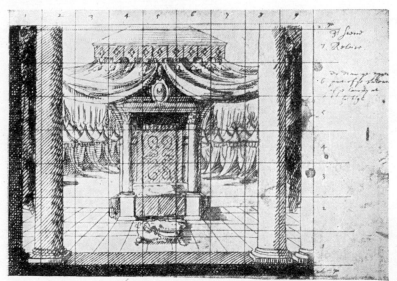

FIG. 188. DESIGN FOR A "RELEIVE" IN "THE SIEGE OF RHODES," SCENE III, BY JOHN WEBB
From the original in the possession of the Duke of Devonshire.

(iv) PLANS FOR THEATRES BY CHRISTOPHER WREN

Recently there have been discovered, at All Souls College, Oxford, four designs executed by Sir Christopher Wren during the Restoration period. One of these is almost certainly a cross-section of the Theatre Royal in Drury Lane, and may be considered separately; the other three, unfortunately, cannot be assigned to any particular place or to any particular year. Their interest, however, is great, because they show once more the keen attention which was being paid, in England as on the Continent, to theatrical architecture.

[1] *Supra*, p. 143.

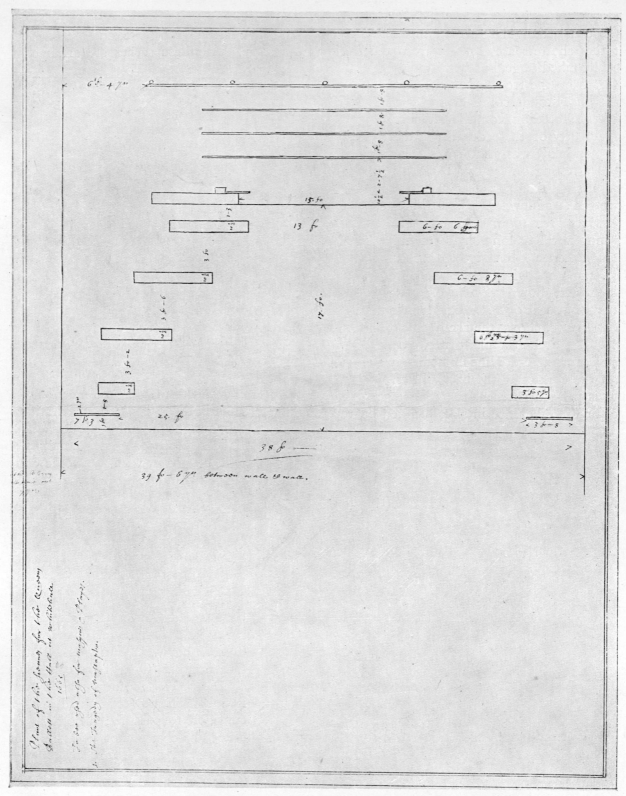

Fig. 189. PLAN OF THE WHITEHALL STAGE FOR "MUSTAPHA" (1665), BY JOHN WEBB
From the original in the possession of the Duke of Devonshire.

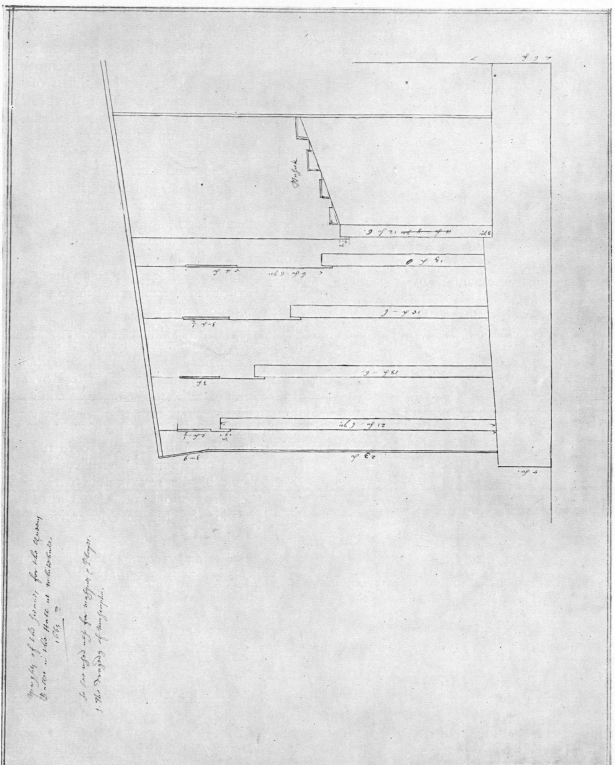

FIG. 190. SECTION OF THE WHITEHALL STAGE FOR "MUSTAPHA" (1665), BY JOHN WEBB

From the original in the possession of the Duke of Devonshire.

By far the most interesting of the three unlocated sketches is that shown in Fig. 191. A plan, a rough cross-section, and a fragmentary elevation of this playhouse are given to us. The auditorium has two galleries set with seats "in segments of circles all struck from the same centre," the spectators being thus given an excellent view of the stage. The segment which marks the seventh row of seats is carried round over the stage space but is cut at two-thirds of the radius by a straight line, which, as we can see, marks the proscenium arch. There is thus left a wide apron bounded on each side by the curving lines of the circle. The cross-section shows that the pit sloped up rapidly to the first tier of boxes and was carried at another steep angle to the second tier. The apron itself was level, but the stage behind, raised above the apron level at a line a few feet behind the proscenium arch, was raked gently. From the sketches which accompany the plans there would seem to be no fewer than four doors at each side under the boxes placed on the apron, unless two of the apertures, which seem to be doors, were in reality stage boxes. It appears just possible, taking into account the fact that the plot of ground which Killigrew leased in 1663 was 112 feet by 59 feet, that these designs were executed for the first Theatre Royal in Bridges Street, although it must be confessed that there is no evidence to show that Wren was in any way connected with the architecture of that house. Still, the plans would roughly fit the space of ground to be filled, and the arrangement of the seats would correspond with the descriptions of Count Lorenzo Magalotti and of M. de Monconys. The latter declares that

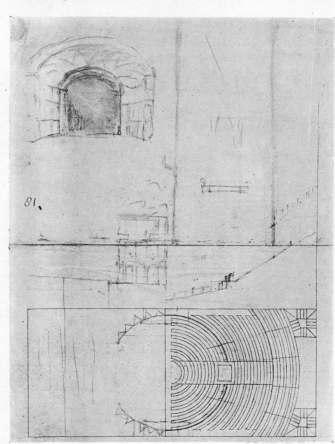

Fig. 191. Theatre Plan by Sir Christopher Wren

From the original at All Souls College, Oxford.

> Tous les bancs du parterre où toutes les personnes de condition se mettent aussi, sont rangez en amphithéâtre, les uns plus hauts que les autres.[1]

If Wren's plan were for the first Theatre Royal, his pit would undoubtedly have seemed to a visitor to be "en amphithéâtre" with the broad sweep of the benches and the soaring floor of the house.

The second sketch (Fig. 192) is much less interesting. Here is shown an almost completely semicircular auditorium with a broad apron framed by what no doubt are two doors on each side. Behind is a square stage space. More finished in detail is Fig. 193, obviously an experiment in design. A highly unsatisfactory auditorium is arranged in an oval shape with eleven sections. There is a rectangular apron and an exceedingly narrow proscenium opening, with, in the rear, a deep, wide stage. Barely one-half of the spectators in this theatre could have had a view of any scenic effects behind, and some could have seen only the front portion of the apron.

---

[1] "All the benches of the parterre where even the people of quality sit are arranged as an amphitheatre, one row higher than another."

Obviously the design is one unsuitable for an ordinary public playhouse, although it may have been made for some projected Court theatre. Its detail and finish suggest that it was more than an academic exercise.

(v) Wren's Design for Drury Lane

Finally we come to what is by far the most important of the four Wren drawings. This (Fig. 194) is a carefully executed section of a theatre 112 feet in length, no doubt, as Mr Hamilton Bell has suggested, an original drawing for the new Theatre Royal in Drury Lane. The general arrangement of the house is made fully apparent in the sketch, but a summary may be given of its principal features. A slightly raked apron extends 17 feet from the proscenium

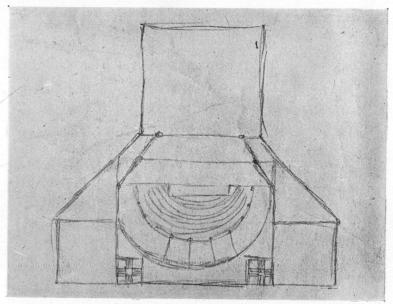

Fig. 192. Theatre Plan by Sir Christopher Wren
From the original at All Souls College, Oxford.

arch, leaving about 15 feet of stage depth behind. In this back portion of the stage provision is made for four side-wings (or flats) and there are three grooves behind for "shutters." Over the apron on each side are two boxes, beneath which are two doors. The pit slopes upward as in Fig. 191, and there is provision for two tiers of 'boxes,' four on each side being enclosed, the rest arranged merely with dividing pillars. A top gallery faces the stage, but is not carried round the sides of the house.

Unfortunately, we possess no print of this time showing the interior of the theatre, except a highly fantastic frontispiece to the opera of *Ariane* (1674) which shows us a front view of the proscenium and of the apron (Fig. 195). In the *Ariane* design the only part which seems realistic is the proscenium pillars on each side. The apron is far too small, and the conventional buildings were most certainly not solid as they seem to be in the engraving, but merely

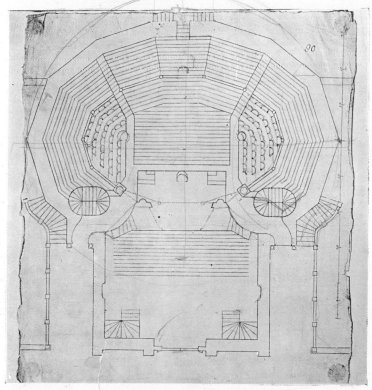

FIG. 193. THEATRE PLAN BY SIR CHRISTOPHER WREN
From the original at All Souls College, Oxford.

simulated by a series of side-wings. Still, taken with Sir Christopher Wren's sketch, it aids us in our endeavour to picture the interior of a theatre which had such a distinguished history, which echoed to the voice of a Betterton and a Garrick, and in which were produced so many comedies which to-day we treasure for their incisiveness and refinement of style.

(vi) THE DUKE'S THEATRE IN DORSET GARDEN

Of the Duke's Theatre we have no plan, but we do possess, in its stead, an exceedingly instructive series of engravings published in 1673 with the text of Settle's *The Empress of*

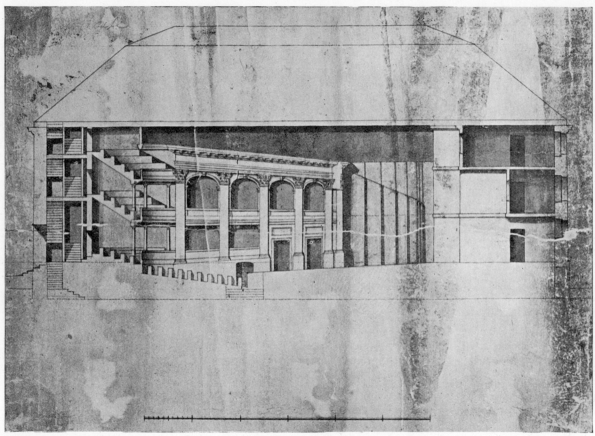

Fig. 194. SECTION OF A THEATRE, PROBABLY DRURY LANE. DESIGN BY
SIR CHRISTOPHER WREN
From the original at All Souls College, Oxford.

Morocco. All of these engravings have at various times been reproduced, but perhaps the collected group of them here may be convenient for reference (Figs. 197 and 198). Each design shows a scene from the play, enclosed in a rather realistic framework—a delineation of the proscenium of the theatre. The first thing that strikes us is the elaborate decorations which made this theatre at Dorset Garden the most gorgeous of its time. Instead of Corinthian (or other) pillars, the proscenium arch is decorated with a formal pattern, and at the top there is a kind of half roof which may be a relic of the "heavens" of the early part of the century. Above this two figures, evidently representing Thalia and Melpomene, stand at each side of a curtained window with leaded sashes opening inward. Similar windows appear in the curves to the right and left of the emblematic statues. On the ledges underneath these two side windows are pictured a drum, a trumpet, and a violin, whence we may conclude that these were the windows of the music room.   The drawing cuts off all but a few feet of the apron, but enough is left to show the edge of the stage boxes and the beginnings of the pro-scenium doors.   Save for the presence of the music room, the arrangements were evidently not very different from those obtaining at the Theatre Royal.

FIG. 195.   FRONTISPIECE TO "ARIANE" (1674), AS PLAYED AT DRURY LANE

Countless references there are to the gorgeous appearance of this new house.   Its managers pro-fessed that they were but seeking the good of the public; the managers of the rival Theatre Royal retorted by "odious" references to show and spectacle and meretricious splendour.   After a time,

Teütsche
Schawbühne.
1655.

FIG. 196.   A GERMAN SETTING OF 1655
To be compared with the frontispiece to *Ariane* (Fig. 195).
Here the side-wings are clearly shown, and note should be taken of the candelabra over the stage-front.
From an exemplar in the Darmstadt Landesbibliothek.

of course, both theatres indulged in elaborate effects, but it was Dorset Garden theatre which at first led the way.   In more respects than one it was the representative in London of the Parisian Salle des Machines, for, not only did the directors of the theatre look to the Continent for general inspiration, but they actually took or copied scenery which had been devised in Paris.   The operas produced by Dryden and Shadwell and D'Urfey all had for their object the utilization of effects of the more spec-tacular kind, the description of which, with the many machines, cloud-breakings, and chair-sinkings, remind us irresistibly of descriptions of operatic performances at Bologna or at Paris.

(vii) TYPICAL SCENES AND THEATRICAL CONVENTIONS

It must not be supposed, of course, that for ordinary plays new scenery was painted.   Both the Theatre Royal and the Duke's playhouse had sets of stock flats which must have been used over and over again.   Glancing through the texts of the plays themselves, we realize that conventionalism reigned supreme.   An opera might show surprising terraces and silver moons and poetic hells, but for tragedy there was the Grove, the Palace, the Temple; for comedy the Room, the Hall, the Garden, and the scene of London life.   The Mall,

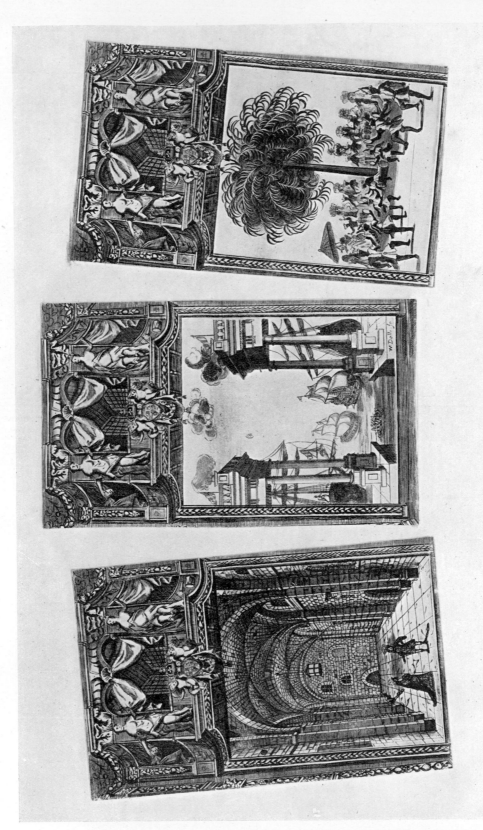

Fig. 197.   Three Settings in "The Empress of Morocco" (1673)

St. James's Park, the New Spring Garden—all appear among the lighter plays of the period. The management must have constantly added to these stock scenes, but, working with a repertory of constantly changing plays, they obviously could not indulge in fresh scenery for each production, and frequently a spectacle from the opera, painted by an Aggas, a Streeter, a Stevenson, or a Robinson, may have been dragged in, tarnished and tawdry, for an ordinary show.

All these scenes, as has been noted above, were arranged by means of flats and back-shutters. The grooves for the former could serve for side-wings or else for scenes which ran together in the centre and thus gave an opportunity for the setting of a full-stage effect. In most

Fig. 198. TWO SETTINGS IN "THE EMPRESS OF MOROCCO" (1673)

of the plays of the time we can easily work out the scene plan in this manner, front stage and full sets alternating in regular series. The fashion was set which for many years ruled dominant in the theatre. The curtain was hardly ever employed during the performance of a play, merely rising at the commencement of the action and falling at the close, so that the scene-shifting took place in full view of the spectators. It is obvious that, as the lights could not be lowered so easily as the electric globes in a modern playhouse, the audience was, at each change, rapidly rushed from locality to locality. Still further, actors could remain on the front apron while an alteration in setting was made behind so that they, without moving a step, had passed from one place to another. In many plays we find that some characters are bidden to go out or to move "within the scene," that is to say, behind the proscenium arch. Another character or other characters step forward on to the apron. Then the flats click together in the middle, shutting off those who had gone "within" and transporting those on the apron to an entirely new setting. I am not aware that this convention obtained on the Continent; it seems to be a relic of Elizabethan practice, itself based on medieval traditions.

167

(viii) THE PROSCENIUM DOORS

It must have been observed that the typical Restoration playhouse differed from that of the Continent in that it possessed a wide and deep apron extending forward from the proscenium arch as far as the stage proper stretched behind.   It is undoubted that this apron is a relic of the Elizabethan platform stage, the apron corresponding to the platform even as the stage within or beyond the proscenium arch corresponded to the inner room revealed through the central

Fig. 199. MODEL OF DORSET GARDEN THEATRE BY HERBERT NORRIS
The setting is for a scene in Dryden's *All for Love*.

doorway. Just as in Italy the scene space developed out of the *periaktoi* set within the archways, so in England the scenic part of the stage developed from that room in which Shakespeare had shown Ferdinand and Miranda playing their amorous game at chess. The wide apron, however, made necessary a different technique for the actor. Clearly, a continual series of entrances and exits behind the proscenium arch would have been awkward, and accordingly there was retained that set of doors which had been typical of the Palladian theatre at Vicenza. There the arrangement of the scene wall had been rectangular. With Jones it became curved (Fig. 149).   In the Restoration theatre the four doors were relegated to the *versurae* placed in a curve round, or at right angles to, the proscenium arch. Through these doors the actors normally came and went, the entrances sometimes marking a definite locality (*e.g.* the outside door of a house), sometimes being merely conventional means of getting upon or off the stage. These proscenium doors, then, are among the most important features of the Restoration stage. As many references of the early nineteenth century show, they gave the actors a special style, so that there was almost a mutiny when it was proposed to cut them down. Lingering on in provincial playhouses to within living memory, they serve to mark out a distinct break between the normal theatre of the Continent and the typical London playhouse.

(ix) ACTORS AND ACTRESSES

For one other innovation the Restoration period is of importance. In Elizabethan days, as in classical Greece, all women's parts had been taken by boys. The Continent already had actresses in the late years of the sixteenth century, but a kind of Puritan conscience forbade their presence in London until the " Merry Monarch," Charles II, came to his own again. True, he had to profess that his authorizing of actresses arose out of a desire to promote morality in the theatre, but we may suspect that the wording of the warrant was more than a trifle cynical.

RESTORATION THEATRES

About 1661 the first woman actress—if we except Mrs Colman who sang the part of Ianthe in *The Siege of Rhodes* in 1656—appeared in the part of Desdemona with a prologue specially penned for her by the pageant-writer, Thomas Jordan. From this time on the boy-actor disappeared. Perhaps for the first few years actresses of talent were difficult to obtain, but soon a Mrs Davis with her nimble heels, a Nell Gwyn with her nimble tongue, a Mrs Barry with her tragic intensity, came to exercise a potent influence upon dramatic endeavour. Perhaps something of the new spirit which breathes through the comedy of manners comes from this source.

Both actresses and actors at this time were social figures of no mean importance. The society of a Betterton and a Harris was sought for by semi-courtiers such as Samuel Pepys, while a Nell Gwyn queened it at Whitehall. The audience of the Restoration period was, we must remember, small and select. Only two theatres were open from the early years of the age to 1682; from 1682 to 1695 one alone served the needs of London. As very often the actors could obtain 'houses' of a size barely sufficient to cover the cost of the candles, we may say that only the Court party, a comparatively small section of London's population, attended the playhouses. Elizabethan England had seen many public theatres open at one time in the metropolis, for then citizens as well as aristocrats patronized the performers. Now, however, Puritan sentiment prevailed among the middle classes, and the theatre was shunned by them because it breathed of that licence and flagrant immodesty which the gay Charles had brought back with him from France and Spain and Italy. In reality the Restoration playhouses were more akin in spirit to the strictly private theatres of Ferrara and of Paris than they were to their Elizabethan forerunners. A new type of aristocratic comedy and a new type of hopelessly heroic tragedy were the results. Remembering these facts, we must realize that there was much more direct intimacy in this theatre than there is in theatres of to-day. Probably three-quarters of the audience were personally acquainted with the actors and the actresses. The same spectators came day after day, and accordingly grew accustomed to idiosyncrasies of behaviour and of gesture. The actor was merged in the part, and as a consequence, when we read the Restoration dramatic literature in the light of the theatre, we can see why types were repeated over and over again. All those villains of Restoration tragedy are not villains of personality—they are but shadows of Sandford, an actor who, it is said, only once appeared in an honest part; and then was not allowed by his auditors to continue beyond the third act. So too all those merry maidens of Dryden's earlier fancy— they are not individualized pictures of girls of that age, but reveal in every movement, in every line, the form of bright-eyed Nell Gwyn, so soon to become a king's companion, to lose her art in luxury.

On this subject we cannot linger here, but it is one of which due account must be taken in our study of the main theatrical tendencies of the time.

CHAPTER X

THE ENGLISH THEATRES OF THE EIGHTEENTH CENTURY

(i) AUDIENCES AND THEATRES

IT is impossible, of course, to draw a sharp dividing line between the period 1660–1700 and the eighteenth century, but we are aided in making some kind of distinction because of the arrival of a new line of sovereigns, because of the emergence of a new type of writers, and because of the gradual disappearance of that peculiarly virulent Puritanism which still ruled in the hearts of many subjects of Charles II. In speaking of this period we must remember, of course, that we are dealing with a whole century and that we can in no way make generalizations covering the entirety of the period. On the other hand, some deductions can be made concerning the typical spectators of the time. In the first place, we note that, while the theatre still retained its air of fashion, the focus of public attention was no longer the Court. Anne rarely went to the public playhouses, and her successors, the Georges, for the most part followed her example. Moreover, a subtle change was coming over the aristocracy. Middle-class people were edging their way into the ranks from which hitherto they had been debarred, and, while the middle-class people aped a good deal the follies and the fashions of the more nobly born, they brought a new taste to the theatre. It is only by studying the gradual alteration in audience that we can explain the rising of the sentimental comedy and of the bourgeois tragedy. Lillo's *George Barnwell* could never have appealed to the spectators of 1670, and, conversely, no Wycherley or Congreve could arise to delight the hearts of eighteenth-century auditors. This is not to say that the same *blasé* air did not hang over at least one section of the theatre. From the early years of the century to the last we have reference to that aristocratic boredom which bestirred itself when a new play was being performed, so that parties repaired to the playhouse determined to mock the silly fool, the author, and damn his comedy or tragedy, whether it were good or bad. Perhaps mediocre dramatists of the time over-emphasized this aspect of the age, but that it existed in one form or another there can be not the slightest doubt. I feel certain that Bodens was painting from the life when, in *The Modish Couple* (1732), he drew the portrait of Grinly. This young gentleman is speaking to a companion of the playhouse, and says :

> I will wager you now five hundred Pounds that half a score of us shall quite demolish the best Piece that can come on any Stage. . . . Very well, Sir ; but now comes our Time, for the third Act being begun ; the first piece of wit that is utter'd, *Hiss* cry two or three of us—In a little time after, a stroke of Humour comes out, *hoh, hoh, hoh,* cry others. Then perhaps a serious Scene comes in Play, *Yaw* say the rest, and so on, till the Play is pretty well over. And for the last two or three Scenes, where the silly Rogue thinks he has shewn his Judgment the most, and on which the whole Business of the Piece depends, we strike up such a Chorus of *Cat-calls, Whistles, Hisses, Hoops,* and *Horse-laughs,* that not one of the Audience can hear a Syllable, and therefore charitably conclude it to be very sad Stuff.—The Epilogue's spoke, the Curtain falls, and so the poor Rascal is sent to the Devil.

Reading such a passage as this, can we wonder that authors preferred to write spectacular pieces, and that actors more and more inclined toward the pantomime where action took the place of dialogue and chequered Harlequin kept the audience in roars of good-humoured laughter ? It was in this period that some of the traditions of the *commedia dell' arte* became thoroughly established in England; John Rich (Lun) made his name not as a regular performer in classical tragedy and comedy but as a nimble pantomimic actor. Successful plays of former times were reduced to forms which admitted the display of his genius, thus securing a new lease of life. Probably the most famous of all these shows, *Harlequin Dr Faustus*, was thus based ultimately upon Marlowe's sixteenth-century tragedy. These conditions are maintained throughout the whole of this century. Pantomime dominated even over David Garrick, and it was still flourishing in the nineteenth century. With it prospered the many comic operas and musical interludes and melodramas of the age.

(ii) The Playhouses

All through the eighteenth century the two patent theatres maintained their position of complete or of partial monopoly. The Dorset Garden house was very early disused, largely, it would seem, because the acoustics were not all that could be desired. In its place rose the house employed by Betterton and his actors, a playhouse in Lincoln's Inn Fields built in the old tennis court which had once housed D'Avenant's players. During the early part of the century Drury Lane and another small theatre in Lincoln's Inn Fields (opened in 1714) were the privileged houses; after 1732 Covent Garden took the place of the latter. These two theatres, however, were rivalled by many another. Without taking into account the booths at Bartholomew Fair, May Fair, and Southwark Fair, or the later places of entertainment such as Sadler's Wells, the Royal Grove, and the Royal Circus, we find before the passing of the Licensing Act in

Fig. 200. Delpini as Pierrot at Sadler's Wells (early Nineteenth Century)
From a print in the British Museum.

1737 the presence of a small theatre in the Haymarket and of a theatre at Goodman's Fields. The Licensing Act theoretically closed every playhouse save those at Drury Lane and Covent Garden, but in various ways the managers of the minor houses succeeded in evading the law, while Samuel Foote, in the latter years of the century, was given a special licence for summer performances at the little theatre (Theatre Royal) in the Haymarket. Nor must we forget the opera house. Italian lyric drama had been introduced into London during the first years of the eighteenth century and soon had gripped the attention of the fashionable part of the town. A home for it was found in the large Queen's Theatre in the Haymarket, built by Vanbrugh in 1705 for regular plays, but soon abandoned for that purpose. In spite of frequent financial losses due to the enormous salaries which the singers demanded, the managers of this house—a motley crew—struggled on year after year, bringing to England some of the finest Italian voices and the most famous Italian operas. It was here that G. F. Handel reigned supreme in the mid years of the century.

It is useless to enter more fully into the stage history of the time; enough has been said to show that London, in spite of fettering restrictions, was much more adequately supplied with houses of entertainment than it had been in the Restoration period; a new audience was being born.

(iii) THE PROSCENIUM DOORS

One of the most important changes made in the structure of the new or of the altered theatres was the cutting away of one pair of proscenium doors. About 1696, Colley Cibber tells us, Rich, the manager of Drury Lane, determined on a modification of the original Wren plan.

> It must be observ'd . . . that the Area or Platform of the old Stage projected about four Foot forwarder, in a Semi-oval figure, parallel to the Benches of the Pit [*i.e.* in earlier times]; and that the former lower Doors of Entrance for the Actors were brought down between the two foremost (and then only) Pilasters, in the place of which Doors now the two Stage Boxes are fixt. That where the Doors of Entrance now are, there formerly stood two additional Side Wings, in front to a full Set of Scenes, which had then almost a double Effect in their Loftiness and Magnificence.

> By this Original form the usual Station of the Actors, in almost every Scene, was advanc'd at least ten Foot nearer the Audience than they now can be, because, not only from the Stage's being shorten'd in front, but likewise from the additional Interposition of those Stage Boxes, the Actors (in respect to the Spectators that filled them) are kept so much more backward from the main audience than they us'd to be; but when the Actors were in possession of that forwarder Space to advance upon, the Voice was then more in the Centre of the House, so that the most distant Ear had scarce the least Doubt or Difficulty in hearing what fell from the weakest Utterance.

From Cibber's account we can see what happened. The front, or lower,

Fig. 201. THE AUDIENCE AT SADLER'S WELLS

From a water-colour sketch in the British Museum.

Fig. 202. THE FITZGIGGO RIOT, 1763

Note may be taken of the Eastern costumes of the two central figures (*cp.* Figs. 220 to 225), and also of the methods of illumination.

door on each side was converted into a stage box, while behind the proscenium arch—so great was the force of tradition—were built two other doors. The "former" upper doors now became the lower doors. The arrangement of these is well shown in the prints which illustrate the Fitzgiggo riots of 1763 (Fig. 202).

Here the stage boxes are plainly apparent, with the doors behind them. This change naturally brought about a shortening of the apron, and a few minor innovations in the general disposition of the stage-front. At the Royalty Theatre in 1787 (Fig. 203) the doors are set slantwise from the curving sides of the boxes, reminding us a trifle of Jones' proscenium for a Court theatre (Fig. 150). It may be observed that in the Royalty Theatre the boxes over the doors had latticed windows much in the style of the music room at Dorset Garden. In a cross-section of the Haymarket

Fig. 203. THE ROYALTY THEATRE, 1787

Theatre (Fig. 204) we are again shown obliquely set doorways with windows above. Attention may be drawn to the fact that here the windows would be of practically no use for spectators, as they almost directly face the auditorium. They were, no doubt, reserved for actors only, as in Elizabethan times.

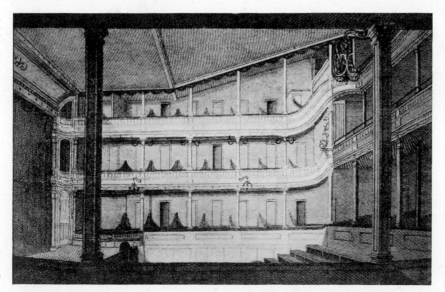

Fig. 204. CROSS-SECTION OF THE HAYMARKET THEATRE, 1807

(iv) THE MISE-EN-SCÈNE

In the matter of scenery the eighteenth-century managers, at least up to the latter years of the period, continued on the way mapped out for them in earlier times. We can still trace the Palace, Grove, Garden, Temple, and Prison scenes which were conventionally employed for tragedy and for opera, although pantomime gave an impetus to the origination of new theatrical machines and delighted in all that was new and costly and wonderful. There seems, however, to have been less experimentation even on machines than there had been in Restoration times. For general purposes we may assume until 1760 the continuance of those methods and those devices which had been employed in Betterton's theatre.

After 1760, however, some new spirit entered into the playhouse. Romanticism in the world of literature was by this time well under way, and was leading men to seek for something different from the conventionalism of pseudo-classic art. Some sought for truth in a new realism, looking at nature direct and not through the medium of antique description ; others sought for it in imaginative realms where gloomy mountains and ruined Gothic cathedrals played a dominant part. Realism, with a delight in the majestically grand, and a general reaction to Augustan conventionalism ever mark the romantic movement. Remembering this, we can easily explain the various tendencies in late eighteenth-century scenic design.

First perhaps may be chronicled new methods of securing the effects. Up to 1760 and even for long after that date most settings were made up of side-wings and back-shutters. Thus when a room was shown upon the stage the walls at the side were conventionally marked by two or three of these side-wings set in the manner established by Inigo Jones in the early seventeenth century and used, as we have seen, by Juvarra in the eighteenth century. These are clearly marked in Fig. 205. The box-set still had not been thought of, nor was it established until many years had passed by. So far as exteriors were concerned, however, the late eighteenth century saw the introduction of three-dimensional forms calculated to provide a greater approach to reality than might be afforded by painted flats. The utilization of built-up scenery—even when that was combined with older conventional forms—necessitated a complete revising of those theatrical aims which had served since the seventeenth century. From about this time comes the beginning of a fresh approach on the part of scene-designers. Progress, no doubt, was slow, but we can easily trace the stages by which the newer romantic conceptions, reacting against classical method, grew into the familiar naturalistic forms of the later nineteenth century.

Fig. 205. Scene in "The Heiress" (1786)
This shows well the arrangement of side-wings to represent an interior.
From Odell, *Shakespeare from Betterton to Irving.*

New devices, however, are really of less importance than new styles of treatment, and of these there were several during the last years of the century. In general, we may say that the romantic movement led men away from Augustan conventionalism, but obviously a reaction to conventionalism may take one of many forms. It may strive toward the capturing of archaeological correctness, or it may endeavour to reproduce the living shapes of nature. Whichever form it may assume, it still strives against that conventionalism which is present in neo-classic art. Of the two main tendencies of the age that heralded by William Capon (1757–1827) is probably the more important. Capon's predilections were all on the side of antiquarianism, which, it is true, had been gaining ground for some few years in the theatre. For the new Theatre Royal opened on April 21, 1794, Capon executed a number of special scenes, obviously destined to become stock properties, but displaying what were then novel features. The artist based his designs for these upon ancient Gothic architecture, striking thus away from the would-be classical temples and palaces favoured in England and on the Continent since the time of Serlio. The " Ancient Palace of Westminster " as it had been at the close of the fifteenth century formed one of these settings; the Tower of London in the time of Richard III was another; while various street scenes were devised out of faithful reproductions of a series of picturesque Elizabethan houses. Most of these original flats or drop-curtains were intended for the revival of Shakespeare's plays—for J. P. Kemble was then in charge of Drury Lane —but various contemporary dramatists gave the artist ample opportunity to display his skill. George Colman the younger thus provided him with *The Iron Chest* (Drury Lane, 1796) set in the reign of Edward IV, while M. G. Lewis indirectly aided him through his novel, *The Monk*, which was drama-

Fig. 206. ANCIENT STREET SCENE FOR JOHN KEMBLE'S SHAKESPEARIAN REVIVALS AT COVENT GARDEN, 1809. DESIGN BY WILLIAM CAPON

From *The Magazine of Art*.

tized by Boaden as *Aurelio and Miranda*. Here obviously was material for illustration in gloomy Gothic style. When Kemble occupied Covent Garden in 1809 Capon continued the same style of work there; the accompanying design of a street scene will give some idea of the general effects at which he aimed (Fig. 206).

The second tendency of the period is more clearly 'romantic' in the ordinarily accepted sense of the term, and may be associated with the scenic art of Loutherbourg (about 1735–1812), an Alsatian, who was engaged by David Garrick for Drury Lane some twenty years before Capon worked there. Loutherbourg, it is true, worked mainly in the region of the 'Entertainment' and of pantomime, but his importance cannot be under-

Fig. 207. SCENE FOR "A CHRISTMAS TALE" (1776) BY LOUTHERBOURG

From Odell, *op. cit.*

estimated when we consider his later influence. Loutherbourg was a romantic realist. A tour in Derbyshire provided him with a series of sketches from which he designed the scenery for *The Wonders of Derbyshire, or Harlequin in the Peak*, produced at Drury Lane in 1779, while Garrick's *A Christmas Tale* (Drury Lane, 1776) evidently allowed of free scenic embellishment in the same style (Fig. 207). Palaces, mountains, catacombs he produced in regular series, winning on all sides applause for his work. That applause came not merely because of his sense of artistic proportion and because of his skill as a draughtsman. He proved himself in every way a genius in his own sphere, introducing many novelties from the Continent and inventing many scenic devices himself. Thus his effects were secured by means other than the then usual back-shutter and triangularly arranged side-wings. For O'Keeffe's panto-mimic piece called *Omai* he executed scenery which evidently attracted attention. According to the author,

Fig. 208. Side Lighting in a German Theatre, 1790

he had previously invented transparent scenery—moonshine, sunshine, fire, volcanoes, etc.—as also breaking the scene into several pieces by the laws of perspective, showing miles and miles distance. Before his time, the back was one broad flat, the whole breadth and height of the stage.

This " breaking the scene," particularly with the use of built-up scenery, seems to have been Louther-

Fig. 210. Woodward as Mercutio
From Odell, *op. cit.*

Fig. 209. Romeo and Juliet in the Eighteenth Century
From a print in the possession of Mr Herbert Norris.

bourg's chief innovation, but the transparent scenes and the scenes of elemental effects were also highly applauded. He busied himself too with various methods of simulating thunder and lightning, and was one of the very first in England to give due care to the illumination of his scenes. Coloured or stained glass he used regularly for his lamps, and it is said that for the *Eidophuskion*, a spectacular entertainment devised by him in Spring Gardens, he went so far as to remove the now habitual footlights, illuminating his scenes from the top and the sides. This *Eidophuskion* made a considerable appeal to contemporaries, so that when Kean revived *King Lear* in 1820 he had in it "A Land Storm. After the manner of *Loutherbourg's Eidophuskion*," in which a most realistic storm howled round the head of the aged King.

It is impossible and unnecessary here to speak in greater detail of the exact means by which Loutherbourg and others secured their effects. We are dealing here with main tendencies only, and those have been sufficiently outlined in the preceding sections.

(v) COSTUME

It is necessary, however, to present a broad and selective survey of stage costume during these years. As a general rule, it may be stated broadly that up to 1760 or 1770 practically no attempt was made to secure historical accuracy in the dressing of various characters; but it must not be presumed that eighteenth-century, or, for that matter Elizabethan, performers habitually wore

Fig. 211. GARRICK AND MISS BELLAMY AS ROMEO AND JULIET

Note should be taken of the 'romantic' setting in this and in Fig. 212.
From an engraving by Ravenel after Wilson, 1763.

the garments of their own day. Rather, we may say, there was a definite convention in stage-costuming which, originated in the late sixteenth century, was passed on with minor modifications to the time of Garrick.

Looking at the theatrical prints of these years, we easily distinguish several sets of costumes for actors—actresses, be it noted, had a system all of their own.[1] We find (1) costumes of the day, (2) costumes *à la romaine*, (3) costumes for Eastern potentates, and (4) special costumes used mainly for Shakespearian plays. Comedy here we need not consider, for comic plays usually were 'clothed' in the most fashionable garments of the period, nor need we consider

Fig. 212. GARRICK AND MRS PRITCHARD AS MACBETH AND
LADY MACBETH

From a mezzotint by Green after Zoffany, 1776.

[1] *Infra*, p. 182.

pastorals, where fantastic garments of one sort or another—not always very Arcadian—were regularly worn. Our survey must be one of tragic types.

(1) The ordinary clothes of the time are shown in a number of eighteenth-century prints. Mercutio (Fig. 210) is generally a fashionable man of the time, as, in their own ways, are Romeo (Fig. 211) and Macbeth (Figs. 212 and 213). Hamlet is regularly habited in a contemporary but sombre suit of black as in the character-print of Henderson (Fig. 214). The list of examples, of course, might be increased a hundred-fold, but it may be assumed that knee-breeches, coat, and cravat were regularly used by the actors taking those parts.

Fig. 214. HENDERSON AS HAMLET, 1776

(2) When a Roman play was in question, however, there entered in that semi-classical costume which we have seen already adumbrated in Elizabethan times. Sometimes it is fairly accurate, sometimes it consists of little more than a breast-plate and a plumed helmet. Various 'styles' are shown here in the accompanying set of prints (Figs. 216, 218–220).[1] Thus was Antony and thus was Julius Caesar habited.

Fig. 213. GARRICK AS MACBETH

Fig. 215. FRONTISPIECE TO ROWE'S "HAMLET" (1709)

(3) Eastern heroes also wore plumes on occasion, but they had besides a very special costume of their own. The prints are so unanimous that we are bound to assume a definite continuity of tradition. Bannister as Zaphna in Miller's *Mahomet* wears tight-fitting boots, roomy breeches, a sash, and a long dressing-gown-like coat, trimmed with fur. A plumed turban completes his outfit (Fig. 217). As Hippolitus Lewis has the roomy trousers, the boots, and the coat, adding a curved scimitar. A peculiar turban sits on his head (Fig. 223). Mossop as Bajazet lacks the boots but has the other features identical (Fig. 222), while Barry as Othello varies the costume only by the adoption of an Indian tunic instead of the breeches (Fig. 226). Benson as Timurkan, later in the century (Fig. 225), while

---

[1] Compare also the frontispiece to Addison's *Cato*, reproduced in *British Drama*.

trying to secure Chinese local colour, obviously has remembered some of the outstanding peculiarities in the dress of his predecessors. These prints may be regarded as typical, and from them we may deduce the fact that Othello, like other Eastern characters, regularly appeared in a conventional costume which included Central Asian

Fig. 216. Quin as Coriolanus, 1749

Fig. 217. Bannister as Zaphna, 1778

boots, Turkish trousers or Indian tunic, sash of Arabia, furred coat of doubtful origin, and turban of India. The curved scimitar was associated with the type even in Shakespeare's earliest days.[1]

Fig. 218. Garrick as Demetrius, 1777

Fig. 219. Murray as Demetrius, 1797

Fig. 220. Lewis as Pharnaces, 1795

Clearly this costume has considerable value, for do the eighteenth-century prints not preserve the main features of the original costume worn by the actor who created Othello in the early

[1] *Supra*, p. 137.

years of the seventeenth century? Traditionalism, we must remember, ruled dominant in the theatre till 1800.

(4) It is a most strange fact that for Shakespeare's plays certain characters were dressed in

Fig. 221. Mossop as Zanga, 1776

Fig. 222. Mossop as Bajazet, 1778

Fig. 223. Lewis as Hippolitus, 1777

garments peculiar to themselves even while others in the same drama wore contemporary costumes. Let us take as an example the popular type of Falstaff. In the library of the Duke of Devonshire at Chatsworth there is a sketch by Inigo Jones made for the Brachmani

Fig. 224. Barry and Mrs Barry as Bajazet and Selima, 1776

Fig. 225. Benson as Timurkan, 1796

in Sir William D'Avenant's masque *The Temple of Love* (1635). One of the figures there has a hat with an upturned brim and a long gown or cloak with full sleeves. The interest of the sketch consists in a note inscribed by the artist in which he describes a roabe of russet Girt low wᵗ a great belley like a swoln mã long miſtchaheos [mouſtaches] the sleeues shorte . . . buskines to shew a great swolen lege on his head a capp comĩng fourth beefore like a peake . . . a hood gatherd behind a great head and balde,

Fig. 226. BARRY AS OTHELLO, 1777

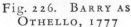

Fig. 227. POPE AS VARANES, 1793

and then, most important of all, " like a Sʳ Jon fall ſtaff." We next turn to the early eighteenth century and see Falſtaff in *Henry IV*, *Part II*. He has the large buskins, an Elizabethan collar, a cloak, and a wigless head, although his two companions are dressed in eighteenth-century ſtyle (Fig. 228). Later ſtill, in 1778, his coſtume is fundamentally the same,

except that the cloak has given way to a coat of semi-Georgian cut (Fig. 229). The hat, the collar, and the boots are there, so that we feel assured that we are in the presence of one of the essentially traditional Shakespearian coſtumes. Shylock is another figure who is honoured with a special dress. The two prints of Macklin in this rôle, with the long black ' gaberdine ' and the white necktie (Figs. 230 and 231), give a

Fig. 229. HENDERSON AS FALSTAFF, 1778

Fig. 230. MACKLIN AS SHY-LOCK, 1777

Fig. 228. FRONTISPIECE TO ROWE'S " HENRY IV, PART II "

fair idea of its main features. Special note should be taken in Fig. 231 of the fact that while Antonio and Bassanio wear eighteenth-century coſtume with wigs, Shylock is

wigless. The wigless types are the traditional ones. Among the other characters who wear peculiar coſtumes may be mentioned Dromio in *The Comedy of Errors* (Fig. 232), Poſthumus in

Cymbeline (Fig. 233), and King Lear (Fig. 234). The last-mentioned is clad in knee-breeches of the period, a white shirt, and a peculiar coat trimmed with ermine. No explanation can be offered for the curious fact that Lear was thus distinguished while Macbeth appeared in ordinary contemporary dress; that is one of the strange elements in a stage tradition which undoubtedly takes us back to Shakespeare's time.

Fig. 231. MACKLIN AS SHYLOCK
From an engraving by Nutter after Boyne.

Fig. 232. BRUNSDEN AS DROMIO, 1779

The actresses mostly took their own line, one dictated to them by the fact that they did not wish to appear in anything but the most fashionable dress of their time. While Barry as Bajazet (Fig. 224) wears Eastern costume, Mrs Barry as Selima is clad in a costume of the eighteenth century. Mrs Hartley as Cleopatra (Fig. 235), the same actress as Andromache (Fig. 236), Miss Younge as Merope (Fig. 237), Mrs Oldfield as Rosamond (Fig. 238), Mrs Melmoth as Queen Elizabeth (Fig. 239)—they all wore garments of the same type. A few exceptions, however, must be noted. We need not here dwell on the Indian costume of feathers which Mrs Behn gave the theatre in the early years of the Restoration, but we may note the fact that Mrs Quickly, Doll Tearsheet, and their crew seem to have worn costumes which carry us back to Elizabethan days. In Fig. 228 they are sufficiently distinguished in this way. Mrs Woffington as Mistress Ford (Fig. 240) seems also to retain something of earlier dress. The actresses, however, rarely liked thus to distinguish themselves, and long after the time when Mrs Siddons started the fashion for 'Grecian' draperies we find the women playing in contemporary costumes while the men were historically clad. Miss Wallis as Palmira (Fig. 241) marks about the furthest limit to which they allowed themselves to venture.

About the sixties or the seventies in England, however, changes in the

Fig. 234. GARRICK AS KING LEAR, 1779

Fig. 233. REDDISH AS POSTHUMUS, 1777

traditional costuming began to creep in, the dresses being thus brought gradually into harmony with the new scenic effects. These changes, of course, did not come into being in one decade: indeed they had been heralded years before their actual introduction by theorists both in England and on the Continent. In the early Renascence period di

Somi [1] had suggested the advisability of dressing characters in accordance with historical fashions, but di Somi in many ways was a lonely prophet with ideas far beyond those of his

Fig. 235. MRS HARTLEY AS CLEOPATRA, 1776

Fig. 236. MRS HARTLEY AS ANDROMACHE, 1777

Fig. 237. MISS YOUNGE AS MEROPE, 1777

own time. The demand seems next to have been made in the preface to Antonio Conti's *Il Cesare* (1718), and was repeated by the later dramatist Martelli.[2] Possibly it was from these men that Gottsched in Germany took his ideas. About 1741 this playwright-theorist persuaded the actress Carolina Neuber to put on *Der sterbende Caton* with classical costumes, but unfortunately the effort was not successful, the audience treating the whole affair as an excellent joke. No doubt the English dramatist Aaron Hill may also have known of Conti's and Martelli's proposals, for he was deeply interested in the Italian opera of the age; at any rate in October 1724 he enunciates a similar suggestion for

Fig. 238. MRS OLDFIELD AS ROSAMOND, 1778

Fig. 239. MRS MELMOTH AS QUEEN ELIZABETH, 1779

productions in London theatres. For a play of his own in 1731 he sketched " a few light drawings," beautiful and inexpensive, yet presenting " a novelty in the old *Saxon* dresses." A decade later Macklin seems to have been thinking about accuracy in costume ; it was he who caused a revolution in method by habiting Macbeth in " the old Caledonian habit." Garrick himself grew

[1] See Appendix B.   [2] On this see J. G. Robertson's *The Genesis of Romantic Theory*, p. 106.

interested in the innovation, and capped Macklin's experiment by providing old English costumes for *King Lear*.

A further study of the development of this historical costuming must be reserved for the next section;[1] here it may be noted that up to 1800 the results achieved were not always as perfect or as complete as the play-bills would lead us to imagine. Many contemporary records prove to us that it was often only the 'star' who boasted the 'correct' garments, the rest of the company being furnished with costumes "which had done service for other times and for other nations." Macklin, Garrick, and Kemble all seem to have been guilty of this hopelessly reprehensible vice which is the peculiar property of stars—of all times and of all nations. Similarly, the contemporary records show that by 'historical' the managers of this time meant merely "not conventional or contemporary."

Fig. 240. Mrs Woffington as Mistress Ford

From a mezzotint by Faber after Haytley.

Fig. 241. Miss Wallis as Palmira, 1795

If Henry IV was clad in the gown which a real Henry VI might have worn all was well; Edwardian, Henrician and 'ancient British' costumes might often serve to costume heroes of any one time.

[1] See p. 191.

CHAPTER XI

THE THEATRES OF THE NINETEENTH CENTURY

(i) THE THEATRES

THE nineteenth century as a whole gave little to scenic artistry. This categorical statement, of course, will require a certain amount of qualification, but the fact remains that the period merely carried on traditions which had been set in the ages which preceded. Gas and, later, electricity gave new instruments to the managers, but the careful placing of the means of illumination, the blending of colours, and the general artistic effects to be secured thereby had occupied the minds of many men from the times of Serlio and of Inigo Jones to those of Loutherbourg. 'Transparent' scenery, gauze, and all the various tricks of the scenic art had been tried long before the vaunted triumphs of the eighties and the nineties. Still, however far the pioneer work had been carried by previous artists, we must not by any means despise the nineteenth-century theatre. It had for the most part an honest aim, and it succeeded in realizing, at least partially, its desires.

There is not much necessity here to chronicle the tumultuous stage history of the period, but attention may be drawn to one or two of the most salient characteristics of the theatres of the time. From the beginning of the century to the end there was a tendency toward the enlarged house. Drury Lane had been entirely rebuilt in 1794, with a vastly increased seating capacity—nay, planned "upon a much larger scale than that of any other theatre in Europe." It had a proscenium opening of 43 feet by 38, with a stage depth of no less than 92 feet. This gorgeous structure, which aroused contemporaries to paeans of admiration and surprise, was burnt to the ground on February 24, 1809, and three years later (1812) was opened the present Theatre Royal, with a proscenium opening of 33 feet and a seating capacity of well over 3200. It may be remarked that, while the acoustic properties of this theatre are now excellent, those of the original playhouse built in 1812 were far from being so. Alterations were made both in 1814 and in 1821 for the purpose of improving the defects. The respective playhouses in Drury Lane may well be studied in Figs. 242, 243, and 244.

A new Covent Garden too rose in 1809 out of the ashes of the old house, which had been destroyed by fire on September 20, 1808 ; it also was considerably larger than the theatre the place of which it took. The auditorium was 51 feet by 52, with four tiers, each containing twenty-six boxes. The width of the proscenium was 42 feet with a height of 36, while the stage itself was 68 feet by 82. It held some 2800 or 3000 spectators (Fig. 245).

This tendency toward the use of a large theatre was, of course, countered to a certain extent by the 'minor' playhouses, which naturally increased rapidly in importance after the new bill destroying the monopoly of the patent theatres was passed in 1843. Even before this date, however, Sadler's Wells, Astley's Amphitheatre, and the Royalty competed not unfavourably with Drury Lane, Covent Garden, and the Italian Opera. In 1810 a special licence for "English Opera" was granted to Arnold for the Lyceum, while other 'minors' spectacularly displayed melodrama and farce. It would take pages here to chronicle the mere advent of the many houses—Princess's, His Majesty's, Royalty, Prince of Wales's, and what not—which were erected during the last years of the century or in the first years of our own period.

Fig. 242. DRURY LANE IN 1775

The three 'galleries' should be contrasted with the five of the later house.
From a print in the Victoria and Albert Museum.

THE THEATRES OF THE NINETEENTH CENTURY

Unfortunately, for the earlier period, the minor theatres served to intensify an evil which was rapidly gathering way in the patent houses. It was soon found that both sight and hearing were bad at Drury Lane and Covent Garden. Countless are the complaints, the satirical references, and the jests made concerning this. The actors and actresses coarsened their methods, but in vain; they could no longer make the appeal which they had made before. Scenery, spectacle was all that could help them to hold the attention of the audience, and as scenery had so dominated the thoughts of the Capons and the Loutherbourgs all went merrily forward. A subsidiary incentive came, too, from the minor theatres. These had been condemned to musical and spectacular pieces, and as a result set a fashion which soon came to dominate the entirety of the theatrical world.

This attention paid to spectacle led, naturally, toward the disappearance of the repertory system. It has often been pointed out that a 'run' of three days was normal for a new play in the Restoration period, and that the first really long 'run' was that of *The Beggar's Opera* in 1728—extending to just over a month. While many plays and operas had similar successes before 1800, the modern run is first approximated most closely in several spectacles which were presented at Sadler's Wells, at the Royal Circus, or at the Royal Grove about the years 1788 to 1795. Not only did some of these continue from an original production in April till the

Fig. 243. DRURY LANE IN 1808
From Odell, *op. cit.*

following October, but they had a corresponding run during the same months of the year following. It is here that we meet with the first definite establishment of that pernicious custom which has had such a deleterious effect on the fortunes of modern English drama.

In structure, the most important change in the theatres was the cutting away of the apron and the proscenium doors. For a long time the players, accustomed to their easy exits and entrances, opposed any alteration, and relics of the ancient doors—a link with Shakespeare and Palladio—existed in the provinces up to comparatively recent years. These doors disappeared in the London houses about the middle of the century. The Haymarket, we know, got rid of them in the winter of 1843, for an advertisement informs us that

> During the recess, the theatre has undergone Extensive Alterations, the Proscenium has been entirely remodelled, and the whole of the Interior decorated in the most Costly and Elegant Style. By a curtailment of the useless portion of the Stage in front of the Curtain, and advancing Orchestra and Lights near the Actors and Scenic Effects, the Lessee has been enabled to appropriate the portion so obtained, to form a certain number of Orchestra Stalls, which can be retained for the parties taking them the whole of the Evening.

With this notice we are on the threshold of the modern theatre, with its proscenium arch cutting the play off from the audience, with its reserved stalls, and its loss of the proscenium doors.

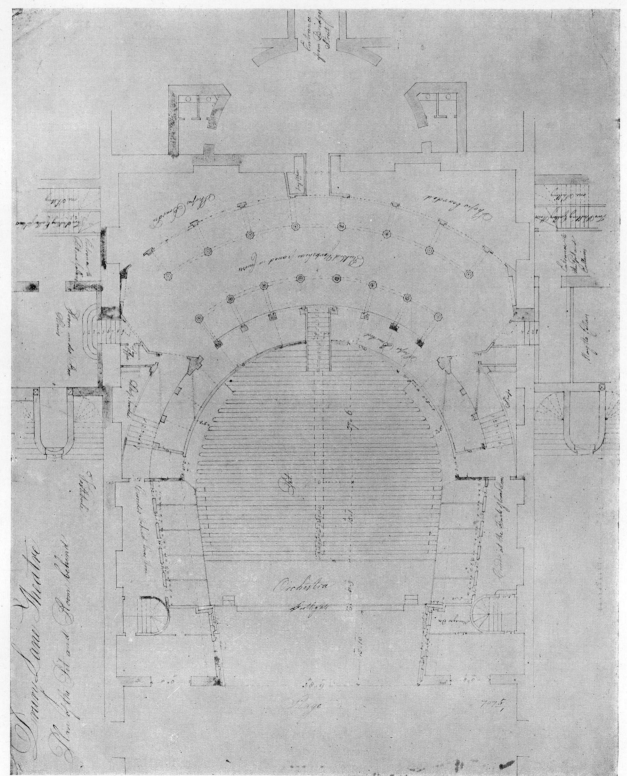

Fig. 244. Plan of Drury Lane, 1809.
From the original in the Victoria and Albert Museum.

Fig. 245. COVENT GARDEN IN 1810

From *The Covent-Garden Journal.*

Fig. 246. A STEAMBOAT SCENE IN A TRAVESTIE OF "THE TEMPEST"

Frontispiece to *The Enchanted Isle*, as acted at the Adelphi, 1848.

Fig. 247. AN EXTRAVAGANZA SETTING IN THE NINETEENTH CENTURY

Frontispiece to *The Golden Branch*, as acted at the Lyceum, 1848.

Fig. 248. A GREEK SCENE IN NINETEENTH-CENTURY BURLESQUE

Frontispiece to *The Sphinx*, as acted at the Haymarket, 1849.

THE DEVELOPMENT OF THE THEATRE

Perhaps the disuse of the apron was partly responsible for the increased employment of the curtain. Slowly but surely managers, authors, and actors came to realize what a benefit this could be. 'Discoveries' could be readily made by its means; it could descend to conceal satisfactorily some thrilling tableau; it provided an opportunity of indicating those intervals so necessary for the setting of the ever more and more elaborate scenic effects. In any case, by 1850 the end of an act meant "Curtain," and the beginning of the next act meant the rising of the curtain, generally to reveal a new set.

One other general movement in the period is to be noted, and that is the dominance of the star. In earlier times a Burbage and a Betterton might be of greater magnitude than others acting with them, but their names were not billed large, and the audience did not come for them alone. From David Garrick's time, however, a new movement was set on foot, and the principal actor completely eclipsed his unhappy companions. In the nineteenth century a Kemble, a Macready, a Samuel Phelps, a Charles Kean, a Sir Henry Irving, and a Beerbohm Tree organized performances in which each was the central figure, each the centre of the scenic effect, each the point on which all eyes must be fixed. O'Keeffe's *Recollections* show us that it was not the nineteenth century which invented those many tricks and devices intended to attract the attention of the public to one spot or one person, but the nineteenth century certainly did establish as a principle the actor-manager system with all its accompanying disadvantages and misfortunes.

(ii) The Scenic Art of the Period

The main tendencies of nineteenth-century scenic art may be summed up in the words spectacular and antiquarian. The Grieves at Astley's playhouse devised wonderful and perhaps often beautiful effects, and other theatres eagerly copied their efforts. Equestrian shows and aquatic shows throng the earlier years of the period; Vestris naturally required rich scenery for her terpsichorean burlettas which J. R. Planché so liberally provided. A "Programme of Scenery, &c." for his *The Sleeping Beauty in the Wood* (Covent Garden, 1840), described as "An Original, Grand, Comic, Romantic, Operatic, Melo-dramatic Fairy Extravaganza," may give some idea of what was attempted:

PART FIRST.—Period 1583.
BOUDOIR OF THE FAIRY BANEFUL. . . .
Banquet Hall in the Castle of the King of Noland.

PART SECOND.—Period 1601.
VESTIBULE IN THE ROYAL CASTLE.
Apartment of the Princess in the Octagon Tower. . . .
Lobby and Lumber Room at the very Top of the Castle.
State Bed Chamber.

PART THIRD.—Period 1701.
MAGIC FOREST.
Castle Gates. Moat and Drawbridge. Old Palace Yard,
And Re-view of a Company of the " Old Guards."
Quick-set Hedge, and a merry Green Wood in the Spring-time of the year.
The State Bed Chamber (Exactly as before.) . .
Illuminated Palace and Gardens of the Fairy Antidota.
Fete Al-fresco. . . .
Departure of the Seven Fairies, in a Patent Safety " Fly,"
constructed by Mr. W. Bradwell, " time out of mind the Fairies' Coachmaker."

All this, it is true, is in a " Fairy Extravaganza," but it was the Fairy Extravaganza which set the tone for so much of the scenic art of this age.

The result of all this was that Shakespeare took on a new lease of life. The actor-manager wished to make a success in the plays of Britain's Greatest Bard, and as a consequence revived tragedy and comedy alike, always reserving for himself the sympathetic rôles. At the same time the actor-manager found that Shakespeare lent himself as much to spectacle as did a Planché. What an opportunity for gaunt castles and medieval chambers in *Macbeth* and *Lear* ; what a host of fairy 'business' could be brought into *A Midsummer Night's Dream* ; and what a charming play *The Tempest* was for the attentions of the scenic artist ! Still, a new public, tutored by romantic sentiment, had arisen, and these wished their spectacles to be correct in all details. The actor-manager, therefore, following Capon, turned scholar, and posed as an instructor as well as an artist.

The first sign of development in this direction appeared in the Kemble production of *King John* in 1823, when J. R. Planché, an enthusiastic antiquary as well as an indefatigable playwright, persuaded the manager to allow him to habit the piece. With the assistance of a number of learned enthusiasts, and fortified by a close study of illuminated manuscripts, Planché put on what was undoubtedly the first completely 'historical' production of Shakespeare's drama, for he paid attention not only to the hero's costume but to those of the meanest underlings. The result was that " receipts for 400 to 600 pounds nightly soon reimbursed the management for the expense of the production," and, this being so, quite naturally " a complete reformation of dramatic costume became from that moment inevitable upon the English stage." From now on the revivals of Shakespeare's plays are billed as dressed in correct, authentic garments, and in the advertisements the various 'authorities' are duly printed. The crisis, if not the catastrophe, is reached in the versions prepared for the stage by Charles Kean. Plentiful record remains in the newspapers of the time regarding these revivals, but we need do no more, in our endeavour to estimate the tendencies of the time, than turn to the printed texts of the plays. How erudite are the notes to difficult passages in the dialogue, and how anxious the actor-manager is to convince his public that he has consulted all the possible sources of information, and that his settings and costumes do not conflict with historical fact ! The preface to *The Merchant of Venice* (Princess's, 1850) informs us that

> the costumes and customs are represented as existing about the year 1600, when Shakespeare wrote the play. The dresses are chiefly selected from a work by Cesare Vecellio, entitled " *Degli Habiti Antichi e Moderni di diverse Parti del Mondo*. In Venetia, 1590 " : as well as from other sources to be found in the British Museum.

The procession which opens the comedy " is copied from a print in the British Museum, by Josse Amman, who died in 1591," while the text is generously padded out with a series of lengthy " Historical Notes."

For *The Merchant of Venice*, for the tragedies and for the histories, of course, all was plain sailing. The manager had merely to look up the historical sources for the reigns of King John or of Henry VIII and reproduce " the costumes and customs " on the stage ; but a difficulty obviously arose when *The Winter's Tale* was revived. Kean's preface to this play as performed at the Princess's in 1856 is so illuminating that parts of it may be quoted in full. While recognizing the " charming " nature of the drama, the actor-manager grumbled loudly at the fact that Shakespeare had

> left the incidents of the play . . . alternating between Sicily and Bohemia, without assigning any specific date to the time of action. Chronological contradictions abound throughout the five acts ; inasmuch as reference is made to the Delphic oracle, Christian burial, an Emperor of Russia, and an Italian painter of the sixteenth century.

N

Fig. 249. A Dance of Fairies in Kean's Production of "A Midsummer Night's Dream." Design by Grieve

From the original in the Victoria and Albert Museum.

Surely this was a hard nut for an antiquarianly minded manager to crack. Typical is the manner in which Kean solved his difficulty. He may be allowed to tell his own tale:

> It is evident that when an attempt is made to combine truth with history, conflicting epochs cannot all be illustrated; and I have therefore thought it permissible to select a period which, while it accords with the spirit of the play, may be considered the most interesting, as well as the most instructive.
>
> The pivot on which the story revolves, is in fact the decision pronounced by the oracle of Delphi; and taking this incident as the corner stone of the whole fabric, I have adopted a period when Syracuse, according to Thucydides, had, from a mere Doric colony, increased in magnificence to a position in no way inferior to that of Athens herself, when at the summit of her political prosperity. An opportunity is thus afforded of reproducing a classical era, and placing before the eyes of the spectator, *tableaux vivants* of the private and public life of the ancient Greeks, at a time when the arts flourished to a perfection, the scattered vestiges of which still delight and instruct the world. Assuming that the civilization of Athens was reflected by Syracuse, I feel that no period could have been selected more interesting and suggestive, or more likely to give additional zest to those who wish to contemplate the manners and habits of a country once " the centre of ancient civilization, and the fruitful mother of so many illustrious sons," but which can now, alas! boast of nothing beyond its history and its ruins.
>
> To connect the country known as " Bohemia " with an age so remote, would be impossible: I have therefore followed the suggestion of Sir Thomas Hanmer, in his annotations on Shakespeare, by the substitution of *Bithynia*. The difference of name in no way affects the incidents or metre of the play, while it enables me to represent the costume of the inhabitants of Asia Minor at a corresponding period, associated so intimately with Greece, and acquiring additional interest from close proximity to the Homeric kingdom of Troy.
>
> The Phrygian dress presents a marked distinction between the two races that constitute the chief actors in the drama, while at the same time scope is afforded for the introduction of customs common to both. A leading instance is furnished in the pastoral scene of the fourth act, where the festivities applicable to the season of sheep-shearing take place, and in which Shakespeare brings in, for the purpose of a dance, twelve rustics, " who have made themselves all men of hair, and call themselves Satyrs." I have here ventured to introduce one of those festivals in honour of Bacchus, known under the title of " Dionysia," wherein similar disguises were used, while the actors indulged in mad enthusiasm and extravagant merriment.
>
> For the purpose of presenting with closer accuracy the domestic manners of the period, Leontes and his Queen Hermione, together with their Kingly guest, are first discovered towards the termination of a *Feast*. . . . As dancing and music invariably formed a portion of such entertainments, a representation of the celebrated *Pyrrhic Dance*, so popular throughout the principal states of Greece for its martial character, has been attempted.
>
> Later in the play, " TIME, as CHORUS," has been restored, in accordance with the poet's conception. By this restoration, the lapse of sixteen years, supposed to have taken place from the birth of Perdita until she is seen as the shepherdess in the fourth act, is rendered more intelligible. To carry out the idea, a classical figure, more in accordance with the character of the play as now represented, has been preferred to the ordinary old man with his scythe and hour glass, who was unknown in classic ages. CRONOS, the ancient representative of Time, has been chosen, and I have ventured to associate him with an allegorical tableau of Luna and the Stars (personified), sinking before the Car of Phoebus, which rises with all its attributes of splendour. Each figure is taken from an antique, or from the works of Flaxman.

Kean has obviously " ventured " much, but he has done so in good company. " Eminent Professors " are referred to; the architecture has been superintended by George Godwin, F.R.S.; thanks are given to " George Scharf, Esq., F.S.A. (author of the Hand-book to the Greek and Pompeian Courts at the Crystal Palace)"; the " vegetation peculiar to Bithynia is adopted from his private drawings, taken on the spot "; " James A. Davies, Lecturer on Ancient Music," has given his valuable aid; while a host of artists, including Grieve, Telbin, W. Gordon, F. Lloyds, Cuthbert, Dayes, and Morris, were responsible for the scenery. Truly an awe-inspiring production, beautiful perhaps in some ways, but not Shakespeare, not even genuine theatric art, something which, to use Kean's own words, is " an exhibition of pageantry appealing to the eye " and " an illustration addressed to the understanding." Pageantry is not scenic art, and historical instruction—what on earth is it doing in this galley?

It is hardly necessary to state that these historical efforts of Kean, which he had inherited from Macready, who in his turn had them from Capon and Kemble, were passed on to Tree and to

Irving. The gorgeous state and panoply of a production at His Majesty's was no new thing ; it sprang from that craze for ' processions ' which we find established at a very early period, added to the falsely directed antiquarianism of player and of artist.

This antiquarian-spectacular movement is unquestionably, for our purposes, the most important in the age. At the same time it must be noted that spectacularism of the kind described above was not opposed to a genuinely realistic movement ; indeed, it sprang ultimately from a desire to reproduce as faithfully as possible the buildings and the costumes contemporaneous with the action of Shakespeare's tragedies and comedies.[1] Obviously the same tendency could find application in plays written of later conditions, an endeavour being made to present in strictest faithfulness the current phenomena of ordinary existence. Such an endeavour led to the exploring of new possibilities. More and more the old flats disappeared, their place being taken by structures built in greater solidity, and the frankly conventional arrangement of the scenery gave way to illusionistic effects. Perhaps the treatment of interiors provides us with as good an example as any. Throughout the eighteenth century a room was shown by means of a back-drop and pairs of side-wings. Clearly this room was far from a representation of reality, and when the desire for realism came sweeping over the theatre during the period with which at present we are concerned efforts were made to secure a greater verisimilitude. Hence came the revolution which banished the wings and substituted flats arranged so as to form three sides of an interior. With the introduction of a ceiling in place of the old flimsy sky borders the box-set had arrived, and with it the consciousness of that gaping ' Fourth Wall ' the presence of which before had hardly been realized. Closely allied to this alteration in basic stage-planning goes the substitution of real objects for things which in former days had been merely symbolic or frankly presented in a conventional manner. Tom Robertson's doorknobs are notorious ; their introduction was thoroughly symbolic of what was happening during those days in all branches of theatrical activity. In 1800 a door set in a flat could be taken for nothing but a framework of laths covered with painted canvas ; Robertson wanted something more—he desired that his doors should be solid with handles fixed to them, and not merely delineated by a scene-painter's brush. Nor was this desire just the idiosyncrasy of an individual playwright ; Robertson's doorknobs were precisely what the public of his time most wanted. They were tired of convention and thrilled to see presented before them lamp-posts and cows and hansom-cabs, finding in the contemplation of these common objects in unfamiliar surroundings a strange attractiveness and charm.

Revolutionary methods of securing effects and the supplanting of the conventional by the real are, however, only partial results of this new tendency. During the pseudo-classic period, as has been seen,[2] familiar scenic types (Grove, Temple, and Prison) were accepted by dramatists and audiences alike ; with the clamouring for realism these could no longer serve. Realism demands particulars where conventionalism seeks for principles and generalities. Not surprising, therefore, is it to discover that during these years interesting experiments were being made in entirely new types of settings. Apart from the frequent use of the *Eidophuskion* and of similar panoramic effects, we find even before the middle of the century quite a number of interesting innovations. In one play the setting is a side-view, from the wings, of a fictional stage with a section of an imaginary audience glimpsed beyond ; in another play two rooms in one house are set one above the other on separate planes, action going on in both. No longer were men satisfied with the commonly accepted and the traditional ; they sought to achieve both a surer reproduction of what they might see around them and the delineation of scenes which their forefathers would never have dreamed of representing on a stage.

---

[1] *Supra*, pp. 174–175, 190–191. 　　　　[2] *Supra*, pp. 165–167, 173.

THE THEATRES OF THE NINETEENTH CENTURY

(iii) LIGHTING

Obviously all this endeavour is intimately related to stage illumination. So long as candles and lamps were the only means of lighting the stage little in the way of an illusionistic effect could be hoped for. Serlio in the Renascence playhouses and Loutherbourg at Drury Lane had done their best with glasses of coloured liquids or tinted panes, but to expect much from these primitive instruments would have been lunacy. Often in history we find that an invention is prepared for by a need and a desire: gas illumination came at a time when men were craving for a means which should give them greater control. The introduction of gas made new wonders possible. The stage might be brilliantly illuminated or it might be completely darkened, not by a laborious process of kindling and quenching hundreds of candles but by the mere turning of a screw. More important still, the lighting of the auditorium might be similarly controlled, so that no longer did spectators need to sit in brightness during the enacting of scenes supposed to take place at night.

From the use of gas to the use of electricity was but a step, and with electricity came greater brilliance, ease in placement of the source of illumination, safety, and the opportunity of introducing 'magical' effects impossible before. Moonlight and sunlight might now be simulated with reasonable success and soon the projection of slides was to introduce a new 'heavens' undreamed of in days of solid board or canvas sky borders. During this period the new methods of illumination were employed either for attaining greater verisimilitude or for increasing the spectacular appearance of the scenery. But it must be realized that fundamentally the substitution of gas and electricity for candles and lamps has not merely improved the means at the command of the theatrical director; it has introduced an entirely new element in the production. The fact that the lamps and candles could not without very grave difficulty be controlled during the course of a performance meant that, in essence, the theatre of the eighteenth century was not far different from the open-air theatres which had preceded it. Unquestionably from the sixteenth century onward theatre artists had been aware of the possibilities of artificial lighting in their new indoor playhouses, but little could be done to bring their ideals to realization. Only when they were enabled to work with gas and electricity could they hope to achieve what their fancies had immaterially suggested. The theatre of earlier times had three main elements. The actor stood on a platform backed by scenery which by the operation of machinery might change and present startling appearances to the eyes of the spectators. Stage, scenes, and machines were all. Now a fresh element, lighting, was introduced, and gradually theatre workers came to recognize that, in addition to the securing of richer and more illusionistic effects, light might serve, along with scenery, to create a definite impression and so play its part in the whole production. If need be, the light might be employed in a frankly arbitrary manner—colours, brilliance, and shade all being used to arouse emotion, without immediate reference to the 'reality' of the set. Before the opening of the present century, however, these things were barely appreciated. The theatre, gripped by the love of spectacle and excited by the overthrow of older conventions, seized upon the newly invented gas-jet and electric bulb as things likely to serve its immediate purposes. In recent years only has come the utilization of the new instruments in diverse ways, and perhaps even now we have not arrived at a full recognition of all that might be accomplished in this direction.

CHAPTER XII

THE THEATRES OF THE MODERN PERIOD

(i) THE REALISTIC SCHOOL

THE preceding two chapters have endeavoured to trace the slow but determined growth of the realistic movement. Realism, of course, is a relative term, and we must recognize that from the beginnings of the romantic movement about 1760 on to our own days the attempt to present illusionistic forms in the playhouse has taken a diversity of shapes. Earlier romantics delighted in the realism of history, in the realism of wild nature, as opposed to the conventional treatment of life and of past ages. Later realism did not look at the picturesque but at the ugly, the drab, and the material. It came to prefer a labourer's cottage, a slum-tenement, a house of prostitution, to a view of soaring mountains or a wide expanse of seascape. It felt, consciously or unconsciously, that the romantic realist, in looking at flowers and clouds and trees, had missed the misery of human life, had deliberately substituted the beautiful for the true. Throughout this period, indeed, there is manifested a confusion between realism considered as a method whereby an attempt is made to reproduce natural forms illusionistically upon the stage and realism considered as a choice in material—a choice which selects the darker sides of existence and concentrates upon hopelessness and pain rather than upon joy.

Here, in dealing with the theatre as distinct from the drama, we are concerned mainly with the former interpretation, although the other sense must be appreciated fully if we are to understand what was happening during those years. The steady movement toward the building up of exact illusion in the theatre may be traced in hundreds of experiments and ventures between 1850 and 1900. In England Tom Robertson insists on a greater truth to life in his dialogue and characters, and demands that these should find a harmonious setting in stage rooms which are more solid than those of the past. After Robertson come Pinero and Jones, who carry the work farther, and with their efforts make his seem artificial. The German Saxe-Meiningen company, with its more naturalistic treatment of crowds and its careful stage-management, stimulates thought in every country of Europe. Ibsen steps forward as a champion of the new realism, and soon in the greater capitals 'independent' theatres spring up to provide opportunity for the presentation of the new plays. London's Independent Theatre, the Théâtre Libre of Paris, and Berlin's Freie Bühne, all established about the year 1890, mark the last stage in this battle for theatrical reality. The Moscow Art Theatre, more enduring in its efforts and less dogmatically extreme in its aims, was born of the same general movement.

The struggle went on until the end of the century, when victory remained with the realistic rebels. The old theatre of conventionalism vanished. Drearily kitchen succeeded kitchen, and drawing-room followed drawing-room demurely. The style is still with us, and it may take decades to remove it, but within the past few years clear dissatisfaction, both with its tenets and with its practical manifestations, has been demonstrated among the most vital of theatrical workers. Fundamentally, it is being recognized that the essential philosophic belief of the realistic school is false. This belief presupposes that art should be, or should seem to be, an excerpt from life, that a play ought to represent three hours seized bodily out of the rushing hours of existence,[1] that the art of the theatre is an art of pure illusion. The fallacy inherent in this belief is immediately apparent, but not so apparent are the ways of escape.

Clearly, if illusion be our aim, we shall endeavour to make our settings as lifelike as possible. Shaky flats will go completely. Our walls must be so solid that a man may fall against them without fear of their trembling ; or, if the scene represented be a modern-built bungalow, they must be of just that requisite jerry-built flimsiness which will make the illusion complete—for we must be careful not to let our endeavours carry us beyond this truth to reality. Everything on the stage must be exact and genuine : genuine liquid for the teacups and tankards, genuine butter for the plates. For this illusion obviously some frame is required, and the modern proscenium arch, devised after the travail of centuries, cannot be dissociated from the aims and achievements of the realistic school. The problem of the Fourth Wall could never have troubled an Elizabethan mind, for in an Elizabethan theatre no walls had existence. When you are forced to imagine three walls the absence of a fourth does not matter. But once the architect has made a frame and the scenic artist has put in that frame three sides of an interior together with a ceiling, we begin to worry about the gaping space immediately in front of us. No one in real life ever saw a room which had only three walls and a row of footlights ; no person in real life would act and talk so intimately did he know that a thousand spectators were watching him. Frantic efforts have been made to evade this difficulty. One producer will carefully lay a fender and fire-irons facing the footlights and audience, bidding his actors pretend to warm themselves at the possibly rather chilly atmosphere of the auditorium. Such a device, which once seemed so clever and up-to-date, does little more than call attention to the basic fallacy already referred to. Whether the actors pretend to warm themselves or not, the audience knows perfectly well that it is not a fireplace. And it knows, too, that it is not the Hudson river—so that the attempt made in the New York production in 1935 of Sidney Kingsley's *Dead End*, in which the orchestra pit was transformed into the piles at the river-bank and sirens instead of bells summoned the audience to their seats at the conclusion of the intervals, must be deemed untrue to the essential spirit of the theatre. Technical brilliance was here and sure accomplishment, but in many ways the endeavour to reproduce reality defeated its own ends.

The only logical solution, of course, is that proposed cynically by the Russian dramatist Evreinov. In effect his thesis goes as follows. If you wish realism, if you do hold this philosophy, for heaven's sake be reasonable. Never let a play be acted in English or in Russian the characters of which are supposed to be Swedes or Germans. Never employ a careful reproduction of a fourteenth-century oak table ; always purchase an original specimen. Don't bother about the audience : be bold and build up that fourth wall. Then, and then only, will your play, your acting, come close to real life.

Pirandello carries us a trifle farther still. Even with this, he declares, your play will not be realistic. Your actors, after all, are only actors pretending to be something they are not. Still more, even if we were to dismiss these actors, and employ a labourer, a clerk, a typist for their ' real ' parts, they could not produce in absolute sincerity the words, the intonations, the passions which they might have uttered or experienced at some chosen crisis in their careers. The only ' realistic ' play, we may declare, is to be found in the ordinary conversation and customary actions of daily life. Such logical application of the realistic theory results in a familiar *reductio ad absurdum*.

The trouble is that absurdities have an unfortunate way of clinging tenaciously to life. Our public, particularly in England and America, has become so thoroughly accustomed to seeing scenes

---

[1] It is important, of course, to distinguish between naturalism, wherein the utmost endeavour is made to reproduce reality, and realism (or selective realism), wherein a choice is made of such real objects as may best convey a theatrical impression. In general, the ordinary public will make small distinction between these, for both eschew the conventional and the element of choice in the latter is commonly overlooked.

of reality set before them on the stage that they have lost a true feeling for the essentially theatrical. To realize the justice of this statement we need do no more than consider the manner in which the word 'theatrical' itself has come to be used. Once 'theatrical' meant only 'that which appertains to, or is associated with, the theatre,' but since the growth of realism men began to display a certain sense of shame when they looked upon the art of acting, with the result that the adjective 'theatrical' developed a pejorative significance. To be theatrical in the theatre—absurd though it may seem—was regarded as a fault.

(ii) THEATRICALISM REBORN

Fortunately, as has been noted, there are not wanting signs to indicate that dissatisfaction with this prevalent realism is increasing, and at the same time that a new foundation is being sought. We are beginning to realize that the art of the theatre is an art, and that, being so, it has to be based on convention like all things aesthetic. The 'illusion' of the playhouse, we dimly perceive, should never be so complete that we forget the skill of the performers in front of us or the identity of ourselves as spectators. Above all, we are coming to recognize that our imaginations should be released by an avoidance of that detailed copying or imitation which characterized the thoroughgoing naturalistic production.

No movement in art is without its earlier analogues, and it is not surprising that many of the most forward-looking artists find a hope and an encouragement from contemplation of an earlier theatre. The Greek stage, symbolic and conventional, has assumed for us a new

FIG. 250. A SETTING FOR CHECHOV'S "THE THREE SISTERS" AT THE MOSCOW ART THEATRE
From Bashky, *The Path of the Russian Stage.*

importance; the Chinese formalism and the formalism of the Japanese Nō are fraught with new significance; out of the Middle Ages comes a dramatic expression which, although naïve, has much to give to us. Mere imitation, of course, can lead us nowhere: but from intelligent adaptation much may come. Nor is it to be supposed that the new way will take only one shape: vitality will be expressed through variety and diversity in effort.

For a time, it is true, the basic elements of the naturalistic ideal are being conserved by the activities of those who expound the mode of selective realism. Seeing that pure naturalism is impossible, but unable to escape from the illusionistic theory, these men claim that the true art of the theatre consists in presenting a choice of subjects from reality or in deviating just so slightly from reality as to make the stage picture, viewed at a distance, seem true to life. They have noted, for example, that a gesture or a costume which might be perfectly ordinary and acceptable if seen in a real room may become absurd or ineffective when, set upon the theatre's boards, it is looked at from the auditorium. A genuine snore might thus be considered artificial by an audience, and a sincere laugh savour of the unnatural. Everything, they have realized, that is introduced in a production requires controlling, augmenting, or restraining; otherwise, instead of giving an impression of the actual and the commonplace, there will be created an impression of unreality. In so far, therefore, the adherents of this school break with nineteenth-century methods, substituting a kind of theatricalism

Fig. 251. A Setting for Chechov's "A Month in the Country" by M. V. Dobujenski
(Moscow Art Theatre)

Fig. 252. Alexander Tolstoi's "Tsar Feodor Ioanovitch" as presented by the Moscow Art Theatre (1922)

for the earlier styles in faithful reproduction, but it is obvious that they are yet clearly wedded to the same ideal. They also want the theatre to be a place of illusion; only the means of attaining that end are different. In this school we have to recognize, not something new, but rather the last efforts, the final blossoming, of a plant which soon must perish. The achievements, genuinely worthy, of the Moscow Art Theatre should not blind us to the fact that out of such endeavours will not grow the theatre of the immediate future. The Moscow Art Theatre certainly still endures, and Stanislavski's ideals in histrionic method are eagerly studied by young enthusiasts in countries far removed

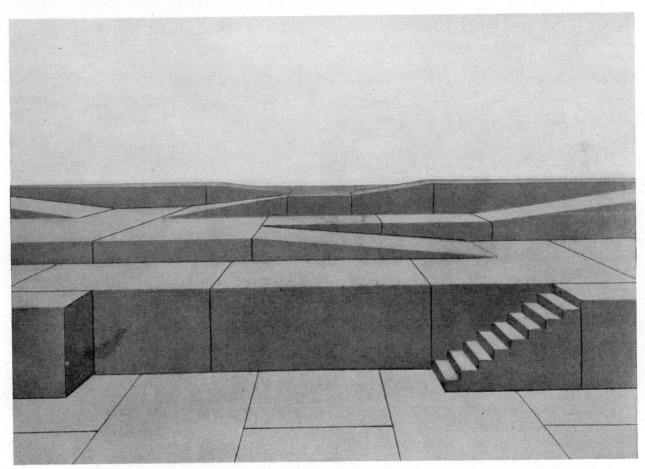

Fig. 253. A Setting for Gluck's "Orpheus" by Adolphe Appia

from his own. The future, however, belongs to those who react against the essential dogmas of his stage and who aim at things vastly different from those which animate his actors. Such reaction, it should be remembered, was born many years ago. As early as 1902 a Russian critic was proclaiming against the excesses of naturalism, and by his side creative artists were dreaming of other things to come. Even in the midst of that period when the realistic style was most markedly developing the ground beneath its feet was being undermined. For convenience we may consider the force of reaction to have taken two main forms, forms determined by the particular emphasis and interests of the revolutionaries. Naturalism demands as complete illusion as possible both in the setting and in the acting: one man may start to reform the first; another's aim may lie largely in reconstituting the histrionic basis of performance.

A start may be made by devoting some attention to those who sought a completely revised conception of the scenic accompaniments of drama. The battlecry was first raised by an Englishman, Gordon Craig, the son of London's most famous actress, Ellen Terry. Whether Craig's designs are adaptable to this theatre or that is a question which need not worry us here; all we are concerned with is the tendency of his work. It may be, as Lee Simonson declares, that his settings are theatrically impossible because conceived in terms too vast for any existing playhouse; it may be, as is asserted in *The Mask*, that many of Reinhardt's most vivid *décors* were but adaptations of Craigian conceptions—with these problems we have nothing to do. What it is important to note is the general tendency, the basic ideal, on which Craig has founded his work. Expressed simply, this ideal may be described as a revolt against the falsity of the realistic method, a determination to dismiss the trivialities which only too often do service for art on the stage.

For those falsities he would substitute symbolic form, and to dismiss the trivialities he would make the theatre once more a temple. Mass of light and shade he substitutes for naturalistic detail, suggestive shapes of a statuesque kind he brings in place of illusionistic interiors, and different planes of action he provides for the more adequate display of the actors. Easily is it seen that with these ideals Craig draws near to the theatre of the Greeks; from it he derives inspiration and strives to draw things which will be of service to a later age. Designing a set for the *Electra* of Sophocles, he fills his stage with " a vast and forbidding doorway "— hardly more than that, reality reduced to its simplest forms. To evoke the mood of *Hamlet*

Fig. 254. A Setting for "King Lear" at the Deutsches Theater, 1908. Design by Karl Czeschka
From Sayler, *Max Reinhardt and his Theatre.*

he gives us great hanging curtains to establish the sense of loftiness, diverse planes for the actors to move on, and, for suggesting the outer world, a glimpse of sky seen through parted folds with a glimpse of the wandering moon.

Craig uses curtains on occasion, but in his work the prevailing element is three-dimensional form. He attacks the naturalistic theatre, but he also attacks the painted theatre. There is practically no 'decoration' in his designs; mass solely is used to convey his effects. In this he allies himself to another pioneer, the Swiss Adolphe Appia, whose work, although usually emphasizing the horizontal in place of Craig's typically vertical lines, resembles his in its rejection of detail and of painted ornamentation. In both, to secure variety, light plays its part, creating mood quality besides supplying illumination by which the actors may be viewed and which is devised to imitate the sunlight or moonlight of nature.

The Craig-Appia method may be taken as the first path of escape. Three-dimensional, extremely simple in its masses, with ample space for the actors, it forms a basis from which many artists have taken their ideas. To trace such artistic borrowings in detail would be a lengthy and laborious task.

A few examples may serve to indicate how diverse is the imitation. In such a design as Karl Czeschka's palace for *King Lear* (Fig. 254), as produced at the Deutsches Theater in 1908, there is evident the same use of severely unadorned masses of light and shade, an elimination of detail, and a consequent endeavour to evoke mood and to arouse imagination by conventional means. Far removed from this is Ernst Stern's doorway for *The Miracle* (Fig. 255), with its stained-glass windows; yet here, too, some of the Craigian ideas are working. The plain walls, the vastness of proportion, recall the general conceptions animating Craig's work. Still other artists, who otherwise may deviate far from these general conceptions, have found inspiration in the various planes of action. The notorious steps of Leopold Jessner at Berlin's Schauspielhaus are a direct result of this part at least of Craig's revolutionary activities.

The simple, three-dimensional masses, familiarized throughout Europe by many reproductions, did more than merely suggest subjects for imitation. From them sprang still further styles, some so far removed that at first glance we should hardly dream of seeing any connexion between them and the earlier efforts of Appia and Craig. In Terence Gray's cubes of different sizes, so constructed that they might be fitted together into any desired scenic shapes, one recognizes merely a device whereby settings of the simple mass kind could be easily built up; but in essential aim the methods used by Gray differed in all but one respect from Craig's. For the latter the scenery was of prime import; at least, for him the setting had to be an artistic unity conceived of and appreciable without the introduction of actors. That actors make the play no one realized better than Craig, but that does not imply that the background against

Fig. 255. A Setting for "The Miracle" (1911), by Ernst Stern
From Sayler, *op. cit.*

which the performers stood and the levels on which they moved should not thrill and awe and please for its own beauty. In Terence Gray's hands the masses of simple planes became for the most part merely acting space; the set as such had lost its meaning and could be vested with significance only when the business of the stage was in action before and upon it.

The Terence Gray style forms a transition which leads us onward to constructivism. Alexander Tairov in the Kamerny Theatre, Vachtangov's work enshrined in the Third Studio of the Moscow Art Theatre, Mardshanov with his ideals for a synthetic theatre, Meyerhold eager for bio-mechanics, Foregger bringing play-acting to the level of acrobatics, and Eisenstein devising new staging for the Proletkult Theatre may here be considered together. Fundamentally all believe that the theatre must be based on the work of the actors, that the theatre must strive to be conventional, and that the 'setting' must become dynamic in the sense that its significance will derive solely from the movement of the human figures associated with it. Mardshanov's ideal player who is singer, actor, and dancer in one is the basis of all this endeavour, and naturally in the search for support recourse has freely been made to the ancient *commedia dell' arte*, the performers in which, barely removed from their companions of the mountebank stages, were gymnasts, contortionists, and jugglers as well as artists in the realm of improvisatory prose and operatic aria. Not all, of course, subscribe to the same specific aims. For Tairov scenery was significant and valuable; to Meyerhold it seemed a snare, deluding with false loveliness. Alexandra Exter's constructivist design for Calderon's *La Dama duende* (Fig. 257) has a beauty of its own besides providing free planes for histrionic action, whereas Meyerhold's ideal tends toward the bare walls relieved only by a few pieces of property, mostly for the sake of gymnastic display (Fig. 258).

Obviously in all of these, modern tendencies in pictorial art have freely been utilized. Cubism has provided ideas for the employment of various planes; Italian futurism has given suggestions for the simple massing of form; the anticipatory movements leading toward present-day Surrealism

Fig. 256. "PRINCESS TURANDOT" AS GIVEN BY THE MOSCOW ART THEATRE

adumbrated the use of symbols and intensified the reaction to earlier naturalistic endeavours. Dynamic vitality is sought for here in place of static beauty. Constructivism banishes scenery as we know it, substituting in its place an unadorned stage set with scaffoldings which support platforms and raised passage-ways to provide amplitude of acting level. With their machine forms these enthusiasts stress the mechanical and dynamic quality of our age, and strive to give us the modern equivalent of that conventionality so patently captured for the seventeenth century in Callot's etchings and for the nineteenth in the gaudy series of prints "twopence coloured." The naturalistic decorum, imitative of the quiet life of ordinary existence, is banished, and in its stead comes a new flamboyancy, a fresh theatricalism.

Closely associated with the entirety of this activity from Craig to Eisenstein are the formal 'architectural' settings of the Redoutensaal at Vienna and of the Théâtre du vieux Colombier at Paris; but perhaps it will be best for the moment to leave these aside in order to discuss the counterpart of

Fig. 257. Constructivist Setting for Calderon's "La Dama Duende" by Alexandra Exter

Fig. 258. Ostrovsky's "The Forest" as given by the Meyerhold Theatre (1924)

the three-dimensional theatre, for amid all the questing of recent years the substantial, practicable set has not alone occupied the stage. Quite evidently reaction to the realistic stage picture could take one of two directions. On the one hand, men might endeavour to simplify, render symbolic, or utterly banish the ordinary elements of the set; on the other hand, they might try to get back to conventionalism by frank painting of three-dimensional forms, perhaps emphasizing the artificiality by false perspective and bizarre exaggeration. For a time painted sets of this kind attracted much attention because of the work of many talented artists who were employed by the Russian ballet, nearly all of whom owed allegiance to that extraordinary genius Leon Bakst. That Bakst's inspiration goes back to early Byzantine art is obvious. From it he has taken his rich colours, his grotesque conceptions, his formalism. Greece has influenced him too: but the gods of ancient Athens relive their existence here in a light which is tinged always with the hues of the ikon; perhaps one might say that the element which most appealed to him in Grecian art was precisely that

formalism which, in an extreme form, grew into the unreality of the Byzantine miniature. Bakst was a theatrical innovator who had a thorough knowledge and love of the theatre, and that passion for the stage he handed down, together with much of his inspiration, to his immediate followers. Gontcharova too is animated by the Byzantine formality (Fig. 262), carrying that style still farther in theatrical expression, while many elements in Bakst's artistry are transformed into abstractions by Larionov or into strange bizarreries by Poshedaiev.

So long as the painted set remains vitalized by theatrical effectiveness it is a worthy and stimulating form; its dangers become apparent when that

FIG. 259. A SETTING FOR "DIE WÜPPER" (1919), BY ERNST STERN
From Sayler, *op. cit.*

knowledge of the stage which Bakst possessed so markedly are absent. When Diagkeliev came to Paris the Russian style was dominant on his stage; but only too soon he started to encourage French artists—Picasso, Braque, Bauchant, and others—to design for him. Many of these men were purely easel painters, and often their conception of a theatrical setting was simply a canvas enlarged to sufficient size for a back-drop. Like cinematic close-ups, huge shapes of animals and humans hung in devastating immobility behind the dancers, who once had received added grace and value from the closely harmonized union of physical movement and painted settings. In this style can reside naught of theatrical virtue.

The painted set and the three-dimensional set are distinguished by their methods of securing certain preconceived ends, but in the revolt against the exact naturalism of the nineteenth century must be noted one other development which is marked out not by method, but by fundamental conception. Surrealism has recently achieved a certain popularity in intellectual circles; but so far we are more familiar with Surrealist experiments in painting and in verse than with attempts to express similar aims in theatrical form. Basically Surrealism represents a reaction against the utilization of that ordinary 'reality,' the common phenomena of daily experience, which art since the time of the Renascence has striven to capture and present aesthetically in enduring shapes; in this reaction an

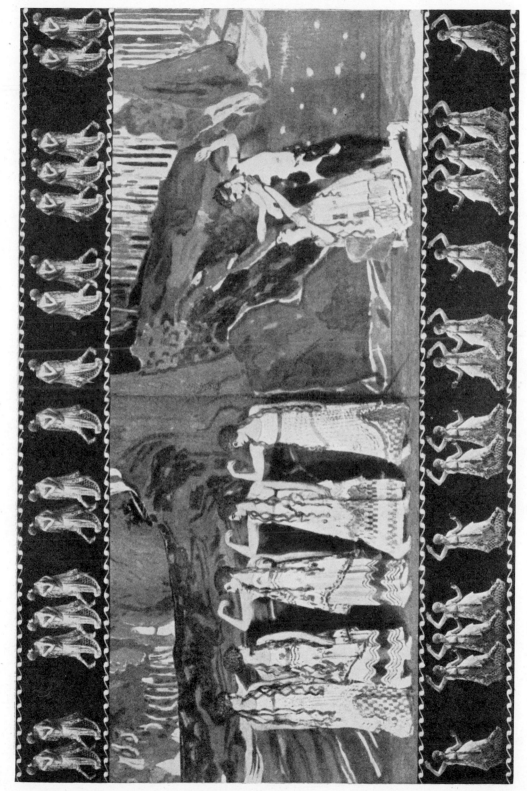

Fig 260. A Setting for "L'Après-midi d'un Faune," by Leon Bakst

endeavour is being made, not to present such phenomena in 'stylized' manner, but to discover an essentially fresh foundation. They have read Freud and Jung, these Surrealists, and have entered into the world of the subconscious; the dream is to them what walking vision was to their predecessors. Caviare still to the general, there is to be discerned here a movement which has seized

Fig. 261. A FIGURE STUDY FOR "L'OISEAU DE FEU"
BY BAKST

on many imaginations and which is intimately to be related to kindred tendencies in the modern novel, as well as in poetic circles not owing strict allegiance to the Surrealist masters.

All these movements, and many others too numerous to chronicle here, are independent, yet ultimately the source of each is to be traced back to one desire common to all—the wish to cast aside and to destroy the realistic theatre which was the child of nineteenth-century romanticism. True, realism still rules among the general public; yet one need not be temerarious to assert that the realistic theatre is dying or dead. The reason is, of course, a simple one. Historical realism and the realism of daily life were in the nineteenth century exciting things because hitherto unattempted and barely dreamed of ; now the stage equipment has reached such a perfection that a naturalistic effect which would have startled audiences sixty years ago is the common expectation in any metropolitan playhouse. Art can subsist only when there comes with it an element of the unexpected and the hardly won, and realism accordingly must go, leaving the path open for a conventionalism from which may be wrested things more worthy and more enduring than the problem dramas of a Pinero and a Jones.

It is, of course, not to be expected that any one of the more revolutionary tendencies should seize sole hold of the stage either now or in the immediate future ; audiences still find a certain pleasure—the pleasure, perhaps, of familiarity—in seeing theatrical representations of a naturalistic kind, but already these same audiences are manifesting a willingness to accept conventionalities of a sort which would have been odious to their generation immediately preceding. In England Lovat Fraser brought to Sir Nigel Playfair's productions at the Lyric, Hammersmith, a pattern and a sense of style both of which were essentially 'artificial,' and the more noted scene-designers of London, men such as Paul Shelving, Oliver Messel, Aubrey Hammond, Norman Wilkinson, George Sheringham, and Albert Rutherston, are constantly striving to break from the imitative methods of the past. The same is true of America. There too the designers, Robert Edmond Jones, Lee Simonson, Donald Oenslager, Norman Bel Geddes, Jo Mielziner, and others, while frequently they are compelled to give an impression of reality with solidly built-up scenes, set their imaginations free and take delight in a deliberate theatricalism which borrows from, or independently re-creates, many conventions long banished from the stage. All countries have shown the same desires. Of present-day Germany it is impossible to speak, but in the Germany of

Fig. 262. A Figure Study by Natalie Gontcharova

1918–28 the newer aims were predominant. Predominant, too, were those aims among the leaders of the Parisian 'Théâtre d'avant-garde,' as well as in most European capitals. Everywhere has been manifested a desire to start afresh on a basis which, while novel, at the same time reproduced the forms cast over by the theatre of the nineties. So far, it is true, we cannot point to any single co-ordinating principle (as we may, for example, when we turn to the days of the Athenians and of Elizabethan London), but possibly we are only waiting for a crystallization of thought and for a theatre structure in which these things may adequately find expression.

Fig. 263. Scenery for "L'Oiseau de Feu" (Act II) by Natalie Gontcharova

MALVERN FESTIVAL 1934.
THE INTERLUDE OF YOUTH

Fig. 264. A Setting by Paul Shelving for "The Interlude of Youth," as produced at Malvern, 1934

Fig. 265. A Setting by Aubrey Hammond for "Acropolis," by Robert E. Sherwood

Fig. 266. A Setting by Lee Simonson for "Marco Millions"

Fig. 267. A Setting by Donald Oenslager for "The Emperor Jones," by Eugene O'Neill, as presented at the Yale University Theatre

Fig. 268. Design by Jo Mielziner for Maxwell Anderson's "Winterset" (1935)

Fig. 269. Design by Robert Edmond Jones for "Macbeth"

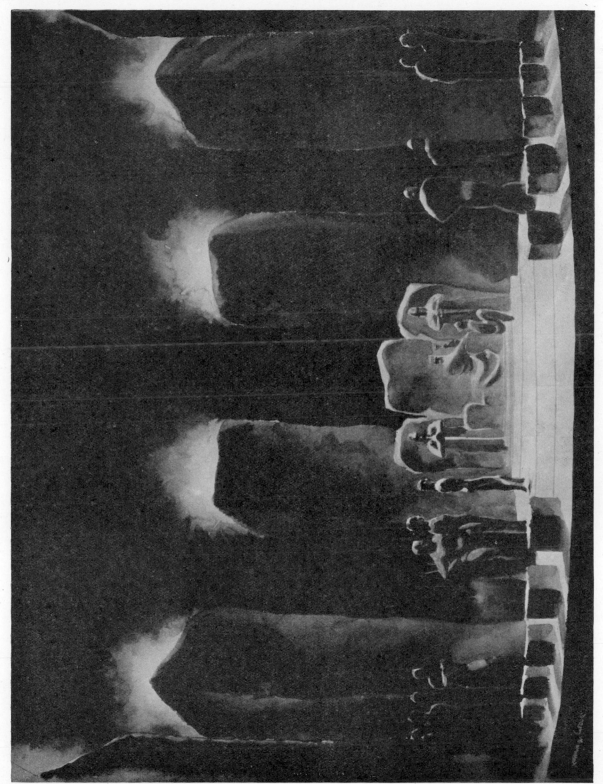

Fig. 270. Design by Norman Bel Geddes for "King Lear"

(iii) The Complex and Simple Theatre

The theatre structure is truly of fundamental import, for in nowise can we hope for a free and fitting realization of the aims until the playhouse itself is harmonized to their mood. Already it has been shown how the familiar 'picture-frame' stage, the final achievement of the nineteenth-

Fig. 271. A Setting for "The Unknown Soldier" (Kamerny Theatre, Moscow, 1932), by Leonid Pervomaiski. Design by V. Rindin

century theatre, was the obvious result of the naturalistic ideal. By a strange paradox men found that to secure realistic illusion the audience had to be separated from the actors, with the result that playhouses which, in Greek and medieval and Elizabethan times, had brought public and performers into closest association now were divided into two portions, separated both materially and by the operation of light: there was, on the one hand, a darkened auditorium, and, on the other, a brightly lit stage framed by the proscenium arch and the row of footlights. As realism demanded fresh worlds for the conquering this simple picture-frame playhouse became gradually more complex. The auditorium remained virtually unaltered, but the stage grew into a wondrous machine. To build up a solidly constructed set is not so difficult a task, but theatre workers found that but few modern dramatists were satisfied with a single locality for their action, and that the ' classic ' playwrights, such as Shakespeare, were so criminally lavish with their scenes that even a murderous revision of the text could not reduce the localities below ten or a dozen. Obviously, therefore, something had to be done to the theatre itself. In the good old days a set was altered by the simple expedient of running in a fresh set of wings on grooves attached to the acting floor and of changing the backcloth ; no longer was this possible. To alter one of these new realistic interiors to another demanded a considerably greater expenditure of energy and often of much more time than an audience might reasonably be asked to endure.

Fig. 272. A Setting for "Una Familia" (Teatro de Orientación, Mexico City, 1933)

Hence the period between 1880 and 1920 is marked by the erection of ever more ornately constructed theatres, with mechanical contrivances calculated to make easier the presentation of realistic settings. In America an inventive genius, Steele MacKaye, was dreaming of some way to overcome these difficulties, and in 1879 he filed a patent for a " double stage," a stage realized in the Madison Square Theatre. Driving the orchestra to the top of the proscenium arch (the position it occupied in London's Dorset Garden Theatre), MacKaye built an elevator platform so devised that while a scene was being played below a new scene might be set above, ready for lowering when the time came. This, it seems, was the very first of the mechanical theatres, but soon the idea was seized upon in Germany, and, because of its development there, it is to Germany our thoughts turn when we think of these things. Diverse were the methods devised. Sometimes the stage was made to slide to right or left ; sometimes a sliding device was combined with an elevating one ; sometimes the revolving stage, as introduced by Lautenschläger at Munich in 1896, was employed (Fig. 274). Nowadays our predilections normally turn in other directions, but even in 1934 the Stratford

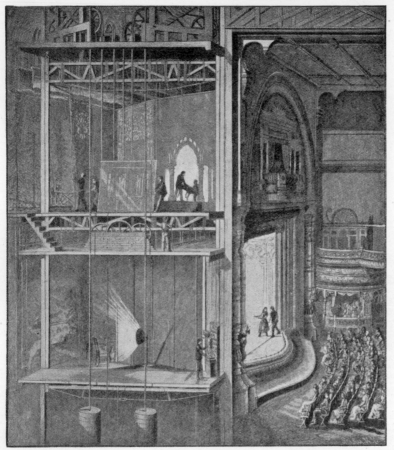

Fig. 273. THE MADISON SQUARE THEATRE, NEW YORK, 1879

authorities determined on this type of playhouse for the new Shakespeare Memorial Theatre. Here a combination of mechanical aids has created a stage which might have been the ideal of a director in 1900.

So soon, however, as realism is abandoned such theatres clearly become useless. In the days of conventional side-wings and backcloths no more could have been achieved by the use of these mechanical stages, supposing they had been in existence at that time; and to-day those who embrace the more recently developed forms of theatrical conventionalism discover that the vast machines invented in the immediate past are not only negatively useless but positively cumbersome and restrictive. The enormous revolving and sliding stages of the Continent are, thus soon, rendered old-fashioned, the antiquated relic of an age that is nearly gone.

The mechanical stage, the instrument of realism, naturally required a closely defined proscenium frame. Sometimes the frame too might become mechanized and be contrived so that its shape altered at the will of the director, but, fixed or mobile, large or small, it had to be there in order to conceal the workings within. Reaction to realism, on the other hand, has most commonly led to a breaking of the fourth wall. So far the efforts have been tentative, and, being so, have often sought for support in past achievements. Maybe we shall be permitted to set aside the revival of 'Elizabethan' stages, sponsored so enthusiastically by William Poel, regarding such a revival as a kind of outgrowth from the earlier historical realism; but we cannot thus set aside the deliberate seeking for inspiration in the Athenian and eighteenth-century theatres. For a time the Greek ideal

Fig. 274. A MODEL OF THE REVOLVING STAGE AT THE DEUTSCHES THEATER

From Sayler, *op. cit.*

220

dominated in the mind of Reinhardt. The Grosses Schauspielhaus in Berlin, with its carefully planned stage and ' orchestra,' its towering dome of innumerable lights, its vast seating accommodation, demonstrably springs from study of the Dionysian theatre at Athens. All that remains of the old proscenium is a rectangular frame serving to mask what is now a mere background for the actors. Audience and players are once more united.

After the Grosses Schauspielhaus Reinhardt turned to the Redoutensaal at Vienna. This beautiful ballroom, once the delight of Maria Theresa, he converted into a theatre of purely formal design. Here too the ' proscenium ' is moved back of the actors. A central aperture and four

Fig. 275. The Grosses Schauspielhaus, Berlin
From Sayler, *op. cit.*

doors, reminiscent of the Teatro Olimpico, becomes a setting for all kinds of plays. Locale, instead of being illusionistically displayed, finds suggestion merely by the placing of a few properties on the stage, chairs, tables, trees in tubs, screens, serving to indicate for the audience the surroundings of the actors. Reinhardt's Redoutensaal is no solitary experiment. A similar stage resulted from the efforts of Jacques Copeau at the Parisian Théâtre du vieux Colombier. From a small stage steps lead down to the ground-level. A wide aperture is at the back, doors give exits left and right, and the whole is framed within a series of three arches. Again a few properties, the use of a screen or a curtain, serve to indicate the locality and the atmosphere.

In none of these theatres are audience and actors separated. Directional method, too, tends to make use of every means for binding them together ; kindred directional method may be found even in playhouses originally designed for the naturalistic style. Periodically one finds performances wherein players are brought up through the auditorium, or where the boxes are used, not to seat spectators, but to provide additional acting space. At the best, methods of this kind applied to the picture-frame stage are but a makeshift, and the combination of two ideas generally results in a feeling of dissatisfaction; but no other way is open when the theatrical structure has not been specifically built to accord with the non-realistic approach. The truth is that stage architects in general have somewhat lagged behind their fellows, the scene-designers. The latter have repeatedly broken away along new lines, but when new theatres are being built hardly ever is there a thought of escaping from the tyranny of the proscenium frame. In England almost the only playhouse provided with a more adaptable arrangement was the Festival Theatre at Cambridge, designed by Terence Gray.

Fig. 276. JACQUES COPEAU'S STAGE AT THE VIEUX COLOMBIER, PARIS

The picture-frame form really suits only one style of approach; for that it was conceived, and to that properly it belongs. What modern theatre workers require is something less finally fixed, something which will give them the opportunity of harmonizing the directional treatment and the spirit of the play. The poets once more are beginning to arouse themselves and appreciate the possibilities of the theatre. Sean O'Casey writes *Within the Gates*, T. S. Eliot writes *Murder in the Cathedral*, Maxwell Anderson writes *Winterset*, and Gordon Bottomley experiments in novel choric types. These plays return to an older conventionalism. Fundamentally they find closer kinship with the extreme artificiality of the Chinese and Japanese dramas than they do with *A Doll's House* or *Strife*. Each one cries out for the re-establishment of a playhouse which shall acknowledge frankly the value of pure theatricalism.

In the search for this new theatre the efforts of the past have had much to contribute and are likely to contribute still more. From the Greeks we may learn, and from the medieval stage and from the stage of the Renascence—from the playhouses of those times when the naturalistic ideals were absent and unconceived. Genuine and valid utilization of past efforts, however, may be reached only when we understand fully the co-ordination of all things pertaining to the stage during each period. To rebuild a Shakespearian Globe Theatre may be interesting and valuable; significant may be the presentation of Greek tragedies in their original surroundings; but we could not hope to adapt either the one method or the other and use that as the basis for a modern playhouse. Before we can use these significantly we need to know all that may be learned concerning the relations between the particular stage and its actors, between audience and playwrights, between the social conditions of the spectators and the ideas expressed in the plays. Herein precisely lies the value of studying in meticulous detail the theatre that has gone. Hardly any art is so perishable as the art dramatic. A performance vanishes as soon as it has been presented : nothing remains but the bare text of the play which gave it occasion. At first we might imagine that, the theatre being thus a transient thing, an insubstantial pageant and a baseless fabric, it were mere waste of time to investigate the conditions which gave it birth. The more we see of the theatre, however, the more we realize that inspiration for the future is to be sought for in days that are beyond us. Gordon Craig knew this ; this has been one of the secrets of Reinhardt's success. If our own days, as seems likely, are to see the building up of a new playhouse, with ideals far removed from those of Charles Kean and David Belasco, we may rest assured that the basic aim granting it life and interest, animating all its parts, and giving it harmony of expression, will be closely related to other aims which once inspired playwrights and actors in bygone eras. The new aim will not, if it be truly worthy, merely copy these, but it will embody their essential principles in a corporeal frame apt to appeal to audiences of our time.

APPENDIX A

A NOTE ON COSTUME ON THE ELIZABETHAN STAGE

THE question of Elizabethan stage costume, touched upon briefly at pp. 136–137 and 177–183, is one which has been peculiarly neglected. Sir Edmund Chambers apparently does not deal with it at all in his *Elizabethan Stage*, and, although Professor Creizenach and Professor Thorndike note in passing that certain conventional dresses were used in Shakespearian playhouses, the general assumption is that throughout the sixteenth and early seventeenth centuries plays were put forward in contemporary costumes. It is this assumption which has led to the production of *Hamlet* (and other plays) in 'modern dress.' A more careful analysis, however, of Elizabethan conventions tends to prove that Oscar Wilde's overstrained and not always scholarly thesis in *The Truth of Masks* possesses more than a stylistic value, and that the general assumption is based on a too hurried examination of the evidence at hand, or even is due to a complete neglect of it.

The subject, as I have endeavoured to show, cannot be rightly considered until we take into our survey the theatrical traditions, not only of the Elizabethan, but of the Georgian era as well. The eighteenth-century prints, some of which I have reproduced in this volume, may tell us much of the conditions operating in the seventeenth-century playhouse. So too a study of French and Italian stage dresses often has a very direct bearing upon the conventions of the Elizabethan stage. Such a study, however, cannot be entered into here, and I wish merely to draw attention to a few indications in plays and property lists which seem to have a connexion with this subject.

That Hamlet, Macbeth, and others normally wore Elizabethan dress no one can deny ; the later prints prove that Garrick and his compeers retained what was undoubtedly an ancient tradition. The fact remains, however, that other characters, distinguished by country or age, abandoned Elizabethan costume in favour of robes more correct historically or imaginatively more appealing. It may not be inopportune here to indicate some references to the types of special costumes outlined in Chapter X (pp. 177–183). These may best be considered separately.

(1) TURKISH COSTUMES

" iiij genesareyes [janizaries'] gownes . . . iiij Turckes hedes . . . j Mores [Moor's] cotte " are mentioned by Henslowe in his 1598 inventories. The " hedes " may refer to turbans or headpieces : thus in Kyd's *Soliman and Perseda* Lucina asks Basilisco :

> But how chance,
> Your turkish bonnet is not on your head ?

and he replies :

> Because I now am Christian againe,

proving that the " turkish bonnet " had been worn in the earlier part of the play and was some typical headgear. We may, it seems to me, refer from public stage costumes to those worn at Court ; while it would be foolish to suppose that the ordinary playhouse costumes were as rich as those worn at royal festivals, it must be presumed that there would not be a vast cleavage

225

between the two. In Professor Feuillerat's *Documents relating to the Office of the Revels in the Time of Queen Elizabeth*[1] we learn that Turkish commoners in 1560 wore "hedpeces of yellowe golde sarsnet" and "longe gounes of damaske," while Turkish magistrates had "longe streighte turkye gownes of redd cloth of gold," with "longe Sleves" and "Capes of the same figured clothe of gold." Among Inigo Jones' drawings for *Britannia Triumphans* is a 'Turk' dressed in wide trousers, a close-fitting jacket, and a turban.

From these notices, added to the *Titus Andronicus* sketch (Fig. 152), we may hazard the suggestion that Eastern characters wore (1) either wide "Turkish trousers" (like the figure to the extreme left of the last-mentioned drawing) or tights (like Aaron), (2) close-fitting boots, as shown in Aaron here or in eighteenth-century prints, (3) a close-fitting tunic with puffed sleeves which could be rolled back, (4) a turban, and often (5) a loose dressing-gown-like robe with long sleeves. As a weapon the Eastern characters normally carried a scimitar—assuredly not an Elizabethan instrument of offence. This curved scimitar is shown in the *Titus Andronicus* drawing, and is referred to frequently in contemporary drama.

> He dies vpon my Semitars sharpe point

cries Aaron in *Titus Andronicus*, while Basilisco in *Soliman and Perseda* declares that

> with this Semitor,
> [I], alle on foote . . .
> Endured some three or foure howers combat,

and Soliman remarks that Perseda's white neck

> Will breake the edge of my keene Semitor.

The Prince of Morocco in *The Merchant of Venice* is made to swear

> By this scimitar
> That slew the Sophy.

(2) ROMAN COSTUMES

The Roman costume is less easy to disentangle and define, although there are examples of it among Inigo Jones' drawings. It is probable that the figure second on the left in the *Titus Andronicus* sketch is in this dress. Gowns must have been worn by persons of higher estate, and Shakespeare, following Plutarch, seems to make special use of the "woolvish gown" which had to be worn by the candidate for the consulship. The eighteenth-century prints show well the mingling of contemporary and ancient in this conventional dress.

(3) ALLEGORICAL COSTUMES AND COSTUMES OF DEITIES

There are many indications in plays and elsewhere that allegorical figures and the classical deities wore distinctive dress. It is impossible here to indicate all the types mentioned, and the following list must, accordingly, be regarded as severely selective.

i. *Neptune*. "j sewtte for Nepton" is mentioned by Henslowe, and the same inventory chronicles "Nepun forcke & garland."

ii. *Juno*. Henslowe records "Junoes cotte," and Inigo Jones has a sketch of her costume (Inigo Jones, *Masque Designs*, Malone and Walpole Societies, No. 102, Plate XIV).

---

[1] I omit references here to the other volume of Revels accounts, although that contains many matters of interest concerning costume at an earlier period.

iii. *Phaeton*. Henslowe has "j Faeytone sewte" as well as "ij leather anteckes cottes with basses, for Fayeton."

iv. *Dido*. In Henslowe we find mention of "Dides robe."

v. *Iris*. "Ierosses head, and raynbowe" appear in Henslowe. Inigo Jones has a sketch of Iris (*op. cit.*, No. 7, Plate III) and another along with Juno (*op. cit.*, No. 102, Plate XIV). It will be remembered that both of these appear in Shakespeare's *The Tempest*.

vi. *Mercury*. "Mercures wings" appear in Henslowe, and no doubt the "Cadeseus" was used by this divinity.

vii. *Ghosts*. Henslowe mentions "j gostes sewt, and j gostes bodeyes" as a special property. The stage directions in dramas bidding some character to "enter like a ghost" no doubt refer to this, a particularized, costume.

(4) Animal Costumes

There is frequent mention of animal costumes both in Henslowe and in the Revels accounts. Shakespeare has his ass's head and lion in *A Midsummer Night's Dream* and his bear in *The Winter's Tale*. Among Henslowe's entries are "j lyone skin . . . j bears skyne . . . j bores heade . . . j dragon . . . j lyone . . . ij lyon heades . . . j great horse . . . j black dogge." Twelve "Lyons heades counterfeicte" were made for the Revels' Office in 1578, while an "artificiall lyon, and horse" appear in a 1581 account. Inigo Jones has a human lion of this type among his drawings for *Tempe Restor'd* (*op. cit.*, No. 146); among these drawings may be noted also an ape (No. 147) and an ass (No. 148). Along with these animal costumes should be recorded "Serberosse [Cerberus'] iij heades" in Henslowe.

(5) Professional, Foreign, and Similar Costumes

That Portia wore a lawyer's gown we must assume, and that the artizans of *A Midsummer Night's Dream* were distinguished in costume from the aristocrats is certain. The habiliments of the various trades and professions must have appeared regularly on the Elizabethan stage. Again a few references must stand for many. Henslowe records several times "freyers gownes" with "hoodes to them," and friars are of frequent occurrence in sixteenth- and seventeenth-century drama. "j senetores gowne, j hoode, and 5 senetores capes" points to a regular dress for civic authorities in foreign-set plays; the costumes of the Venetian senators in the Revels accounts may be compared with these. Shylock wears his Jewish gaberdine. Among Henslowe's records are frequently mentioned special garments for Robin Hood plays: "j green gown for Maryan . . . vj grene cottes for Roben Hoode . . . Roben Hoodes sewte"— all of these point to specialized costumes. Among the others we may note "ij whitt sheperdes cottes," "j fooles coate, cape, and babell," "Merlen gowne and cape," "j carnowll [cardinal's] hatte," and "j hode for the wech." Some foreign nationalities, and some particular foreign characters, seem also to have been thus distinguished. "ij Danes sewtes, and j payer of Danes hosse" are mentioned, as are also Spanish dresses. In addition we find "j payer of hosse for the Dowlfen," "Vartemar sewtte," "Tamberlynes cotte, with coper lace . . . and . . . Tamberlanes breches, of crymson velluet." Special properties were apportioned to such characters. "j helmet with a dragon," "j poopes miter," "iij Imperiall crownes" and "j crown with a sone" could have been worn only by certain marked characters. Perhaps among these figures may be noted the Druid pictured by Inigo Jones (*op. cit.*, No. 320) for Carlell's play of *The Passionate Lovers*.

(6) Historical Costumes

When we turn to the Folio, open it at *Henry VIII*, and read the following passage we feel that Shakespeare or Fletcher (for our purpose it matters not which) was not so blind to the purely pictorial value of the history he dramatized as we often assume.

THE ORDER OF THE CORONATION

1 *A liuely Flourish of Trumpets.*

2 *Then, two Iudges*

3 *Lord* Chancellor, *with Purse and Mace before him.*

4 Quirristers *singing.* Musicke.

5 Maior of London, *bearing the Mace. Then Garter, in his Coate of Armes, and on his head he wore a Gilt Copper Crowne.*

6 Marquesse Dorset, *bearing a Scepter of Gold, on his head, a Demy Coronall of Gold. With him, the Earle of* Surrey, *bearing the Rod of Siluer with the Doue, Crowned with an Earles Coronet. Collars of Esses.*

7 Duke of Suffolke, *in his Robe of Estate, his Coronet on his head, bearing a long white Wand, as High Steward. With him, the Duke of* Norfolke, *with the Rod of Marshalship, a Coronet on his head. Collars of Esses.*

8 *A* Canopy, *borne by foure of the* Cinque-Ports, *vnder it the Queene in her Robe, in her haire, richly adorned with Pearle, Crowned. On each side her, the Bishops of* London, *and* Winchester.

9 *The* Olde Duchesse of Norfolke, *in a Coronall of Gold, wrought with Flowers, bearing the Queenes Traine.*

10 *Certaine* Ladies *or* Countesses, *with plaine Circlets of Gold, without Flowers.*

The average Elizabethan, no doubt, had but a vague conception of the details in the dress of his forefathers, but we can hardly suppose that he was totally ignorant of the fact that costumes had changed, nor can we suppose that the complete presentation of an historical tragedy in Elizabethan doublet and hose would have appeared to him perfectly fitting. Once more, we may hardly presume a complete cleavage between court or university plays and plays given in the public theatres; at least part of the audience for both was the same. That thoughts of historical costume stirred the universities is amply proved by the letter sent by the Master of Trinity on January 28, 1594(5), to the Chancellor, requesting the loan of some special dresses:

> Whereas we intend . . . to sett forth certaine Comoedies and one Tragoedye, there being in that Tragoedie sondry personages of greatest estate to be represented in auncient princely attire wch is no where to be had, but within the office of the Roabes at the Tower: it is our humble request . . . that upon sufficient securitie we might be furnished from thence with such meete necessaries as are required . . . wch favor we have founde heretofore.

Among Henslowe's records, besides a collection of general attributes of royalty and the like, including " j globe, & j golden scepter . . . j wooden hatchett . . . jx eyorn targates . . . j copper targate . . . iiij wooden targates . . . j playne crowne . . . j crown with a sone," we have mention of " j greve armer," and " j longe sorde," which seemingly were " auncient." " Haryc the v. satten dublet " and " Harey the fyftes vellet gowne " seem to point to a special dress—otherwise they need hardly have belonged to a particular character, but could have served for many. Shakespeare's *Henry VI* makes mention of tabards and crested helmets, characteristics of a bygone age, while in the *Richard II* play contained in the famous Egerton manuscript reference is made to those strange toe-chained shoes which had, in the Elizabethan age, long vanished from men's memories.

In surveying this whole question it appears to me that too much is made of the references in Shakespeare's historical and Roman plays to 'caps,' 'bonnets,' 'doublets,' and the like. There is no doubt that Elizabethan features must have appeared in all costumes, but that does not militate against the supposition (which seems to me almost a certainty) that along with certain elements of Elizabethan dress went special characteristics intended to be symbolic of past ages or of other lands. If this be assumed we find that nearly every play of Shakespeare's will contain some character or characters distinguished by particular dress. One might assume that most of the persons in *Romeo* were in Elizabethan garments, but the friar and perhaps the apothecary would give a flavour of antiquity. *Troilus*, *Coriolanus*, *Titus*, *Timon*, *Julius Caesar*, *Antony*, and *Pericles* might all contain elements of Roman costume, which might also appear, with other features, in *Cymbeline*. For *Hamlet* we must remember Henslowe's " Danes' suits," for *Macbeth* the witches' garments, for *Lear* the costume shown in the *Titus Andronicus* drawing, and for *Othello* the Eastern dress. Several of the comedies, of course, are set in almost contemporary times, and, in any case, we do not need in comedy the same atmosphere as we require in history play or tragedy. Yet even here there are fools, fairies, artisans who grow asses' heads, magicians, friars, lawyers, Russians, Jews, and bears—a pretty little collection of characters who would appear in diversified garments on the contemporary stage. The assumption that by putting Shakespeare in modern dress we come back to Elizabethan methods of staging is not so certain as it appears at first sight ; perhaps that escape for the modern producer is as false as the methods employed by an Irving and a Tree.

APPENDIX B

THE DIALOGUES OF LEONE DI SOMI

The *Dialogues on Stage Affairs*, by Leone di Somi, are here presented for the first time in their complete form. Although noted as early as 1789 by Risbaldo Orsini di Orbassano, they have never before (even in the original Italian) been printed as a whole; only small portions have hitherto been translated into English. Why they have not been put to greater use is a mystery, for they constitute an invaluable commentary on stage practice and on histrionic method at the period of their composition, probably about the year 1565, approximately when Shakespeare was born.

The author, Leone di Somi, belonged to a Jewish family of Mantua, that of the Portaleone, highly distinguished for its contributions to the art of science and medicine. Its real founder was Guglielmo Mizolo, who acted as body-physician to Ferdinando I of Naples, Galeazzo Sforza of Milan, and three Mantuan princes—Lodovico, Federigo, and Francesco Gonzaga. So richly were his talents regarded at Naples that he was accorded there the rare honour of knighthood—the only Jew of his age distinguished as a *cavaliere*. Guglielmo's two sons, Abraham and Lazzaro, were also doctors. The former acted for a period as court physician to Guidobaldo, Duke of Urbino, but toward the end of his life returned to his native Mantua under Federigo Gonzaga. His brother likewise left Mantua in his youth, attaching himself to Count Giovanni Sassatelli, general of the Venetian army, and he too found his way back under Lodovico Gonzaga. Lazzaro's two sons, Abraham and David, were during the early years of the sixteenth century duly licensed court physicians to Duke Federigo. David's son was still another Abraham, known to historians as the author of *Shilṭē hag-Gibbōrīm* (Mantua, 1612), and *De Auro, dialogi tres* (Mantua, 1584). David's line carries us, in a succession of notable doctors, well past the middle of the seventeenth century. His brother, Abraham, also had children, and from one of these was descended the author of the *Dialogues*. He was born at Mantua in 1527.

From 1567 to the time of his death we can trace this man's varied activities. Patronized by Mantuan nobility, he evidently became chief purveyor of theatrical entertainments to the court, and even projected the scheme for having a permanent public playhouse opened in his native city. From his activities he gained the distinction of becoming official *scrittore*, or author, to the famous Accademia degli Invaghiti, directed by Cesare Gonzaga. To commemorate the death of this prince he wrote and produced an " heroic pastoral," entitled *I doni*. Until his death in 1592 he seems to have proved an indispensable official in Mantuan service.

His activities embraced much more than the theatre. The social and religious work of his community occupied his attention. He founded a synagogue in Mantua; he was a noted writer of scrolls; and he came forward in his youth as a poet with a series of Hebrew and Italian verses " In Defence of Women." These are preserved now in a manuscript at the Bodleian Library, Oxford (Bodl. 2251). Another work, apparently even more interesting, is a comedy, discovered and described recently by Schirmann. An Italian play, *L'Hirifile*, is all that remains of the large collection of his writings once preserved in the Biblioteca Nazionale in Turin.

Of the *Dialogues* there is extant only a copy, now in the Biblioteca Palatina of Parma. When these were written is a trifle difficult to determine. The address to the readers is dated 1556, but internal evidence demonstrates that, though they may have been begun in that year, they were certainly not completed until at least a decade later. The surest clues are the reference to Flaminia and to Leono

Arctino. Flaminia made a great stir when she came to Mantua in 1567, and Leone Aretino's work for Duke Guglielmo's wedding was carried out in 1561. One might suggest that the composition of the original manuscript was undertaken about this time; it may be that the copyist's date 1556 was put in error for 1565.

Portions of the *Dialogues* are printed in Luigi Rasi, *I Comici italiani* (Florence, 1905), i, 106–112, and Alessandro D'Ancona, *Origini del teatro italiano* (Turin, 1891), ii, 411–422; short passages in English rendering appear in Winifred Smith, *The Commedia dell'Arte* (New York, 1912), and Kathleen M. Lea, *Italian Popular Comedy* (Oxford, 1934). The list of di Somi's works once preserved at Turin will be found in B. Peyron, *Codices Italici . . . qui in Biblioteca Taurinensis Athenaei . . . asservabantur* (Turin, 1904). The Portaleone family is dealt with in M. Mortara, *Un important document sur la famille des Portaleone* (*Revue des études juives*, 1886, xii, 113–116), David Kaufmann, *Leone de Sommi Portaleone* (*The Jewish Quarterly Review*, 1898, x, 445–461) and *Leone de Sommi Portaleone der Dramatiker* (*Gesammelte Schriften*, iii, 1915, 303–315), Vittore Colorni, *Note per la biografia di alcuni dotti ebrei vissuti a Mantova nel secolo xv* (*Annuario di studi ebraici*, 1934, i, 169–182), Luigi Carnevali, *Il ghetto di Mantova con appendice sui medici ebrei* (Mantua, 1884). Letters and documents relating to Leone's biography are presented in A. D'Ancona, *op. cit.*, B. Peyron, *Note di storia letteraria del secolo xvi tratte dai manoscritti della Biblioteca Nazionale di Torino* (*Atti della R. Accademia delle Scienze di Torino*, 1884, xix, 743–759), Charles Dejob, *De la Condition des juifs de Mantoue au seizième siècle* (*Revue des études juives*, 1891, xxiii, 75–84), and A. Bertolotti, *Musici alla corte dei Gonzaga in Mantova del secolo xv al xviii* (Milan, 1890), 92. For the Accademia degli Invaghiti see Michele Maylender, *Storia delle accademie d'Italia* (Bologna, n.d.), iii, 363–366. Leone's Hebrew comedy is discussed in detail by J. Schirmann, *Eine hebräisch-italienische Komödie des xvi Jahrhunderts* (*Monatsschrift für Geschichte und Wissenschaft des Judentums*, 1931, lxxv, 97–118).

THE DIALOGUES OF LEONE DI SOMI

TO THE READERS

1556

I believe that these four Dialogues—which truly were composed more for my own personal convenience than from any desire of securing fame—may be of use to others and to myself as a set of rules, or at least as a record of what must be done in writing or in producing any dramatic poem; otherwise, I have no doubt, they would prove but useless and ill-pleasing. I earnestly beg whoever reads these dialogues for utility to accept whatever is to his purpose (for it is impossible that they can be entirely without service) and pardon me for the rest on account of the difficulty of my theme. I warn any persons who are not seeking for matter of information that they may expect neither usefulness nor pleasure in these writings, since my principal aim in this heavy task has been only to record, rather for myself than for others, in due order those more important rules and more necessary precepts of which I myself have often had to avail myself when obeying the commands of the authorities. Such rules and precepts have been taken from the writings of good authors whom I have not alluded to here lest I may seem to become by turns what one is accustomed to call familiarly a boorish pedant and a familiar Gratiano.

Sᴿᴱ. LEONE HEB°. DE SOMI

Assuredly with justice this terrestial existence has been styled by many philosophers both ancient and modern an earthly scene; for, while they stay on this earth, men must act even as the performers act on the stage. Just as the performers in tragedy, comedy, or similar pieces are costumed by the director—one set up as a prince and another as a citizen, one as a yeoman and another as a slave, others still in stranger guises—and then are turned forth on the stage each one to represent as well as he can the person he is told to interpret; and lastly, when the show is over, all are stripped of their borrowed clothes and returned to their former state, with praise or blame meted out in accordance with the manner, good or bad, in which they essayed their *rôles*; even so one sees men at birth tricked out in various guises by the Ruler of the universe, each one coming to play a part as best he can or as far as he wills till the drama of life arrives at its conclusion. Then, stripped and naked as he came, each one returns, bearing praise or blame—rather say, reward or punishment—

according to the way he acted in the state and profession that was given him. But since not all men are accustomed to act at one time in the same play—some being introduced to-day in tragedies, others to-morrow in comedies, others only in farces or eclogues or in similar pastoral shows, others again in mimes, others in satires—so it happens that every man may frequently become, if he so desires, a spectator of many of his companions, and from the actions of others (if he be wise) can draw both use and pleasure ; from their example he may profit, so that what he is called upon to do on this earthly stage will become such a show for the others as will leave no room for blame from those Arguses and Momuses who are ever lying in wait to blame us. This undoubtedly ought to be the aim of all dramatic performances ; especially is it the scope of all the tragedies and comedies which are produced in well-regulated cities for honest entertainment—namely, to reveal those virtues which are to be imitated and those vices which are to be avoided and condemned. Thus, by such examples, is every one made aware of the manner in which he should govern his own actions. If, then, these dramatic performances (I refer, of course, to those which are worthy of esteem) have so much power to make us skilled in our own affairs—nay, if they are so prized that the whole world is none other than a scene or theatre where a continual spectacle is made of our actions—it seems to me that this dramatic method deserves to be dealt with much more carefully and in much greater detail than has been hitherto done by any writers ancient or modern. Hence—not in the belief that I can here entirely satisfy the need, but rather for the purpose of encouraging others to fill in what I leave blank—I have deemed it no vain task to set down these talks lately made by some of my friends on this subject. Since these conversations were entered into familiarly by men who make no pretensions to rhetoric or literary style, I have left them unaltered in their original purity, believing that often a meagre portion of natural beauty is more agreeable and valuable than a richly ornamented, but artificial, loveliness. With the same object, therefore, in which these four dialogues originated and with the same method and aim in which they were familiarly discussed by men who, as I said, made no professions toward poetry or oratory, I send them to your Illustrious Highness, so that by association with the glory of your name and the purity of your rare virtues the lowly state of that interlocutor who appears here under the name of Veridico may be granted a tinge of illustriousness. Veridico speaks without pomp of words and without intricacy of style ; he would rather be held sincere and dutiful than witty and ambitious, learned and ingenious.

FIRST DIALOGUE

Interlocutors : Massimiano, Santino, *and* Veridico

Massimiano. Let us call on Veridico, the embroiderer. I want to ask how he has got on with the cloak and circlet I ordered from him. I am very much afraid they won't be ready in time.

Santino. All right : let's go in. I should like to see the things.

Massimiano. And of course it's just possible we might be able to see a rehearsal of his play.

Santino. Oh ? So the play we are to see at Tuesday's carnival is his doing, is it ?

Massimiano. I believe so ; and I should expect we'll see something rather fine. He has given good proof of his skill in these things on more than one occasion.

Santino. It is hard to credit that an ordinary workman can write a poem worthy of critical praise.

Massimiano. I tell you his talent is not to be laughed at. He is a most versatile man, and he excels particularly in playwriting. If I can persuade him I'd like you to see a rehearsal to-day. You would be surprised, I'm certain.

Santino. There's nothing I should enjoy more.

Massimiano. Here he is. Good day, my dear Veridico.

Veridico. Good day, sir, and good day to your friend. Pray be seated.

Massimiano. Well, how are my things getting on ?

Veridico. Those two lads at the loom there are busy on them now ; they say they'll be finished to-morrow morning. If you trust my word I'll stand surety for them.

Massimiano. That's all right, then.

Santino. What extraordinary costume is that you are holding ? It is heavily ornamented with gold, and to me seems most effective and of a new cut.

Veridico. This is a costume designed for a Rainbow who is to conduct a noble lord to the lists at Sunday's tourney.

Massimiano. You don't tell us his name, eh?

Veridico. No, sir: just as I don't give up your secrets to others.

Santino. Just look, Massimiano, at that queer device on the shield over there.

Massimiano. I noticed it as we came in. I like it very much indeed. It shows a winged child throwing a stone into a river and watching the ripples circle outward in the water; childishly he seems to be trying to catch them. And the motto reads, " I catch naught." Besides being brief and from a well-known author, it is a most striking device.

Santino. Yes, but I rather suspect that those who refuse to admit the human figure into things of this kind will be inclined to condemn it.

Veridico. Pedants such as those do not worry me. The lord who is to bear this shield and I, its maker, might bring forward many arguments in its favour, but for us all that really matters is that this winged child harmonizes excellently with my lord's object and with his relations to his lady. She, I expect, will recognize the force of the motto and agree that the device is skilful and effective.

Massimiano. I think you are right.

Santino. And what new kind of headgear is that hanging there?

Massimiano. They are decidedly out of the common and pleasant to look at.

Santino. We won't ask whose they are, for you won't tell us; but I'd gladly know if they are to be used in our tourney or intended for some masquerade.

Veridico. Neither. To tell you the truth, confidentially, they are to be used in our play. The setting is supposed to be Constantina, and some of the women characters are dressed as Greeks with those ornaments in their hair.

Massimiano. I am simply dying to see your play. I'm sure I shall see and hear—in the poet's words—" things 'bove nature high and rare."

Veridico. May I remind you that in jesting at me you are jesting at one who is your most sincerely devoted servant?

Massimiano. Indeed, I protest, as I am your friend, as we came along here together we talked about you and agreed you have such talent (particularly in things of this kind) that we were certain to get from you not only the exquisitely beautiful but the novel and the fresh. But let that pass. Could we possibly be granted the favour of seeing a rehearsal of your play to-day?

Veridico. Not to-day, sir. I gave no instructions for the actors to meet to-day. To fetch them now would be a difficult task—nay, almost impossible.

Massimiano. I know what a job it is to collect people together even when they've had notice. At least, however, will you grant us the favour of entertaining us for half an hour—for we have nowhere special to go—saying something about this playwriting business?

Veridico. What do you want me to tell you?

Santino. What, in your opinion, is a play? Who first wrote plays? Of what use are they? Ought they to be in verse or in prose? Why are they divided into five acts? Things of that kind.

Veridico. These questions are difficult to answer: all the more so since those authors who have dealt with such subjects have treated them most confusedly. For my part, if I must, to please you, speak about this matter, I protest that I should not wish to repeat much of what others have written on this theme—not because I am so bold as to disagree with judgments made by men much wiser than myself, but because it were mere labour lost to repeat opinions of others regarding plot and plot-arrangement, decorum, and the various rules. In any case, since I am speaking to persons well skilled in these matters and well endowed with talent, I should like to leave all this aside.

Massimiano. Without any ceremonies, then, would you not say something on this subject for the brief period we are at leisure? We should esteem it and feel much obliged to you.

Veridico. Obliged to me? No, for it is my duty to do all in my power to serve you. Your request for me is a command. Here, then, I stand, prepared to give answers (though I know how inadequate they must be) to the questions you propose.

APPENDIX B

Massimiano.   Without any further ceremony, then—save only that I must repeat how highly we esteem your skill in these matters—let us first put Santino's initial question : What is a play, and how did drama arise ?

Veridico.   Drama, according to the best authorities, is simply an imitation or mirror of human life, wherein vices are attacked and made odious and virtues praised in such a manner as to make people wish to follow them, by methods which will be more apparent when we have dealt with its origin and the manner by which it was introduced.   Some think that the Athenian peasants were the first to provide an example of acting in that they, enraged at the authorities and having no other means of self-defence, used to march by night through the city streets traducing their oppressors ; this, they say, developed to such an extent that crowds gathered to listen to their scandals, just as to-day love-lorn girls and lively youths gather on pleasant evenings for conversation.   Since, however, opinions regarding this matter are diverse, and since I personally do not think it is of much importance to know who was the first actor, it being of far greater value to discover the first person who, in a dignified and judicious manner, composed a play suitable for and worthy of histrionic interpretation, I venture to put forward my own rather bold opinion on that subject.   Very strongly do I object to our granting all credit to the lying Greeks.   These Greeks have often laid claim to the glory of others, although in several ancient and sacred records we find ample proof of the existence of these arts and virtues long before their time.   Tentatively, then, and rather as a theme for discussion than as an affirmation, I suggest that just as modern writers inherited the art of writing plays from Livius Andronicus, who is said to have been the first in time among the Latin dramatic authors, and later from Plautus and Terence, while these and other Romans inherited this art from Aristophanes, Menander, and possibly the still more ancient Eupolis, among the Greeks, so I believe that these Greeks might have learned the art of introducing diverse characters and of making them converse from the still more ancient sacred books of the Hebrews ; this method may have been imitated later by Plato, and then came drama's first beginnings.   If this be so, then Drama was not invented by some rude peasant, as others would have us imagine painting, kindred art to poetry, primarily arose. These critics say that a rustic shepherd standing with his flock in the sun saw the shadow of a goat cast on the ground and began idly to trace its outlines on the sand with his staff—hence the origin of that fine art which provides so gracious a mirror of nature.   Not so, I say, do I believe drama to have been invented— neither by chance nor by rustic intellect.   Drama is an imitation or mirror of human life, and I conceive it established by divine ordinance.   The sublime genius of the holy legislator Moses, the famous leader of the Jews, after he had written his five books of divine law as delivered to him by oracle—nay, from the lips of Almighty God Himself—in 5550 verses, produced, as is demonstrated in the literature of the Jews, the magnificent and philosophic tragedy of Job, introducing therein just five human characters.   No doubt this was not written to be represented on the stage (although it has been so represented many times since then), but it was cast in the form of a dialogue or discussion in which various characters took part—that is to say, in the form assumed by every poem suited for dramatic representation.   One might perhaps believe that the first things recited publicly were (as the critics say) rustic colloquies, since some indication of this is given by the word ' scene,' which may be derived from *scigni*, the significance of which both in Greek and in popular Italian is ' leafy,' in allusion to the places where these primitive folk acted their rustic plays.   Hence, they say, the origin of satyr plays and of pastoral eclogues.   On the other hand, *scèhonà* is a Hebrew word meaning ' way ' or ' street ' where there is a group of houses, and it seems to me more likely that the first plays were presented by city folks in a habited spot with settings akin to those we have now.   Of this I wish, at a more fitting time, to speak later.   To add further proof, I may mention that I have translated from the Chaldean a most ancient work, called *The Course of Life*, in which is introduced a youth inexperienced in the ways of the world and a guardian angel who briefly but skilfully and with mysterious power extorts him to live a good life and counsels him to go dressed in a simple costume of pure white linen given to him by the angel.   The youth seems well disposed to follow his advice, but when left alone he allows the Tempter, who appears before him with lovely aspect and conceals his monstrous horrid features, to flatter him with his lies and dress him up in rich, proud garments.   On hearing this his better angel reproves him, and he, repentant, casts off the costly raiment. Then anew he is suborned by the Tempter, assuming once more the world's delights and all its transitory joys. In the end, after a long debate, through the admonitions of the good angel, who makes him look into a mirror, he recognizes his true self : in astonishment he looks—sees himself in the twinkling of an eye turned into an aged man—and in a fit of repentance strips off all those damnable worldly clothes of his.   Then, with a devout and pious prayer, he submits to God's will. This piece is written so excellently and so well planned that one must assume it was composed for representation, and, indeed, that it was probably acted in public. From this, and for many other reasons, I argue that the origin of drama lies far back in the past—farther back than Greek authors would lead us to suppose. Thus—to continue with the main subject of our discussion—I declare that, in my opinion, I am right in affirming that from the afore-mentioned poem of Job (more ancient assuredly than any other of which we have record) these first poets must have derived the dramatic method ; from this poem, too, I am prepared to believe they may have drawn the practice, much observed among the ancients, of making tragedies out of real events and historical episodes—for I assume, as many do, that the story of Job is literally true. Even if those are right who regard this holy poem as of divine but fictional invention for the purpose of introducing the concepts of the philosophers, and so of aiding the listeners (the genuine end of every theatrical work)—even following their opinion, we must agree that here there is the tragic weaving of some familiar tale with moral aim and theological purpose. Although some moderns may believe that a poet be permitted to invent the whole subject of a tragedy (as, it seems, Aristotle does in the *Poetics*), they do not deny that it is better to search for a true tale, and that, unless there is any special reason against its adoption, this should be utilized ; the reason being that a spectator, knowing that what he sees before him has a basis in truth, will be moved to greater terror and pity as he watches the tragic events and characters, and, being more deeply moved, will have his mind better purged of vices, will derive, too, more profit from the examples set on the stage, since these will be regarded as verities and not as fictions. Such tragedies, both in dialogue and in action, are to be expressed with an imagery the more vivid and the more elevated than that of comedy as the regal majesty of tragedy is elevated above the ordinary. Yet both tragedy and comedy are designed as things to give pleasure, even while they present warnings whereby may be learned, by means of eminent fictions and exemplars, the way to a good and temperate life ; this is the end of every tragic poem and of every comic poem alike, whether put into representation or only described. The only essential difference between them is this, that tragedies introduce as their chief characters royal persons speaking serious dialogue in a majestic way and involved in terrible actions, all conceived in a style suitable to their grandeur, whereas in comedy (which is but a mirror of ordinary life) only honest citizens and their manners are depicted, in a style harmonious with their character, all for the purpose of taxing vice and lauding virtue. Here the terrors of tragedy are transformed into such pleasant delights as are suitable to comedy, the object of which is to instruct by example and rouse delight by means of quip and jest.

Santino. If it is only thus they differ—or, to be more correct, present variation—why are so many things allowed in the one which are regarded as faults in the other ?

Veridico. What do you mean ?

Santino. Is it not the peculiar property of tragedy to have a sad ending and of comedy to have a happy conclusion ?

Veridico. No, sir, it is not the happy ending or the sad that gives to a poem the title of tragic or comic ; the distinction lies in the quality of the persons introduced and of the situations in which they are involved. Indeed, we find tragedies which end on a note of consolation (as in the poem of Job I mentioned, although it starts with many horrors, disasters, and deaths). I share the view of the best critics that we cannot lay down any exact rule limiting tragedy to an unhappy ending. This, indeed, has led some to hazard the opinion that deaths and disasters are not prohibited to comedy, even although comedy does not deal with characters permitted, through their position of authority, to do with themselves or others what they please, as is true of the persons playing the principal *rôles* in tragedy.

Santino. Supposing—but not granting—that it is true, according to these critics' views, that so much is proper to tragedy as is allowed to a king or a great noble, and also that comedy may introduce only private citizens, may we not trace beyond that, in the matters that do not depend on this social difference in the characters, some measure of distinction between the two kinds ?

Veridico. As for instance ?

Santino. Well—say the introduction of an innocent virgin on the stage in a speaking part. This would be regarded as a great fault in comedy, and yet is readily allowed in tragedy.

Veridico. That, too, depends on the difference in position of the characters. It is easy to decide, when we wish to do so, what ought to be the actions of kings and what of citizens. I say what they ought to be, and not what they are, because the poet (as Aristotle says) must always represent things in the most perfect way possible.   Here another thing occurs to me, and I trust you will permit a slight digression.   It is important to observe that to this more than to anything else the poet ought to devote attention, for, if he does not give to all his characters the most perfect and natural existence, he will endeavour in vain to convince us that he is doing something worthy of esteem.   He must apply to each one (as Horace indicates well in his *Poetics*) the qualities proper to their age, position, and profession, as well as to the situations in which they are placed—all in the manner most worthy of imitation.   The ancients, therefore, did well in accepting the law that a virgin should not be permitted to appear in comedies lest by such an example citizens' daughters, who ought to be bashful and retiring, might be induced to gad abroad and engage in public gossip.   On the other hand, a prince's daughter might be allowed to appear in public, for the reason that few would be so bold as to dare attack the honour of such a woman—where there is no hope love clearly can take no root.   Love is universally recognized as arising from a certain equality between lover and object—equality in blood or constellation or position ; speaking generally, where there is inequality there can be no love.   Daughters of princes, therefore, may go out and speak to others in the streets, both because their position makes them freer and, more particularly, because it is presumed that no one will violate their honour, there being few persons (and those far distant) of an equality with them.   Such procedure is not allowed to citizens' daughters because in the city there are thousands of their own class ; going out of doors, therefore, brings to them much danger of evil hap.   She who values her honour must avoid the chance of scandal, even if that be purely baseless.   Comedy, therefore, which is designed to present good examples, ought not to permit anyone to say a word or to indulge in an action contrary to that person's position and quality.   Although it does not seem wrong to bring in, say, a malicious and astute servant, a bold and shrewd waiting-maid, a flattering and mendacious parasite, a suspicious and avaricious old man, it would be an intolerable fault to apply these vices to a young gallant, a noble student, an honest girl, or an aged and wise father of a family.   On the other hand, it is true that the poet is allowed—and often by this means gives great delight to his auditors—to tax vice by introducing a person marked by some single vice.   Thus, in order to attack some contemporary social error (and particular attention ought to be given to this) there may be brought on the stage a doctor, or rather a prescription-monger, who thinks far more of his pennies than of curing his patients, endeavouring always to pocket some money, instead of honestly aiming at bringing health ; or else a doctor of laws who cheats his client because he has been bribed by the other party in the case ; or an old man whom love has turned into a fool and who is thus involved in ridiculous action.   Such satirical touches not only are permitted, but give great delight when their object is to condemn vice or expose knaveries for the spectators' benefit.   To conclude, I say that our first aim must be to treat everything in a natural manner, and that we must always think of giving instruction—otherwise we land ourselves in the booby's mathematics where naught from naught is naught.

Massimiano.   I doubt not that, precisely because they aimed at this naturalness you speak of, the ancient writers of comedy refrained from introducing more than three speaking characters on the stage at one time, or, if they did introduce a fourth, from giving him more than a few lines of dialogue.   For it is not natural that cultured men should indulge in confused conversation.

Veridico.   Yes, indeed, and hence, too, comes the rule that no character should don disguise when he is actually on the stage, since it is unlikely that a person who changes his costume in order to go unrecognized, or for some other secret purpose of his own, should do so in public.   For the same reason one of our playwright friends has made a rule in a new comedy he has written that none of his characters should utter any lengthy soliloquies.   All he has permitted is that some of them should make a few short jesting or angry asides.   This gentleman declares it as his opinion that, just as it is esteemed a fault for an actor on the stage to address his remarks to the spectators, for these spectators never are in the place where the actor is supposed to be, so he deems it unfitting that a person who is supposed to be in a public street should raise his voice in long soliloquies beyond the custom of nature and, contrary to every practice of civilized life, talk like an idiot to himself—since, as has been pointed out, he has not the authority to address the spectators directly.

Massimiano.   So far your answers, all concerned with our first question, have been most satisfying. In addition to having had a direct reply, we have learned about the origin of comedy, what comedy is, and how it has for its object the condemning of vices and the praising of virtues.   Now I should like you to give us your opinion concerning the form to be employed in comedy—whether you think it should be in verse or in prose.   I suppose we may put rimed verses out of account, since I imagine it is commonly agreed that such verse is unsuited for such dramatic compositions.

Veridico.   This is a question on which opinions differ very considerably and each critic brings forward his own special arguments, authorities, and examples.   The learned Bibiena, who was perhaps the first to produce a true vernacular comedy worthy of the name, wrote his *Calandria* in prose and had good reason for so doing.   For if the value of a comedy (presupposing, of course, that it be substantial in content and well planned) is increased by its fidelity to nature, and so by its power of convincing the spectators into the belief that what they see before them are real events happening casually, and not merely things imagined by the poet, then its worth will be still further augmented if it be composed, not in verse, but in prose.   It is obvious that in familiar speech we do not observe regularity of rhythm, and, however expert the actor may be, he cannot in speaking verse always conceal the presence of the verse form ; indeed, many critics have attacked prose writings where some passages fall into verse rhythm through the carelessness of the authors.   On the other hand, the judicious and truly unique Ariosto (whose comedies perhaps take first place among those written in Italian, even although they contain little of the purely laughable, which alone seems to please contemporary popular tastes), although he once held to this opinion, changed it later ; all his prose comedies he rewrote in blank verse.   So, too, the illustrious Ercole Bentivoglio, whose high genius and prime authority is universally recognized, has written all his comedies in verse, not so much, I believe, for the purpose of imitating the ancient Romans and Greeks and Hebrews as in the belief that so lovely and useful an art as comedy, to attain the rank of a perfect poem, demanded the dignity and the harmony of verse utterance.   Truly, considering the matter generally, it would appear that this view is the just one ; but, considering it particularly, it is obviously necessary to compare the nature of verse, especially dramatic verse, among the ancients with our vernacular verses.   When this is done it will be immediately realized that, whereas theirs were excellently suited to comic composition, ours are but poorly adaptable for such a purpose.   The chief reason is that our verses of eleven syllables, as opposed to those of the Romans, Greeks, and Hebrews, move so swiftly and end in such a regular note that we cannot escape in it a fettering and resonance which, in relation to the domestic subjects ordinarily introduced into comedy, become thoroughly artificial.   The authors I have mentioned and other gifted modern writers have realized this, and (to avoid such a fault) have been consequently forced to make use of weak endings, so providing a lighter close to the line and a greater linking of verse to verse.   Clearly this is nearer to the prose of common speech.   So far as tragedy is concerned, we note that there has never been any author who made use of aught but verse for this kind of drama.   Nor can I, for my part, counsel a change in such a method by the substitution of tragic dialogue in prose ; for truly verse is more suited to the dignity out of which the tragic impression arises.   The majesty inherent in the theme, the appearance of a king, of a queen, and of suchlike persons who are the normal characters in tragedy, seem to demand a speech more weighty and more rhythmical than that of common men.   Of course, the poet must take care to avoid over-use of consonants in his verses and the repetition of sounds ; he must, too, be careful to see that sentences do not always end at the close of verses, so escaping that severe rhetoric and that boring resonance, which, already condemned in comedy, would become unutterably monotonous in tragedy.   By frequent breaking of the lines, while keeping them pleasing and harmonious, the poet's verses will gain in dignity and nobility and at the same time they will have the ease of prose when they are recited ; the combination of this ease with the majesty of verse produces an enjoyable and gracious effect.   Furthermore, since tragedies and comedies are written to be presented on the stage as well as to be read, the author must take care, when introducing any subject, to relate it to the action and to the dialogue.   The comic poet, indeed, can have no success unless he has qualified actors to interpret his work.   Concerning these actors—a most important subject—I wish to speak to you later ; so, too, I want to say something about the settings, for the stage, as the saying goes, is the trial of the play and many things delightful in the reading will be insipid when produced, and *vice versa*.   Since I have touched on this matter—which is of much greater significance than most people realize—I may take an example to demonstrate what I mean.   Among his prose tales Boccaccio introduces a charming one wherein Bruno and Buffalmacco persuade Calandrino that he has become invisible because of the Heliotropia he imagines he has discovered.   With many jests they proceed to stone him—and the tale is most charming in the reading.   I have, however, seen this plot reproduced on the stage in a blank-verse comedy, and the whole thing proved most boring—partly because of the regularity of the verse, which gave it a sing-song quality, but chiefly because of the abstract nature of the theme, which is ill-adapted for stage presentation.   The spectators always had in front of their eyes this fool who thought he was invisible and consequently refused to believe that he could possibly be such a booby as to think no one saw him.   Thus by these two things the naturalness of the story disappeared, and, deprived of that, it may be said to have been reft of its very spirit.   Hence the great master of poetry well admonishes us that we ought rather to attempt a description of impossible or unnatural things than endeavour to introduce them physically on the stage. Thus, to conclude, it seems to me that both in words and in actions the author must employ those means which seem most natural and pleasing ; hence, too, I deem, as I have said, that in comedies we ought to use prose, as being more fitting for familiar dialogue, while for tragedy verse, as possessing more of the majesty and loftiness suitable to the tragic mood, is to be preferred.   Even here, however, it is desirable that the verse to be recited on the stage should approximate so far as possible to prose utterance.

Santino.   You have expressed it as your belief that comedy and tragedy both spring from the same source and that both have the same aim, each in its particular manner pointing out virtues by good examples and discrediting vice.   Yet, so far as medium of expression is concerned, you seem to allow a vast measure of difference between them by granting verse to the one and prose to the other.

Veridico.   On the contrary, the difference is but a slight one.   Ultimately each introduces simply a collection of words ; the only distinction is that in verse the arrangement is more rhythmical and harmonious and consequently verse is, as I have said, more fitted for the majesty of a regal tale ; while prose, because it is more colloquial and familiar, seems better suited for the easy tone of a less exalted theme.   Please note, however, that I assume that this prose should ever have its own measure of perfection.   Just as verse must have a measure of perfection of its own, we should recognize that prose too must possess its own fundamental standards and move on with a pleasing vigour, without lapsing into limping or insipid phrases.   Prose has an art form of its own, together with rules that apply specifically to it and to it alone ; and when it is judiciously written there is to be recognized in it a kind of rhythmic flow akin to that observable in formal verse.

Massimiano.   There seems to me to be indeed great force in your arguments, and I believe there is no contradiction in your remarks.   On just one matter I should like further explanation before you proceed to other things.   What did you mean when you spoke of comedies having an entire theme ?   In other words, what kind of themes do you accept as entire and which do you reject ?

Veridico.   By an entire theme I mean that which contains a double plot, since comedies with but a single development or of simple plot were little esteemed among the ancients and by us are regarded as of slight value. The reason is that double plots well harmonized together seize more powerfully on the imagination of an audience and avoid monotony by the variety of action introduced.   Hence those comedies are worthy of greatest praise which cheat spectators into the belief that one action must end in a particular way and then conclude in another, for every one derives greater pleasure from witnessing a fresh and unexpected termination of events.

Massimiano.   I think, Veridico, that so far you have answered our queries in a most able manner.   Now will you please tell me about the division of comedies into five acts ?   Do you consider that this is done of conscious design or that the division is purely fortuitous ?   At the same time I should much like to know why these divisions are termed acts.

Veridico.   It is my firmly held belief that, just as comedy was not of chance origin but, as I said, derived by imitation from a divine poem, so it was divided into five acts not fortuitously, but of set purpose.   To reply briefly first of all to the second part of your question before proceeding to deal in greater detail with the original query—I should say that these parts of a comedy are called acts because of the actions occurring in them, since, as you are aware, comedy of movement is more worthy of esteem than static comedy, actions or deeds, together with the dialogues, being the principal means by which this kind of art is expressed.   As I said before, the perfect comedy does not consist merely in fine descriptions, but demands also suitability for good stage representation.

Santino.   Pray, before you proceed further, tell me—for I do not know it—the derivation of the word ' comedy.'

Veridico.   The professors of Greek inform us that ' comedy ' is derived from *chomi*, meaning ' song,' and *odi*, meaning ' discourse ' ; or else from *comos* and *ode*, which signify a rustic ditty.   The latter derivation would be based on the assumption that, as we saw above, peasants were the first actors.

Q

Santino.   And how did the actors come to be called *histrioni* ?

Veridico.   They say that the ancient Tuscans, who are descended from the Lydians, employed the word *hister* for the entertainer who postured both in private houses and on the stage.

Massimiano.   I am anxiously waiting now for you to tell us why comedies are divided precisely into five acts, and also—if this does not lie entirely outside the scope of the question—why the ancient comic dramatists did not permit their actors to come upon the stage more than five times.

Veridico.   The latter is a rule which is but little observed even among the ancients, yet I trust I shall satisfy you that——

Santino.   Wait a moment, please.   Two, three, four, five.   It is five o'clock, Massimiano—we are due at the castle.

Massimiano.   Bother the necessity of service—I almost called it by a worse name !   I am really grieved that it prevents me from hearing an answer to the question I was so eager to get answered.

Veridico.   Every living person must serve some one ; and he who serves so courteous a lord as yours is need not complain and style his service slavery.   Go where your duties summon you, and I shall defer that last part of our discussion till to-morrow, when your costume will be finished.   I shall then conclude our discourse, God willing, and seek as best I can to give you full satisfaction.

The *Second Dialogue* wherein there is a discussion concerning the division of comedy into five acts and concerning the arrangement and proportion to be desired in a dramatic poem.

SECOND DIALOGUE

Interlocutors : SANTINO, MASSIMIANO, *and* VERIDICO

Santino.   Every hour seems an age to me, so anxious am I to hear what that excellent man has to say about the division of comedies into acts.

Massimiano.   There he is.   Look—under the loggia, sitting and picking his teeth after dinner.   Good day, Veridico.   How are you ?

Veridico.   Good day, gentlemen.   Since you have come so soon, I know now that no time had to be lost in getting your costume ready.   Here it is all ready and carefully finished.

Massimiano.   It was not for the costume we came so soon, although I am glad to see it finished.   We have hurried back because we are so eager to hear what you have to say about the division of comedy into acts, and, too, about some other matters on which we want to ask you questions.   First of all, will you give us your opinion concerning the rule proposed by certain of the ancients which would prohibit actors from entering the stage more than five times ?   I know, of course, that the moderns pay but scant attention to it.

Veridico.   This rule of the grammarians seems to me to be utterly false whether we consider it generally or in its particular application.   Terence—assuredly a most scrupulously exact playwright—broke it frequently.   In the *Andria* he makes Davus come on the stage seven times, and in the *Heautontimoroumenos* I believe Chremes enters eight times.   You will find the same licence, I think, elsewhere in plays I have not carefully examined from this point of view.   Granted, however, that some persons think this rule should be kept, I am inclined to believe the reason that the early comic actors were not permitted to enter more than five times is the same that governs the division of comedy into five acts.   In discussing this division perhaps we shall also indirectly resolve the other question.   So far I have discovered no references of any kind to this subject.   I do not propose at present to say much concerning the general significance of the number five, although that has a decided bearing on the point at issue ; I shall limit myself to one explanation—a very pertinent one, methinks—of which I am rather proud.   I shall indeed rejoice if it pleases you : should it not, then take it as propounded rather as part of a familiar discourse for the purpose of meeting your inquiries than as a formal argument intended to bring absolute conviction.

Santino.   I know well we cannot but be satisfied ; but please do not put aside this lengthy discourse which, you say, may be delivered on the number five.   At least give us such part of it as is intimately related to our particular theme.

Veridico.   The number five, as you are aware, includes within itself a two and a three—let us call them the even and the odd in one.   The even is related to the feminine, and the odd, as being more perfect, to the masculine ; whence the Pythagoreans called five the matrimonial number and the Gentile philosophers applied it to Mercury, god of sciences, particularly of mathematics, arithmetic, geometry, and music.   In addition to this, we find that the number five is the mediator or mean of all numbers ; these, as we all know, extend only to ten and are then repeated ; hence the philosophers style it the number of justice.   This is the first number which, multiplied by itself, returns to itself ; just as the circle, a perfect figure, turns within itself. Doubled, it makes the entire number—as compasses, opened a further space, form a circle of double size. It is said, too, that this number five has great power over evil spirits, and one learns from occult philosophy that it is particularly potent against poisons.   The swallow, which possesses such wonderful properties in matters supernatural, produces its young in fives.

Santino.   May I interrupt to ask you one question ?   What are these properties ?

Veridico.   I shall not speak here of the virtue of certain stones which grow in its stomach or of some marvellous properties these birds have in relation to love and hate ; sufficient be it that magicians lay great store on their plumage.

Santino.   I myself have noted one extraordinary thing in connexion with swallows which I had certainly thought you would have mentioned.

Veridico.   And that is—— ?

Santino.   I have pierced the eyes of young swallows in the nest and left them there.   Then the mother returned, found them blind, and by the aid of a herb restored their vision.

Veridico.   Yes, I have often heard of that and of many other marvellous qualities they possess.   However, lest we wander too far from the subject, let us get back to the question of the fivefold division of comedy. To begin at the beginning, I say that comedy—as, indeed, I indicated before—is nothing but an imitation or speculum of civil life, and , since its end is society, it is clear that the closer its relationship is to man the greater will be its perfection.   Now, I need only show you that this form of art is an exemplum of human life to demonstrate that its structure is as mysterious and perfect as is the structure of man.   That man is perfect, not only as being human but also as participating in the divine, is sufficiently manifest, since he includes within himself both the quality of this inferior world and that of the heavenly and divine.   Because of this the Greeks termed man the microcosm, indicating thus that within himself he embraced something of the whole universe— the inferior world, the celestial world, and the spiritual—as, indeed, is affirmed by the authority of Holy Scripture, where (to select only one example from the beginning of Genesis) it is said, " God created man in his own image, in the image of God created he him."   Man's structure, then, is sublime and perfect ; and at once we recognize that he is made up in terms of five—five senses—seeing, hearing, tasting, smelling, and touching ; five psychological qualities—vegetable, sensible, lustful, irascible, and rational ; five extremities— head, two hands, and two feet (just as the world is divided into five zones).   Not only has our body these five extremities, but each one of these extremities is divided into five : five fingers to each hand, five toes to each foot, five parts to the head—eyes with visual sense, ears with sense of hearing, nose with sense of smell, mouth with sense of taste, and finally, although the sense of touch is spread through all our members, we get the fifth, the sense of touch, specifically related to the supreme intellect, whose seat is in the brain.   To sum up, there are five extremities to this microcosm, each with its own five extremities.   Furthermore, we realize that the whole human body is made up of five chief parts—bones, nerves, veins, muscles, and flesh.   The sacred law, therefore, which is divine and granted directly by God to mankind, was for this reason (among others more mysterious and arcane) divided into five books, which are to be read with but five principal vowels ; on the front page of this law we see written the great name of God expressed in five letters, by means of which the cabalists declare the whole world was created.   In five books and no more the Psalmist, Prophet, and King, David, composed his famous Song of Songs, and this truly cannot have been by chance, but must have come of set purpose for reasons partly revealed, partly shaded in solemn darkness.   And so Moses, who was imitated by David and others, in instructing those early fathers in divine law and civil government, inspired by the Holy Spirit and with the consent of the All-Highest, chose this division by five—itself a symbol of the divine and intimately related to the essential nature of the microcosm, as we have already demonstrated.   In writing his significant and philosophic poem of Job Moses, moreover, made use of but five characters.   This being so, what better division could be sought for or discovered by the ancient Greek and Roman poets when they came to compose comedies—that most useful form of art, designed solely to instruct others delightfully how to pursue virtue and avoid vice ?

Massimiano.   We are to take it, then, from your discourse that comedy ought to be an image or mirror of a perfect human being ?

Veridico.   So I believe.   Not only should there be five acts, corresponding to the five extremities of the human figure and to the five extremities of each of these taken separately, but every individual act must be associated with one of the extremities—the first with the head, the second with the left hand, the third with the right, the fourth and fifth with the left and right feet respectively—the whole taking shape as a well-planned organism, unified by a dominant spirit.   Its soul will be the main theme which will give life to all the various parts, each of which must be proportioned to the shape of the entire body and not presented as though it was monstrously formed or maimed.

Santino.   This I should like dealt with in greater detail.

Veridico.   Well, just as a man sees and hears and understands through the senses located in his head, so the first act of a comedy with its exposition, which we might style the demonstration of the argument, must present to the understanding and sight the principal bases of the plot.   Similarly, just as the left hand, being the weakest, does not aid man much in defending him against dangers, unless he is able to employ his stronger right hand to realize his aims, so the intrigues and mischances which ought to be introduced in a well-planned comedy throughout the course of the second act, would result in utter disaster were it not that, quite naturally, the third act carried these affairs to a happier conclusion.   And just as we should, in traversing the ways of this weary world, stumble into many of the pitfalls and precipitous dangers placed around us were it not for the firmness of our right feet which God has given us as our stay and support, so the disasters and threats which occur at the climax of the intrigue—or, rather, the epitasis of the fourth act—might result in complete ruin for the characters and plunge our minds into hopeless gloom, if it were not that the fifth act, introducing catastrophe and peripeteia, brought everything to a fortunate conclusion.   Summing up, we may say that, even as the heart distributes its spirit to all man's members, so the theme of a play should send its spirit into all the parts of the work, giving the impression that nothing has been brought in needlessly or without purpose any more than any member of our body has been created in vain.

Massimiano.   We are to assume, then, that in your opinion the first act of a well-constructed comedy should contain the argument and exposition, in the second we should see various disturbances and hindrances, in the third some adjustment must be made, ruin and disaster must threaten in the fourth, while in the fifth a solution is to be reached, bearing all to a joyous and happy ending.

Veridico.   Yes, that is my idea.   At the end all the characters must reach a state of happy contentment.

Santino.   According to your able demonstration, it is clear that comedy has been given five acts, neither more nor less, because of careful forethought.   I am prepared to believe that the actors were forbidden to leave the stage empty except between these five acts in order that the audience should not imagine the play to be divided into more portions.

Veridico.   I should think that was the reason.

Santino.   A comedy, then, is divided into five acts.   Now, every act is divided into scenes—have you by chance any opinion to express concerning the number of scenes each act should have ?

Veridico.   The number of scenes introduced in an act is left to the discretion of the author.   I am inclined to accept the common view that an act should not include less than two scenes or more than nine.   It is well, I think, to keep to these limits.

Massimiano.   In accordance with what you have said, Veridico, I suppose you will not deny that those plays which have only three acts—called, I know not why, farces—are imperfect.

Veridico.   Such plays cannot be termed imperfect simply for that reason.   Granted that they are written cleverly and according to the rules, they deviate from the others only in having a simple theme.   The comedies of double plot which, counting in the intermedii (of which we shall speak later), are designed to last in performance for four or five hours would certainly become boring without the provision of suitable intervals. The fivefold division, besides the reasons for its observance given above, has this virtue, that it provides the author with a period between each act which may stand for four, six, or eight hours, a lapse of time frequently necessary between one episode and another in a comedy which introduces various themes.   But those pieces which in plot and scope did not come within the sphere of true comedy, and yet would be tedious in performance were they not provided with any intervals, were divided into three parts only. They could not bear the perfect fivefold division, the symbol of the human figure, but approached that human figure as nearly as they might. Please note that, although I have demonstrated the fivefold division to be that natural and proper to comedy, it by no means follows that poems unsuited to this division are consequently imperfect. Rather may we say that farces or eclogues with simple plots find their most fitting arrangement in three parts. This, too, harmonizes with the human figure, which may be considered as threefold also, a likeness of the three worlds. From the stomach, called the diaphragm, down to the legs man corresponds to the lower world; from the waist to the throat he corresponds to the celestial; while the head, the highest part of the body, is the genuine image of the spiritual world. All this I could easily demonstrate in detail if that had been the main subject of our talk. Moreover, we see that man is made up of soul, body, and spirit, the last uniting the first two. Thus it will be realized that farce adopts the same method of division as comedy—that is to say, it has the same number of acts as the parts of the body. Indeed, it may be argued in favour of this division that the five extremities of the human body are reducible to three—the head, the two hands taken together, and the two feet. And although it seems a little beyond our present subject, I should like to remark that verse is better than prose in satyr-plays and eclogues, since these are works wherein under the guise of shepherds, gods, and goddesses we see reflected that simplicity, purity, and joy of the early ages imaginatively described by our famous poets. I do not, of course, wish to affirm that no author may invent out of his own imagination tales and plots (provided they be full of marvels) in order to weave these into pastoral settings; on the contrary, I believe that such a licence is granted to them, as it is to writers of comedy. And, since the men of these times must be represented not only as happy in their sincerity but also virtuous and of high genius, it is fitting that they be brought on the stage embellished with certain resplendent and good qualities apt to arouse in the audience both commendation of the honesty existent in those times and admiration of the cultured genius and the integrity of the men of that period, alike in word and action. Just as verse, as being more choice and refined than common speech, is used in these works, so the presence of gods, denied to comedy, is permitted here. The tragic poet is, of course, allowed to introduce gods (perhaps following the example of Moses, who brought in the deity as a speaking character in his tragedy of Job); similar introduction of gods is permitted in pastoral plays even in our days. It cannot cause any hurt to religion, for there is no fear that such foolish idolatries should cheat men into error; we realize now throughout the whole world that there is only one God worthy of true adoration and reverence. I have touched on this subject to combat the views of some hypocrites, who in a pretence of devotion are used to condemn the appearance of pagan gods in plays of this kind, declaring that they present a bad example. These fools do not realize that such profane superstitions may be treated humorously in a way we could not permit with things sacred and divine.

Massimiano. In referring to these hypocrites you have brought to my mind an objection made by a certain zealous friend of ours who would not allow in any comedy the slightest word or phrase of a licentious kind. What do you think about this?

Veridico. There is no doubt that if comedies were to be witnessed always by wise and virtuous people they would be the more praised the farther removed they were from every lascivious and obscene thought. But since there will ever be among the audience more licentious persons stained by some vice than wholly virtuous ones, and since their humour must be met, I think that the introduction of a few licentious phrases in a comedy will not come amiss. Just as we praise a doctor who conceals a bitter medicine with a jam pleasing to the corrupt taste of his patient, so we should not blame the poet who, desiring to present in his plays salutary material, conceals this sometimes by appealing to the corrupt taste of an infirm age. The true beauty of comedy, after all, consists in its power to give entertainment to every one—and this particularly in our times. To do this adequately it must, as modestly as it may, appeal to men of every type, and endeavour to hold the attention even of those who will fall asleep during the philosophic scenes and moral discourses by which the poet interests others and will be aroused only by laughter at vulgar and immodest jests. These men are like the blacksmith's dog who sleeps through the sound of the hammer by means of which his master gains his livelihood, but wakens up at the sound of his master's teeth when he starts eating the bread he has won by his toil. Hence I should not condemn the introduction of some small obscenities in a comedy any more than I should condemn the human body, from which comedy takes its perfect form, because some of its limbs are shameful. Indeed, since comedy (as I have said) ought to follow otherwise the proportions of our bodies, so it undoubtedly ought to in this. Just so much and not more should it be allowed of licentiousness as is the proportion of shameful parts in respect of man's other members. This will not take from comedy the unity we have credited it with, but rather will make it more perfect and complete. Be this observed, however, that, as Nature places these shameful parts of the human body in a position easily concealed, so the poet ought, in his mirror of civil life, to hide every vicious element. And since all civilized men cover those parts either with clothes or animals' skins or at least leaves of the trees, it should be noted that every vulgar phrase ought to be concealed with virtuous words. This is easy to accomplish and is highly laudable. Here let us finish our talk for to-day.

Santino. In your speaking about these matters you have more than once said that you would tell us something about the stage business and the intermedii and the methods of acting. We don't want to tire you too much just at present, but we shall hold you to your promise and shall content ourselves now by hoping that you will fulfil it. Now we are going off. Good-bye.

In the *Third Dialogue* there are treated the rules of acting, the method of costuming, and everything that appertains to the stage, with many valuable comments.

THIRD DIALOGUE

Interlocutors : SANTINO, MASSIMIANO, *and* VERIDICO

Santino. We shall be in luck if this excellent fellow gives us as good material on the producing of plays as he has given in his other talks. I like his way of always presenting valid reasons for all his arguments.

Massimiano. For my part I should think his talk to-day will be even better than the others, because he has directed more plays than he has written. He is therefore likely to be more expert in matters of production than in those of play-construction. But here he is himself.

Santino. Dinner-time seemed an age to us, Veridico, we so longed to hurry over to you to get you to pay the debt which of your own volition you owe us.

Veridico. I am most glad to see you. Will you not sit down ?

Massimiano. Perhaps we are disturbing you. I see you are engaged in some arithmetic.

Veridico. No, no. This is not an account of debit and credit. Indeed, it has to do precisely with the subject you wish to talk about.

Santino. In what way ?

Veridico. This is a list I have made of the costumes and properties belonging to our actors. I drew it up so that we may be quite prepared when the time of performance comes.

Santino. Now we are here I propose to pounce directly on our prey. Let's start by inquiring how you would set about getting a play ready, supposing, say, the Prince ordered you to start producing one immediately.

Veridico. You are presuming, are you, that he has chosen the piece already ?

Santino. No. I presume that you have the job of finding one.

Veridico. Well, first of all I should endeavour to obtain a play that satisfied me, one presenting those qualities which I said specially concern such works of art, above all written in a good prose style and not made tedious by many soliloquies or long-drawn-out episodes or useless dialogue ; for I agree with those who declare that a play is perfect when the omitting of the smallest part renders it imperfect. If possible, I should try to get a new play, or at least one little known, avoiding as far as I could those already in print, however masterly they might be ; partly because every novelty gives pleasure, and partly because it is certain that those comedies which the audience knows beforehand have little interest. There are many reasons for this, chief among which, I believe, is the fact that, since the actor has to try as hard as he can to cheat the spectator into the belief that what he sees on the stage is true, if the auditor knows already the dialogue and the action of the piece the cheat seems too open and absurd, the plot loses that impression of reality with which it must always be associated, and the spectator, as if he imagined that he had been laughed at, not only condemns the show but chides himself for having childishly gone, as the proverb says, on a wild-goose chase. This does not occur in the presentation of new plays, for, however much the spectator realizes from the beginning that he is going to listen to fictional things, yet as he remains intent upon the novelty of the events it seems that little by little he voluntarily permits himself to be cheated until he imagines—if the actors are as accomplished as they ought to be—that he is really looking upon an actual series of real events.

Santino.   Certainly all you say is true, for I myself have attended good performances of really fine printed plays, and I, in common with others, have found myself dissatisfied.   On the other hand, I have derived immense pleasure from seeing other plays which, while they were not nearly so good, were new to me.

Massimiano.   Now you have told us about choosing a play would you say a few words about your method of production ?

Veridico.   First I have all the parts carefully copied out and then choose the actors who seem to me fittest for the various *rôles* (taking as much stock as possible of those particular qualities which I shall deal with later). I then gather them all together in one room and give each one that part for which he is most fitted.   I get them, after that, to read the whole play in order that they, even the children who take a share in it, may learn the plot, or at least that portion which concerns them, impressing on all their minds the nature of the characters they have to interpret.   Then I dismiss them and give them time to learn their parts.

Massimiano.   This presents a clear start.   Now we come to the question of choosing the actors and distributing the *rôles*—truly a most serious matter.

Veridico.   You may be surprised to hear me say—indeed, I should set it forth boldly as a fundamental principle—that it is far more essential to get good actors than a good play.   To prove the truth of this it is only necessary to call to your minds the number of times we have seen a poor drama succeed and give much pleasure to the audience because it was well acted ; and how often a fine play has failed on the stage because of the poor performance.   Now, supposing I have a good number of men skilled in acting and ready to follow my directions, first of all I endeavour to select those who speak with a good accent—for that is the primal consideration—then I consider their physical suitability for the part.   Thus a lover must be handsome, a soldier stoutly built, a parasite fat, a servant nimble, and so on.   I pay also great attention to their voices, for this I find of major importance.   I should not give the part of an old man, unless I were positively forced to do so, to an actor with a childlike voice, or a woman's part (particularly the part of a girl) to a deep-voiced actor.   So, too, suppose I had to choose some one for a ghost in a tragedy, I should endeavour, in order to produce the impression demanded, to secure an actor with naturally shrill tones or at least one who could counterfeit a trembling falsetto.   I should not pay so much attention to the actual facial features, since so much can be done by the aid of make-up in the way of altering the colour of a beard, simulating a scar, turning the cheeks pale or yellow, or rendering an appearance of vigor, ruddiness, weakness, or darkness as occasion demands.   Masks and false beards I should never employ, since they impede the voice too much.   If I were forced to give an old man's part to a beardless actor I should simply paint his chin to make him appear shaven, with a fringe of hair showing under his cap ; I should give him a few touches with the make-up brush on his cheeks and forehead, and by so doing I should make him seem aged, decrepit, and wrinkled.   Now, since I can't think of anything else concerning the selection of play or actors, I shall let you ask any questions that occur to you.

Santino.   I should like to inquire first of all what precepts and methods have to be followed by these actors.

Veridico.   You set me a very hard task.   To give you a general idea of the way I set about this matter, I shall say that in the first place I tell them all to speak firmly without raising their voices to shouting pitch ; I instruct them to speak in such a manner as to make their words clearly audible to all the spectators, thus avoiding those uproars which often occur among those in the back seats who cannot hear and which completely disturb the action of a play.   The only remedy is having an actor with a naturally fine voice, which, as I said, is the next necessity after a good pronunciation.

Massimiano.   That is very true.

Veridico.   I prohibit entirely as a very serious fault any tendency to haste in utterance : nay, I am always counselling them to go as slowly as possible.   For this purpose I make them pronounce their words very deliberately, without letting their voices drop on the last syllables.   Through this fault the spectators often lose the ends of sentences.

Santino.   If, as I think, the actors have to imitate ordinary speech I should have imagined that this slow and deliberate utterance would have seemed unnatural.

Veridico.   No, it does not in the least, for, apart from the fact that this slow enunciation is no bad thing in itself and is the special feature of dignified persons—those, indeed, who should be imitated by us—the actor must watch to give time to the auditors for appreciating the poet's words and relishing his sentences, which are by no means ordinary and commonplace.   I should like you to observe that, while an actor may think he is talking slowly, the spectator does not get that impression, provided that the words are not separated but given continuous delivery without being so mannerized as to raise annoyance.   Regarding other rules or methods of acting I do not believe I can say anything precise.   In general let us state that, granted the performer has a good accent, good voice, and suitable presence, whether natural or achieved by art, it will be his object to vary his gestures according to the variety of moods and to imitate not only the character he represents but also the state in which that character is supposed to be at the moment.

Massimiano.   Could you make that a trifle clearer, Veridico ?

Veridico.   Well, to take an example.   It will not be enough for a person taking, say, the part of a miser to keep his hand always on his purse as if he were constantly in terror lest the key of his desk should be lost ; he must learn as occasion demands to imitate the frenzy (for instance) he will experience when he learns that his son has stolen some of his money.   If the part is that of a servant, then the actor must learn how, on an occasion of sudden joy, to break into a lively dance ; in a moment of grief to tear his handkerchief with his teeth ; in a moment of despair to pull his cap to the back of his head, and so on with suitable effects which give life to the performance.   And if he has the part of a fool, besides speaking ill to the point as indicated by the author in his dialogue, he must learn on occasion to play the ninny, catching flies, searching for fleas, and suchlike.   If he is taking the part of a waiting-maid he must learn to make an exit by tossing up his skirts in a vulgar manner or biting his thumb and so on—actions which the author has not been able explicitly to indicate in his script.

Massimiano.   I remember hearing of some actors who were able to make their cheeks go pale on hearing bad news as though in reality they had experienced a great misfortune.

Veridico.   This is referred to by the immortal Plato in his dialogue on poetic fury.   He makes Ion say, " Every time I recite a mournful poem my eyes fill with tears ; every time I come on some terrible passages my hair rises on my head," and so on.   But in fact these things cannot be displayed very well on the stage, and certainly cannot be learned if they do not come by nature.   Although there are references among the ancients to many skilled players, and although one recognizes that theirs was a peculiar art, yet we cannot frame any rules for this profession ; truly it must be born in the individual.   Among the many gentlemen who take delight in acting to-day (such as the wonderful Montefalco, the excessively witty Verrato of Ferrara, the piquant Olivo, sharp Zoppino of Mantua, and that other Zoppino of Gazzolo, besides many others we have witnessed) I have always thought and still think that the acting of a young Roman girl called Flaminia is the most extraordinary.   Besides being gifted with many beauteous qualities, she is judged so unique in her profession that I do not believe the ancients ever saw or the moderns are likely to see a more brilliant actress. When she is on the stage the audience gets the impression not of a play composed and finished by an author, but rather of a series of real events taking shape before them.   She so varies her gestures, tones, and moods in accordance with the diverse nature of her scenes that every one who sees her is moved to wonder and delighted admiration.

Santino.   I remember hearing her, and I know that many wits, inspired by her rare playing, have written sonnets and epigrams and other poems in her praise.

Massimiano.   I should like to hear one of these.

Veridico.   I remember only two—one is " Mentre gli occhi fatali hor lieti, hor mesti, etc.," and the other " Donna leggiadra a cui la più gradita, etc."   Now, to get back once more to acting in general, let me say again that the performer must have a natural disposition for his work, otherwise he can never succeed.   On the other hand, the man who learns his part well and has the requisite skill finds movements and gestures of an appropriate kind to make his part seem real.   For this, as for other things, it is useful to have the author of the play as a director ; he generally has the ability to demonstrate some ideas not expressed in the text which improve the play and consequently make the actors seem more lively.   I say lively, for above all other things the actor must be vivacious and bright in his diction, except, of course, when he has to express grief, and even on such an occasion he must express it in a vital manner so as not to bore the audience. In fine, just as the poet has to hold the attention of the spectators by a seeming naturalness and a well-planned vivacious dialogue, so the actor has the business of keeping the variety of his actions appropriate to the situations, of maintaining a constant alertness, and of avoiding a tedious dullness ; this last simply bores an audience in the theatre and comes from cold interpretation, lacking the necessary fire and fitting power. To remedy this defect the actors (and particularly those who are not very expert in their art) must introduce this vivacity I have spoken of even in their rehearsals ; otherwise when they appear before the public they show up but ill.

Santino. Assuredly the actor takes a greater place in a play than I imagined. I suppose few realize this.

Veridico. I have spoken already to you about actions and words and have indicated that a comedy is built up from them, as our bodies are composed of flesh and spirit ; the poet corresponds to one of these parts, the actor to the other. The actor's movements, styled by the father of the Latin tongue the body's eloquence, are of so great importance that perhaps the power of words is not more than the power of gesture. Proof of this is to be found in those silent comedies familiar in certain parts of Europe, wherein the story is so clearly and pleasantly presented by means of action alone that only those who have witnessed this kind of play would credit its force. To this corporal eloquence, although it is of tremendous importance, called by some the soul of rhetoric, and consisting in dignity of movement in head, countenance, eyes, hands, and body, we can apply no laws. I can say only that the actor ought in general to have a lithe body with free-moving limbs, not stiff and awkward. He must place his feet on the ground naturally when he speaks, move them easily when occasion demands, turn his head without artificiality—not as though it were fastened to his neck by rivets. His arms and hands, too, when there is no need to make gestures with them, ought to hang naturally at his sides. The actor should avoid the manner of those many persons who introduce inappropriate gestures and seem to know not what they are doing. To take an example, if a woman playfully puts her hand on her hip or a young man puts his on his sword, neither should remain standing in this position for long ; whenever the situation that called for this action is over a change should be made and another gesture should be adopted suitable to the speech that follows. When an appropriate gesture cannot be found or when no movement is called for, then the actor should, as I said, leave his arms and hands in a natural position, loose and easy, without raising or folding them as though they were attached to the body with sticks. He should always employ in his actions just such demeanour as is demanded from the character he represents ; and likewise in the tone of his voice, now arrogant, now calm, now timorous, now fervent, with due emphasis on the essential points. In all he has to observe and imitate the natural manner of those persons whom he represents, above all avoiding as a capital crime what I shall call, for want of a better word, a pedantic manner of interpretation, after the style of school-children repeating their lessons before their master. That method of acting, I say, which makes the words seem like a passage learned by rote, must be avoided ; and endeavour must be made above all other things to render whatever is spoken thoroughly effective, with suitable alteration of tones and appropriate gestures. The whole dialogue must seem like a familiar talk, wholly improvised. Beyond this I can give you no rules ; and since I suppose this subject in general is sufficiently understood, let us dwell on it no longer, but pass on to the question of costume. In speaking about costume—and leaving aside the methods of the ancients whereby old men were all dressed in white and youths in coloured robes, parasites in folded cloaks thrown over their shoulders, and courtesans in yellow garments, because such symbolic indications, owing to variety in usage, would now be useless or but little appreciated—I may say that I always aim, first of all, at dressing the actors as richly as possible, yet with proportionate variations, since sumptuous costumes (particularly in these times when show is at its highest, and above all things we must consider time and place) seem to me to add much to the beauty of comedies and more so to that of tragedies. I should not hesitate to dress a servant in velvet or coloured satin, provided that his master's costume had sufficient embroidery and gold ornament to make a proper distinction between them ; nor should I endeavour to clothe a waiting-maid in a torn skirt or a valet in a shabby doublet ; on the contrary, I should give to the former a fine petticoat and to the latter a magnificent jacket—increasing at the same time the richness of their master's clothes to match the brightness of the servants' dresses.

Massimiano. Unquestionably the sight of those rags which are sometimes worn by a miser or a servant detracts from the impression created by a play.

Veridico. A miser or a servant may be clad in garments which have something rich about them and yet are true to nature.

Santino. That is true, particularly when one takes into account what you said about the usages of our own times.

Veridico. I try so far as possible to give the actors widely differing costumes. This is of double service in that the variety adds to the beauty of the show and at the same time aids in making the plot clear. For the latter reason, I believe, rather than for any other, the ancients employed characteristic dresses with particular colours allocated to the social position of the persons. To take an example, supposing I had to provide costumes for three or four servants, I should clothe one in white with a hat, another in red with a small cap, another in mixed livery, while to the fourth I might give a velvet hat and a pair of knitted sleeves should his position permit this. (I am speaking, of course, of a comedy introducing Italian fashions.) Similarly, if I had to dress two lovers I should try both in the colours and the cut of their suits to make them as different as possible. One would wear a cape, the other a short cassock ; one would sport some feathers in his cap, the other a gold ornament without any feathers. All would be contrived in such a way that as soon as either came on the stage he would be immediately recognizable, not merely by his countenance, but by the form of his clothes, so that the audience would know who he was without having to wait for him to announce his identity. I may observe that the method of wearing a hat is the most distinguishing characteristic in both men and women ; for that reason these should be as different as possible, in both colour and shape.

Santino. How often have I been in doubt for a time about the identity of a particular character on the stage, precisely because he is not dressed differently from another actor or servant !

Veridico. The diversity of colours gives great pleasure in the theatre. In general the costumes ought to be worked out in clear and bright shades. Black should be used as little as possible, and also any sombre tones. Not only do I aim at contrasting one actor with another, but I try to transform each one so that he shall not be immediately recognized by those spectators who have daily business with him. Of course, I endeavour not to fall into the error of the ancients who, to conceal the real identity of their players, painted their faces with wine-lees or mud. I am content to transform, not to transfigure, them, trying as much as I can to make them seem persons unknown to the audience. When a spectator recognizes an actor he loses some of that pleasant pretence which it is our object to maintain ; for we must always try to make him believe that our play is a real series of events. But, since novelty is always sure to please, an audience takes delight in seeing foreign and strange costumes on the stage ; it is for that reason that comedies in the Greek style are usually so successful. For this more than for any other reason I have contrived that the setting of the comedy you are to see on Tuesday should be Constantinople, so that I can introduce men's and women's dresses of a kind we do not wear. I hope by this means to add not a little to the beauty of the show, and, apart from that, there is the fact that theatrical situations affecting strange persons we do not know invariably seem more probable than the situations introduced into most of our comedies where the characters are citizens with whom we have daily business. And if this plan is good for comedy, as experience amply shows us, it is still better for tragedy. In costuming tragedies a careful producer must not be satisfied with modern clothes, but must dress his actors after the fashion of antique sculptures or paintings, with those mantles and attires in which these persons of past centuries were so beautifully depicted. Since, too, the finest stage spectacles have introduced a troop of armed men I recommend that where possible there be brought in as a bodyguard to a king or a general some soldiers and gladiators, costumed in antique style after the manner of old paintings.

Santino. Certainly it is true that such spectacles are poor unless they are presented by princes who have sufficient grandeur of spirit to spend lavishly on the settings and accoutrements.

Veridico. I don't want to speak about the settings to-day ; to-morrow, I promise, I shall come back to that subject. But, lest you fall into the error of supposing that one needs a whole treasury to furnish out a tragedy, let me just say that no prince's wardrobe is so poorly equipped as to lack materials for the dressing of a great tragedy so long as the producer is a clever man who can make use of what is given him and who has the skill to convert pieces of stuff, draperies, and the like into mantles, cloaks, and vestments, with girdles and knots after the antique fashion, without cutting or destroying them at all.

Massimiano. Assuredly a whole treasury (as Santino said) would have to be expended if one wanted to make all these dresses especially for the occasion.

Veridico. Yes, a whole treasury, or little less, would have to be expended on even a comedy or a pastoral play if all the dresses had to be specially made. Because of this we generally contrive to use up existing material.

Massimiano. Now you have brought it to my mind I should be glad if you would tell us something about these costumes and scenes suitable for pastoral plays. I personally do not think I have ever seen one on the stage.

Veridico. I shall deal with pastoral settings to-morrow when I turn to the subject of scenery in general. Concerning the manner of costuming, I should say that if the poet has introduced a god or a similar imaginative character we must try to follow his intentions ; but for pastoral costumes generally the same rule holds good as appertains to comedy—namely, that the characters must be dressed as differently from one another as possible. In general the method of costuming such persons is as follows : the legs and arms are covered with flesh-coloured cloth, or if the actor is young and handsome they are left naked. No actor, however, must go barefoot ; a well-fashioned cothurnus or the sock has to be worn. He should have a small, sleeveless shirt of taffeta or of some similar material pleasantly coloured ; and over this two leopard or other skins such as were described by Homer in his account of the Trojan shepherd, one worn on his breast, the other on his back. The legs of the animals' skins should come over his shoulders and under his thighs ; but variety may be introduced by making a few characters wear them over one shoulder only. Some of the actors should have at their girdles a small flask or a wooden bowl ; others a pouch slung over the shoulder and hanging down on the opposite side. Each one ought to have a stick, some of these sticks being cut and polished, others left untrimmed—the more extraordinary they are in shape the better. Their hair may be either natural or false, some curly and others combed out straight. Thus are the shepherds suitably dressed according to their positions and distinguished from one another by their colours, different kinds of skins, varying complexions, and variously arranged headdresses, as well as by other devices determinable only through actual experimentation. For the nymphs, after a careful examination of their qualities as outlined by the poets, there will be found necessary sleeved slips variously embroidered. I personally am in the habit of soaking the materials in starch so that when the dresses are bound with jewellery or else with coloured or golden girdles they spread out and present a pleasing picture to the eyes. In addition skirts of good coloured material are worn, girdled up so as to show the instep. The feet are clad either in elegant golden shoes of an antique pattern or else in boots of coloured leather. Finally a sumptuous mantle is demanded, passing from one of the hips and gathered together at the opposite shoulder. These nymphs ought to have thick, fair hair so as to seem natural, some flowing freely over their shoulders with a small garland ; others, for variety's sake, may have a frontlet of gold, and still others may bind their locks with silk ribbons and cover them with such thin veils floating down on their shoulders as in ordinary dress add so much beauty to a woman's costume. This, I say, is permissible even in pastoral shows since generally the floating veil is the principal head ornament worn by women and yet has a sufficient appearance of innocence and simplicity to accord with the dress of a wood-nymph. Some of these nymphs should carry bows with a quiver at their hips, others should merely carry a hunting spear, while still others may be equipped with both. He who attempts one of these pastoral shows must be a real expert, for it is much more difficult to win success in them than in comedies, although when success is secured the spectacle assumes much more gracefulness and beauty.

Santino. You do not, I suppose, include under the name of nymphs all kinds of women appearing in these plays—any more than you would include under the name of shepherds all the men ?

Veridico. Assuredly no ; for if, for example, the poet were to introduce in such a play the person of a witch we should have to dress her in fitting robes ; or if a peasant we should have to put him in coarse rustic garments. Should shepherdesses be introduced, then the nymphs' dresses will serve, with the exception that no cloak will be worn and nothing held in the hands save a crook. The costumes may vary from the plain to the elaborately rich. It adds to the spectacle if the shepherds bring in one or two dogs, and I like to see some of the nymphs bringing them in too. The latter, however, should be more graceful dogs, with pretty collars and light coverings. To conclude what I have to say about these plays, I shall affirm that, just as verse is required for their dialogue, so an harmonious accompaniment is needed in the costuming and direction as well as in the stature and movements of the players.

Massimiano. I should not imagine that it would be possible to assign more particular rules than those you have already given to these pastoral plays. Let us therefore get back to our former theme—the arrangements to be made for the prologues to comedies.

Veridico. Before one comes to the prologue, however, one must run over the characters to see if all are provided with such things as they may require; these things must be noted down in a property list (such as that which I was but now engaged in preparing), for to forget even some small article may put the players very much out. Besides this, I personally am in the habit of doing another thing which is very useful and necessary; I note down all the scenes in order, with the names of the characters appearing in them, together with an indication of the house or street by which they are to enter, their cues, and the first words they have to utter on the stage; by the aid of this plan the director can arrange always to get all the actors ready in time at their places of entrance, to put them on stage at their cues, and prompt them with the first words they have to speak.

Santino. With this device there is no danger of the stage remaining empty between one scene and another. Now let us go to the question of the dropping of the curtain, or *sipario*, as the ancients called it.

Veridico. Before the curtain falls I recommend the sounding, after the fashion of the early actors, of trumpets or flutes or of similar loud instruments. This has the effect of awakening interest, which may be flagging owing to the long wait which commonly the great majority of the spectators have before the beginning of the play. It serves also to give warning to the groups of actors.

Massimiano. My experience is that this does make a strong impression. Now let us come to the question of prologues and their forms.

Veridico. So far as kinds of prologues are concerned, I believe that those have greatest dignity and are most fitting which were used by the ancients. In these an actor clad in a toga and crowned with laurel, dressed in a sumptuous yet dignified costume, entered in the guise of the poet. It adds much to place under the wreath a false wig, both to conceal the actor's individuality and to make him seem an antique character. He must come on stage, immediately the curtain falls, walk very slowly and with dignified demeanour from the extreme edge of the stage, and, when he has at last arrived in the very middle, remain motionless for a time until he recognizes that the chatter common in such places is quite stilled. Then with smooth diction he may commence. I do not counsel him to move; it is much better for him to stay in one spot as he majestically delivers his words; should he be forced to move from one position to another he may take a single step, or two, but slowly, without turning his back on the audience. Since I have referred to this, it may be appropriate to mention that neither the speaker of the prologue nor any of the actors should ever turn their shoulders to the audience; this is a universal rule. Also it is always well for them to act as much in the middle of the stage and on the proscenium line as possible, and to face the spectators. The actor should also try to avoid going too close to the scenic perspectives, since if he gets near them they lose their verisimilitude, while the distance he actually is from them seems but slight to the audience. This is well proved in practice. In general, too, I may say that while an actor is speaking he ought never to walk about unless he is forced thereto by great necessity.

Massimiano. That is assuredly true. Now please tell us this: if the scene is supposed to be, let us say, Rome, and the play is being acted, say, in Florence, whom is the actor speaking the prologue to address and where is he supposed to be?

Veridico. Leaving aside just now those fantastic prologues where gods and other extraordinary characters are introduced (of these we shall deal when speaking of visible intermedii), I may say that the person who, speaking in the name of the poet, delivers the prologue must always directly address his speech to the spectators (contrary to what the actor has to do) and make himself seem their fellow-citizen, giving them information regarding the city represented in the setting, the nature of the play, and its title, besides begging their silence, and other similar things.

Santino. You don't want to say anything to-day about the intermedii?

Veridico. I want to leave over till to-morrow this question of stage intermedii. I shall then give you my opinion concerning the way in which they may add to or detract from the plays with which they are associated. Just now, however, I shall say that plays need musical intermissions at least, both to refresh the spectator's minds and to grant the dramatic poet (as I started to tell you yesterday) an interval to give proportion to his play, since every one of these intermedii, however brief, may serve to indicate a space of four, six, or eight hours.

APPENDIX B

Obviously the play, however long it may be, cannot last more than four hours, yet the action often spreads over a whole day and sometimes half of another; the fact that during the interval no actors are on stage makes the fictional passage of time more efficacious.

Massimiano. What kind of intermedii seem to you best adapted to the needs of tragedy and pastoral?

Veridico. Tragedies, as I believe I have indicated before, do not need to be divided into acts (although the moderns so divide them on their own authority), and the choruses which are introduced in them by the poets ought to serve for that part which marks the passage of time from one action to another. But as it is the custom in our times to distinguish separate acts (owing to the fact that the moderns introduce lengthier themes) I shall tell you to-morrow what kind of intermedii may be judged most fitting. At the same time we shall talk about the intermissions suitable for pastoral plays. To-day our discussion has been long enough, and, indeed, it is time that I tried out the lighting for our comedy, to see that nothing is amiss. Therefore with your leave I shall make an end of my discourse, unless perchance you too wish to come and see the rehearsal.

Santino. We certainly do wish to accept this gracious invitation—do we not, Signor Massimiano?

Massimiano. Undoubtedly.

Veridico. Let us go, then, to the theatre.

Santino. Yes, let us go.

FOURTH DIALOGUE

Interlocutors : Veridico, Santino, *and* Massimiano

Veridico. Quick, Marcletto, and you, you booby, get one of these ladders each and start lighting the lamps. We shall sit here, gentlemen.

Santino. I should like to sit a trifle farther back, so as to see better the excellent effect of that perspective.

Veridico. All right: I too will come over there. Ready? Light all these reliefs.

Massimiano. Assuredly this art of painting is a wonderful thing when it is in capable hands. Standing here, I am completely cheated by the illusion. Though I know, of course, that there is only a flat cloth in front of me, I seem to see a real street running back a good half-mile.

Veridico. Precisely the same power is at the command of the accomplished actor. Though you are perfectly well aware that he *is* only play-acting, if he does his part well a series of real events will seem to unfold themselves before you.

Massimiano. That is quite true.

Santino. Apart from the painting, the architecture of this set appears to my eyes to be excellent. I do not recall having seen so beautiful buildings at Naples or Rome or Florence or Milan.

Veridico. I do not wish to speak at large about the special qualities of the scenery, partly because my business is not that of architect or painter, partly because it would be impossible to provide you with adequate examples. The manners and styles of the painters vary considerably, and the material they work in is infinite; equally varied are the settings which they may devise—house fronts, squares, porticoes, streets embellished with arches, columns, statues of diverse kinds—the models being taken from this city or that, ancient or modern, according to the demands of the script. However, just as I said that the actors' costumes should be rich in appearance, so I say that the sets ought always to be based on the finest possible models. The details of such matters I leave to those who practise such arts, but I may remark—with all due deference to the moderns—that the sets of which we have so full descriptions among the ancients must have possessed an almost absolute beauty. On this subject Ercole Bentivoglio touches pleasantly and briefly in one of his prologues, when he declares that:

> Marcus Scaurus, citizen of Rome,
> So beauteous a theatre made, and scene,
> Of glass and marble joined in harmony,
> With rich carved columns all embellishèd,
> And statues hewn by sculptors famed.

'Tis said another theatre was made,
By Caius Antonius, a glittering dream
Of silver ; and of gold a third Petreius
Fashionèd ; of ivory white was that
Of Quintus Catulus. Most marvellous
Were those two theatres of Curio,
Which wondrously did turn and, facing each
To each, an amphitheatre made—

and so on. From these accounts we may deem that our modern sets, lovely as they may seem, are but shadows to those of that more glorious time. During that period plays were held in greatest esteem, their end being, as I have said, the civil institution. Because of this, theatres were erected among the more important civic buildings ; as Vergil, in the first book of the *Aeneid* observes, concerning the founding of Carthage :

And then the firm and ample base was laid
For the great stages.

Massimiano. In my opinion that was a magnificent setting which his Highness the Duke of Mantua caused to be erected in the courtyard of his castle for his wedding celebrations. Though it was not used for anything but the tourney held that evening, it would have served excellently for the presentation both of comedies and of tragedies.

Veridico. Cavalier Leone, accomplished architect as he is, could not have created anything but what was perfect ; and that set, I agree, was perfect—enriched with so many reliefs, embellished by such admirable architecture, with such variety of lovely inventions.

Santino. Had it been constructed of firm and durable substance, maybe one might have compared it—perhaps even put it above—those settings you have just been speaking of. Unfortunately, it was made entirely of lath and plaster.

Veridico. But all the greater was Duke Guglielmo's magnanimity in spending so many thousands of ducats on that marvellous set and then destroying it when it had served its immediate purpose.

Santino. Perhaps so, but let us dwell on this subject a trifle longer. I want you to tell me one thing, Veridico. Here on your stage are many lighted lamps, giving ample illumination and making a most lovely show ; what, then, is the use of and how originated those many lamps burning on the roofs of the stage-houses ? They do not seem to me to aid the perspective, and for ordinary purposes of illumination there are torches enough.

Veridico. I think I have said more than once that plays are produced for the purpose of providing pleasant instruction and of alleviating noyance of mind. Whence I declared, and again I repeat it, the actor should above all other things endeavour to enunciate his lines in a bright and joyous manner. Such, granted that the author provides us with a pleasant, charming plot and that the actor gives to this a vivid interpretation, surely it is equally essential that the architect should represent gladness and joy on the stage. Now it has been a custom, both in ancient and modern times, to light bonfires and torches in the streets, on the housetops, and on towers, as a sign of joy ; and hence arises this theatrical convention—the imitating of such festive occasions. The lights are put there for no other purpose but to imitate, in the very first scene, this mood of gaiety.

Santino. I suppose, then, that these lights would not appear in a tragedy.

Veridico. Perhaps they would not be so wholly out of place even in such a play. Quite apart from the fact that there are tragedies with happy endings, we note that nearly all tragedies open in a happy strain ; and consequently it will not be unfitting to arouse the mind, so far as we may, to this happiness, although disasters and deaths are to ensue later. I remember once I had to produce a tragedy of this kind. During all the time when the episodes were happy in mood I had the stage brightly illuminated, but so soon as the first unhappy incident occurred—the unexpected death of a queen—while the chorus was engaged in lamenting that the sun could bear to look down on such evil, I contrived (by prearrangement, of course) that at that very instant most of the stage lights not used for the perspective were darkened or extinguished. This created a profound impression of horror among the spectators and won universal praise.

Santino.   It could not have called forth anything but praise.

Massimiano.   Will you now please tell us why most of your lights have in front of them transparent or coloured glasses ?

Veridico.   This was invented by some men who realized a little-appreciated fact—that a brilliant light striking directly upon the eye for any length of time becomes exceedingly irritating.   Since, then, the spectator must keep his eyes fixed on the stage, watching the actions proceeding now on this side, now on that, the shading of the lights was devised to minimize the annoyance.

Massimiano.   I should be willing to bet that not ten persons out of a hundred who make use of these shades appreciate their object.

Veridico.   They would at any rate say that the shades were used to produce a more beautiful effect, and in so doing they would be enunciating part of the whole.   Not by my own theorizing, certainly, but from long practice and experience I have made observation of these things and have tried to get at their origins.   I have found that it was the ancients who, as the saying goes, snatched them from obscurity.   While we are dealing with this subject I should like to point out also that the small mirrors which some managers set at appropriate places in the perspective settings and the far sides of the wings are very effective.   They reflect those concealed lights which the architects cleverly place behind columns and in the openings between the wings, thus serving to make the set more gay and bright.   Not only can these reflections give no annoyance to the eyes ; they have the further advantage that here we obtain light without smoke—a great consideration.   I may take this occasion to remark that the producer who does not take care to have a number of holes made behind the scenes so that the smoke from the lamps may have a means of escape will land himself in serious difficulties, for otherwise this smoke, gradually increasing and becoming thicker, will produce so effective a screen that before the second act be done the actors will seem to be not men but shadows, while the spectators, as if blinded, will, without realizing the cause, get the impression that they are losing their sight.   Great care ought to be taken of this, though it is a matter to which few pay sufficient attention.   So far as my experience goes, there is no real difficulty provided adequate pains are taken beforehand.

Massimiano.   Now that you bring these things to my attention I do recall that at the close of plays we have often found our eyes smarting uncomfortably and that we have not been able to see nearly so much as we did at the beginning.   I realize that this must have been due to the cause you have referred to.

Veridico.   To avoid the smoke screen I have found that the best remedy is to open as many windows as possible under the proscenium, so that the air, entering from below, drives all the smoke through the holes bored in the roof behind the scenery.

Massimiano.   That, I believe, would be an excellent device.

Veridico.   It is, I assure you.

Santino.   I see, Veridico, that on your stage there are many lamps both behind the scenes and in front of them ; yet in the auditorium here you have made arrangements for but twelve standing candelabra.   The reason I can't imagine ; for I have often counted as many as 250 torches in this large hall.

Veridico.   It is a natural fact—as no doubt you are aware—that a man who stands in the shade sees much more distinctly an object illuminated from afar ; the reason being that the sight proceeds more directly and without any distraction toward this object, or, according to the peripatetic theory, the object impinges itself more directly upon the eye.   Wherefore I place only a few lamps in the auditorium, while at the same time I render the stage as bright as I possibly can.   Still further, these few auditorium lights I place at the rear of the spectators, because the interposition of such lights would but be dazzling to the eyes.   Over them, as you see, I have made small openings so that their smoke can cause no damage.

Santino.   By thus introducing only a few lights in the auditorium, then, you obviate the trouble of smoke-fumes and to a certain extent you render the seeing clearer.

Massimiano.   There is yet another advantage : he saves the Duke fifty ducats in respect of the torches usually set in the hall.

Veridico.   That, I confess, had not come into my mind, nor does his Excellency need to think of such economies, but, as the proverb says, in the end every good proves good.

Santino.   Concerning the illumination of the scene you have said, in my opinion, all that can be said; concerning the details of the set you yourself declared you were unwilling to say more since you are not an architect by profession. But would you not now care to tell us something about the pastoral settings, since for those at least a knowledge of architecture is not demanded ?

Veridico. At your request, then, I shall say this : If the pastoral play which is to be produced demands the usual setting of an open country in summer-time, then the scene will have to be rich and full of foliage. On being discovered to the spectators it ought to give an impression of great loveliness. This is best done by using leaves and flowers and fruit-trees to represent a summer season, with, among the branches, diverse birds whose songs may arouse a feeling of joy. At times, too, one may cause various animals, such as rabbits and hares and so on, to wander over the stage. Thus the likeness of pleasing landscapes and solitary woods may be drawn to the life. Similarly, prospects may be shown of mountains, valleys, cottages, springs, caves, and suchlike, according to your desire—the distant views, of course, being rendered in conformity with the laws of perspective. At the front so much space, adorned to represent a flowery field, may be left clear for the ordinary purposes of the play as the stage permits. If, however, a night scene is demanded, then painting must be employed, and special care must be taken to see that the lamps are concealed as much as possible. No more can I say about such settings in matter of detail ; one must depend on the judgment of the writer of the play and the skill of the director, just as is the case in scenes of a maritime sort.

Santino. What do you mean by maritime scenes ?

Veridico. Such as I saw not many years ago in Portugal. The set called for a great ship in the harbour at Rhodes. This indeed made a brave show, both because of the great colossus which, according to the ancients, once stood above this harbour, its legs straddling over the ships that sailed in or out, and because of the number of characters who in the various scenes performed now on shore, now on board ship.

Santino. That, I doubt not, was a novel and beauteous show. Now would you not be so good as to say a few words concerning the method of presenting perspective or open scenes which, it is said, is frequently used—indeed, generally used—in Spanish theatres ?

Veridico. By open scenes I presume you mean those where we look into a room and see some one acting there ?

Santino. Yes, these are the kind I refer to. What do you think of them ?

Veridico. Although there is a certain beauty in seeing presented on the stage an open, well-appointed room in which, for example, a lover has an interview with a bawd, and although this gives a strong impression of verisimilitude, yet it goes so contrary to reality—in that the room is lacking (as it must) a fourth wall—that it appears to me rather awkward ; besides which, I am by no means sure that the actor in such a scene can be said to be on a stage at all. One might, of course, avoid these inconveniences by opening the scene on a loggia or a terrace where some persons come to converse, but, for myself, I should not take the licence to leave the front stage otherwise empty and accordingly should contrive that such conversations appeared at the end or the beginning of an act—so that they might almost be called intermedii. Since I have thus made reference to visible intermedii, I may give you a few thoughts on this subject. First of all, in regard to extraordinary prologues, I should say that those of a fantastic kind do not harmonize very well with plays, for plays, after all, ought to deal with things which may seem natural. However, when these prologues have some connexion with the plot or with the occasion of the performance, then they will become more tolerable.

Santino. Would you be so good as to give us an example ?

Veridico. Well, this will do. Suppose in a comedy designed to celebrate the establishment of a new prince we introduce, say, a god who, drawing lots with his brothers, gains the rule of the heavens, and suppose this god is made to say something concerning the good governing of a state. Similarly if the performance were to take place on the occasion of the birth of a prince, then we might, for example, introduce a Lucina to prognosticate immortal glory arising from his birth. Or else at a nuptial festival one might introduce a Hymen. Indeed, it is easy to invent suitable topics for all sorts of occasions.

Santino. And if it were not for any special performance, but merely, as is more usual, for a carnival show, how would the poet harmonize his matter to the occasion ?

Veridico. Easily, for there is no lack of subject-matter having some bearing on the plot.

Santino. What do you mean ?

Veridico. I shall give you some examples from those which a few years ago we saw in this city ; these will make it all clear to you. Don't you remember the success of the prologue to that tragi-comedy presented last carnival, when the poet introduced an argument between Comedy and Tragedy ?   Do not you recall also the prologue to *Fortunata*, a comedy acted four years ago, in which appeared a new show of Fortune and Fame ?

Santino.   Of course I do ; but surely one could not find similarly appropriate prologues for all plays ?

Veridico.   I grant that : but when this is the case it is always possible to bring in matter relating to the city or to the places in which the plays are given—one might introduce the rivers that irrigate the surrounding country, the men who first built the town, those born there who had become famous for their heroic virtues. A friend of ours did this when in a Mantuan play he introduced Virgil ; another time he brought in a Mincio, and still another the Theban Manto—thus varying his fancies in the prologues to diverse plays.   However, I do not want to spend too long a time on this matter, since I want to speak of visible intermedii.   Such, I say, are little suitable for comedies, since by their novelty they so distract the mind of the spectator that when he turns again to the plot of the drama it seems to him less interesting, for truly we shall be more powerfully attracted by the spectacle (say) of a Cadmus sowing the teeth of the slain dragon and raising his crop of armed men, or of a Perseus ascending on his Pegasus to defend an Andromeda, than when we watch a slave astutely disentangling himself from the dangers encompassing him or a lover planning a *tête-à-tête* with his adored one. Hence I say that when a play has such extraordinary fancies in the intermedii these will be more looked to, and the play as a consequence fail in its success.   Sometimes, however, we see certain bizarreries which, without drawing away the attention, give a good deal of pleasure.   Thus, for example, between two acts of a play eight or ten artisans might come on the stage from different streets ; these might sing in concert, and on entering each might indicate his profession, some of them playing on instruments concealed in the tools of their trade.   Thus a small lyre would be in the locksmith's pan, a violin in a boot belonging to the mender of old shoes, a flute in the handle of the broom borne by the chimney-sweep, a harpsichord in the basket of the pastry-cook, with similar other devices which, being things commonly seen in cities, do not draw away the mind and detract in no wise from the interest we take in the plot of the play.

Santino.   Of this sort were the intermedii brought forward by our own Cardo ; he introduced four pilgrims who went about singing and with a number of engaging quips, begging alms from the ladies.   In another intermedio he called for four porters, who, after a brief argument in rustic terms concerning the division of some money, came to blows and kicks, all in morris time.

Veridico.   We may conclude, then, that those intermedii which are concerned with such ordinary things as one may see in comedies may be tolerated.   Those of an extravagant kind, introducing matters of an unnatural sort, seem to me to be entirely inappropriate.   In tragedies divided into acts and also in pastoral poems undoubtedly may be permitted things more out of the ordinary, since in the body of the play itself appear ghosts, furies, gods, and strange characters ; but unquestionably these intermedii will be the better the more definite relationship they bear to the plot.   Thus, for example, in a play which is to bring ruin or death on the stage the Fates may be introduced ; these may sing as they spin and wind on their distaffs the thread of a king or a queen until it is violently cut by Clotho.   Or else one may bring on the Furies of Hell, with burning torches in their hands ; these, moving about in morris time, would set alight Rage and Ruin around some royal palace.   Things of this kind would make pleasing shows without entirely distracting attention from the subject-matter of the play.

Massimiano.   Verily I believe that any man of good judgment could easily discover diverse extravagant fancies of this sort, for most legends and many historical anecdotes could readily be dramatized in this way. For instance, at Bologna I saw some years ago an intermedio which brought on an Amphion ; at the sound of his music the rocks began to pile up one on top of the other, and thus were reared the walls of Thebes.   In the second intermedio an eagle appeared to seize a Ganymede.   During the interval of the third act Deucalion and Pyrrha came on and threw stones over their shoulders, whence arose little by little tiny nude children. The fourth intermedio introduced a giant, who brought on an enormous globe and placed it in the middle of the stage ; after he had given it some blows with a club the ball opened, and out stepped four satyrs, who executed a delightful morris dance.   In a tragi-comedy recently presented here in our city I saw a battle between the three Horatii and the three Curiatii, produced so effectively to the time of a morris dance, with real weapons, that it made a magnificent show.   In conclusion I say that I believe that any man might easily invent things of this kind, although the harmonizing of them to the theme of the play seems to me rather difficult.   Wherefore I should like to have some specific example.

R

Veridico. I wish to give you to read a pastoral in five acts. You will find that the intermedii introduced in it are so thoroughly appropriate that they seem almost part of its structure. I am sure you will not regret looking at it. While I am searching for it among my books I shall take the opportunity of telling you about a pastoral feast which followed this play. It proceeded thus. Our illustrious Lord had got built in a great hall two orders of square rustic columns, evenly spaced and bearing vaulted arches. Although it was winter-time, these were all covered with green boughs. Thus were formed two lovely, long, and leafy loggias with diverse festoons of fruits and flowers, some artificial (since it was out of their season), some real. Within the columns (which were hollow) there had been concealed many lamps, which, shining forth from shades made of coloured glass and skilfully placed, illuminated the whole room in a delightful way; still greater splendour was provided by several great globes filled with water, cleverly set in the middle of each archway. Above these, lamps had been placed in such number that each arch seemed lit up by a blazing sun. Indeed, it seemed brighter than at high noon. Between the two loggias was a space of about ten cubits; it was considerably higher than the two loggias and was entirely roofed with a blue sky set with stars and having a magnificent great moon in the middle. The rays from this moon fell on a deliciously set table which stretched the whole length of the open space, and on which was spread a rich supper of diverse fruits—mostly artificial sugar fruits or else real fruits preserved in sugar. As soon as the play was over—this was given in another hall and had marvellous success—an Orpheus appeared, followed by many shepherds and nymphs. In a few lines of verse, to the harmonious accompaniment of a lyre, he invited the assembled audience to a pastoral and rustic feast; and accordingly the accompanying shepherds—following their instructions—went off to welcome the guests. Each shepherd acted as escort to one of the gentlemen, masked or unmasked as the case might be; similarly every nymph took one of the ladies under her guidance; and so, couple by couple, all the guests were led into the room set apart for this purpose—the sudden sight of which caused great wonderment among them all. The lord of the feast, who was masked as a shepherd, together with many of his men, took the mask from his face, and they all followed him. Then, after some pleasant jesting, they washed their hands and sat down in festive spirit at the table, where they were richly served by the shepherds and the nymphs, without the least confusion or disorder.

Massimiano. You have filled me with delight by the mere retelling of this device. Just imagine how transported I should have been had I actually been present.

Veridico. And what would you have done had you seen all the dishes borne with various devices to the table?

Massimiano. Then some art was employed in bringing the food to the table?

Veridico. Yes, indeed; that was the best part of the feast. Nothing was brought in already cooked; but the contents of each dish were first displayed either alive or uncooked, with a series of delightful fancies.

Massimiano. Please give us an example so that we may imagine the rest.

Veridico. Willingly. First there appeared four youths clad as monks; these, bearing baskets of various rich salads, greeted a sister of the Lord who sat at the head of the table, and on behalf of the Mother Prior gave them to her as an offering of affection. Then, seeing all the company were seated at the table, they sang a lovely benediction in unison, and meanwhile the dressed salads were brought in. And since the banquet was a sumptuous one, when the fish arrived there appeared first a number of fishermen, each dressed in the fashion of a different locality, and as they made their bows at those moments the produce of their various regions were brought in. Similarly when the time came for kids or other like domestic meat a shepherd or a peasant arrived to lead them in alive; he would then present them to the lord and to the guests with many witty remarks, and immediately the table would be served with these courses. In the same way, before the bird course came, hawkers brought them in alive, accompanying them now with music, now with verses, now with doggerel rimes. Similarly before the meat was served a number of hunters appeared with sound of horn and hounds, and presented to one guest a boar's head, to another a hare, to this man a deer and to that a roe, and so with all. What, however, aroused the greatest amount of pleasant laughter was that certain vile, lecherous, or vicious things were presented by two facetious persons (not to call them buffoons)—an old man and a youth who had been called in specially for this purpose. When they brought in their various objects they aroused great laughter by the variety of their witty remarks.

APPENDIX C

DESIGNS BY GIACOMO TORELLI DA FANO (1608–78)

AMONG the greater scenic artists of the seventeenth century Giacomo Torelli da Fano is by no means the least interesting or the least important. Not only was he styled in his native country *il grande stregone*—" the great sorcerer " [1]—but he was one of those scenographers who helped to carry the Italian theatre ideals to the rest of Europe. His services were early sought and obtained for the royal performances in France, and some of his greatest triumphs were those associated with the ballets, operas, and tragedies produced at the Court of Louis XIV. At Paris he worked till 1660, when, on his retirement, his envious successor, Gaspare Vigarani, wilfully destroyed what remained of his scenes and his machine effects. Happily, however, many engravings were made of his stage designs, and these at once served to spread his influence during the seventeenth century and serve now to indicate his aims and the achievement of those aims. The designs reproduced in this appendix are taken from four important collections: (1) *Il Bellero Fonte . . . rappresentato nel Teatro Nouissimo in Venetia . . . Giacomo Torelli Da Fano Inuentore delli Apparati*, 1642; (2) *Apparati scenici per lo Teatro Novissimo di Venetia Nell' anno 1644*; (3) *Feste Theatrali per la Finta Pazza drama del Signor Givlio Strozzi Rappresentate nel piccolo Borbone in Parigi quest anno* MDC.XLV; and (4) *Scene e Machine preparate alle Nozze di Teti Balletto Reale representato nella sala del piccolo Borbone*, 1654. The settings, therefore, illustrate Torelli's work both at the Venetian theatre and at the Parisian Petit Bourbon. They may be classified according to the collections in which they appear.

(1) The interest of Figs. 277, 278, 279, and 280, taken from *Il Bellero Fonte*, is twofold. In the first place, a comparison of these with the design for *Ariane* (Fig. 195) will show that the last-mentioned, if not actually copied from the others, has been at least deeply influenced by the Torelli manner. The buildings forming the side-wings in *Ariane*, both in respect of general architectural effect and in respect of the superimposed statues, at once recall the side-wings in Fig. 279. The background of the *Ariane* engraving is formed by a patch of water ending in a bridge and buildings faintly outlined. Cupids sport in the sky, and a shell, drawn by dolphins, nears the shore. Fig. 277 shows a very similar background. The stretch of water, the distant buildings, the airy figure and the shell—this time drawn by sea-horses—all indicate the connexion between the two designs. Fig. 278 has been added here in order to show the use of a different back-cloth (with the same side-wings) for the purpose of a scenic change. In Fig. 280 (from the same performance) the side-wings have been altered, but it seems probable that the stretch of water between the stage level and the distant prospect formed a constant feature through most of the scenes (Fig. 280). The Romanized costume of the characters, the fiery dragon, and the winged Pegasus all deserve particular notice in the last-mentioned design.

(2) The three designs (Figs. 281, 282, and 283) from the *Apparati scenici* of 1644 have their own interest. Fig. 281 shows a very typical satyric setting such as we find ever associated with the pastoral. The cloud effects and the presentation of deities are here somewhat original. The

---

[1] There is a story that he was actually attacked in Venice as a servant of the devil.

second illustration shows a temple with the heavy stage perspective beloved of the period, while the third, Fig. 283, is an equally typical re-rendering of a Serlian tragic scene (*cf.* Figs. 80, 82–84, and 151).

(3) Fig. 284 (the proscenium arch as well as the setting is illustrated), from the *Feste Theatrali*, again suggests the tragic scene, but there is this particular interest in the print, that the divided buildings in the background give more than a mere suggestion of the various passageways shown in the Teatro Olimpico (*cf.* Figs. 85–89). The deities in the clouds bring to mind some of Inigo Jones' designs (*cf.* Fig. 148), and the costumes of the human characters are worthy of special attention.

(4) Finally, we reach the designs for the *Nozze di Teti* of 1654 (Figs. 285, 286, and 287). These plates are accompanied in the collection with lengthy descriptions of the scenic action, and it may not be uninstructive to quote at least part of these accounts. Regarding the first setting (Fig. 285), which shows the Grotto of Cheiron, we read the following :

> La prima Scena dell' Atto primo rappresenta la Grotta di Chirone Centauro, è composta tutta di sassi, e scogli horridissimi, e coperta da vn vastissimo volto pure di sassi, rende insieme vaghezza, & horrore. Nell' alto si vede vn' apertura, per la quale la Grotta riceue il lume, e per doue si vedono le strade di vna montagna, e paesaggio di fuori, che conduce all' entrata della sudetta Grotta, che aprono due porte di rustica architettura fabricate d'vna parte, e d'altra. Si vedono molti, e diuersi sepolcri di maestosa costruttura che chiudono quegli Eroi, che sono stati degni di morir discepoli di cosi grand maestro. Sotto la medesima apertura dell' alto, se ne vede vn' altra, che mostra i più intimi luoghi della sudetta habitazione ; e con ingegnosa regola di prospettiua appare di lontano il fondo, in cui vedesi ancora vn più superbo sepolcro de' gli altri. Quì all' incanto de' maghi, addittati da Chirone, frà tuoni e lampi sorge un carro, sopra di ciu montata Peleo, si leua in aria in mezzo di fiamme, e fumosi vapori, che lasciati à mezzo corso, vola à trauerso della Grotta, vscendo per la sudetta apertura, il fumo suanisce in aria, e la fiamma ricade al fondo.[1]

The presentation of Cheiron and the costumes of the sorcerers are to be noted in this illustration. Fig. 286 shows the same ' side-scenes ' with a different prospect behind. Again we may turn to the description :

> Quì cangiata tutta la prospettiua della Grotta, in luogo di vna lontananza di scogli, si vede vn placidissimo mare, circondato di riue piaceuoli, de colli ameni, e deliziose habitazioni. Comparisce da vna parte vna gran conchiglia piena di pescatori di coralli, che sostenendone nel mezzo loro vn' altra più picciola, n'è portata Teti Dea maritima. Viene sorgendo dal mare di lei inuaghito Nettune, accompagnato da vn coro di Tritoni, e Sirene. . . . Gioue intanto apparisce in aria . . . mentre Giunone gelosa discende su'l proprio carro . . . egli se ne vola al Cielo sù l'aquila, e fa chiudere Dei gran nuuola. Gioue intanto, chiamate dall' inferno le furie ; sorge dalla terra vna testa di formidabil mostro, che esalando fiamme, e fumi sulfurci, vomita quattro furie.[2]

[1] Translation (this and the following translations have of necessity to paraphrase rather than render literally some of the Italian descriptive passages) :

The first scene of Act I, which shows the Grotto of the Centaur Cheiron, is wholly composed of stones and fearsome rocks ; this, being vaulted with stones, gives an impression at once of beauty and horror. Above, an aperture is seen whence the grotto receives its light, and through which is to be discerned a landscape with mountain paths which lead down to the entrance of the grotto. Two doors of rustic architecture open one on each side. There are to be seen many diverse tombs of a majestic type which enclose the remains of those Heroes who had been worthy to die disciples of so great a master. Beneath the high opening is another which reveals the furthest parts of this dwelling. By the ingenuity of perspective the background seems very distant. There, a more superb tomb than the others can be seen. At the incantation of the sorcerers directed by Cheiron a chariot bearing Peleus rises with thunder and lightning. This rises into the air in the midst of flames and smoke, crossing the grotto and departing through the aperture. The smoke vanishes into the air and the flame recedes into the background.

[2] Here all the perspective of the Grotto changes. In place of a distant view of rocks there is to be seen a calm sea surrounded by lovely shores and gentle slopes and pleasant houses. On one side appears a great shell full of coral fishers who support in their midst another smaller shell which bears Thetis, the goddess of the sea. Neptune, in love with her, and accompanied by a chorus of Tritons and Sirens, rises from the sea. . . . Jove meanwhile appears in the air. . . . Juno, in a fit of jealousy, descends in her own chariot . . . he flies off to Heaven on his eagle and causes the gods to close the great cloud. . . . Juno [" Gioue " above must be an error for " Giunone "], meanwhile, having called the furies from hell, a head of a horrible monster rises from the earth and, with clouds of sulphuric smoke and flames, casts up four furies.

APPENDIX C

This illustration is specially interesting for the costumes displayed and for the use of a monster's head which recalls the Hell-mouth of centuries previous (*cf.* Figs. 59, 60, and 63). Fig. 287 shows the setting for a later scene. The immediately preceding scene had been that of Thetis' palace, and now changes come to that as to the others:

> Ercole in fine con Prometheo liberato conducono le Arti liberali sue figliuole, che danzano mentre che dal Cielo cominciano à scendere sei nuuole da' fianchi con diciotto persone sopra. . . . Di sopra si vede vn' altra apertura, doue siedono dalle parti diciotto persone, che sono le Intelligenze celesti, che . . . attendono Giunone, e Imeneo.[1]

---

[1] At the end Hercules with the liberated Prometheus leads forward the Liberal Arts, his daughters, who dance while six clouds, with eighteen characters on them, begin to descend at the sides from heaven. . . . Above is to be seen another opening, where eighteen characters are seated. These are the Celestial Intelligences who attend on Juno and Hymen.

Fig. 277. Theatrical Design by Giacomo Torelli

Fig. 270. Theatrical Design by Giacomo Torelli

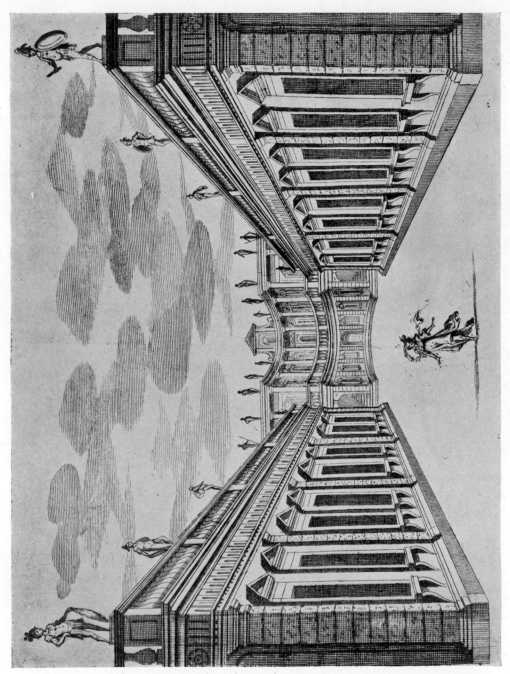

Fig. 279. Theatrical Design by Giacomo Torelli

Fig. 280. Theatrical Design by Giacomo Torelli

Fig. 281. Theatrical Design by Giacomo Torelli

Fig. 282. Theatrical Design by Giacomo Torelli

Fig. 283. Theatrical Design by Giacomo Torelli

Fig. 284. Theatrical Design by Giacomo Torelli

Fig. 285. Theatrical Design by Giacomo Torelli

Fig. 286. Theatrical Design by Giacomo Torelli

F. Franciart del.   I. Torelli in.   I. Silvestre F.

Fig. 287.   Theatrical Design by Giacomo Torelli

APPENDIX D

SOME DESIGNS ILLUSTRATING THEATRICAL DEVELOPMENT DURING THE SEVENTEENTH AND EIGHTEENTH CENTURIES

THE designs presented in this appendix have been selected from the collection of photographs at Yale University.

Fig. 288.   SETTING FOR ONE OF THE INTERMEZZI GIVEN AT FLORENCE IN 1589.
DESIGN BY BERNARDO BUONTALENTI

Engraved by Agostino Carracci.

Fig. 289. SETTING FOR A THEATRICAL PERFORMANCE AT FLORENCE, 1589.
DESIGN BY BERNARDO BUONTALENTI

Fig. 290. DESIGN FOR PERSPECTIVE SIDE-WINGS

These are probably Italian in origin. Preserved among the sketches of Inigo Jones, they are
reproduced here by permission of the Duke of Devonshire.

FIG. 291. SETTING FOR "LA CONTESA" (FERRARA, 1632). DESIGN BY FRANCESCO GUITTI

Particularly to be noted are the steps leading into the auditorium and the painted panels above the proscenium. The latter may be compared with those shown in Fig. 289; the print of the Red Bull Theatre (cf. Fig. 137) also shows such panels.

Fig. 292. SETTING FOR "IL TOBACCO" (TURIN, 1650)

This and the immediately following designs (Figs. 293–299) are reproduced from the originals now preserved in the Biblioteca Nazionale, Turin.

Fig. 293. SETTING FOR "LA PRIMAVERA TRIONFANTE" (TURIN, 1657)

Fig. 294. Cloud Machine in "L'Unione perla Peregrina" (Turin, 1660)

Fig. 295. Practicable Ship in "La Primavera Trionfante" (Turin, 1657)

Fig. 296. SETTING FOR "LA PRIMAVERA TRIONFANTE" (TURIN, 1657)

Fig. 297. SETTING FOR "IL DONO DEL RE" (RIVOLI, 1645)

Fig. 298. Setting for "Il Gridellino" (Turin, 1653)

Fig. 299. Scene in "L'Unione perla Peregrina" (Turin, 1660)

Fig. 300. Setting for "L'Oronte" (Salvator Theatre, Munich, 1657).
Design by Francesco Santurini

Fig. 301. Setting for "Antiopa Giustificata" (Munich, 1662). Design by
Francesco Santurini

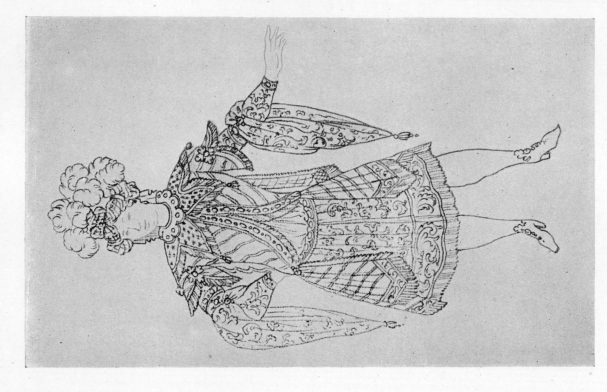

Fig. 302. Costume Design by Jean Berain (c. 1680) for the Paris Opéra

Fig 303. Costume Design by Jean Berain (c. 1680) for the Paris Opéra

Figs. 302–307 are reproduced from the originals now preserved in the Bibliothèque de l'Opéra, Paris.

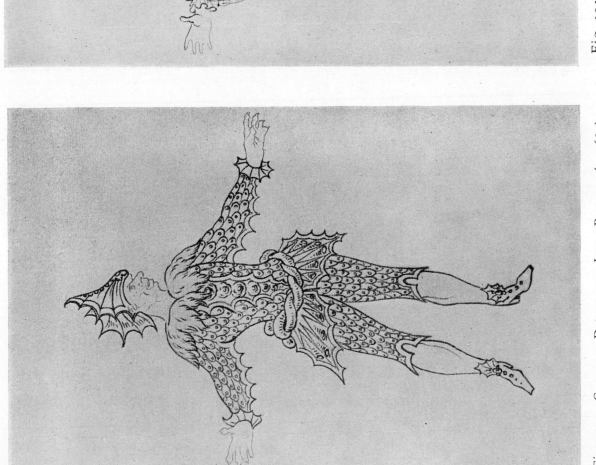

Fig. 305. Costume Design by Jean Berain (c. 1680) for the Paris Opéra

Fig. 304. Costume Design by Jean Berain (c. 1680) for the Paris Opéra

Fig. 307.   Costume Design by Jean Berain (c. 1680) for the Paris Opéra

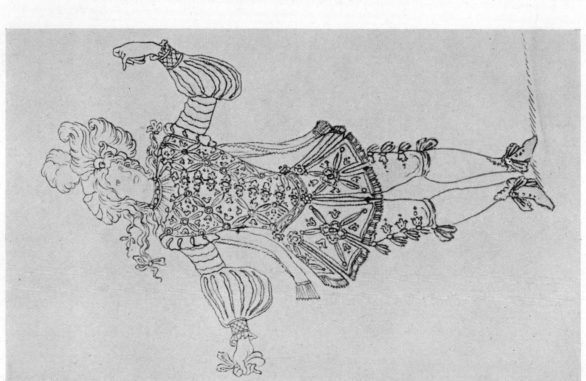

Fig. 306.   Costume Design by Jean Berain (c. 1680) for the Paris Opéra

Fig. 308. Setting for "L'Idea di Tutte le Perfezioni" (Parma, 1690). Design by Ferdinando and Francesco Bibiena

Fig. 309. The Imperial Theatre, Vienna, c. 1690. Built by Lodovico Burnacini

Fig. 310. Stage-setting by Domenico Mauro (1700)

Fig. 311. STAGE-SETTING, *c.* 1700

This shows clearly the arrangement of sky borders used in the seventeenth and eighteenth centuries.

Fig. 312. Interior Setting by Kleiner (Eighteenth Century)

Engraved by J. G. Pintz.

Fig. 313. The New Theatre at Amsterdam, c. 1774

BIBLIOGRAPHY

THE following list of books is selective only. Its object is not to provide anything approaching an exhaustive account of theatrical literature, but merely to indicate a few of those works which may prove useful to the student who wishes to pursue further this subject of playhouses and their *mise-en-scène*. It will be noted that no mention is made here (1) of volumes on dramatic literature, (2) of actors' biographies, and (3) (in general) of contemporary periodical literature, although many of these works contain matter of interest for our purpose, and all must be studied by the person who would devote himself to a particular period. It must be remembered, also, that books do not form by any means the whole, or even the chief, material for such a student. Actual theatres and theatre remains as well as contemporary drawings, sketches, and prints deserve more attention than printed commentary. There are valuable collections of scenographic work in America (notably those arranged by Mr Robert Gould Shaw at Harvard, by Professor Brander Matthews at Columbia, and by the late Mr H. H. Houdini in New York City), in England (the Victoria and Albert Museum and the British Museum), in Germany (especially the collections at Munich and Dresden), and in Austria (Vienna State Museum). Many Continental theatres possess specialized or general collections, among which may be specially mentioned the Museo Teatrale, housed at the theatre La Scala, Milan; and the Musée of the Comédie-française. (See G. H. M. Monval's *Les Collections de la Comédie-française*, 1897, and E. Dacier's *Le Musée de la Comédie-française*, 1905.)

(i) GENERAL

There are few works which deal with the development of the theatre in its entirety. The best-known book is *La Scenografia* (1902) by Giulio Ferrari; but this, like Karl Mantzius' *A History of Theatrical Art in Ancient and Modern Times* (1903-9), is lacking in exact scholarship. The former, however, gives a full and accurate account of the great schools of scenic artists in seventeenth- and eighteenth-century Italy. More scholarly in aim are J. Gregor's *Wiener szenische Kunst. Theaterdekoration* (1924), H. v. Hofmannstal's *Denkmäler des Theaters* (1925), Adolphe Winds' *Der Schauspieler in seiner Entwicklung vom Mysterien- zum Kammerspiel* (1919), and Christian Gaehde's *Das Theater vom Altertum bis zur Gegenwart* (1921). Quirino Angeletti has a suggestive study entitled *Scenografia passata e presente* in *Architettura e Arti decorative* (v, 1926). The *Essai sur l'histoire du théâtre* (1893) of Germain Bapst contains valuable matter, but is now largely out of date. For those who read Russian the Очерки по истории Европейского Театра, prepared by a group of experts (1923), is very useful. Valuable selections of illustrations are provided in A. Streit's *Das Theater : Untersuchungen über das Theater-Bauwerk bei den klassischen und modernen Völkern* (1903), and Carl Niessen's *Das Bühnenbild : Ein kulturgeschichtlicher Atlas* (1925). No attempt has been made to make a full bibliography of theatrical books, but the following contain the records of important collections : *Catalogo generale della raccolta drammatica italiana di Luigi Rasi* (1912) (*cf*. E. Maddalena's *Luigi Rasi e il suo museo drammatico*, 1905), J. de Filippi's *Essai d'une bibliographie générale du théâtre* (1861), R. F. Arnold's *Bibliographie der deutschen Bühnen seit 1830* (1909), P. A. Merbach's *Bibliographie für Theatergeschichte, 1905-10* (1913), G. Weisstein's *Theater : Bühnengeschichte, Gesellschaften, Ballet* (in *Bibliothek Weisstein*, 1913), and the *Catalogue of the Allen A. Brown Collection of Books relating to the Stage* (1919, Boston Public Library).

Some of the theatrical, as distinct from dramatic, dictionaries are particularly useful. Among these may be numbered the *Allgemeines Theater-Lexikon oder Encyklopädie alles wissenswerthen für Bühnenkünstler, Dilettanten und Theaterfreunde* (1846), C. M. E. Béquet's *Encyclopédie de l'art dramatique* (1888), F. A. A. Paroisse-Pougin's *Dictionnaire historique et pittoresque du théâtre et des arts qui s'y rattachent* (1885), and A. Bouchard's *La Langue théâtrale* (1878).

Most of the volumes mentioned below in this list contain specialized bibliographies on their own themes, and these, of course, will be used by the student who wishes to study some particular manifestation of theatrical art. Special attention should be paid to the various periodical Almanacs (Almanach, Almanacco, Annuaire) issued at various times in connexion with particular towns and theatres. Among modern journals *The Mask*, *The Theatre Arts Monthly*, and the *Rivista teatrale italiana* are all of importance, for reproductions as well as for articles dealing with ancient and modern theatres. Note should be taken likewise of occasional studies in journals such as *The Architectural Review*. Recently a series of most suggestive articles from the pen of Corrado Ricci, covering scenic art from classic to contemporary times, appeared in *Il Secolo* (1926, March 24, 29, April 10, 30, and May 10). The volumes of the *Theatergeschichtliche Forschungen* (from 1891) contain matter of considerable interest, and attention should be paid to the publications of the *Gesellschaft für Theatergeschichte*. The *Archiv für Theatergeschichte* (1904–5) was continued in the *Kleine Schriften* of that society. The *Bulletin* (1902–3) of the *Société de l'histoire du théâtre* likewise includes articles of value ; special attention may be drawn to the reproductions from and comment on the " Terence des Ducs " (No. 1, January 1902), by Henry Martin, and to Charles Malherbe's study of *Les Costumes et Décors d'Armide*, ' *L'Armide*,' *de Lulli* (No. 2, April 1902).

While no attempt has been made in the text of this volume to deal with the Oriental theatres, the student may be referred to various monographs on the Chinese, Japanese, and Indian stages. J.-J. Ampère has a study *Du Théâtre chinois* in the *Revue des deux Mondes* (September 15, 1838) ; this is of less value than *Les Chinois peints par eux-mêmes : le théâtre des Chinois* (1886) by Tcheng-Ki-Tong. The standard work on the subject is A. E. Zucker's *The Chinese Theatre* (1925). B. S. Allen's *Chinese Theatres Handbook* (1925) may also be referred to. On the popular theatre of Japan Zoë Kincaid's *Zabuki* (1925) is invaluable, and E. F. Fenollosa and E. L. Pound have a work on ' *Noh* ' *or Accomplishment : A Study of the Classical Stage of Japan* (1917). S. Lévi's *Le Théâtre indien* (1890) and Émile Senart's article on the same subject in the *Revue des deux Mondes* (May 1, 1891) are both of interest. Other Oriental countries are touched on in *La Danse au théâtre* (1924) by André Levinson and in *The Dramas and Dramatic Dances of Non-European Races* (1915) by W. Ridgeway.

(ii) THE GREEK THEATRE

Most of our knowledge of Greek theatres and methods of staging is due to German industry and research, but A. E. Haigh's *The Attic Theatre* (3rd edition revised by A. W. Pickard-Cambridge, 1907) is an invaluable text-book for students who cannot read German, and may well be supplemented by R. C. Flickinger's *The Greek Theater and its Drama* (1918), and by Octave Navarre's *Le Théâtre grec* (1925). The first contains an excellent summary of theatre structure and of theatrical conditions ; the latter is especially valuable for its succinct expression of the main results of modern research. In addition to these books, there are, of course, important articles on various detailed points in such periodicals as *The American Journal of Archaeology*, *Studies in Classical Philology*, and *The Hellenic Journal*.

The German contribution to this subject can be outlined but briefly. The centre of recent discussion is *Das griechische Theater* (1896) by W. Dörpfeld and E. Reisch, in which it is argued that the ancient classical theatre was innocent of a raised stage. Previous to the appearance of this work, and not entirely out of date, may be mentioned the great compilation of Albert Müller, *Lehrbuch der griechischen Bühnenalterthümer* (1886), G. C. W. Schneider's *Das attische Theaterwesen* (1835), E. Bodensteiner's *Scenische Fragen im griechischen Drama* (1893), E. J. A. Bethe's *Prolegomena zur Geschichte des Theaters im Alterthum* (1896), and Weismann's *Die scenische Aufführung der griechischen Dramen* (1893). The various views, theories, and controversies will be found in a variety of books, German, French, and English, among which the most important are O. Puchstein's *Die griechische Bühne* (1901), Fiechter's *Die baugeschichtliche Entwicklung des antiken Theaters* (1914), E. Bodensteiner's *Das antike Theater* (1902), the work on the same subject by G. Öhmichen, E. Petersen's *Die attische Tragödie als Bild- und Bühnen-Kunst* (1915), *Skene tragike* (1915) by Noack, *Die altgriechische Bühne* (1917) by Frickenhaus, and *The Greek Theatre of the Fifth Century before Christ* (1919) by J. T. Allen. There are, besides, many individual works and articles on separate theatres. Important notes have appeared in *Athenische Mittheilungen*, *Jahrbuch des archäologischen Instituts*, *Hermes* and *Philologus*, and the following volumes contain detailed studies of individual playhouses : E. A. Gardner and others, *Excavations at Megalopolis* (1892), F. Versakis' *Das Scenengebäude des Dionysos-Theaters* (at Athens) (*Kaiserlich deutsches archäologisches Institut : Jahrbuch*, vol. xxiv, Berlin, 1910), A. von Gerkan's *Das Theater von Priene* (1921), K. Dumon's *Le Théâtre de Polyclète* (1889), Defrasse and Lechat's *Épidaure* (1895), G.-E. Rizzo's *Il Teatro greco di Siracusa* (1923), and *Das Theater in Ephesos* (1912), by G. Niemann, R. Heberdey, and W. Wilberg.

Vitruvius' work on architecture (*De Architectura*) was first published in 1486, and was frequently reprinted in Italy during the sixteenth and seventeenth centuries. In 1521 appeared an Italian version, in 1547 a German and a French, in 1602 a Spanish, while in 1692 was issued an English abridgment of the famous later French translation by Claude Perrault (1673). For English readers *The Ten Books of Architecture* (1914), rendered by H. H. Martin, is unquestionably the best edition. The study by E. Capps, *Vitruvius and the Greek Stage* (1893), might be consulted. The *Onomastikon* of Pollux, a typical late Greek encyclopaedia, was first printed at Venice in 1502, and was reprinted several times during the sixteenth and seventeenth centuries. The best modern edition is that of Bethe. The Greek text is almost untranslatable, but the Greek-Latin edition published at Amsterdam in 1706 (*Julii Pollucis Onomastikon Graece et Latine*) may be found useful.

Most of the works on the Greek theatre cited above contain plans and illustrations, and many of these, with

BIBLIOGRAPHY

new material and valuable commentary, are included in the magnificent work of Dr Margarete Bieber, *Die Denkmäler zum Theaterwesen im Altertum* (1920). Additional pictorial evidence will be found in Baumeister's *Denkmäler des klassischen Alterthums* (1888), and in Wieseler's *Theatergebäude und Denkmäler des Bühnenwesens bei Griechen und Römern* (1851).

The best study of stage masks (confined, however, to the realm of comedy) is Carl Robert's *Die Masken der neueren attischen Komödie* (1911), which contains many illustrations and a full discussion of the categories of Pollux. To this might be added a series of essays and articles, including Dierk's *Über das Costüm der griechischen Schauspieler in der alten Komödie* (*Archäol. Zeitung*, xliii), Hense's *Die Modificirung der Maske in der griechischen Tragödie* (1905), and C. A. Böttiger's *Die Furienmaske* (1801). The illustrations in the MSS of Terence are dealt with by Engelhardt in *Illustrationen der Terenzhandschriften* (1905). On the chorus see J. Pickard's *Der Standort der Schauspieler und des Chors im griechischen Theater des 5ten Jahrhunderts* (1892). Weil's *Études sur le drame antique* (1896) has notes on the act division in ancient drama.

Fuller bibliographies will, as was noted above, be found in the separate works mentioned, and this list by no means exhausts the books and monographs which will be found of value by the student.

(iii) The Hellenistic and Roman Theatres

Most of the works which deal with the classical Greek stage treat also, directly or indirectly, of the Hellenistic and the Roman. To those mentioned may be added G. Körting's *Geschichte des griechischen und römischen Theaters* (1897), R. Opitz' *Schauspiel und Teaterwesen der Griechen und Römer* (1889), C. C. Saint-Saëns' *Note sur les décors de théâtre dans l'antiquité romaine* (1886), and B. Varneke's Очерки изъ исторіи древне-римского театра (1903). Mau's *Pompeii* (1907) has a section on the theatres, and Piranesi's *Teatro di Ercolano* (1783), although early, will be found useful. A. L. T. Vaudoyer has a *Description du théâtre de Marcellus à Rome* (1812); Gsell's *Monuments antiques de l'Algérie* (1901) surveys the stage relics in North Africa; while A. N. Caristie's *Monuments antiques à Orange* (1856) and the *Conférence sur le théâtre antique d'Orange faite devant le Congrès de la Société-française d'archéologie* (1883) deal with the famous Gallic theatre. Performances there are described by Fernand-Michel in *Le Théâtre antique d'Orange et ses représentations modernes* (1894), and by T. A. Janvier in *The Christmas Kalends of Provence* (1902). Literature on the Terence MSS has been cited above; there may also be added *Costume in Roman Comedy* (1909) by Catherine Saunders.

On the Phlyakes there are some important notices in the *Jahrbuch des Kaiserlich deutschen archäologischen Instituts* for 1886 and 1893, while there is a little library of articles and essays on the *Fabula Atellana*. Martin Schanz in his *Geschichte der Römischen Litteratur* (1909) provides a useful summary and quotes most of the important references to this type of entertainment. The stock characters are discussed by K. Sittl in *I Personaggi dell' Atellana* (*Rivista di storia antica*, 1895, i, 3) and by F. Graziani in a study of the same title (*Rivista di filologia*, 1896, xxiv). Fragments of the Atellan farce appear in O. Ribbeck's *Comicorum Romanorum fragmenta* (1898), and there are some special studies such as D. A. H. van Eck's *Quaestiones scenicae Romanae* (1892), R. Maffei's *Le Favole Atellane* (1892), and E. Munk's *De Fabulis Atellanis* (1840). E. Bethe deals with the subject in his above-cited *Prolegomena* (1896).

(iv) The Medieval Theatre

Unquestionably the most important work on the traditions of the Roman and Greek mime is Hermann Reich's *Der Mimus: Ein litteratur-entwickelungsgeschichtlicher Versuch* (1903), although a few studies, such as C. J. Grysar's *Der römische Mimus* (*Wiener Akademie der Wissenschaften*, philos.-histor. Klasse, 1854, xii, ii, 237–337), Führ's *De Mimis Graecorum* (1860), C. Magnin's *Les Origines du théâtre moderne* (vol. i only published, 1838), A. Dieterich's *Pulcinella* (1897), Édélestand Du Méril's *Origines latines du théâtre moderne* (1849) and M. Scherillo's *Die Atellanen und das heutige Volkslustspiel Neapels* (*Das Ausland*, 1884), had all discussed or made some approaches toward his final conclusions. To these might be added, as containing matter of interest, the *De ludis scenicis mimorum et pantomimorum* (1713) of N. Calliachius, *Über die Pantomimen der Römer* (*Rheinisches Museum für Philologie*, 1834, ii) by C. J. Grysar, O. Driessen's important monograph, *Der Ursprung des Harlekin* (1904), and P. S. Allen's *The Medieval Mimus* (*Modern Philology*, viii, January and July 1910). F. Ficoroni in his *Dissertatio de larvis scenicis et figuris comicis antiquorum Romanorum* (1750) presents a series of engravings from Roman terra-cottas and gems, with commentary. A number of frescoes in the church of St Sophia at Kiev are reproduced and discussed by N. P. Kondakov in an article О Фрескахъ лѣстницъ Кіево-Софійскаго собора (Записки императорскаго русскаго археологическаго общества, New Series, iii, 287–306). Most of the references to the medieval mime and to the decisions of Church councils are given in Reich and D'Ancona (see below), but the student could turn to original sources such as J. Hartzheim's *Concilia Germaniae* (1759–90), J. Douhet's *Dictionnaire des Mystères*, J. P. Migne's *Patrologiae cursus completus* and J. D. Mansi's *Sacrorum Conciliorum Nova . . . Collectio* (1769–92).

To outline even the most important works on the medieval pageants and performers is well-nigh impossible, for almost every introduction to the text of a medieval play contains some matter of interest. The standard English work on the subject is Sir Edmund Chambers' *The Medieval Stage* (1903), which includes a fairly full bibliography to the date of publication. Not much space, however, is devoted in this work to pageants and methods of production, and it must be supplemented by many independent studies. W. Creizenach's *Geschichte des neueren Dramas* (1893–1907) is a famous work which gives full attention to methods of presentation.

Much study has been devoted to this subject in France. The works of the Parfaict *frères* are now largely out of date, but still contain some points of value. More important for our purpose are the various books by Petit de Julleville: *Les Mystères* (1880), *La Comédie et les mœurs en France au moyen âge* (1886), *Les Comédiens en France au moyen âge* (1889; a valuable summary of the performers in French medieval dramas), and *Répertoire du théâtre comique en France au moyen âge* (1886; a survey of extant comic works with notes on performances). É. du Méril's *Histoire de la comédie: Période primitive* (1864) is important, as is M. Septet's *Le Drame chrétien au moyen âge* (1878). All these have references to methods of performance. É. du Méril's *Origines latines du théâtre moderne* (1849) and C. Magnin's *Les Origines du théâtre moderne* (1838) have less interest theatrically, but are of considerable general value. Other specialized information will be found in the *Dictionnaire des mystères* (1854), by Jules, Comte de Douhet, *Les Prophètes du Christ* (1878), by M. Septet, *Drames liturgiques du moyen âge* (1861), by E. de Coussemaker, *Drames liturgiques de la Cathédrale de Rouen* (*Annales de la Faculté des Lettres de Caen*, 1888), by A. Gasté, *Mystères inédits du xvᵉ siècle* (1837), by M. L. A. Jubinal, *Études sur les mystères* (1837), by O. Le Roy, *Essai sur la mise-en-scène depuis les mystères jusqu'au Cid* (1836), by É. Morice. Most valuable of all, however, is the detailed study by G. Cohen on the *Histoire de la mise-en-scène dans le théâtre religieux français du moyen âge* (1907). This may be supplemented with A. Veselovski's Старинный театръ въ Европе (1870), and M. Paushkin's Средневековый театръ (1914), both careful studies of medieval theatrical enterprise. Émile Male's *L'Art religieux* has been referred to in the text.

Considerable attention has been paid to the subject both in Germany and in Italy. F. J. Mone's *Schauspiele des Mittelalters* (1846) is an important early work. Among a multitude of others C. Lange's *Die lateinischen Osterfeiern* (1887), G. Milchsack's *Die Oster- und Passionsspiele* (1879), and A. H. Alt's *Theater und Kirche in ihrem gegenseitigen Verhältniss* (1846) may be mentioned. R. Froning's *Das Drama des Mittelalters* (1891) contains interesting texts and commentary, while Leibing has a valuable account of a Lucerne play in *Die Inscenierung des zweitägigen Luzernes Osterspiels* (1869). The standard Italian work is *Origini del teatro italiano* (1891) by Alessandro D'Ancona. This includes most of the material presented in such monographs as Lumini's *Il Drama nelle sacre rappresentazioni dei secoli XIV, XV, e XVI* (1875), Ignazio Ciampi's *Le Rappresentazioni sacre nella parte comica* (1865), and Emiliani Giudici's *Storia del teatro italiano* (1869). Consultation might be made of Mazzatini's article on *I Disciplinati di Gubbio e i loro Uffizj drammatici* (*Giorn. di Filol. Romanza*, iii, 85), and Monaci's *Uffizj drammatici dei disciplinati dell' Umbria* (*Rivista di Filologia Romanza*, i, 256).

Articles and essays abound on various aspects of this subject, and the indexes of *Notes and Queries*, *The Modern Language Review*, *Modern Philology*, *Anglia*, *Englische Studien*, and similar periodicals may be referred to. Among miscellaneous studies G. R. Coffman's *A New Approach to Medieval Latin Drama* (*Mod. Phil.*, 1925, xxii, 3), and the same author's *A Note concerning the Cult of St Nicholas at Hildesheim* (*Manley Anniversary Studies*, 1922) should be mentioned. J. J. Jusserand's *English Wayfaring Life in the Middle Ages* (1892) presents the social background with vividness, and marionettes are well dealt with by C. Magnin in *Histoire des marionettes en Europe depuis l'antiquité jusqu'à nos jours* (1862), and by H. S. Rehm in *Das Buch der Marionetten: Ein Beitrag zur Geschichte des Theaters aller Völker* (1905).

Special studies on national theatres contain matter of general interest. The early Russian stage is discussed in P. O. Morozov's magnificent compilation, История драматической литературы и театра (1903), and in Очеркъ историй театра в Западной Европе и Россий (1911). P. de Corvin has also a study on *Le Théâtre en Russie depuis ses origines jusqu'à nos jours* (1890). The fortunes of the Spanish theatre are traced in E. Catarelo y Mori's *Estudios sobre la historia del arte escénico en España* (1896–97), J. Yxart's *El Arte escénico en España* (1894–96), H. A. Rennert's *The Spanish Stage in the Time of Lope de Vega* (1909), and A. F. von Schack's *Geschichte der dramatischen Litteratur und Kunst in Spanien* (1854). The stage of the Netherlands is well treated in E. Vander Straeten's *Le Théâtre villageois en Flandre* (1881), in F. Heller von Hellwald's *Geschichte des holländischen Theaters* (1874), and in H. J. E. Endepols' *Het decoratief en de opvoering van het middelnederlandsche Drama volgens de middelnederlandsche tooneelstukken* (1903). Reference may also be made to another general study, K. Nyrop's *En Theater forestilling i Middelalderen* (in *Studier fra Sprog- og Oldtidsforskning*, 1892).

BIBLIOGRAPHY

(v) EARLY RENASCENCE THEATRES

Full details concerning some of the earlier efforts are to be found in D'Ancona, *op. cit.*, and Ferrari gives a good summary of performances and of *mise-en-scène*. The woodcuts in the editions of Terence are noted in M. Herrmann's *Forschungen zur deutschen Teatergeschichte des Mittelalters und der Renaissance* (1914). E. Flechsig has a special study of *Die Dekoration der modernen Bühne in Italien* (1894). Lily B. Campbell's *Scenes and Machines in the Renaissance* (1923) is an interesting study of classical origins and one of the best books on the subject. The relevant portions of S. Serlio's *Architettura* (1551) are reprinted in Sir Edmund Chambers' *The Elizabethan Stage* (1923). The discussion of theatrical methods is given in Book II, which appeared in English as *The second Booke of Architecture* (1611). N. Sabbatini's *Pratica di fabricar scene, e machine ne' teatri* (1638) is summarized in Ferrari's monograph. With these works should be taken into account a number of contemporary essays on (1) theatre practice, and (2) the rules of perspective. A. Ingegneri's *Della poesia rappresentativa e del modo di rappresentare le favole sceniche* (1598) is of special importance, as is the earlier MS. *Dialoghi in materia di rappresentazione scenica* by L. de' Sommi, of which a few selections are given in Appendix D. A select list of books on perspective is given by Ferrari (pp. 275–76), dating from 1504 to 1827. Among and in addition to these there may be signalized Scipione Chiaramonti's *Delle scene e teatri* (1675), Giulio Trioli's *Paradossi per pratticare la prospettiva senza saperla* (1683), and L. Sirigatti's *La Pratica di prospettiva* (1596). *Del Teatro Olympico* (1733) by G. Montenari, *Il Teatro Olimpico* (1847) by A. Magrini, and *Il Forestiere instruito delle cose più rare di architettura e di alcune pittura della città di Vicenza* (1761) give accounts of the Palladian stage. A very important work on seventeenth-century theatrical activities is Angelo Solerti's *Musica, ballo e drammatica alla corte medicea dal 1600 al 1637* (1905), which gives, besides some valuable illustrations, an enlightening series of entries from a diary kept by Cesare Tinghi. C. H. Kaulfuss-Diesch's *Die Inscenierung des deutschen Dramas an der Wende des 16. und 17. Jahrhunderts* (1905) and E. Schmidt's *Die Bühnenverhältnisse des deutschen Schuldramas im 16. Jahrhundert* (1903) both contain matter of value. Notes on English stage-lighting appear in an article by W. J. Lawrence in *The Stage Year Book* (1927).

(vi) THE COMMEDIA DELL' ARTE

The literature on the Italian improvised comedy is vast; a good bibliography is appended to the second edition (1926) of the exceedingly well-illustrated and entertainingly written study on *La Comédie italienne* by Pierre Louis Duchartre. This volume, however, may be supplemented by others. In addition to several works on the relationship between the classical and modern comedy, cited in Section III, there may be mentioned L. Stoppato's *La Commedia popolare in Italia* (1887), M. Scherillo's *La Commedia dell' arte in Italia* (1884), and N. Signorelli's *Storia critica dei teatri antichi e moderni* (1813). On the general history of the type C. Miclashevski's *La Commedia dell' arte* (1914; in Russian), and L. Rasi's *I Comici italiani* (1897–1905) are among the more valuable works, but these do not render obsolete some earlier books such as I. Ciampi's *Studio sulla commedia italiana nel secolo xvii* (1856), Maurice Sand's *Les Masques et bouffons de la comédie italienne* (1859), G. Cocchi's *Studio sulle maschere italiane* (1891), E. Ferretti's *Le Maschere italiane nella commedia dell' arte e nel teatro di Goldoni* (1904), and A. Agresti's *Studii sulla commedia italiana del secolo xvi* (1871). W. Smith has a study in English on *The Commedia dell' Arte* (1912). L. Riccoboni's *Histoire du théâtre italien* (1730) is an interesting early account, as is A. Perrucci's *Dell' Arte rappresentativa premeditata ed all' improvvisa* (1699). The story of the Gozzi-Goldoni controversy can be studied in the former's *Memoirs* (translated by J. A. Symonds, 1890), and in O. Marchini-Capasso's *Goldoni e la commedia dell' arte* (1912). There are various special monographs on individual types of the improvised comedy, of which the following may be singled out: on Arlecchino—Driessen, *op. cit.*, A. Graf's *Arlecchino* (*Giornale storico della letteratura italiana*, 1886, ix), and C. Nerucci's *Arlecchino* (*Giornale di erudizione di Firenze*, 1898, vii); on Pulcinella—Dieterich, *op. cit.*, M. Scherillo's *The Genealogy of Pulcinella* (*The Mask*, iii), V. Fainelli's *Chi era Pulcinella?* (*Giorn. stor. d. lett. ital.*, 1909, liv), and B. Croce's *Pulcinella e il personaggio del napoletano in commedia* (1899); on the Captain—F. De Simone Brouwer's *Capitan Fracassa* (1900), U. Fleres' *Ancora del Capitan Fracassa* (1880), B. Croce's *Lo Spagnuolo nelle commedie* (*Atti dell' Acc. Pont*, xxvii), and G. Senigaglia's *Capitan Spavento* (1899); on Scaramuccia—A. Constantini's *La Vie de Scaramouch* (1695); on Stenterello—G. Jarro's *L'Origine della maschera di Stenterello* (1898).

The iconography of the improvised theatre is large, the most important collections being those of J. Callot (*Balli di Sfessania*), C. Gillot (*Le Théâtre italien*), and F. Bertelli (*Il Carnevale italiano mascherato*). A. Frizzi's *Cinquanta maschere italiane illustrate nei loro costumi* (1888) is also of interest.

Many *scenarii* have been collected. Flaminio Scala's *Il Teatro delle favole rappresentative* (1611) contains fifty titles; and others are given by A. Bartoli (*Scenari inediti*, 1880), E. Maddalena (*Uno Scenario inedito*, in *Sitzungsberichte der wiener K. Akad. der Wissenschaften*; phil.-hist. Klasse, 1901, cxliii), P. Toldo (*Uno Scenario inedito*, in *Giorn. stor. d. lett.*

ital., 1905, xlvi), V. Rossi (*I Suppositi dell' Ariosto ridotto a scenario*, 1895), A. Neri (*Una Commedia dell' arte*, in *Giorn. stor. d. lett. ital.*, 1883, i), and G. Martucci (*Uno Scenario inedito*, in *Nuova Antologia*, May 15, 1885). G. de la Porta's *Delle Commedie* (1726) may also be consulted. Various specimens too remain in manuscript. The more important collections are those of B. Locatelli (MS Rome, Bibl. Casanatense, F. iv, 12–13, Cod. 1211–1212 ; see A. Valeri's *Gli Scenari inediti di Basilio Locatelli*, 1894), and of J. D. Biancolelli (MS Paris, Bibl. de l'Opéra, in a French translation of 1760), and the anonymous gatherings at Naples (Bibl. Nation.), Rome (Bibl. Corsini, Cod. 652. 45. G. 6 ; Cod. 976. 45. F. 1 ; and Bibl. Casanatense, 4. 302–4.386) and Venice (Museo Civico). Gherardi's French collection of the seventeenth century is well known, and may be read in many editions. L. Moland deals with the influence of this form on literature in *Molière et la comédie italienne* (1867). A posthumous work by Enzo Petraccone entitled *La Commedia dell' Arte : Storia, Tecnica, Scenari* (Naples, 1927) presents an unusually valuable series of historical texts and selected *scenarii*. It will undoubtedly form an important ' source-book ' on the subject.

(vii) Early French Theatres

The most important document in this section is H. C. Lancaster's *Mémoire de Mahelot* (1920), which presents the sketches made for the Hôtel de Bourgogne. The accompanying text is presented and discussed in E. Dacier's *La Mise-en-scène à Paris au xvii* siècle* (*Mémoires de la Soc. de l'hist. de Paris*, 1901). In addition H. Prunières' *Le Ballet de cour en France avant Benserade et Lully* (1914), E. Rigal's *Le Théâtre français avant la période classique* (1901), E. Despois' *Le Théâtre français sous Louis XIV* (1874), E. Rigal's *La Mise-en-scène dans les tragédies du xvi* siècle* (*Revue d'hist. litt. de la France*, 1905, xii, i), J. Haraszti's *La Comédie française de la renaissance et la scène* (*Revue d'hist. litt. de la France*, 1909, xvi), Ludovic Celler's *Les Décors, les costumes et la mise-en-scène au xvii* siècle* (1869), and G. Despierres' *Le Théâtre et les comédiens à Alençon au seizième et au dix-septième siècle* (1892) are all of considerable value for the student. The question of the influence of Italian comic practice has been discussed in a variety of volumes among which G. Apollinaire's *Le Théâtre italien, avec une étude sur le théâtre italien en France* (1910), O. Klingler's *Die Comédie italienne in Paris nach der Sammlung von Gherardi* (1902), and A. Baschet's *Les Comédiens italiens à la cour de France sous Charles IX, Henri III, Henri IV et Louis XIII* (1882) are the most valuable. A considerable number of more literary surveys, such as the *Histoire générale du théâtre en France* (in progress), by Eugène Lintilhac, deal also with the theatre, and there are special volumes on individual theatres, such as the *théâtres de la foire* (*cf.* M. Albert's *Les Théâtres de la foire* (1660–1789), 1900, and N. M. Bernardin's *La Comédie italienne en France et les théâtres de la foire et du boulevard* (1570–1791), 1902). J. L. A. Jullien surveys costume on the French stage in his *Histoire du costume au théâtre depuis les origines du théâtre en France jusqu'à nos jours* (1880).

(viii) Elizabethan Theatres

The earlier morality stage is dealt with in *The Medieval Stage* (1903) of Sir Edmund Chambers, whose *Elizabethan Stage* (1923) is an invaluable compilation of fact and theory relating to the later playhouses. This latter work includes the results of most of the earlier writers on this subject, such as Albright, Quincy Adams, Thorndike, Reynolds, and others. The survey, however, ends with the year 1616, and other authorities must be used for the later decades. On the history of the theatres and companies J. Quincy Adams' *Shakespearean Playhouses* (1917) is the best authority, and the fullest study of staging is that by A. H. Thorndike (1916). This may be compared with G. F. Reynolds' *Some Principles of Elizabethan Staging* (*Mod. Phil.*, 1905, i and ii), and R. Crompton Rhodes' *The Stagery of Shakespeare* (1922). W. J. Lawrence's *Elizabethan Playhouse and other Studies* (1912 and 1913) as well as his articles, *New Light on the Elizabethan Theatre* (*Fortnightly Review*, May 1916) and *Night Performances in the Elizabethan Theatres* (*Englische Studien*, 1915, xlviii), contain many facts and suggestive theories. G. F. Reynolds, in addition to his general study, has an article on *What we know of the Elizabethan Stage* (*Modern Philology*, 1911, ix) which surveys the materials at the command of the student.

The Revels Office documents have been collected in two series by A. Feuillerat (1908–14), while Henslowe's *Diary* has found an excellent editor in W. W. Greg. Many documents relating to the theatres of the time are reprinted in the Malone Society *Collections*, and others have been given in the publications of the New Shakspere Society. The *Records of Sir Henry Herbert* have been edited by J. Q. Adams (1920), while E. Hyder Rollins has collected some new facts in *A Contribution to the History of the English Commonwealth Drama* (*Studies in Philology*, 1921, xviii). It must be added that references to the stage appear in almost all the literary histories enumerated in the Elizabethan section of *British Drama*.

On the masks R. Brotanek's *Die englischen Maskenspiele* (1902) and Paul Reyher's brilliant study of *Les Masques anglais* (1909) are standard authorities. The Malone and Walpole Societies in 1924 issued a monumental illustrated catalogue of Inigo Jones' masque designs, and there are several articles on his work and on that of his assistant, John

BIBLIOGRAPHY

Webb, among which may be mentioned: H. Bell's *Contributions to the History of the English Playhouse* (*Arch. Record*, 1913), and W. G. Keith's *The Designs for the First Movable Scenery on the English Stage* (*Burlington Magazine*, 1914, xxv), *A Theatre Project of Inigo Jones* (*Burl. Mag.*, 1917, xxxi), and *John Webb and the Court Theatre of Charles II* (*Arch. Review*, 1925, lvii).

(It must be noted that no mention is made in this section of books or articles which deal exclusively with the Elizabethan theatre before 1616, as these are all chronicled in Sir Edmund Chambers' *The Elizabethan Stage*.)

(ix) Continental Theatres of the Eighteenth Century

Ferrari's account of the eighteenth-century Italian theatre artists is particularly full, and he has included important reference lists of the scenographers of different schools. Corrado Ricci has issued a beautiful collection of Bibiena designs (1915), Paul Zucker's *Theater-Dekoration des Klassizismus* and *Theater-Dekoration des Barock* (1925) contain representative designs, while both J. Gregor's *Wiener szenische Kunst* (1924) and the vast *Monumenta Scenica* (1925, in progress) devote considerable space to the eighteenth century. Andrea Pozzo's *Prospettiva dei pittori e architetti* (1692–1700) presents a variety of stage designs, as do Ferdinando da Bibiena's *Direzioni della prospettiva teorica* (1732) and his *Disegni delle scene* (1714). Giuseppe Bibiena has his *Architetture e prospettive* (1740), many plates in which were reproduced in *Theatre-Dekorationen* (1888). *Opere varie di architettura e prospettiva* of G. B. Piranesi was issued in 1750. There are many collections of engravings by other and later artists. The importance of Martelli's engravings (1735) is called attention to by Hugh Quigley in *Notes and Queries*. Some attention is devoted to scenery and costume in M. Aghion's *Le théatre à Paris au xviii⁰ siècle* (1925).

On the theatres of this time there are numerous general and specialized works. P. Patté's *Essai sur l'architecture théâtrale* (1782) contains interesting plans. Plans of the various theatres at Rome are included in the *Descrizione istorica del Teatro Tor di Nona* (1795). Information on the structure of these houses will be found in the *Traité de la construction des théâtres* (1886), by A. Gosset, *Architectonographie des théâtres, ou, parallèle historique et critique de ces édifices considérés sous le rapport de l'architecture et de la décoration* (1837), by A. Donnet, *Parallèle des principaux théâtres modernes* (1870), by J. de Filippi, and *Storia e descrizione de' principali theatri antichi e moderni* (1830), by G. Ferrario. Corrado Ricci has an important study on *I Teatri di Bologna* (1888), Benedetto Croce another on *I Teatri di Napoli* (1891), and M. Scherillo has written on the *Storia letteraria dell' opera buffa napolitana* (1883), with notes on the popular playhouses. For the Teatro alla Scala at Milan see G. Piermarini's *Teatro della Scala in Milano* (1826), and for the San Carlino at Naples see S. di Giacomo's *Cronaca del teatro San Carlino* (1895). On the German theatres Petersen's *Schiller und die Bühne* (1904), Eduard Devrient's *Geschichte der deutschen Schauspielkunst* (1848), and M. Hammitsch's *Der moderne Theaterbau* (1906) may be consulted. Information on stage machinery will be found in E. M. Laumann's *La Machinerie au théâtre depuis les Grecs jusqu'à nos jours* (1897). The older methods may be compared and contrasted with those described in G. Moynet's *La Machinerie théâtrale: trucs et décors* (1893), A. de Vaulabelle's *La Science au théâtre* (1908), and J. Lefèvre's *L'Électricité au théâtre* (1894).

(x) Restoration Theatres

Various documents and a brief survey of Restoration stage conditions will be found in the present writer's *History of Restoration Drama* (1923). R. W. Lowe presents a picture of a playhouse in his *Thomas Betterton* (1891), while L. B. Campbell deals with the period generally in her above-cited *Scenes and Machines*. The theatre chapters in G. C. D. Odell's *Shakespeare from Betterton to Irving* (1924) are important and cover theatrical history from 1660 to the present time. There are many contemporary sources of information, the chief being John Downes' *Roscius Anglicanus* (1708), and Colley Cibber's *Apology* (1740). The latter should be read in R. W. Lowe's excellent reprint. Various details are discussed by W. J. Lawrence (*op. cit.*), W. G. Keith, and Montague Summers (see particularly Summers' introductions to various reprints).

(xi) The Eighteenth-Century Theatres

For the eighteenth century R. Farquharson Sharp's *A Short History of the English Stage* (1909) is particularly full. The various works by J. Doran and P. Fitzgerald are interesting, but not always accurate. Documents and sketches of playhouse conditions are presented in the present writer's *History of Early Eighteenth-Century Drama* (1925) and *History of Late Eighteenth-Century Drama* (1927). E. Thaler's *From Shakespeare to Sheridan* (1924) contains interesting commentary on stage practice but little on theatre settings. The many contemporary works on the theatre are enumerated in R. W. Lowe's *Theatrical Literature* (1888). Valuable collections of playbills and press-cuttings are preserved in the British Museum (especially the Burney collection) and in the Victoria and Albert Museum. An interesting survey of histrionic costume from 1660 to 1824 is contributed by L. B. Campbell to the *University of Wisconsin Studies* (1918, ii), while W. J. Lawrence has two essays on William Capon and P. J. de Loutherbourg in *The Magazine of Art* (xviii).

(xii) THE NINETEENTH CENTURY AND AFTER

The nineteenth century teems with works on the theatre and with actors' memoirs. Many illustrated papers and playhouse 'souvenirs' contain examples of theatre design. The original sketches for Kean's performances are preserved in the Victoria and Albert Museum. Hardly any single works can be mentioned here, but Errol Sherson's *London's Lost Theatres* (1926) and Watson's *Sheridan to Robertson* (1926) are excellent playhouse guides. Descriptions of the early theatres will be found in *The Covent-Garden Journal* (1810) and in Gilliland's *Dramatic Mirror* (1808).

The modern theatre has seen considerable treatment. Adolphe Appia's *La Mise-en-scène du drame wagnérien* (1895) and *Die Musik und die Inscenierung* (1899) suggest the lines taken by that great innovator, while Gordon Craig's *On the Art of the Theatre* (1911), *Towards a New Theatre* (1912), *The Theatre Advancing* (1921), and *Scene* (1923) all present examples of that artist's work. A. M. S. Rocca's article on Craig's work in *Comoedia* (1924) is an interesting study. H. K. Moderwell's *The Theatre of To-day* (1914), C. Van Vechten's *Stage Decoration as a Fine Art* (in *Music after the Great War and other Studies*, 1915), K. Macgowan's *Continental Stagecraft* (1922) and *The Theatre of To-morrow* (1921) present the main pre-War tendencies. The later movements have not been fully 'written up' as yet, but examples of the newer work have appeared in *The Theatre Arts Monthly*, while Alexander Bakshy (1916), Huntly Carter (1924), and Leo Wiener (1924) have dealt with post-War Russian scenography. The work of the Moscow Art Theatre has been much discussed : Stanislavski's *My Life in Art* (English translation, 1926) is the most important document concerning the great *régisseur's* methods, but Oliver M. Sayler's *Inside the Moscow Art Theatre* (1925) might also be consulted. A monumental and fully illustrated historical record, Московский Художественный театр *1898–1923*, was prepared by Nicolai Efros in 1924. A similar record of the Moscow Grand Theatre was published in 1925 (Московский Большой Театр *1825–1925*), and there is an interesting monograph on modern Russian film-work (which is there intimately connected with the theatre) entitled Кино (1925). Alexander Bakshy's *The Path of the Modern Russian Stage* (1916) deals suggestively with the earlier movements. Oliver M. Sayler's *Max Reinhardt and his Theatre* (1924) is a magnificently illustrated account of German endeavour, and other tendencies there are well dealt with by Oscar Fischel in *Das moderne Bühnenbild* (1918). Among Italian works there may be mentioned A. G. Bragaglia's *Del teatro teatrale* (1926) and *La Maschera mobile* (1926), C. Pavolini's *Arte teatrale* (*Le Arti plastiche*, 1925), E. Prampolini's note on modernist aims in *Rivista d'Arte Futurista* (1924), and P. Gori's *Scenografia* (1927). Sheldon Cheney's *The New Movement in the Theater* (1914), *The Art Theater* (1917), and *The Open-air Theater* (1918) treat mainly of American endeavour. Irving Pichel's *Modern Theatres* (new ed., 1925) should also be consulted. In addition to these there are some more general works, such as Huntly Carter's *The New Spirit in Drama and Art* (1913), H. B. Sell's *What is it all about?* (1914), and Albert Rutherston's *Decoration in the Theatre* (1919).

(xiii) SOME BOOKS ON SPECIAL THEATRES

It may be worth while to add a note on some books which deal with particular theatres or theatrical endeavour apart from chronological divisions.

(a) *England*. Farquharson Sharp's essay on the English stage has already been mentioned ; H. B. Baker's *The London Stage* (1889) is less satisfactory. H. Saxe-Wyndham's *The Annals of Covent Garden* (1906) traces the fortunes of one of the two patent houses, L. Bayliss does the same for *The Old Vic* (1925), and Nigel Playfair for *The Lyric, Hammersmith* (1925).

(b) *France*. There are many general works on the French theatres, among which J. Moynet's *L'Envers du théâtre, machines et décorations* (1873), Adolphe Jullien's *Les Spectateurs sur le théâtre* (1875), C. A. Mendès' *L'Art au théâtre* (1897–1900), A. Muriel's *Le Théâtre aujourd'hui* (1855), and A. Zola's *Le Naturalisme au théâtre* (1881) are of special interest. J. É. V. Arago in *Foyers et coulisses* (1852) and *Physiologie des foyers de tous les théâtres de Paris* (1841) has some notes of value. Many books have been devoted to the Comédie-française ; the following will be found useful : J. Bonnassies' *La Comédie-française : histoire administrative* (1874), C. G. Étienne and A. L. D. Martainville's *Histoire du Théâtre-français* (1802), A. Houssaye's *La Comédie-française, 1680–1880* (1880), A. Joannidès' *La Comédie-française, 1901–14* (1902–15), F. and C. Parfaict's *Histoire du Théâtre-françois* (1745–49). An equally extensive library is devoted to the Opéra. F. H. J. Blaze traces the history of *L'Académie impériale de musique* (1855); N. Desarbres has an essay on *Deux Siècles à l'Opéra, 1668–1868* (1868); the history of the theatre may be traced in the *Histoire du théâtre de l'Opéra* (1753), by L. Travenol and J. B. Durey de Noinville, and in the *Histoire de l'Opéra* (1875) by A. Royer. There is an interesting *Album de l'Opéra* (published *c.* 1850) showing the "principales scènes des meilleurs ouvrages" presented there, and A. Guillaumot has a set of *Costumes des ballets du roy* (1885) with twenty colour-plates of eighteenth-century designs. P. D. Parfouru and G. H. M. Monval have a work on *L'Odéon : histoire administrative, anecdotique et littéraire* (1876–82). L. O. A. Heulhard's *Jean Monnet* (1884) is an interesting study of eighteenth-century theatrical endeavour, and valuable plates are given in J. Huret's *Le Théâtre national de l'opéra comique* (1898). *Le Théâtre libre illustré* (1890), by R. Darzens, with sketches by Lucien Métivet, and A. Thalasso's *Le Théâtre libre* (1909) preserve records of the famous nineteenth-century effort, while in 1917–18 appeared *A New French Theatre in America : Théâtre du vieux Colombier*, giving a succinct account of Copeau's work.

(c) *Germany*. The earlier stage history has little but dramatic interest, and may be traced in the many works on the Englische Komödianten. M. Martersteig's *Das deutsche Theater im neunzehnten Jahrhundert* (1904), F. J. von Reden-Esbeck's *Caroline Neuber und ihre Zeitgenossen* (1881), J. C. Stümcke's *Die deutsche Theaterausstellung* (1910), and F. H. O. Weddigen's *Geschichte der Theater Deutschlands* (1906) all deal with general stage development and present important illustrations. *Die Theater in Berlin* (1886) gives seven plans, and L. Heim and G. Buss' *Das Königliche Opernhaus für Berlin* (1910), and H. C. G. Schliepmann's *Die neuen Entwürfe zum Berliner königlichen Opernhaus* (1913) both contain illustrations. O. A. Banck in *Aus der deutschen Bühnenwelt* (1865) deals with Dresden, and plans are provided in G. Semper's *Das Königliche Hoftheater zu Dresden* (1849). O. J. Bierbaum writes of *Fünf und zwanzig Jahre Münchner Hoftheatergeschichte* (1892); E. Giesenberg has a monograph on *Das Opernhaus zu Frankfurt a. M.* (1883), while A. H. E. von Oven deals with an earlier period in *Das erste städtische Theater zu Frankfurt a. M.* (1872). C. F. Langhans has a work on *Das Stadt-Theater in Leipzig* (1870). Wagner's experiments are dealt with in the *Handbuch der Architektur* (1885). Friedrich Michael's *Deutsches Theater* (1923) is a very useful cheap survey, which may be supplemented by Julius Petersen's *Das deutsche Nationaltheater* (1919).

(d) *Austria*. The stage in Vienna is dealt with in a number of volumes : A. W. von Weilen's *Geschichte des Wiener Theaterwesens von den ältesten Zeiten bis zu den Anfängen der Hof-Theater* (1899), and F. L. von Holbein's *Deutsches Bühnenwesen* (1853) are among the more important. Later efforts are treated of by H. Bahr in his *Wiener Theater, 1892–98* (1899), and in *Die Theater Wiens* (1893–1909), issued periodically by the *Gesellschaft für vervielfältigende Kunst*. The Kaiserlich-königliches-Hofburgtheater is dealt with by J. Bayer (1894), while J. E. Schlager has a monograph on the old playhouse in the *Wiener kaiserliche Akademie der Wissenschaften*, phil.-hist. Klasse, 1851, vi. R. Lothar's *Das Wiener Burgtheater* (1899), and E. van der Nuell and A. von S. von Siccardsburg's *Das Kaiserlich-königliche Hof-Opernhaus in Wien* (1885), give many illustrations of other Viennese playhouses.

(e) *Russia*. To the special studies mentioned above may be added an interesting essay by N. D. Berstein, *Russlands Theater und Musik zur Zeit Peters des Grossen* (1903) and P. de Corvin's general survey, *Le Théâtre en Russie depuis ses origines jusqu'à nos jours* (1890).

(f) *Switzerland*. Bächtold's *Schweizerische Schauspiele des 16. Jahrhunderts* (1890–93) and A. Beetschen's *Das Theaterwesen in der Schweiz* (1897) give an account of the Swiss theatres.

(g) *United States of America*. Much research has been devoted to the history of the American stage, but there is little until modern times that calls for attention here. T. A. Brown's *A History of the New York Stage from the First Performance in 1732 to 1901* (1903) provides a general survey of theatrical events in New York City; G. O. Seilhamer covers the whole of the United States in his *History of the American Theatre* (1888–91). In 1879 T. J. McBride collected an interesting set of *Diagrams of the Leading New York Theatres*. Many plans and settings of modern date are presented in *The Theatre Arts Monthly*.

(h) *Arabia, Turkey, etc.* Besides the books on the Chinese, Japanese, and Indian theatres mentioned above, there are several which deal with other Eastern countries. These are of value for purposes of comparison. P. E. Kahle has an essay *Zur Geschichte des arabischen Schattentheaters in Egypten* (1909). A. Thalasso's *Molière en Turquie : étude sur le théâtre de Karagueuz* (1888) has interest for the mime tradition, and there is much that is suggestive in *Das türkische Volksschauspiel Orta ojnu* (1908).

(xiv) MISCELLANEOUS

(a) *Costume*. A few works on theatrical costume have been cited above. Most of the books of this type deal more with civil and military than with stage dress, but the following contain matter of interest : the costume plates published under the direction of M. Trentsensky in London in the fifties of the nineteenth century, the collection of stage costumes designed by A. Garnerey and H. Lecomte published in the early nineteenth century in Paris, the costume plates in *La Scène* (1877–81), Lacy's collection of costume plates (1865 and 1868), and *Costumes of the Modern Stage* (1880–90). E. Aria's *Costume : Fanciful, Historical, and Theatrical* (1906), Böhn's *Das Bühnenkostüm* (1920), and O. Bie's *Das Theater : Bühnenbilder und Kostüme von Karl Walser* (1912), show interesting modern plates. Designs for costumes naturally appear in many of the works on the modern theatres (*cf.* Oliver M. Sayler's *Max Reinhardt* and the various works on the Moscow Art Theatre), many of Inigo Jones' designs are given in the Catalogue cited above, and the *Monumenta Scenica* devotes several plates to this subject. An important work is J. Gregor's *Wiener szenische Kunst, Band II, Das Bühnenkostüm* (1925).

(b) *The Ballet and the Dance.* As intimately connected both with the origins of drama and with later theatrical spectacle, the dance deserves some attention from students of the playhouse. G. Desrat's *Dictionnaire de la danse, historique, théorique, pratique et bibliographique, depuis l'origine de la danse jusqu'à nos jours* (1895) is an ambitious and useful compilation. There are various works on the history of dancing ; L. de Cahusac's *La Danse ancienne et moderne ou traité historique de la danse* (1754) among older books, and the anonymous *The Dance* (1911) and E. L. Urlin's *Dancing, Ancient and Modern* (1912) among more modern books are probably the most valuable. The late Cecil Sharp's works should be considered in connexion with the rise of medieval drama. M. L. Becker's *Der Tanz* (1901), C. Blasis' *The Theory of Theatrical Dancing* (1888), C. F. Menestrier's *Des Ballets anciens et modernes selon les règles du théâtre* (1682) have all historical value. For the Russian ballet *The Decorative Art of Léon Bakst* (1913) and the various souvenir programmes give illustrations of settings, costumes, and groupings.

(c) *Pantomime.* Intimately connected with the ballet is the pantomime. R. J. Broadbent's *A History of Pantomime* (1901) gives a general account of the *genre*, and M. Willson Disher's *Clowns and Pantomimes* (1925) contains lively notes on the later developments of the type. J. Weaver has an early essay of no great value on *The History of the Mimes and Pantomimes* (1728), and P. Hugounet has left a volume entitled *Mimes et pierrots : notes et documents inédits pour servir à l'histoire de la pantomime* (1889). Obviously this subject must be connected with the mimic art of earlier periods as outlined in Sections I and II.

I have made no mention here of books on acting, as the subject is not directly touched upon in the text of this book. A fairly full collection of such works will be found in the catalogue of the Allen A. Brown collection. Most of these do not concern the student of the theatre, since their notes and advice are largely practical ; but some, such as W. Archer's *Masks or Faces?* (1888), contain important discussions regarding the psychology of the art, and others, such as L. B. Campbell's *The Rise of a Theory of Stage Presentation in England during the Eighteenth Century* ("Publications of the Modern Language Association of America," xxxii, ii), discuss the actor in connexion with the theatre and the setting.

ADDITIONAL NOTES

Since the preparation in 1927 of the select bibliography to this volume there have appeared many books and articles which are of fundamental importance to the student of the theatre. While not all of these could be listed here, attention is drawn to some likely to be of particular service to those engaging in more advanced investigation of particular or general problems. Perhaps reference may, in the first place, be made to the lately established Theatrical Collection at Yale University, where an attempt is being made to gather photographic reproductions of designs, plans, and documents covering the entire range of theatrical practice. An important feature of this collection is the cross-index catalogue of the prints that are filed in it. Rosamond Gilder and George Freedley have prepared a most useful guide to *Theatre Collections in Libraries and Museums* (1936).

(i) GENERAL

In this section several books of value have been issued during the past ten years. Lee Simonson's *The Stage is Set* (1932) presents an entertaining survey of the theatre from the point of view of a practical scene-designer who is also passionately interested in stage history. Joseph Gregor's *Monumenta Scenica* (1925–30) gives splendid reproductions of many early designs and prints. Rich illustrative material is incorporated in Lucien Dubech's *Histoire générale illustrée du théâtre* (1931–35). *Theatre Arts Prints* forms a convenient series for easy reference.

Sheldon Cheney's *The Theatre : Three Thousand Years of Drama, Acting, and Stagecraft* (1929), Thomas Wood Stevens' *The Theatre from Athens to Broadway* (1932), and Joseph Gregor's *Weltgeschichte des Theaters* (1933) are all interesting surveys of theatrical development through the ages. *Stage Decoration* (1930), by Sheldon Cheney, deals specifically with scenic design and will be found particularly useful. Among other works may be mentioned Oskar Fischel's

BIBLIOGRAPHY

Das Bildnerische der Szene (1931). General bibliographies are provided by Rosamond Gilder in *A Theatre Library* (1932) and by Blanch M. Baker in *Dramatic Bibliography* (1933).

Acting (1930), by Lane Crauford, surveys the histrionic art of past times and present; entertainingly Rosamond Gilder investigates the importance of women players in *Enter the Actress* (1931).

On the Chinese drama there is an informative book by L. C. Arlington, *The Chinese Drama from the Earliest Times until To-day* (1930). Frank A. Lombard has *An Outline History of the Japanese Drama* (1929), and *The Masterpieces of Chikamatsu* (1926) has been translated by Asataro Miyamori. *The Sanskrit Drama* (1924) is surveyed in a scholarly manner by A. Berriedale Keith; the modern stages of India have been dealt with by R. K. Yajnik, *The Indian Theatre* (1933), and P. Gula-Thakurta, *The Bengali Drama* (1930). *A Bibliography of the Sanskrit Drama* (1906), by Montgomery Schuyler, Jun., lists such writings on this subject as had appeared before 1905.

(ii) THE GREEK THEATRE

A great deal, both scholarly and 'popular,' has been published on the Greek stage, but references here must be limited solely to those which deal specifically with the theatre and with methods of performance. A particularly important work of this kind is J. T. Allen's *Stage Antiquities of the Greeks and Romans and their Influence* (1927). This contains a serviceable bibliography. The present writer's *Masks, Mimes, and Miracles* (1931) examines popular entertainments from the earliest times to the middle of the sixteenth century. Many references are given there to other works on this subject.

(iv) THE MEDIEVAL THEATRE

By far the most important work published recently on the stage of the Middle Ages is Karl Young's *The Drama of the Medieval Church* (1933). With painstaking care the author has examined the entire range of material relating to the liturgical play; his work, like that of Chambers, is indispensable for a study of this subject. Very useful are the two volumes of Gustave Cohen, *Le Théâtre en France au moyen âge* (1931).

(v) EARLY RENASCENCE THEATRES

The writings of Serlio, Sabbatini, and Furtenbach (see pp. 85–104) are being edited and translated by George Kernodle and John McDowell in connexion with work in the Yale Theatrical Collection. Much of Gordon Craig's *Books and Theatres* (1925) deals with this period.

(vi) THE COMMEDIA DELL' ARTE

Masks, Mimes, and Miracles, cited above, deals largely with this subject. A scholarly survey has been prepared by Kathleen M. Lea, *The Italian Popular Comedy* (1934). Duchartre's volume has been translated into English as *The Italian Comedy* (1928) and Miclashevski's into French as *La Commedia dell' arte* (by "Constant Mic," 1927). The *Recueil de plusieurs fragments des premières comédies italiennes* (1928), edited by Agne Beijer and P. L. Duchartre, contains an important series of early pictorial illustrations. Winifred Smith relates the activities of *Italian Actors of the Renaissance* (1930), and M. Willson Disher's *Clowns and Pantomimes* (1925) treats of their companions on slightly lower stages. Mario Apollonio's *Storia della Commedia dell' arte* (1930) will be found suggestive. J. S. Kennard has a general work on *The Italian Theatre* (1932) and a particular study of the *commedia dell' arte* (*Masks and Marionettes*, 1935). C. W. Beaumont's *The History of Harlequin* (1926) is an interestingly written and well-illustrated study.

(vii) EARLY FRENCH THEATRES

So far as the stage is concerned, the most important of recent publications is S. W. Holsboer's *L'Histoire de la mise en scène dans le théâtre français de 1600 à 1657* (1933). H. C. Lancaster's invaluable *French Dramatic Literature in the Seventeenth Century* (1929–36), while it treats chiefly of the drama, has several notes on methods of staging.

(viii) ELIZABETHAN THEATRES

W. J. Lawrence has recently published several very informative volumes on the Elizabethan stage—*Pre-Restoration Stage Studies* (1927), *Shakespeare's Workshop* (1928), *The Physical Conditions of the Elizabethan Public Playhouse* (1927), and *These Nut-cracking Elizabethans* (1935). A. W. Reed's *Early Tudor Drama* (1926) and F. S. Boas' *An Introduction to Tudor Drama* (1933) deal thoroughly with the predecessors of Shakespeare. W. W. Greg has collected various *Dramatic Documents from the Elizabethan Playhouses* (1931)—an invaluable source volume. M. C. Bradbrook's *Elizabethan Stage Conditions* (1932) is suggestive. Of *The Court Masque* (1928) Enid Welsford has written a carefully studied and informative account. M. Channing Linthicum has a valuable volume on *Costume in the Drama of Shakespeare and his Contemporaries* (1936).

(ix) CONTINENTAL THEATRES OF THE EIGHTEENTH CENTURY

A valuable volume of pictorial material is Corrado Ricci's *La Scenografia italiana* (1930)

(x) RESTORATION THEATRES

Leslie Hotson in *The Commonwealth and Restoration Stage* (1928) has presented many interesting new facts concerning the theatre from 1640 to 1700. Montague Summers' *The Playhouse of Pepys* (1935) deals in great thoroughness with all pertaining to the Restoration theatre. Noteworthy also is Eleanore Boswell's *The Restoration Court Stage* (1932), which presents many newly discovered documents. E. J. Dent gives a thorough account of *The Foundations of English Opera* (1928), with special reference to this period.

(xii) THE NINETEENTH CENTURY AND AFTER

Brief accounts of the theatre in the first half of the century are provided in the present writer's *A History of Early Nineteenth-century Drama* (1930). H. N. Hillebrand's *Edmund Kean* (1933) is a model of histrionic biography and gives an excellent picture of playhouse conditions between 1780 and 1820. Gordon Craig's *Henry Irving* (1931) recreates the fascination of a later actor.

In John Mason Brown's *The Modern Theatre in Revolt* (1929) will be found exceedingly suggestive and thoughtful chapters on various aspects of the modern theatre ; with this may be mentioned the same author's delightful *Letters from Greenroom Ghosts* (1934). The naturalistic movement finds a capable historian in Anna I. Miller—*The Independent Theatre in Europe* (1932). With this may be read S. M. Waxman's *Antoine and the Théâtre Libre* (1926). Later effort is dealt with in Hallie Flanagan's *Shifting Scenes of the Modern European Theatre* (1928), Sheldon Cheney's *The Art Theatre* (1925), *Theatre*, edited by Edith J. R. Isaacs (1927), Roy Mitchell's *Creative Theatre* (1929), *Twentieth-century Stage Decoration*, by Walter René Fuerst and S. J. Hume (1929).

Representative designs will be found in *Adolph Appia* (1929) and in *Goethes Faust . . . als Dichtung dargestellt* (1929). Enid Rose has written an account of *Gordon Craig and the Theatre* (1928). A volume of *Inedited Works of Bakst* (1927) gives reproductions of that artist's work.

(xiii) SOME BOOKS ON SPECIAL THEATRES

Below are listed a few books devoted to particular countries or playhouses.

(a) *England*. The present writer's *The English Theatre* (1936) is a general survey in one volume. *Design in the Theatre* (1927), edited by George Sheringham and James Laver, provides illustration of modern effort with special reference to English designers.

(b) *France*. Raymond Cogniat's *Décor au théâtre* (1930) forms a valuable record of modern scenic design in Paris. With this may be mentioned the magnificent *Tendances nouvelles du théâtre* (1921) of Léon Moussinac.

(c) *Germany*. Hans Rothe's *Max Reinhardt* (1930) is a suggestive study of the work of one of the most famous among modern producers.

(e) *Russia*. A rich array of illustrations and informative text appear in *The Russian Theatre* (1930), by René Fülöp-Miller and Joseph Gregor. Norris Houghton has a stimulating *Moscow Rehearsals* (1936).

(g) *United States of America*. G. C. D. Odell is engaged in the preparation of a monumental *Annals of the New York Stage* (1930–) ; eight volumes have already appeared. A. H. Quinn has an exceedingly useful two-volume *History of the American Drama* (1923–27) ; another account, also in two volumes, was published by Arthur Hornblow in 1919. Eola Willis gives interesting material in *The Charleston Stage in the Eighteenth Century* (1925). The records of Steele MacKaye's activities are presented by his son, Percy MacKaye, in *Epoch* (1927). Valuable illustrations, together with a general account of theatrical development, appear in *The American Stage* (1929), issued by the Yale University Press in its " Pageant of America " series. Another extremely valuable illustrative survey is *Das amerikanische Theater und Kino* (1931), by René Fülöp-Miller and Joseph Gregor. The modern movements are dealt with in Oliver Sayler's *Our American Theatre* (1923), Kenneth MacGowan's *Footlights across America* (1930), and John Mason Brown's *Upstage* (1930). Designs by Robert Edmond Jones (*Drawings for the Theatre*, 1925) and by Norman Bel Geddes (*A Project for a Presentation of the Divine Comedy*, 1924) have been issued by Theatre Arts, Inc. Joseph Urban's *Theatres* (1930) is important.

INDEX

U

INDEX

INDEX